WILLIAM KING

WILLIAM KING

From the portrait by John Williams in the Bodleian Library, Oxford.

William King

TORY AND JACOBITE

BY

DAVID GREENWOOD

CLARENDON PRESS · OXFORD

1969

Oxford University Press, Ely House, London W.1

GLASGOW NEW YORK TORONTO MELBOURNE WELLINGTON
CAPE TOWN SALISBURY IBADAN NAIROBI LUSAKA ADDIS ABABA
BOMBAY CALCUTTA MADRAS KARACHI LAHORE DACCA
KUALA LUMPUR SINGAPORE HONG KONG TOKYO

MADE AND PRINTED IN GREAT BRITAIN BY
WILLIAM CLOWES AND SONS, LIMITED
LONDON AND BECCLES

SODALIBVS
CIRCVLI DVBLINENSIS
SOCIETATIS OXONIENSIS
HOC VOLVMEN
DEDICATVR

Preface

It is a curious fact that, though the history of Jacobitism has been written several times in the past, the principal literary protagonist of the movement has remained so far without a biography. My intention in writing this book has been to fill this gap. That gentle and modest author, Izaak Walton, has already expressed my feelings on completing the work: 'If I have prevented any abler person, I beg pardon of him, and my reader.'

My first debt of gratitude is due to Her Majesty The Queen for her gracious permission to use and quote from the Stuart Papers, now in the Royal Library at Windsor Castle.

Next, I thank His Grace the Duke of Beaufort for his kindness in dealing with several matters connected with the Latin epitaph which King wrote for the fourth Duke, His Lordship the Marquess of Lansdowne for permission to use the Bowood papers, His Lordship the Earl Howe for information on the history of Gopsall Hall, Sir Gyles Isham, Bart., for advice on the archives of Northamptonshire, and Col. Sir Watkin Williams-Wynn, Bart., for counsel on his Jacobite ancestors.

Of the many persons in Oxford to whom I owe gratitude, the first is John Sparrow, Esq., Warden of All Souls College, who allowed me to make use of his private library, including an invaluable collection of the works of King. The University Archivist, Dr. William Pantin, provided kind assistance in making the archives accessible to me. To the Provost and Fellows of Oriel College I am especially indebted, notably to Dr. John Gough for putting at my disposal the collections in the College Library, and to Brigadier Ralph Bagnall-Wild for making available those archives of St. Mary Hall which still remain. The staff of the Bodleian Library has been most helpful: I should mention Bodley's Librarian, Dr. Robert Shackleton; the Keeper of Printed Books, Ian Philip, Esq.; together with Dr. David Rogers and D. H. Merry, Esq. The records of Balliol College were liberally made available by the Librarian, Edward

Quinn, Esq., and those of Exeter College by Dr. J. P. V. D. Balsdon. H. J. R. Wing, Esq., of Christ Church, went to great trouble to seek out relevant material. The Keeper of the Department of Antiquities of the Ashmolean Museum, Robert W. Hamilton, Esq., and the Assistant Keeper of the Heberden Coin Room, J. D. A. Thompson, Esq., both gave of their time and expert knowledge.

In London, the staffs of the British Museum, the Church Commissioners, the Public Record Office, the Principal Probate Registry in Somerset House, the Guildhall Library, and the Library of the University of London in Senate House gave unstinted assistance. I should also thank the Librarians of: Lambeth Palace, E. G. W. Bill, Esq.; Gray's Inn, R. M. Cocks, Esq.; the Inner Temple, W. W. S. Breem, Esq.; the Honourable Society of the Middle Temple, D. V. A. Sankey, Esq.; the Victoria and Albert Museum, John P. Harthan, Esq.; the City of Westminster, K. C. Harrison, Esq., M.B.E.; and the Borough of Tower Hamlets, Herbert Ward, Esq. The Rev. Roderick Gibbs, Rector of St. Dunstan's Church, Stepney, and the Archivist of the same parish, Henry G. Weedon, Esq., spared no pains to help; nor did the Vicar of St. Mary's Church, Ealing, the Rev. G. H. Perman; the officials of the Ealing Local History Society, and in particular Dr. F. A. Toufar and H. D. G. Holt, Esq.; the Director of Research of the Society of Genealogists, Anthony J. Camp, Esq.; and David W. Vessey, Esq., Registrar of the Order of the Crown of Stuart and Editor for the Royal Stuart Society. A special word of thanks is due to the Librarian of the Royal Library, Windsor Castle, Robert Mackworth-Young, Esq.; the Richmond Herald of Arms, J. P. Brooke-Little, Esq., and the other officers of the College of Arms; the Secretary to the Editorial Board of the History of Parliament Trust, E. L. C. Mullins, Esq.; and the Librarian of the Institute of Historical Research, A. Taylor Milne, Esq.

Without the co-operation of county archivists the task of pursuing any aspect of the history of Jacobitism would be incalculably greater: among these I am especially grateful to Sir Edgar Stephens, C.B.E., and Anthony Wood, Esq., of Warwickshire; Miss E. D. Mercer of the Greater London Council; E. J. Davis, Esq., of Buckinghamshire; P. I. King, Esq., of

Northamptonshire; Dr. L. A. Parker of Leicestershire; Maurice G. Rathbone of Wiltshire; E. G. Earl of the Isle of Wight; and Miss J. Godber of Bedfordshire. I am likewise indebted to many librarians, but above all to H. R. Creswick, Esq., Librarian of the University of Cambridge; Peter Pagan, Esq., Director of the Municipal Libraries of the City of Bath; and G. Scholfield, Esq., Librarian of the City of New Sarum, who assisted beyond the call of duty.

In Ireland my obligations are many, especially to the staff of the Public Record Office of Ireland; Dr. R. J. Hayes and the staff of the National Library of Ireland; S. C. McMenamin, Esq., Deputy Keeper of the Records in the Public Record Office of Northern Ireland; the Library Committee of Benchers of the Honorable Society of King's Inns, Dublin; and the staffs of the libraries of Trinity College, Dublin, the Royal Irish Academy, and the Four Courts. The administrators of the Sir John Gilbert Collection made available to me the three copies of the complete edition of *The Toast* which are in their care, and through the good offices of the Honourable Desmond Guinness, President of the Irish Georgian Society, I was able to inspect two further copies of the same work, both now belonging to gentlemen of Naas: a 1732 edition with the signature of Swift's friend Knightley Chetwode on the title-page, and an almost perfect copy of the so-called 1747 version. The owners of these are respectively Captain Tadhg MacGlinchey and Mr. J. Barry Brown. The former Dean of St. Patrick's Cathedral and now the Lord Bishop of Cashel, Emly, Waterford and Lismore, the Right Reverend John Armstrong; Professor Donald Wormell and Dr. John Simms of Trinity College, Dublin; and Alexander Donovan, the author of a useful account of the history of St. Audoen's Church, have also been most helpful.

Though the last edition of any of King's published works appeared a century and a half ago, copies of some of his writings are available in a few libraries in the United States. In consulting as many of these as possible, I have benefited from more acts of generosity than I can document. But at the risk of invidiousness, I should mention the staff of the Library of Congress; Dr. Louis Wright and Dr. Giles Dawson of the Folger Shakespeare Library; Pawel J. Depta of the Harvard College

Library; Dr. Robert O. Dougan and Lyle H. Wright of the Huntington Library, Pasadena; and Dr. James Tanis of the Yale University Library. Professor Leicester Bradner of Brown University gave valuable advice, as also did Professor George Siefert of the Catholic University of America, and Professor Alfred O. Aldridge of the University of Illinois.

For reading and commenting on earlier versions of the manuscript I thank Professor Philip Edwards of the University of Essex and Dr. W. F. Pyle of Trinity College, Dublin. And for their careful attention to the problems involved in printing and publication I am obliged to the Delegates of the Oxford University Press and also to their staff.

While writing this book, I have tried to bear in mind that the majority of readers will have no access to King's works themselves. In these circumstances, it seemed appropriate to describe their contents with somewhat greater comprehensiveness than would otherwise have been necessary. I trust that the descriptions will not be found unduly detailed.

The orthography and punctuation in the quotations from eighteenth-century sources are generally retained as they appear in the cited passages, except that ∫ has been normalized to s. Occasionally I have emended obvious slips. Eighteenth-century spellings of names are retained in quotations and titles, but modernized in the text. In quoting Latin, I have not reproduced diphthongs in the form of ligatures, and have omitted the accents wherever they occurred.

D. G.

Oxford
7 April 1969

Contents

I

King's Early Life

THE subject of this work should not be confused with two of his senior contemporaries who also bore the name of William King. The elder of these was the Lord Archbishop of Dublin from 1703 until his death in 1729; the other, described by Swift in the *Journal to Stella* as a 'poor starving wit', was a don of Christ Church, Oxford, and the author of a number of miscellaneous works of which *An Historical Account of the Heathen Gods and Heroes*, published in 1710 and a standard textbook in the classroom for many years, is perhaps the best known. The fact that all three William Kings were associated with Ireland in various ways has probably helped to increase the number of bibliographical errors which have been perpetrated at different times in relation to these three homonymous individuals.

Less is known today about the subject of the present biography than about either of the other two Kings. Scraps of information are provided by Daniel Lysons,[1] Charles Coote,[2] Alex Chalmers,[3] and one or two other writers, but the earliest account that could in any sense be regarded as biographical is given in a long footnote in John Nichols's *Literary Anecdotes of the Eighteenth Century*.[4] All subsequent writers are indebted to this footnote; indeed, the life of King in the *Dictionary of National Biography*, written by Gordon Goodwin, is in many places merely a paraphrase of Nichols's account.

William King was born in Stepney, now in East London and

---

[1] Daniel Lysons, *The Environs of London* (5 vols.; London: Printed by A. Strahan, for T. Cadell in the Strand, 1792–1800); Vol. II, pp. 232, 236; Vol. III, p. 456. An error occurs in the edition of 1811, Vol. II, p. 699, where the date of King's baptism appears as 11 March 1635.

[2] Charles Coote, *Sketches of the Lives and Characters of Eminent English Civilians* (London: Sold by C. Kearsley, 1804), pp. 111–12.

[3] Alex Chalmers, *A History of the Colleges, Halls, and Public Buildings Attached to the University of Oxford* (Oxford: Printed by Collingwood and Co., 1810), pp. 451f.

[4] John Nichols, *Literary Anecdotes of the Eighteenth Century* (9 vols.; printed for the author, 1812–15), Vol. II, pp. 607–9.

renamed Tower Hamlets, but then in Middlesex. The following entry appears in the Register of Baptisms of St. Dunstan and All Saints' Church, Stepney:

> 1684. March 11, William son of Mr. Peregrine King of Stepney Clerk & Margaret *uxor*. 6 days old.

This date is, of course, given in Old Style; in modern works of reference King's birth is usually ascribed to 5 March 1685. Gordon Goodwin in the *Dictionary of National Biography* gives the date as 16 March 1685, presumably following the information—or misinformation—which is inscribed in the exergue on King's monument, now in the chapel of Oriel College. It still reads

Natus Martis XVI^{to}. MDCLXXXV.

I do not know why the wrong date appears in the very place where one would expect to find the truth. It is possible that whoever composed the inscription was attempting to correct the difference between Old and New Style dates. If so, he made an error of one day: since the normal procedure for converting the diurnal difference between Old and New Style dates in cases prior to the end of February 1700/1 is to add *ten* days to the date in Old Style, the converted date should surely be 15 March 1685.[1]

Very little is known about either of King's parents, but both his paternal and maternal ancestors had maintained for several generations a relationship with the University of Oxford. His father, Peregrine King, was the son of another clergyman of the same name who matriculated at Magdalen Hall on 3 November 1615, aged 17. He is described in the Matriculation Register of the University as Peregrine King of Buckinghamshire, *Plebeius*. On 30 October 1616 he was awarded the degree of B.A., and on 9 June 1619 that of M.A. He incorporated at the

---

[1] Because the year 1700 was a leap year in Old Style but not in New Style, the variation between the two calendars was further increased by one day. This eleven-day difference holds good only for dates between 1 March 1700/1 and 2 September 1752, when the discrepancy was rectified in England by the omission of the eleven days between September 2 and 14. Hence arose the public outcry, 'Give us back our eleven days.'

University of Cambridge in 1621, and in 1637 was appointed rector of the Church of St. Peter and Paul, Motson (modern Mottistone) in the Isle of Wight. He was still in possession in 1654, when he was described as 'an able man and a painful minister of God's word'.[1]

Peregrine junior—William King's father—matriculated at St. Edmund Hall on 30 March 1666, aged 17. He received the degrees of B.A. on 1 February 1669/70, and M.A. in 1672. He was instituted to Rowington (modern Runnington) in Somerset on 24 December 1683, the patron being Charles II. Precisely how long he spent at Rowington is a mystery; the surviving Consignation Books and clergy lists in the Somerset County Record Office are silent on the subject, and a curate is invariably named to this small parish. The reasonable inference which may be drawn from these facts is that Peregrine King was probably an absentee incumbent.[2] In 1684 he married Margaret Smyth, one of the daughters of Sir William Smyth of Radclive, Buckinghamshire, at All Hallows' Church, London Wall, and settled in Stepney. He would appear to have been a resident of Stepney when his children were born, but the nature of his connection with the parish church of St. Dunstan and All Saints is not clear. His name does not appear among the records of the clergy of the church; the Subscription Books and Visitation Books of the diocese of London, at present housed in the Guildhall Library, likewise provide no information on his status. What little evidence there is points to his becoming a Non-juror: one of the approximately 400 Anglican clergymen, headed by the Archbishop of Canterbury, William Sancroft, who during 1689 refused to swear their fidelity to William and Mary by the oaths of allegiance and supremacy, arguing that they had already pledged their loyalty to the now exiled James II. While residing in Stepney in 1701, Peregrine King attorned

---

[1] *The Report of the Commissioners under the [1654] Act for ejecting scandalous, ignorant or insufficient Ministers.* The text of the original Ordinance, dated 28 August 1654, is printed in C. H. Firth and R. S. Tait (eds.), *Acts and Ordinances of the Interregnum, 1642–1660* (London: H.M.S.O., 1911), Vol. II, pp. 968–90.

[2] Some of these details are available in Joseph Foster's *Alumni Oxonienses.* Foster gives the date of the appointment of the second Peregrine King to the rectorship of Rowington as 1684; the date of institution to Rowington given above is taken from the archives of the Somerset County Record Office.

the rectory of Rowington for £20 per annum to James Knight of Chipstable. Towards the close of his life he dwelt at Ealing, at that time in Middlesex, as one of the lessees (or sublessees) of the rectory and its property. His name appears in the Ealing Poor Rate Books intermittently during the early 1700s. The Burial Register of Ealing for 1701–16 gives the date of his interment as 10 August 1714.[1]

King's maternal ancestors are more easily traceable. His great-great-grandfather, Sir William Smyth, was born in 1542 and was a Fellow of New College from 1558 to 1571. He acquired the degrees of B.C.L. in 1565 and D.C.L. in 1573, incorporated at Cambridge in 1583, and became Surrogate for Buckinghamshire and Berkshire. He was also instrumental in obtaining a lease for a thousand years on Akeley manor in Buckinghamshire.[2] Sir William's son, Robert, matriculated at Oxford in 1610, became Principal of New Inn, London, one of the former Inns of Chancery, and was slain in 1645, fighting for the cause of Charles I.

Robert Smyth's elder son, Sir William Smyth of Radclive, Buckinghamshire, had a longer career. Born about 1616, he matriculated at Trinity College, Oxford, on 13 March 1634/5, but left the university without taking a degree. He was elected M.P. for Winchelsea in 1640, and held his seat until he was disabled in 1644. Meanwhile he became a barrister of the Middle Temple in 1641, and received the degree of D.C.L. of the University of Oxford on 10 November 1642. During the Civil War he was governor of Hillesdon House, near Buckingham, where Charles I had a small garrison. King tells the following story of the capture of Hillesdon House by Oliver Cromwell in his posthumously published *Political and Literary Anecdotes*:

This place was besieged and taken by CROMWELL. But the officers capitulated to march out with their arms, baggage, &c. As soon as they were without the gate, one of Cromwell's soldiers snatched off Sir William Smyth's hat. He immediately complained to Cromwell of the fellow's insolence, and breach of the capitulation. 'Sir', says Cromwell, 'if you can point out the man, or if I can discover him,

---

[1] The Ealing Poor Rate Books are deposited in the Ealing Town Hall; the Burial Registers are in the possession of the Church of St. Mary.
[2] See *The Victoria County History of Buckinghamshire*, Vol. IV, p. 145.

I promise you he shall not go unpunished. In the meantime (taking off a new beaver, which he had on his head) be pleased to accept of this hat instead of your own.'[1]

Sir William was deprived of his offices during the period of the Protectorate, but was amply rewarded at the Restoration. On 10 May 1661 he was created a Baronet, and was M.P. for Buckingham from 1661 to 1679. In 1664 he was granted, under a patent of Charles II, the right to hold a weekly market at Ratcliffe Cross, a small hamlet in the parish of Stepney, and an annual fair on Michaelmas day at Mile End Green, also within the parish limits.[2] The Court Rolls of the Manor of Stepney refer to him on 24 April 1665 as one of several persons enfeoffing houses on waste ground in Stepney Manor, and his name occurs in several other legal documents in the manorial rolls.[3] He must have maintained a residence in the parish, for his name is listed on 29 March 1687 with those of the vestry-men in the Vestry Book (1662–1747) of the church of St. Dunstan and All Saints. He is described as living 'In Ratcliffe'. The manorial rolls refer to him again on 18 March 1688/9 as being 'of Stepney', and as a lessor of land in Mile End and Bethnal Green.

It would seem that he was active in upholding the legal privileges of the Church of England against the now illegal claims of the Nonconformists. Almost all religious services other than those of the Church of England were by this time forbidden, so that the position of the Nonconformists became essentially that of subversives, who could be punished severely by the magistrates and other authorities. On one occasion, in December 1682, Sir William and a strong guard went to the meeting house of the Independents in Stepney with a view to enforcing the law. The pastor was Matthew Mead, who had formerly been ejected from Shadwell Chapel. Sir William's body of men pulled down the pulpit and broke up the forms;

---

[1] *Political and Literary Anecdotes* (2nd edn., 1819), p. 63.

[2] See Pat. 16 Car. II, Pt. 11, No. 1, and Pat. 19 Car. II, Pt. 6, No. 8.

[3] The Court Rolls of the Manor of Stepney are deposited in the Greater London Record Office at the County Hall. The significant references are: E/PHI/47 (24 April 1665); M39/90, page 30 (11 August 1669); Q/HAL/293 (1 December 1669); M93/90, page 38 (30 May 1670); C/39/1535 (18 March 1688/9).

Mead himself escaped, though his goods were seized.[1] Sir William died in Stepney in 1696, and was buried, according to his own instructions, in the chapel of the chancel of Akeley Church under the great stone where his grandfather, Sir William Smyth, was buried.

His will, dated 18 August 1694 and proved on 10 February 1696/7, exhibits considerable generosity.[2] It stipulates: '. . . give to the children of my Son[-in-law Peregrine] King my Estate att Ealling which I have settled by deed . . .' Various piece of real estate, including that at Akeley, are assigned to his only surviving son, Sir Thomas Smyth. When Sir Thomas died without issue in 1732, the Akeley property passed to his cousin, Sir William Smyth of Warden, Bedfordshire.[3] A sum of £100 is set aside to buy land, the rent of which was to be administered by New College, Oxford, for the benefit of the poor of Akeley, and there are numerous legacies to other individuals.

King's maternal grandfather married twice. His first wife was Margaret, daughter of Sir Alexander Denton of Hillesden: she died apparently without issue. His second wife, King's grandmother, was Dorothy, daughter of Sir Nathaniel Hobart. She could boast of lofty family connections: Sir Nathaniel's brother was an ancestor of the Hobarts, Earls of Buckinghamshire, while her mother, Anne, was the daughter of Sir John Leake of Wyer Hall, Edmonton, and niece of Sir Edmund Verney. Among Sir William's children by his second wife was Dorothy, who in 1682 was married to Charles Wither (or Withers) of Oakley Hall, Hampshire. Educated at Winchester College, he became High Sheriff of Hampshire in 1686. He died in 1697, but as King later married their daughter, Henrietta Maria, Dorothy Wither became his mother-in-law, as well as being his aunt.

The Register of Baptisms of St. Dunstan and All Saints'

---

[1] See Walter Howard Frere, 'Two Centuries of Stepney History, 1480–1680' (Concluding Article), *The East London Magazine*, Vol. I, No. 16 (November 1891).

[2] Principal Probate Registry, Somerset House, Prerogative Court of Canterbury, 40 Pyne.

[3] Little information is available on this particular Sir William Smyth, but King provides a piece of gossip in *Political and Literary Anecdotes* (2nd edn., 1819), pp. 104f. Sir William Smyth of Warden, Bedfordshire, was the nephew of Sir William Smyth of Radclive, Buckinghamshire, and second cousin to William King.

Church contains entries for two of William's siblings, which read thus:

> 1690. 6 Nov. John son of Mr. Peregrine King of
> Stepney clerk & of Margaret *uxor*
> 15 days old.
> 1691 4 Feb. Robert son of Mr. Peregrine King
> of Stepney clerk & of Margaret *uxor*
> 12 days old.[1]

Another brother, Thomas, appears between William and John in the will of Sir William Smyth of Warden, Bedfordshire.[2] He is referred to as 'my brother Tom' in a rather untypically informal letter which William wrote in 1721, now in the Public Record Office.[3] The name of John King appears in two legal documents now in the Registry of Deeds at King's Inns, Dublin, dated in 1723 and 1726; in documents of 1775 relating to litigation over the manor of Wavendon, Buckinghamshire, once the property of Woburn Abbey; and in conveyances concerning the sale of Warden rectory and some other properties in 1776.[4]

Everything that can now be known about William's childhood must be drawn from what he tells us in his own writings, and principally in the *Political and Literary Anecdotes*. There he writes: 'My mother having died of the small-pox when I was about seven years old, I was sent by my grandfather, Sir WILLIAM SMYTH, to Salisbury, and placed under the care of MR. TAYLOR, the master of the free-school in that city. There were at that time two very flourishing schools in Salisbury.'[5] These two schools must have been the Choristers'

---

[1] In Old-Style dating, the difference between the ages of the two boys is, of course, 15 months.

[2] Principal Probate Registry, Somerset House, Prerogative Court of Canterbury, 319 Spurway. This will was proved at London on 2 November 1741.

[3] King to Captain Charles Halsted, Public Record Office, State Papers Domestic, 35/28, Item 66.

[4] See *The Victoria County History of Buckinghamshire*, Vol. IV, p. 494. The Warden documents are in the County Record Office, Shire Hall, Bedford; particularly significant are those in the Whitbread Collection, nos. 2047–86, and the Garrard and Allen Collection, no. 473. A few leases relating to property at Ealing in the Church Commissioners' collections are signed by a John King who is almost certainly the same individual.

[5] *Political and Literary Anecdotes* (2nd edn., 1819), p. 136.

School in the Cathedral Close, and the City Free School founded by Queen Elizabeth I in 1569. In 1625 its premises in Castle Street were opened, and here King received his schooling.[1] Long hours of study were demanded of the boys; in 1632, when Mr. Nathaniel Ross was the master, the following regulation was established: 'Ordered that the scholars shall not be suffered to go to play on any Monday, Wednesday or Friday, although a remedy [half-holiday] be desired for them by any stranger or other person whatsoever. And they shall not be suffered to go to play on any other day of the week but sparingly and at the master's discretion.'

Despite this apparent severity, King always recollected his time at Salisbury with delight:

THERE IS NO PLACE I have ever seen which I review with so much pleasure and satisfaction as the place of my school education, and the scenes of my boyhood. I feel a thrilling secret joy in every street I pass through. How many agreeable trifles and little amusements do I recollect at almost every step! All my actions were then very innocent, and my errors and follies excusable: not so after I had entered into the great world![2]

A letter written much later in life by King to Lord Orrery provides an intimate glimpse of the schoolboy at Salisbury writing Latin verses for penny-puffs. He first laments that he would think it hard if, at the age of fifty-six, he could not sell his verses for half the money for which he sold them at sixteen, and then continues:

For I can appeal to some honest Clergy-men, who are still living, as well as to the memoirs of Mother Page the Pastry Cook of New Sarum who flourished in that City in the beginning of this Century,

---

[1] See Henry Hatcher, *History of Modern Wiltshire: Old and New Salisbury* (Salisbury, 1843). A slightly different account is provided in an earlier work, Hatcher's *Historical and Descriptive Account of Old and New Sarum or Salisbury* (Salisbury: K. Clapperton, 1834). See also by way of augmentation: Robert Benson, *Facts and Observations Touching Mr. Hatcher and the History of Salisbury* (London: William Pickering, 1843), and *The Victoria History of the County of Wiltshire*, Vol. V, p. 349. The Free School eventually became known as Salisbury City Grammar School; it closed for lack of support in 1883 and its premises were sold in the following year. No records survive from King's period, though Salisbury Corporation still possesses ten title deeds relating to the foundation.

[2] *Political and Literary Anecdotes* (2nd edn., 1819), pp. 136f.

if I did not frequently sell eight verses only for a penny-puff. By the way let no objections be made about the puff, for I might have had my pay in ready money, if I had pleased. But I was then too much a man of honour to take ready money for my work. Your Lordship is to observe that these verses I speak of were Hexameters and Pentameters.[1]

As King relates these early transactions to his sixteenth year, they must have taken place during his last six months at Salisbury, immediately prior to his going up to Oxford.

On 9 July 1701 King was matriculated at the University of Oxford *e Collegio Balliolensi*. No academic record survives of his undergraduate years, nor is there any evidence that he ever supplicated for the degrees of B.A. or M.A. But he did graduate with the degree of B.C.L. on 12 July 1709, and received the degree of D.C.L. on 8 July 1715. The Oxford *Catalogue of All Graduates* (1659–1770) indicates that he was a Grand Compounder, defined in the Preface to the *Catalogue* as 'one who has Forty Pounds per Annum, or upwards, in temporal Estate or Preferment; which must be held for Term of Life at least . . .' It is further explained that no place of preferment in the university made a man a Grand Compounder; the privileges accorded to the title were based ultimately on property. The Preface continues: 'Upon account of the extraordinary Fees a Grand Compounder pays, he has special Honour done him by the University, with special Privileges which he claims, one of which . . . is to preceed all those that take the same Degree that year.' From King's status of Grand Compounder at Oxford it may be assumed that he was fairly affluent, and probably living on the 'small patrimony' which he occasionally mentions in his writings, and which provided him throughout his life with a private income. Thus in his last years he could write: '. . . let me be ever thankful to Divine Providence, that I have never wanted the necessaries, nor even the comforts of life: and what has given me a very singular pleasure, I have always been able to spare something to assist a poor friend.'[2]

It is impossible to form more than the most nebulous picture of King during his periods of residence at Balliol College. The

---

[1] Bodleian Library, MS. Eng. hist. d. 103, p. 20.
[2] *Political and Literary Anecdotes* (2nd edn., 1819), p. 3.

principal sources of information are the Balliol Caution Books
and Buttery Books, the Bursar's Books of Battells, and the
Admission Book of 1682–1833. As an undergraduate commoner
in September 1701 he paid £7 in caution money. Various
amounts of money are credited to his name as battells, though
his expenses do not appear in any way unusual. He does not
seem to have been in residence during the academic year
1704–5; his name disappears from the Buttery Books in March
1704/5. It reappears in 1709; on June 23 of that year King was
promoted from commoner to fellow commoner. His name is on
the books again from 1715 to 1719, when he is described as
D.C.L.

When he was not at Oxford, King presumably resided either
in Holborn or Ealing, where he seems to have succeeded his
father in the lesseeship (or a sublesseeship) of the rectory. The
Allegation of Marriage which King signed in October 1709,
and which is now in the Library of Lambeth Palace, describes
him as being 'of the parish of St. Andrew, Holbourne, in the
County of Middlesex'. His name occurs for the first time in the
Ealing Poor Rate Books in 1712. The entry of 28 May 1712 in
The Pension Book of Gray's Inn refers to him as 'William King, of
Ealing, Middlesex, Esq.'[1] For an indeterminable period he
lived on an estate called Newby, near the parish church; there
is no record of the period he spent occupying this messuage,
though Faulkner describes it as 'many years'.[2] When he was in
London he used to visit King's Coffee House in Golden Square;
its exact location is now unknown.[3]

In 1709 he married his cousin, Henrietta Maria Wither (or
Withers), who was about two years younger than he. She lived
only a few years after the marriage. The licence of the Vicar-

---

[1] Reginald Fletcher (ed.), *The Pension Book of Gray's Inn, 1669–1800* (London,
1910), Vol. II, p. 158. See also: Joseph Foster, *The Register of Admissions to Gray's Inn,
1521–1889* (London, 1889), p. 358.

[2] Thomas Faulkner, *The History and Antiquities of Brentford, Ealing & Chiswick*
(London, 1845), p. 248.

[3] *Political and Literary Anecdotes* (2nd edn., 1819), pp. 237f., 243. The standard
reference work, Bryant Lillywhite's *London Coffee Houses*, does not list a King's
Coffee House in Golden Square. From 1702 to 1714 there was a *Kigg's* Coffee
House in James Street, Golden Square; perhaps this is meant. The more famous
King Street Coffee House, King Street, Golden Square, was in existence about
1770, but I can find no evidence of its date of opening.

General, dated 29 October 1709, indicates the place of the wedding as St. Anne's, Westminster. Presumably the marriage took place some short time after King had signed the Allegation, though there is no record of it in the surviving registers of St. Anne's. By his union to Henrietta Maria, King acquired a brother-in-law, Charles Wither junior, who became, paradoxically, a 'hearty Whig'. His name occurs occasionally in historical documents relating to his official positions: like his father he was High Sheriff of Hampshire, and to this dignity he added that of Commissioner for Woods and Forests in 1720. He was M.P. for Christchurch from 1726 to 1731, the year of his death. His sister bore King two children: Charles and Dorothy. The scanty information available on them may be quickly reviewed.

According to the Registers of St. Anne's Church, Westminster, Charles King was born on 5 January 1710/11, and baptized there on the following March 19. He matriculated at St. Mary Hall, Oxford, where his father was now Principal, on 30 March 1726. His B.A. was conferred on 17 October 1729, and his M.A. on 6 July 1732. He married a Lucy Blythman in 1737, thereby acquiring wealth, and was Vicar of Great Bedwyn in Wiltshire from 1748 until his death in 1759.[1] In an anonymous list of notes on local ratepayers, now preserved at Ealing Central Library, Charles King is described as 'a great speculatist, clever but eccentric'. A few other references to him are to be found in contemporary sources; for example, his name appears in a letter written by Sanderson Miller to Deane Swift, from which we learn that Miller bought Volume I of Clarendon's *History of the Rebellion* from him in 1734,[2] and in a letter written by his father to Lord Orrery on 14 July 1741 we read:

I have a Son in Orders who preach'd our Assize Sermon, and as I am told (for I did not hear him) he performed tolerably well. But that you may be assured he has nothing extraordinary to recommend him, he is undignify'd and un-beneficed without so much as half an ounce of preferment. And Your Lordship knows well, that no man in

[1] Rev. John Ward, 'Great Bedwyn', *The Wiltshire Archaeological and Natural History Magazine*, Vol. VI (1860), p. 269.
[2] Lilian Dickins and Mary Stanton, *An Eighteenth-Century Correspondence* (London: John Murray, 1910), p. 5.

these circumstances was ever allowed to be an excellent preacher. Such as he is however I'll introduce him to Your Lordship the first opportunity. He is a pretty good Classic Scholar and on that account perhaps he may acquire a small portion of your esteem.[1]

He died, according to the note on him in Ealing Central Library, 'in the fields coming from Gunnersbury'.

King's daughter, Dorothy, was the younger of the two children; she married William Melmoth the Younger, and is the 'Cleora' of his *Letters on Several Subjects*.[2] Their marriage took place at St. George's Church, Hanover Square, on 5 March 1738/9, and is alluded to in Fitzosborne's letters. They seem to have resided for a time at Shrewsbury, but also maintained a home at Ealing. Here Dorothy Melmoth died on 21 June 1761. On 26 May 1762 Mr. Melmoth married again: this time a Mary Ogle at St. James's Church, Bath. According to Thomas Faulkner, he 'passed the chief part of his life in retirement at Ealing', and specifically in Ealing House; his first wife must have spent a portion of her married life there.[3]

On 28 May 1712 King was admitted as a Barrister-at-Law of Gray's Inn. On the following July 12 he was called to the Bar, as the entry in *The Pension Book of Gray's Inn* indicates:

1712 July 12
    Ordered that Wm. King Esq. a Member of this Society being Batchelor of Civill Law of the University of Oxford and of Drs. [doctor's] standing there, be admitted to the Barr by the Grace and Favour of the Bench.

To be created a barrister of an inn of court less than seven weeks after admission is indeed unusual. The distinction seems to have been bestowed on King by virtue of his status at Oxford: it was

---

[1] Bodleian Library, MS. Eng. hist. d. 103, pp. 27f.

[2] The first volume of William Melmoth's once well-known *Letters on Several Subjects* was published in 1742 under the pseudonym of Sir Thomas Fitzosborne, and reprinted several times later. A second volume of letters appeared in 1749. Letters 7, 12, 25, 31, and 40 relate to Dorothy. They were renumbered by Harrison in his edition of 1787.

[3] Thomas Faulkner, op. cit., p. 240. It is quite possible that Ealing House was adjacent to Newby; in the relevant Ealing Poor Rate Books William King is described as residing in the house next to that of William Melmoth between 1723 and 1729. Undoubtedly William Melmoth the Elder is here intended.

in the nature of an honorary call to the Bar. He never practised as a barrister professionally, as far as is known, and certainly held no official post within Gray's Inn. He may possibly
have resided there for a time, but since the rent rolls of Gray's
Inn perished in 1941 when the old library was destroyed by
German air attack, there is no means of ascertaining the matter.
Later he acquired chambers in the Temple.[1] For a time he
acted as a Justice of the Peace, as is clear from a roll for the
county of Middlesex, now in the Public Record Office, which
includes King's name among those of the Justices sitting at
Quarter Sessions at Hicks Hall on 13 January 1713.[2] His
signature occasionally appears, with the title of Justice of the
Peace, during 1713 and the following year in the Ealing Poor
Rate Book for 1707–19.

At some time prior to 1715 King was appointed Secretary to
the Chancellor of the University of Oxford, James Butler, Duke
of Ormonde. It is reasonable to suppose that his appointment
to this position reflected the confidence that the authorities
placed in him. Since a good deal of the university's correspondence, especially with Continental institutions, was conducted
in Latin, one of the requisites of the Chancellor's Secretary was
the faculty for writing Latin with elegance and reasonable
celerity, an ability which King unquestionably possessed.
Furthermore, the Duke was a Tory, and no doubt found in his
Secretary a subordinate with whom he had mutual sympathies.
King's relationship with the Duke of Ormonde seems to have
been a congenial one. True, the Dublin-born Duke had been
present with King William's army at the Battle of the Boyne,
but he always showed a measure of personal independence, and
was certainly involved, though to an unknown degree, in
Jacobite designs in the latter part of the reign of Queen Anne.
Shortly after the arrival of George I in England in September
1714 Ormonde was deprived of the Captain-Generalship, and
though on October 9 he was nominated to the Privy Council
in Ireland and confirmed in the Lord-Lieutenancy, he was

---

[1] See Appendix IV.
[2] Public Record Office, E. 362/43/25. King's name appears on the dorse of
membrane 7. The roll is included in a bundle of *estreats* of the fines and amerce-
ments imposed in various courts and sent to the Exchequer.

dismissed from both offices a few days later. On 21 June 1715 Lord Stanhope moved his impeachment, and after a lengthy debate the motion was carried by a majority of forty-nine. Dignified and gracious to the end, Ormonde refused to pursue a conciliatory course, and left for France on the following 8 August. He never returned to Oxford.

Necessarily Ormonde's affairs and movements were partially shrouded in mystery during his last months as Chancellor. He was certainly engaged in preparations for a prospective rising in the West, and was also host to a number of Jacobite gatherings during this final period. King provides an intimate glimpse into one of these, in which most of the principal leaders are assembled.

In 1715 I dined with the DUKE OF ORMONDE at Richmond. We were fourteen at table. There was my Lord MARR, my Lord JERSEY, my Lord ARRAN, my Lord LANDSDOWN, Sir WILLIAM WYNDHAM, Sir REDMOND EVERARD, and ATTERBURY, Bishop of *Rochester*. The rest of the company I do not exactly remember. During the dinner there was a jocular dispute (I forget how it was introduced) concerning short prayers. Sir WILLIAM WYNDHAM told us, that the shortest prayer he had ever heard was the prayer of a common soldier just before the Battle of *Blenheim*, '*O God, if there be a God, save my soul, if I have a soul!*' This was followed by a general laugh. I immediately reflected that such a treatment of the subject was too ludicrous, at least very improper, where a learned and religious prelate was one of the company. But I had soon an opportunity to making a different reflection. ATTERBURY, seeming to join in the conversation, and applying himself to Sir WILLIAM WYNDHAM, said 'Your prayer, Sir WILLIAM, is indeed very short: but I remember another as short, but a much better, offered up likewise by a poor soldier in the same circumstances, '*O God, if in the day of battle I forget thee, do thou not forget me!*' This, as ATTERBURY pronounced it with his usual grace and dignity, was a very gentle and polite reproof, and was immediately felt by the whole company. And the DUKE of ORMONDE, who was the best bred man of his age, suddenly turned the discourse to a different subject.[1]

---

[1] *Political and Literary Anecdotes* (2nd edn., 1819), pp. 7–9. Some additional relevant information is provided in Sir Charles Petrie, 'Jacobite Activities in South and West England in the Summer of 1715', *Transactions of the Royal Historical Society*, 4th Series, Vol. 18 (1935), pp. 85ff.

In September 1715 Ormonde's brother, Charles Butler, Earl of Arran, signified the Duke's resignation from the Chancellorship and was himself elected Chancellor in his place. Ormonde's popularity lived on among students and dons of Jacobite sympathies: in July 1716 a certain Frank Nicholas of Exeter College was fined, imprisoned, and compelled to apologize in Convocation for publicly shouting 'An Ormonde for ever',[1] and there were several similar incidents. The former Chancellor spent the rest of his life on the Continent, mainly in Madrid and Avignon, always residing with great magnificence, and enjoying the titles of Captain-General and Commander-in-Chief in England and Ireland, which were bestowed on him at the Jacobite Court by King James. After his death in 1745 his remains were brought back to England and laid to rest in Westminster Abbey.

The Earl of Arran was, according to Hearne, 'in all respects much like the Duke', but though indubitably a Jacobite, he was in some ways more circumspect than his brother. King was his Secretary from the time of his election on 10 September 1715 until December 1721. From the scanty evidence it appears that they worked together well, though towards the end of King's period as Secretary most of the heads of colleges were trying to influence the Chancellor against him.[2]

Shortly after the elevation of Lord Arran to the Chancellorship the Jacobite insurrection of 1715 took place. There were to have been three separate risings: one in the Highlands of Scotland under the Earl of Mar, another in Cumberland under Thomas Forster, with Lord Derwentwater and Lord Widdrington, and a third in the West of England under the Duke of Ormonde. The first rising fizzled out after an indecisive battle with Government troops at Sheriffmuir, the second was a complete failure, and the third never took place at all. But the authorities were prepared to meet trouble in the West, and dispatched a regiment under a Colonel Pepper to deal with such an emergency. Alarming reports continued to reach London of

---

[1] Register of Convocation BD 31, f. 136.
[2] An example of one of King's official letters to Lord Arran is today in the National Library of Ireland, *Ormonde MSS.*, Vol. 177, p. 221, dated 11 June 1721, and written from St. Mary Hall.

large numbers of Jacobites in Oxford prepared to assist the insurrection, and so Colonel Pepper's regiment was diverted at Banbury on October 8, marched southwards through the night, and reached Oxford at about four o'clock on the morning of October 9. The town was blockaded, and Colonel Pepper was enabled to secure the ten or eleven men whom he had been ordered to apprehend, with the exception of one Owen, who escaped by climbing over the wall of Magdalen College in his nightgown. One of those taken was Captain Charles Halsted, with whom King maintained a correspondence over a number of years. This fact was known to the authorities in London by letters which had been intercepted at the post office.

On 20 January 1716 King was admitted a civilian, and became an advocate of Doctors' Commons.[1] The College of Advocates at Doctors' Commons ceased to exist in 1857, and few of the college records survive. But at the time of his admission he was presumably received with the traditional ceremonial, and, duly armed with the rescript of the Archbishop of Canterbury's Vicar-General, accepted first in the Court of Arches and then in the Court of Admiralty. It is impossible to formulate any clear picture of the part that King played in the life of the college, but it can hardly have been of any special importance.[2]

Most of the documentary information available on King's activities between 1718 and 1722 is to be found in Thomas Hearne's *Remarks and Collections*. In the middle of 1718 King was involved in Hearne's dispute with the Delegates of the Oxford University Press. The Delegates had intimated that they would publish no more of Hearne's works until he had acknowledged, or made satisfaction for, some allegedly offensive passages in the Preface to his edition of Camden's *Annales Rerum Anglicarum et Hibernicarum Regnante Elizabetha*, published in 1717. On 21 March 1717/18 Hearne received a copy of the accusations made against him in the form of a set of Latin Articles. To a modern

---

[1] Charles Coote, *Sketches of the Lives and Characters of Eminent English Civilians* (London: Sold by C. Kearsley, 1804), pp. 111f.

[2] The best account of the history of the College of Advocates is still William Senior's *Doctors' Commons and the Old Court of Admiralty* (London: Longmans, 1922). King's name does not occur in it.

reader these twelve Articles seem trifling; in Article 5, for example, Hearne is criticized for having written '. . . *notissimum est Henricum octavum ipso Nerone pene crudeliorem ac efferatiorem Caligulaque & Elagabulo quasi turpiorem . . .*'[1] He denied the charges made against him in a formal Answer to the Articles, but meanwhile the publication of his edition of *Guilielmi Neubrigensis Historia rerum Anglicarum* was held up in the printing house over the Sheldonian Theatre. On 5 July 1718 he wrote: 'This Day Dr. King (Secretary to my Lord Arran, Chanc. of our University) called upon me, & told me he had carried a Letter from Dr. Mead, signed by, & in the name of, several other Subscribers, to my Lord Arran, requesting him that he would desire the Vice-Chancellor to permitt my Book to go on immediately.'[2] The Dr. Mead here referred to was Dr. Richard Mead, son of the Non-Conformist divine Matthew Mead, who had suffered, *de jure* deservedly, at the hands of King's grandfather. Richard Mead was one of King's several Oxford physician acquaintances. Like King, he had been born in Stepney. He had studied medicine at the University of Padua, been elected a Fellow of the Royal Society in 1703, and secured the degree of D.Med. of the University of Oxford, by diploma, in 1707. Whatever differences their forebears may have had, they were both firmly on Hearne's side in this particular controversy.

On July 9 Hearne wrote:

This Day in the Afternoon, I met my Proctor, Acton, at Dr. King's at Balliol-College. . . . The Dr. told me privately that he believ'd all Things would be ended in a Fortnight's time. He said he must go out of Town next Week. I told him I wish'd he would stay till all was over. Because I was afraid that, in his Absence, some new Tricks would be plaid. He said he believ'd not.[3]

King was evidently doing his best to stop the prosecution, as Hearne attests on July 14:

I was this Morning with Dr. King. He told me he had been with

---

[1] Thomas Hearne, *Remarks and Collections* (11 vols.; Oxford: at the Clarendon Press, 1885–1921), Vol. VI, pp. 351f. The *Alumni Oxonienses*, in the entry under King's name, attributes to Hearne the statement that King was 'perhaps writer of the Gazettes'. Actually Hearne was referring to the William King of Christ Church.

[2] Ibid., p. 375.　　　　　　　　　　　　[3] Ibid.

the Principal of Brazen-Nose, & declared to him that he was to be the next Vice-Chancellor. He told him that he must put a stop to my Prosecution as soon as ever he was in his Office, and immediately upon that to permitt Neubrigensis to go on. After a great deal of Discourse, he brought him to yield to this. So that the only Business now remaining is to get a Letter speedily from the Chancellor, & to have it read in Convocation, w^ch, I am afraid, will not be so soon done as I could wish, it being my opinion that D^r. Baron will defer it as long as possibly he can, tho' D^r. King does his Endeavour to have it done at the Beginning of August.[1]

The Principal of Brasenose was Dr. Robert Shippen; Dr. John Baron, Master of Balliol, was the incumbent Vice-Chancellor. On 3 August 1718 Shippen wrote to Lord Arran to the effect that the time for appointing a new Vice-Chancellor was drawing near, and added: 'Your Lordship will be pleased at your leisure to give Directions to your Secretary to prepare a letter for that purpose to be sent hither some time next month.'[2]

A letter to Hearne from Dr. Mead, headed 'Blomesbury, Aug. 5, 1718', showed that King, though now in London, was still actively helping Hearne's cause: 'This day I waited on my Ld Arran, and delivered to him your letter. D^r. John Friend and D^r. Levet were with me, and D^r. King met us there. My L^d received us very kindly. We layd the whole matter before him, and he seem'd fully convinced of the unreasonableness and injustice of your Prosecution.'[3] In subsequent letters from Mead to Hearne it is made amply clear that King was doing everything in his power to end the matter. He encouraged Lord Arran to appoint Dr. Robert Shippen to the Vice-Chancellariate to replace Dr. John Baron, who was one of Hearne's active enemies. He later persuaded the Chancellor to write a letter to Shippen with a view to concluding Hearne's prosecution. Mead, in his letter headed 'Blomesbury. Oct. 18, 1718', intimates: 'Dr. King proposes to bring my Lord's letter to

---

[1] Ibid., pp. 378f.

[2] National Library of Ireland, *Ormonde MSS.*, Vol. 177, p. 209.

[3] Hearne, op. cit., Vol. VI, pp. 384f. Dr. John Friend or Freind of Christ Church and Dr. Henry Levet or Levett of Exeter College were both Doctors of Medicine of the University of Oxford. Dr. Friend was also appointed Professor of Chemistry in 1704 and elected a Fellow of the Royal Society in 1712. There is a monument to him in Westminster Abbey.

Oxford himself, and is your humble servant.'[1] Eventually the opposition dissipated, the prosecution was abandoned, and Hearne lived to see several more of his books published by the University Press.

Shortly after the start of Hearne's troubles King was involved in another academic controversy, thus briefly described in the *Remarks and Collections*:

1718: Aug. 4 (Mon.). D^r. King, when he was lately in Town, told me that M^r. Digby Cotes, Principal of Magd. [Magdalen] Hall, had not paid him his Fees for being Principal of the Hall. The Fees, as he had it from old Will. Sherwin, are 10 Guineas for being Principal of an Hall, and D^r. King, being Register to my Lord Arran, ought to have it. The D^r. mentioned this in my presence, also to Cooper, the University Register, & said, too, that he should sue the Principal.[2]

It is not surprising that Digby Cotes remained one of King's adversaries: his name will occur again in that capacity.

On 9 December 1719 King was installed as Principal of St. Mary Hall, in succession to Dr. John Hudson, recently deceased. He was the thirty-sixth Principal since the appointment of William Croten in 1436, who, if one disregards the very obscure fourteenth-century claimant, William de Leverton, was the first known holder of that position. King maintained his Principalship of what he used to refer to as 'my monastery' for forty-four years, until his death in 1763. St. Mary Hall was one of the several surviving examples of the medieval non-collegiate academic hall. It had been the parsonage of the rectors of St. Mary's Church until Edward II, in 1325, gave the Church and all its appurtenances to Oriel College. Subsequently it became independent. In King's time it had no corporate body to govern it and no Fellows. The Principal was, in effect, a complete autocrat. Small though it was, it had an excellent reputation: William (later Cardinal) Allen had been one of its earlier Principals, and among its former students were the poets Sir Christopher Hatton, George Sandys, and Ulpian Fulwell, the mathematician Thomas Hariot, and the political writer Marchmont Needham. Sir Thomas More may also have resided

[1] Ibid., p. 397.　　　　[2] Ibid., p. 210.

in the Hall for a time, and, if so, could have been one of the St. Anthony Exhibitioners maintained in the Hall by Oriel College.[1]

Almost all the surviving evidence on the routine administration of the Hall during the Principalship of William King is to be found in the holographic Matriculation Register and Buttery Books preserved today in the Muniment Room of Oriel College.[2] During the years 1719 to 1763 about 170 students matriculated at St. Mary Hall, an average of approximately four each year. The hebdomadal lists in the Buttery Books generally contain about forty names, but the number of members in residence, including the Principal and the Vice-Principal, is rarely higher than thirty, and often much lower. The number of undergraduates listed is never large: twelve to sixteen appears to have been the usual number in residence during full term, and there were fewer in the vacations. Philip Bury Duncan writes of 'the hand-writing . . . which is well ascertained to be Dr. King's in the account-books of St. Mary Hall in Oxford',[3] but it is far from clear to which books he is referring. The Buttery Books of King's period are written in a veritable Vishnu of different hands, and there is no proof that any of them is that of the Principal. Furthermore, there is a manuscript note near the beginning of the *Liber Aulae B.M.V. 1764*, referring to King's successor, which reads:

Thomas Nowell was admitted Principal of St. Mary Hall, the Eleventh Day of January 1764.

Soon after his Admission he enquired for the Register of the said Hall, or Book, in which he supposed the Hall-accounts were enter'd. But he was informed by Dr. King's Executors that no such Book was in their custody.—The only Book deliver'd to Dr. Nowell was that

---

[1] On the history of St. Mary Hall see James Ingram, *Memorials of Oxford* (2 vols.; Oxford: John Henry Parker, etc., 1837), Vol. II, section on St. Mary Hall; and Alex Chalmers, *A History of the Colleges, Halls and Public Buildings Attached to the University of Oxford* (Oxford: Collingwood and Co., 1810), pp. 450ff. Information on St. Mary Hall in the medieval period is provided in *Oxford Studies Presented to Daniel Callus* (Oxford: Oxford Historical Society, 1964), pp. 41 ff.

[2] The formal title of the Matriculation Register is 'St. Mary Hall Matriculations, Principals, Buildings, and History'. The matriculation lists appear to be complete; the other material was never finished for King's period.

[3] *Political and Literary Anecdotes* (2nd edn., 1819), p. vii.

which contains a Catalogue of Books belonging to the Library, and an Account of the Plate.

The enigma of the account books remains unsolved.

Until January 1722 King held his position of Principal of St. Mary Hall simultaneously with the Secretaryship to the Chancellor. The little available evidence—all of a formal nature—indicates that he fulfilled his responsibilities in both appointments with competence and thoroughness. Evidence of an informal kind is even more sparse. Hearne provides a glimpse of King involved in negotiations for the purchase of the library of Robert Betham, Rector of Silchester in Hampshire. Betham had died in November 1719, and had left 'a good Study of Books' which had cost him about £900. Some ten months later Hearne wrote:

Sept. 22 (Th.). Calling this Afternoon upon D^r. King, Principal of S^t. Mary Hall, he tells me that he hath bought Mr. Betham of Silchester's Books, or at least as good as bought them.[1]

In the following month King is shown exhibiting to Hearne a remarkable Jacobite medal:

Nov. 5 (Sat.). Yesterday Morning D^r. King, Principal of S^t. Mary Hall, called upon me, and shewed me the finest Silver Medal that I think I ever yet saw. It is of K. James III$^{d's}$ Queen, by wch it appears that she is a Lady of admirable Beauty. On the obverse Side, CLEMENTINA · M · BRITAN · FR · ET · HIB · REGINA. The Figure of the Queen. Reverse, DECEPTIS · CVSTODIBVS · FORTVNAM · CAVSAMQVE · SEQVOR · MDCCXIX. The Fig. of the Vatican and Trajan's Pillar. Also a Ship, and a Lady (being the Queen herself) in a Chariot drawn by 2 Horses, over wch the rising Sun.[2]

Somehow or other King must have acquired possession of one of several Jacobite medals struck on the Continent, this particular keepsake commemorating the escape of Princess Clementina Sobiesky from Innsbruck on 28 April 1719.[3] It is indeed an

[1] Hearne, op. cit., Vol. VII, pp. 70, 171. See also pp. 97, 299.

[2] Ibid., p. 185.

[3] It is referred to in R. W. Cochran-Patrick, *Catalogue of the Medals of Scotland* (Edinburgh, 1884), p. 65, No. 45*, and Edward Hawkins, *Medallic Illustrations of the History of Great Britain and Ireland to the Death of George II* (2 vols.; London: British Museum, 1885), Vol. II, p. 444, no. 49. Illustrations of both sides of the medal are

exquisite piece of numismatic artistry. On the observe side is a delicately wrought bust of the Princess depicted from the left, her flowing hair decorated with a diadem and wreathed with pearls. She wears a pearl ear-ring and necklace, a gown bordered with jewels, and an ermine mantle. On the reverse side she is seated in a chariot drawn at speed by two horses, with the rising sun in the distance. What Hearne calls the Vatican appears to me more like a part of Rome dominated by the Colosseum, but otherwise his description is unmistakable. The words FORTVNAM CAVSAMQVE SEQVOR are inscribed over the top of the scene on the reverse side, and the words DECEPTIS CVSTODIBVS are in the exergue. The name of the engraver appears on the obverse in very minute letters:

OTTO HAMERANI · F [ecit]

Princess Clementina Sobiesky was the grand-daughter of John Sobiesky, King of Poland, the wife of the Old Chevalier and mother of Charles Edward, the Young Chevalier. Her marriage was opposed by George I of England. The Holy Roman Emperor, Charles VI, seeking to gratify him, arrested her on her journey to Italy and incarcerated her at Innsbruck Castle. She escaped, *deceptis custodibus*, and fled to Bologna, where she was married by proxy to James Edward, who on that occasion was in Madrid. Her father, Prince Louis Sobiesky, commented that she ought to follow her spouse's fortune and cause: hence the wording over the scene on the reverse.

It is occasionally suggested that King took a woman of the same name under his protection in the 1740s and established her at Finsthwaite, a small village near the southern tip of Lake Windermere in Lancashire. This person could not possibly have been the mother of Bonnie Prince Charlie, who left her husband in November 1724, entered a convent, and died in 1735. There definitely was a woman who called herself Princess

to be found in the collection of plates appended to the latter work in 1911: see Plate CXLIII, No. 7. Its diameter is 48 millimetres, and some examples were struck in copper. Specimens in both silver and copper are preserved in the Heberden Coin Room of the Ashmolean Museum, Oxford. A short biography of the engraver, Otto Hamerani, who later became Master of the Mint at Rome, may be found in L. Forrer's *Biographical Dictionary of Medallists*, Vol. II, pp. 404-9.

Clementina Sobiesky and used to be referred to as the 'Finsthwaite Princess'; she died in 1771, and a tombstone to her memory was erected in Finsthwaite churchyard at the beginning of the present century. The identity of this particular lady has been much discussed, but even though there were Kings living in Finsthwaite in the middle of the eighteenth century, no connection has been conclusively established between the mysterious 'Princess' and the Principal of St. Mary Hall.[1]

A little more than five months after King had shown Hearne this remarkable medal, he was a guest of the Marquis of Carnarvon at a reception in Balliol College. A list of the participants has survived in the diary of Erasmus Philipps. Not surprisingly, those present were mainly Jacobites:

1721, April 9. Supped wth the Marquiss of Carnarvon at his Apartments in Baliol College, where were Lord Lusam and Mr. Legh [h]is Brother (sons to Wm Legg, Earl of Dartmouth), and Sir Walter Bagott, Bart, Noblemen of Magdalene College, Dr King, a Civilian, Principal of St Mary Hall; Dr Sedgwick Harrison, a Civilian, and Camden Professor of History; Dr Steward, M.D. (a Scotch Gentleman, and Companion to the Marquiss); Dr Hunt, Fellow of Baliol College (Tutor to the Marquiss); Robert Craven, Esqr. (Bro. to Wm Craven, Lord Craven); Stephen and Henry Fox, Esq^{rs}, sons to the famous Sir Stephen Fox, Kn^t (Gent. Commoners of Christ Church); Mr Lees, Fellow of Corpus Christi; Mr Humphrey Lloyd, B.D., Fellow of Jesus, and my Brother. The Entertainment here was extreamly Elegant, in Every Respect.[2]

An entry in Hearne's *Collections* under 8 June 1721, reads: '. . . D^r. King's Mother is now living near Silchester in Hampshire, but his Father is dead.'[3] The reference to King's mother

---

[1] On the activities of the lady portrayed on the medal see A. Shield and Andrew Lang, *The King Over the Water* (London: Longmans, 1907). On the Finsthwaite character see *Notes and Queries*, 8th Series, Vol. XI, pp. 66, 110, 157; 11th Series Vol. VIII, p. 232 and Vol. IX, pp. 230, 495. Some comments on Shield and Lang's book appeared in R. E. Francillon, *Mid-Victorian Memories* (London: Hodder and Stoughton, 1914?), pp. 290f. Francillon was the principal editor of *The Royalist* (1890–1905), the organ of the Jacobite society named the Order of the White Rose. On the Sobiesky Stuarts in general see Sir Charles Petrie, *The Jacobite Movement* (London: Eyre and Spottiswoode, 1959), Appendix VI, pp. 469–74.

[2] J. P. Phillips, 'College Life at Oxford, One Hundred and Thirty Years Ago', *Notes and Queries*, 2nd Series, Vol. X, p. 366.

[3] Hearne, op. cit., Vol. VII, p. 250.

is not correct if interpreted literally: she died when her son was 'about seven years old', as he makes plain in the *Political and Literary Anecdotes*. Hearne is undoubtedly referring to King's mother-in-law, Dorothy Wither, who was residing in Hampshire at this time, and who lived on until 1732. On May 28 of that year she died, and was buried in the Hampshire village of Dean.

Hearne's entry two days later is of greater value:

June 10 (Sat.). D[r]. King, Principal of S[t]. Mary-Hall, lately told me that he heartily wish'd the whole Body of the University Statutes were printed, so as to be made more common, that the World might see and judge what horrible Tricks are plaid by three or four, or a few more, People here (such as Gardiner, Charlett, &c.), who are for doing everything as they please, & if anything be done contrary to their mind, presently cry out that such as are opposite to them are Enemies to the University, by this means taking upon themselves the name of the University, and excluding all others, whereas in reality they are the Enemies of the University, and do all that possibly they can to disgrace and ruin her. The D[r]. told me he had a good mind to print his own Copy of the Statutes. He said those Fellows I have been speaking of acted most basely by our Chancellour, my Lord Arran, & that my Lord had no Copy of the Statutes at all.[1]

Evidently King was deeply involved in academic politics. The names Gardiner and Charlett refer to Dr. Bernard Gardiner, Warden of All Souls, and Dr. Arthur Charlett, Master of University College, two of the heads of colleges whose hostility towards the cause of Jacobitism was generally acknowledged. King, like Hearne, was antipathetic to both of them and to their supporters. As Vice-Chancellor from 1712 to 1715 Gardiner had been the leader of the anti-Jacobite elements in Oxford, and was still a powerful force against King, who by now seems to have been regarded as the principal protagonist of the Jacobite persuasion. Charlett had opposed King by using his influence against Hearne in his dispute with the Clarendon Press in 1718. Even though the Master of University College was thirty years King's senior, he seems to have exhibited a rather unusual degree of garrulity and also a certain penchant

[1] Ibid.

for double dealing.[1] Both Gardiner and Charlett had often
openly sympathized with the Oxford 'Court Whigs', and both
voted against King in the election for the parliamentary
representation of the university in 1722.

This election deserves special mention since it constitutes
King's only attempt to enter practical politics. The earliest
surviving intimation of King's decision to stand as a candidate
for the university is contained in a letter written by King to
Captain Halsted on 24 October 1721.[2] In it he laments: 'I am
hard pushed here by my brother H—ds and they intend once
more to try their interest with Lord A—n. In the meantime
they represent this attempt of mine as a thing perfectly disagreeable to the O—d family.' Writing to Edward Harley, later the
second Earl of Oxford, Canon William Stratford of Christ
Church commented, on the following November 20, 'I am
afraid we shall have a disturbance in this place. Harrison and
his party now canvass openly for a sorry fellow, Dr. King.'[3]
The 'Harrison' here mentioned is Sedgwick Harrison, Fellow of
Corpus Christi College, and staunch supporter of the Principal
of St. Mary Hall. Needless to say, Canon Stratford was
not sympathetic towards King's cause: he was one of King's
many Whig opponents in orders.

Shortly afterwards King resigned his Secretaryship to Lord
Arran under pressures the precise extent of which is now im-
possible to determine. There are several contemporary refer-
ences to this event. One is contained in a letter written by Dr.
George Carter, Provost of Oriel, to Archbishop Wake on 22
December 1721: 'Dr. King who puts up for Member of Parlia-
ment for the Univ^ty hath quitted his Post of Secretary to our
Chancell^r, & Mr Watkins of X^t church succeeds him in that
Office. Dr King if he stands it out will lose his Election by above

---

[1] Some Christ Church men believed that he had acted a double role in their
earlier controversy with Richard Bentley. He was also suspected of duplicity in the
affair of the dedication of Edward Thwaites's *Heptateuchus, Liber Job et Evangelium
Nicodemi Anglo-Saxonice* to George Hickes. In No. 43 of the *Spectator* Charlett, under
the uncomplimentary name of Abraham Froth, is made to write an amusing letter
dealing with the business transacted at meetings of the Hebdomadal Council.

[2] Public Records Office, State Papers Domestic, 35/28, Item 89.

[3] Historical Manuscripts Commission, *Report on the Manuscripts of his Grace the
Duke of Portland, K.G., Preserved at Welbeck Abbey*, Vol. VII, p. 307.

two to one I believe; All us Whigs are against him to a Man.'[1]
Another is contained in a letter written by Canon Stratford on
2 January 1721/2: 'Harry Watkins is Secretary instead of King.
The Chancellor told King he could keep him no longer, but to
make his dismission less disgraceful gave him leave to resign.'[2]

A much fuller account of what happened was inscribed by
Hearne in his diary:

Jan. 18 (Th.). D^r. King, principal of S^t. Mary Hall, being pitch'd
upon for a Parliam^t Man for our University in the ensuing Election
(provided the Parliam^t should be dissolved, as 'tis much talk'd off),
by many honest Gentlemen of the University, who mightily desire
to throw out D^r. Clarke, this D^r. Clarke's Friends are so nettled at it
that most of the Heads of Houses sign'd a Letter to my Ld Arran,
Chancellour of the University, signifying that D^r. King is a Fomen-
ter of Differences in the University, a Disturber of the Peace, and I
know not what. Upon wch some Passages pass'd between my L^d
Arran & D^r. King, & the D^r. resign'd his Secretaryship to my L^d
(worth above 100 Guineas a Year, as I heard the D^r. say), & M^r.
Henry Watkins, M.A., Senior Student of X^t Ch., is made his
L^{d}ship's Secretary. This base Act of the Heads hath made the D^r.'s
Friends the more zealous, & my Ld Arran is much blamed for his
Conduct, since he hath no reason to countenance Clarke, who, when
in France, would not so much as see my L$^{d's}$ Brother, the Duke of
Ormond, who was Clarke's great Friend.[3]

The University of Oxford was represented in the House of
Commons by two members. For the election of 1722 there were
three candidates: William Bromley of Christ Church, George
Clarke of All Souls, and William King of St. Mary Hall. All
three were Tories, but King was the only self-confessed Jacobite. Bromley was the most popular of the three: his reputation
for sincerity, prudence, and honesty was generally allowed, and
nobody seriously doubted that he would be returned. The real
contest was between Clarke and King. The latter was a
quarter of a century younger than Clarke, but, even so, his
chances of success at first seemed promising. Clarke was temporarily unpopular among different sections of the qualified
voters for two reasons: many of the Whigs recalled how in 1705

---

[1] Christ Church Library, MSS. Arch. Wake Epist. 16, No. 95.
[2] Historical Manuscripts Commission, op. cit., Vol. VII, p. 312.
[3] Hearne, op. cit., Vol. VII, p. 318.

he had taken part in the fierce contest in the House of Commons for the office of Speaker, voted for the Tory candidate, and been ejected from all his political offices by the Whig ministry; many of the Jacobites, on the other hand, felt disinclined to vote for him because of his very moderate brand of Toryism and his obvious interest in retaining the friendship of both Hanoverian Tories and, if the phrase may be permitted, Right-wing Whigs. Furthermore, it must also have been manifest to most of the potential voters in Oxford that Clarke was the choice of the majority of the heads of colleges rather than of the electorate as a whole. Very probably these factors had won King some sympathy. On 4 February 1721/2 he wrote to Captain Halsted: 'My brother heads are grown less violent and treat my friends with more temper and humanity.'[1] On the following March 7 Canon Stratford commented at Christ Church: 'There is some whispering here at present, as though the Whigs of this place would go over entirely to King. I know not what to make of it.'[2] This temporary respite, however, produced no lasting results.

Gradually the direction of electoral sentiment turned against King. He had already been, in effect, forced to resign his special relationship to the Chancellor, and had thereby lost a portion of his indirect power. He was the youngest of the three candidates by more than twenty years, and, unlike his fellow contestants, had had no parliamentary experience whatever. His Jacobitism alienated many Tories who might otherwise have voted for him, and his lack of prudence was later admitted even by himself. He could on occasion exhibit causticity, sarcasm, and egocentricity, characteristics which would hardly have won waverers to his cause under any circumstances. Outside Jacobite circles he had powerful and vociferous enemies who unceasingly inveighed against him. Gardiner and Charlett were among them, but he had another energetic antagonist in Dr. John Gibson, Provost of Queen's College, and cousin of Edmund Gibson, the highly influential Whig Bishop of Lincoln. In his entry for February 11 Hearne reproduced an open letter

[1] Public Record Office, State Papers Domestic, 35/30, Item 27. This letter is addressed to Halsted at the Coco Tree in Pall Mall, an established Jacobite haunt.
[2] Historical Manuscripts Commission, op. cit., Vol. VII, p. 314.

to the Chancellor, which was commonly believed to have been written by the Provost of Queen's. 'It had been', wrote Hearne, 'printed and dispersed, but finding that it rather did the Dr Service than Mischief, great care was taken to have it stifled'. Oxford University, the writer proclaimed, was a 'Sacred Place, where *Peace* and *Order* ought to reign', but if the methods of King were followed, the forthcoming election would be '*Mobbish* and *Popular*':

. . . Strife, Envy, Hatred, and Contention will rove about like devouring Lions: *Order* and *Government* will be no more, but every one will do what is righteous in his own Eyes. If once the *Younger and Unthinking Part of the University* meet with Success against their *Governors*, they, like a furious Horse, will too soon feel their own Strength, and throw off all *Submission*, and, consequently, *Opposition and Rebellion* will be their first Principle.[1]

Dr. Gibson, whether or not he penned this letter, apparently engaged in other political activities not merely epistolary. For example, he successfully dissuaded his brother from voting for King, according to Hearne's later account:

Sept. 20 (Th.). M^r. Gibson of Queen's Coll., Brother of the Provost of that Name, is curate of Pamber and Stadley [Tadley] in Hampshire, D^r. King having been his great Friend there, the D^r.'s Mother in Law living at Wyford, wch is situated between both Places; and M^r. Gibson, being sensible of the Obligation, promised the D^r. his vote for Parliam^t Man, but was drawn off by the Threats and illegal Methods of his Brother, the Provost.[2]

Dr. Robert Shippen, the Vice-Chancellor, voted for King's rivals after what seems to have been a singular sequence of events. Hearne writes:

Sept. 15 (Sat.). D^r. King, withall, assured me that D^r. Shippen, our Vice-Chancellor, in the late Election was at first against D^r. Clarke, thinking to have got in his own Brother, Wm Shippen, Esq., the Project being to have got M^r. Bromley to resign, & to bring in the Honble Robt Digby, Esq., in his Place. And the better to secure an Interest, the V. Chanc. endeavour'd to get D^r. King (who had certainly once a Majority of Votes in Magd. Coll., tho' they fell off afterwards) to desist, & to draw over his Men for his Brother, but

[1] Hearne, op. cit., Vol. VII, pp. 328–9.   [2] Ibid., p. 402.

when the V. Chanc. saw that the D^r. was resolv'd to stand it out, he then appear'd strenuous for Clarke and Bromley.[1]

On account of his influential position, Shippen may perhaps have been more instrumental in weakening King's cause than any other single individual. He undoubtedly exerted *some* pressure on the Chancellor to dismiss King as his Secretary, a singularly ironic situation, in view of the fact that King himself had persuaded Lord Arran to appoint Shippen as Vice-Chancellor in 1718.[2] R. J. Robson has suggested that Shippen's behaviour was dictated primarily by the desire to prevent Government intervention:

> Since the Hanoverian succession the Jacobite proclivities of the University had been restrained by the concern of Convocation and of successive Vice-Chancellors for the 'independency' of the academic body. Politics in the national context must invariably be subordinated to the domestic interests of the University. These would not be promoted by inviting Government intervention, and the main preoccupation of the governing magistrates throughout the reigns of the first two Georges was to keep out the Dragoons and the Whigs. Thus when Dr. William King, the Principal of St. Mary Hall, and a man very zealous for King James, decided to fight the University constituency in 1722 against Bromley and Clarke, thereby splitting the Tory vote and affording the 'squadron of Whiggs' their opportunity, Vice-Chancellor Shippen and the heads of colleges connived at all manner of chicanery to secure his defeat.[3]

Also opposed to King in various ways were Dr. John Morley, Rector of Lincoln; Dr. William Delaune, President of St. John's; Dr. Matthew Panting, Master of Pembroke, and most of the other heads of colleges. King's future enemy, John Burton of Corpus Christi College, was among those who did not vote for him, as also were the Public Orator, Digby Cotes of Magdalen Hall; Henry Watkins of Christ Church, King's successor as Secretary to the Chancellor; Sir Nathaniel Lloyd,

---

[1] Ibid., p. 401.

[2] W. R. Ward, *Georgian Oxford* (Oxford: at the Clarendon Press, 1958), pp. 123f. Ward's account of the affair is excellent, though I question the implied date of Shippen's appointment as the beginning of 1719; Hearne's date is 7 October 1718.

[3] R. J. Robson, *The Oxfordshire Election of 1754* (Oxford: Oxford University Press, 1949), p. 3.

Fellow of All Souls; Canon Robert Clavering, the Regius Professor of Hebrew, and all the other canons of Christ Church who took part in the election. Thus, with so many influential persons arrayed against him, King on the eve of the election could hardly have felt optimistic.

The actual election took place on March 21. A brief report of it was provided by Hearne in his diary entry for the following day:

March 22. (Th.) Yesterday Morning, at 9 Clock, was a Convocation for electing Burgesses for the University. The Candidates were the two old Members, Mr. Bromley and Dr. Clarke, but many having a mind to get Clarke out, D^r. King, Principal of S^t. Mary Hall, was put up against him. The Convocation continued 'till about half hour after four in the Afternoon, when it appear'd that D^r. King had lost it by a very great Majority, the Poll standing thus, the Number whereof on the right hand signifies dubious Votes:—

> Br. 337 — 60
> Cl. 278 — 49
> K.   159 — 36

Upon w^{ch}, the Election was declared, tho', a Scrutiny being desired, the Business was put off 'till this Morning, when there was another Convocation. But there being such a vast disproportion, the throwing out the Bad Votes signify'd nothing to the Interest of D^r. King, who thereupon acquiesc'd, and M^r. Bromley & D^r. Clarke were declared duly elected. I heartily wish D^r. King had succeeded, he being an honest Man, & very zealous for K. James, whereas Clarke is a pitifull, proud Sneaker, & an Enemy to true Loyalty. . . . [1]

All the commentators on the subject agree that King lost the election by a substantial margin, though minor variations of Hearne's aggregates have appeared in the literature of the subject.[2] The only radically different set of results for this poll was provided by Henry Stooks Smith over a century later:[3]

[1] Hearne, op. cit., Vol. VII, pp. 341f. A glimpse of Clarke as a 'sneaker' is provided in his letter to Charlett of 11 May 1721, Bodleian Library, Ballard MSS. 20, fo. 164.

[2] For example, W. R. Ward, op. cit., p. 126, gives Bromley's total of votes as 338 rather than 337.

[3] Henry Stooks Smith, *The Parliaments of England* (2 vols.; London: Simpkin, Marshall, 1844–5), Vol. II, p. 7.

	Plumpers	*Total votes*
William Bromley	1	278
George Clarke	1	213
William King (unsuccessful)	75	142

Smith's figures are sometimes quoted, but it is not at all clear how they were arrived at. Since they cannot be substantiated they are best disregarded.

The large number of dubious votes given in Hearne's account resulted partly from the obscurity surrounding the technical qualifications for the university franchise. In theory the right of voting was confined to doctors and masters *actualiter creati*, who had paid their fees and kept their names on the Buttery Books for at least six months prior to the election. In practice it must have been difficult to assess the qualifications of every individual voter, and some heads of colleges had apparently obfuscated the situation further by examining the Buttery Books, and striking out the names of several Masters of Arts without their consent. According to Canon Stratford, Harrison and King had taken it upon themselves to secure 'many votes, who have no names in any college books, and have left the university many years ago'.[1] But even if all the dubious votes cast for King had been counted, he would still have been defeated in the election. On March 22 he demanded a scrutiny as Hearne indicated, but he had lost by such a landslide that the result was a foregone conclusion.

There are two other contemporary accounts of this election, both published anonymously in the same year: *A True Copy of the Poll for Members of Parliament for the University of Oxford*, and *An Account of the Late Election for the University of Oxford*.[2] According to Hearne, the first of these was a 'most silly Paper', drawn up and published 'by that most egregious Coxcomb and Rascal,

[1] Historical Manuscripts Commission, op. cit., Vol. VII, p. 317.

[2] Another pamphlet published shortly before the election, entitled *Some Thoughts Concerning the Next Election of Members of Parliament for the University of Oxford*, is now lost. It is referred to in a letter written by Canon Clavering of Christ Church to Archbishop Wake (Christ Church Library, MSS. Arch. Wake Epist. 16, No. 97). He explains: 'The Author appears in disguise, and at the same time that he would seem to be for the old Members, does really appear to be serving Dr. King who sets himself up in opposition to them.'

Joseph Bowles, Head Keeper of the Bodlejan Library . . .'. He then continues:

It is call'd a *true Copy*, whereas 'tis a most false one, and the *Explication of the Abbreviatures* (as he calls them), wch is put on the backside of the Title, is as ridiculous as 'tis foolish. All sorts of Persons term him a fool, as well as a Rogue (and very justly), for this and other Things. This very Fellow promised to vote for D^r. King in the Election. Nay, D^r. King says that if he promis'd him once, he promis'd him fifty Times. But when the Election came, he not only voted against him, but was the Writer of the Poll for D^r. Clarke and M^r. Bromley, M^r. Jones of Balliol College being the Writer for D^r. King, & now he hath acted the wretched Part of publishing this very poor, blockish Paper, rendering himself thereby the Scorn of all Mankind. I saw D^r. King & M^r. Web (our Senior Proctor for this year) last Wednesday [i.e. April 11 1722], when they spoke of this impudent Fellow with the utmost Contempt, & D^r. King was pleas'd to say that he hop'd to see that sorry Rascal expell'd the University. There is one Thing I cannot pass by here, and that is, a good natur'd Thing of the B^p of Chester and D^r. Stratford, who lately (before this Paper came out) sent to D^r. King, & desir'd him to take care of this Fellow, Bowles. This D^r. King mentions himself, & takes it very kindly, notwithstanding they voted both against him.[1]

These remarks call for comment. There is now no possible method of determining the veracity of the information given in *A True Copy*. What must have irritated King's supporters was a system of symbols, freely used throughout the booklet, to indicate good, bad, and doubtful votes queried by the inspectors of both sides. A list of thirty-three voters is given under the heading BALIOL College; of these, thirty-one voted for King, nineteen of whom are categorized as casting 'doubtful or bad votes'. All the fourteen electors of University College are listed as approving King's rivals, but the only three queries raised relate to 'good' votes. In St. Mary Hall, King's own institution, there were, according to the writer, fourteen voters; five of these are castigated as polling votes which were 'doubtful' or 'bad'.[2]

[1] Hearne, op. cit., Vol. VII, p. 349.
[2] *A True Copy of the Poll for Members of Parliament for the University of Oxford, Taken March the 21st 1721* (Oxford, 1722), pp. 3f., 14. See also the EXPLICATION on p. 2.

Since the technical difference between good, bad, and doubtful votes is nowhere explained, it is impossible to attach any precise significance to these descriptions. If all votes, regardless of their symbols, are totalled, the results are as follows:

William Bromley	:	337
George Clarke	:	278
William King	:	159

These aggregates correspond exactly to Hearne's, if one ignores *his* list of dubious votes. Such conflicting estimates do, of course, manifest the unsatisfactory administrative arrangements for university elections of that time, and the fact that franchise qualifications were, to some extent, a matter of personal interpretation of unprinted statutes.

The other account is of greater length. Its publication was thus heralded by Hearne:

Aug. 17 (Fri.). There is just come out, in 8vo, *An Account of the late Election of the University of Oxford for Members of Parliament.* I read this Book yesterday. It is well penn'd, and done with good Judgm^t, & the Matters of Fact mentioned in it are too true. So that, to be sure, it will vex most of the Heads of Houses, who us'd such base Methods to put by D^r. King.[1]

This anonymous work is generally attributed to Sedgwick Harrison. It contains no detailed statistical assessments, but it does provide answers to some of the accusations made against King, and also a good deal of background information. Several anecdotes illustrate the alleged pressures exerted by most of the heads of colleges on their subordinates to vote against King. A letter is quoted from Dr. John Gibson, Provost of Queen's, to another member of the college, and described as 'a very modest Performance in Comparison of the rest':

Sir,
    If you are on the Side of the College for the *worthy old Members* against some UPSTARTS, who would bring us into Confusion, you will have the Pleasure and Satisfaction of doing what lies in your Power, to retrieve the *sinking Interest of the University*, which is not a little struck at in this Canvass. The Application of those, who would

---

[1] Hearne, op. cit., Vol. VII, p. 393.

make us unhappy, is, I am told, almost incredible: And it would be an unpardonable Neglect in me not to oppose them to the utmost of my Power.[1]

The anecdotes in this work may be presented with some bias, but the general burden of the argument—that the majority of the heads of colleges sided against King—is indisputably true. In fact only two heads voted for him: the Master of Balliol and the Rector of Exeter. With the exception of St. Mary Hall, Exeter College was the only institution which voted unanimously for King, a significant fact, in view of the disputes which he was to have with the fellows of Exeter in the 1750s.

Despite the fact that King lost in this election, it is remarkable how many Whigs voted in his favour, especially in Exeter, Merton, and Wadham Colleges. Two days after the election Canon Stratford explained a few of these cases thus: 'The Lord Chancellor sent over hither on Monday and Tuesday Sir John Doyly and others who brought over for King four Whigs of Merton and about six of Wadham, whose names are now actually on the poll for King.'[2] A more general explanation of this phenomenon may be found in the fact that all three candidates were Tories, and that the university Whigs were divided among themselves as to the best candidates for their purposes. There were moderates such as Canon Clavering of Christ Church and Dr. John Holland, Warden of Merton, who voted for the two less extreme Tories out of a sense of responsibility for the maintenance of university discipline and to secure a *modus vivendi* with the Government in London. In contradistinction to these 'Court Whigs' were the more radical members of the same party, many of them convinced anti-Jacobites, who were desirous of upsetting the position of the moderates, and who presumably felt that voting for King was their best method of achieving this end. The majority of the voters of Exeter College were in this category. Whatever the cause of King's surprising popularity among the extreme Whigs in 1722, he was never again able to recover his prestige with them after his defeat.

When the result of the poll was made public, King let it be

---

[1] *An Account of the Late Election for the University of Oxford* (London, 1722), p. 25.
[2] Historical Manuscripts Commission, op. cit., Vol. VII, pp. 317f.

known that he was dissatisfied with the manner in which the elections had been conducted. On 25 October 1722 he presented a petition to the House of Commons demanding redress, on the grounds that the Vice-Chancellor, as returning officer, had used illegal practices and thereby enabled Bromley and Clarke to be returned although illegitimately elected. His point of view was corroborated in a similar petition presented on the same day by Sedgwick Harrison of Corpus Christi College, Robert Brynker of Jesus College, Joseph Sandford of Balliol College, and some others. The text of neither petition has been preserved: all that remains now is a brief summary of each in *The Journals of the House of Commons*.[1] No result accrued from these petitions, and no proceedings seem to have followed from them. They were referred to the Committee of Privileges and Elections, but there is no evidence that the Committee took any action on them. Although King had gone to Westminster 'to call Walpole, Bromley and Clarke to account',[2] his mission proved ultimately unrewarding.

Perhaps it is just worth mentioning that the echoes of King's petition were still heard a generation later, in 1755, when a doggerel skit on it was published as the Appendix to the anonymous 'heroic paraphrase' of his oration at the opening of the Radcliffe Camera in 1749.[3] A note in prose at the beginning claims that it 'was the occasion of much pleasantry about the year 1722', when it was still unpublished. It is ostensibly written in imitation of Swift's verse satire *The Humble Petition of Frances Harris*. The author wisely remained *sine nomine*. Considered either as verse or as factual evidence it is valueless, as may be seen from the first six lines:

TO THE HONOURABLE HOUSE OF COMMONS, the
    petition of Dr. *King*,
Whom the Heads of Houses, next to *Dr. Harrison*, hate like
    any thing.
THAT your petitioner was made Head, because there were
    no people in the *Hall*;

[1] *The Journals of the House of Commons*, Vol. 20, p. 43.
[2] Historical Manuscripts Commission, op. cit., Vol. VII, p. 340.
[3] *A Satire Upon Physicians* (London, 1755), pp. 59–63.

That your petitioner having no money, in the late Election
lost it all;
That your Petitioner was called by the sitting Burgesses Dr.
Harrison's Tool,
And so tho' your Petitioner stood for a Parliament Man, yet
he went for a Fool.

When the election was over, some of King's enemies, perhaps
to lessen his political popularity further, claimed to know that
he had made an offer to Sir Robert Walpole to turn informer
against some Oxford gentlemen who were dissatisfied with the
Whig Government. King was indignant, and wrote to *The
Evening Post* on 19 November 1722 to the effect that the report
was entirely false, and that he had 'never had the Honour to wait
on Mr. Walpole, or to write to him upon any occasion whatever'.[1] He further intimated that he regarded what his enemies
had propagated as 'a base and villainous Calumny', adding, 'I
never made any such Offers or Overtures; and . . . I never
gave a Commission to any Person to make 'em in my name. . . .'
On November 27 Canon Stratford declared: 'He denies that he
either *went* to Walpole, or *wrote* to him upon any occasion, but
he does not deny that he ever *sent* any one else to him upon any
occasion.'[2] He posited the suggestion that King sent 'his
brother-in-law, one Withers, a hearty Whig' to Walpole, but
neither this nor any of the other accusations of King's political
enemies was based on more than hearsay.

One indirect result of the parliamentary election, according
to Hearne, was that it influenced the election for the Presidency of Magdalen College on 29 July 1722. The candidate
most favoured was Robert Lydall, 'who had been making
Interest almost, if not quite, as long as he had been of the
College, & might have carried it, had he not acted falsely with
respect to D[r]. King, when he stood lately for Parliam[t] Man for
the Univ. of Oxford, at w[ch] many of the Fellows were angry, &
deserted him, as he had deserted D[r]. King'.[3] The consequence
was that Lydall's junior, D[r]. Edward Butler, was elected.

---

[1] *The Evening Post*, No. 2080, 27 Nov. 1722, and Hearne, op. cit., Vol. VIII,
pp. 21f.
[2] Historical Manuscripts Commission, op. cit., Vol. VII, p. 341. See also p. 345.
[3] Hearne, op. cit., Vol. VII, p. 388.

Even though the affairs connected with the parliamentary election took up a good deal of King's time during 1722, he continued to devote himself to the less spectacular business of academic administration. On September 13 Hearne mentioned that King had recently attended his first meeting of the Hebdomadal Council.[1] The Principal of St. Mary Hall was, apparently, in a characteristically argumentative mood. He disagreed with several of the proposals for administering Bishop Crewe's benefaction to the University of £200 per annum. He protested against the suggestion that the Vice-Chancellor should receive £10 per year, maintaining that he should receive ten times that amount. He also dissented from the proposal to give £20 per year to the Registrar of the Vice-Chancellor's court, urging that the position was worth upwards of £100 per year. He felt that there was no justification for giving Bodley's Librarian a proposed £60 per year, since ''twas very probable that the same Man hereafter would be Librarian of D^r. Radcliff's Library as well as Bodley's, & then 'twould be a most noble Thing of it self, D^r. Radcliff's Salary being 150 libs. per an.' The other heads then apparently interposed that the two librarianships should be distinct. To this objection King is said to have replied, with a typically acrid thrust at Joseph Bowles, '. . . suppose the Bodlejan Library hereafter (for, as to the present Librarian, I suppose he will not be regarded) should be a Man of Worth, & be recommended by some great Man or Men above to be Librarian also to the Radcliff Library, I suppose there will be a Complyance to such a Request, & no one of you the Heads will be ag^t it.' This was certainly strong speaking for a newcomer to the Hebdomadal Council, but Hearne adds: 'To this they could say nothing.'

In determining the precise worth of Hearne's statements on these events one should, of course, bear in mind that they are the informal pronouncements of a staunch Jacobite Tory of much the same political outlook as King himself. Hearne, one of the most outspoken Non-jurors of his day, found it difficult to be charitable even towards Hanoverian Tories, let alone any 'rank stinking Whig'. But compared to his highly coloured opinions on *some* Oxford figures, his views on King are expressed

[1] Ibid., p. 400.

in restrained tones. His attitude is explicable: King had few friends who, to use his own words, were *veros, stabiles, gratos*, and there is no reason for believing that he regarded Thomas Hearne as one of them. Hearne was low-born, a disability for which King vituperated against several other men, and, unlike the Principal of St. Mary Hall, was always of an eremitical disposition. Pope's lines on him in the *Dunciad*—where he is styled Wormius—though quite unnecessarily spiteful, no doubt contain a certain degree of truth. The temperamental differences between the two men tend to enhance the value of Hearne's observations: despite their author's political sympathies, they were not patently influenced by any great measure of mutual *camaraderie*.

One final matter relating to 1722 deserves at least passing mention: the fact that towards the end of this year King appears to have been involved in controversy over the non-payment of sums in arrear charged to him for the relief of the poor of the parish of Ealing. The surviving account in the Ealing Poor Rate Book for 1719–29 is not entirely clear, but evidently King had refused to pay two sums totalling £26 17s. 6d. in poor rates for the years 1721 and 1722, on the grounds that he was not legally a resident of Ealing. By this time he personally regarded Oxford as his legal place of abode. Public vestry meetings to discuss the affair and the problems contingent on it took place on 31 October 1722, and on the following December 12.[1] The case was closed with a judicial decision recorded in the Middlesex Sessions Books on 18 January 1722/3: King is herein described as 'no inhabitant within the said parish, neither is he the occupier of the said tithes'.[2] His name does not occur in later Sessions Books, and there is no evidence of subsequent ill-feeling in the matter. The Vicar, Dr. Thomas Mangey, was on several occasions before his death in March 1755 the Principal's guest at St. Mary Hall, and his son, John, was for a number of years in residence there. It is pertinent to add here

[1] The text of the reports of these meetings in the Ealing Poor Rate Book for 1719–29 is reproduced in full in Appendix III.

[2] Greater London Record Office (Middlesex Records), Middlesex Sessions Books MJ/SBB. 809, p. 57. Relevant to the earlier history of King's successful appeal are MJ/SBB. 751, p. 105 (30 April 1717) and the petition MJ/SP. 1717 Ap/20 (20 April 1717).

that, although King appears to have allowed his interest in the rectorial estate at Ealing to lapse temporarily, he had resuscitated this connection by 28 November 1730, when he signed a new lease for the property, thereby becoming responsible for the upkeep not only of the rectory and its grounds but also of the chancel of St. Mary's Church.[1]

For some time after the close of 1722 King seems to have played little part in university politics or administration. Litigation in Ireland kept him out of the country for long periods, and the affairs of St. Mary Hall absorbed a good part of his energies when he was in Oxford. He was also engaged in composing his mock-heroic epic *The Toast*, which he later regarded as his masterpiece. The events underlying the writing of this setaceous literary effort must now be surveyed in some detail.

[1] See Appendix IV, pp. 373f.

II

The Toast

The Toast is King's longest literary work, and in some ways one of the strangest and most vituperative pieces of writing which eighteenth-century England produced. It purports to be a translation by Peregrine O'Donald of an original Latin poem 'in old monkish rhymes' by a Swede or Laplander, Frederick Scheffer. O'Donald has added copious notes and observations to his English rendering. In 'The Translator's Preface' he explains that the author went up to Oxford in the beginning of Queen Anne's reign when he was scarcely sixteen years old, and continued there until 1710, when he married an English woman. His wife having died soon afterwards, he returned to Sweden. In 1723 he paid a visit to Ireland to recover a sum of money due to him for a freight of copper, and was obliged to prosecute a long and expensive lawsuit before he could obtain any part of his money. What he was awarded after seven years of litigation was only a small part of what was owing him, and insufficient to reimburse him for the costs of the voyage and the law suit.

Scheffer places most of the blame for his losses on the wife of the man to whom he had consigned his effects. O'Donald comments: 'The Wife of this Man was an old Sorceress, the lewdest and most vicious Woman of the Age in which she lived, or perhaps of any other Age since the Creation of the World.' She and her cronies in Dublin carried on a running war against Scheffer, first hiring a set of villains to assassinate him, and then filing four long chancery bills against him, charging him with all the frauds of which they themselves had been guilty. They even took from him by force of arms the land which he had purchased from them at a very high price, attempting to murder his servants, who opposed them, and outrageously insulting the royal authority. But Scheffer bore up against all this violence with great resolution, and eventually won his case. Unfortunately, one of his adversaries, the 'chief agent of the sorceress', prevented the execution of the court decree given in Scheffer's favour, by insisting on his parliamentary privilege, as a member of the Irish House of Commons, of freedom from arrest. Disappointed, Scheffer abandoned the case which had dragged on for so long, and determined to leave Ireland, having arranged a compromise settlement in which he relinquished one half of what was due to him in order to secure the other half. To preserve the memory of this affair, and to transmit the names of his adversaries to posterity, Scheffer wrote this poem in Latin, the language which was most familiar to him.

The truth of the matter is that the entire work was written, for very definite reasons, by King himself. Scheffer's problems were essentially those of King, the story of whose case can be pieced together from the Irish court records and from miscellaneous allusions in the text and notes of *The Toast*.

King's uncle, Sir Thomas Smyth, had, according to *The Toast*, made a secret marriage with the elderly Countess of Newburgh after a long clandestine intrigue. The Countess had been praised in verse on numerous occasions. She had inspired Lord Bolingbroke to write his ode *Almahide*, which was published in 1701. She was the same lady whom George Granville had celebrated as Myra, and to whom he had addressed a series of amorous verses in the manner of Waller: some inscribed simply *To Myra*, and others entitled *To Myra, The Surrender*; *To Myra, Loving at First Sight*; *In Praise of Myra*; *Myra Singing*; *Myra in Her Riding Habit*; *Myra at a Review*; and *Myra's Parrot*, all being in print by 1712.[1] The subject of all these effusions was Frances Brudenell, daughter of the self-styled Francis Lord Brudenell, who was heir-apparent of Robert, Earl of Cardigan.[2] Born about 1672, she was married in 1692 to Charles Livingston, second Earl of Newburgh in the peerage of Scotland. He had one daughter by her, Charlotte Maria Livingston, who succeeded *suo jure* to her father's title when he died,

---

[1] Granville's *Poems upon Several Occasions* appeared in 1712, 1716, 1721, and 1726. The quarto edition of his *Genuine Works* appeared in 1732. All of these editions were published by Tonson.

[2] Frances' father died in 1698, but her paternal grandfather, the Earl of Cardigan, not until 1703, at the age of 96. Her mother was Lady Frances Savile: she died of apoplexy in 1695. See *The Complete Peerage*, Vol. III, pp. 13f. and Vol. IX, p. 514.

shortly afterwards, in 1694.[1] In May 1695 she married
Richard Bellew, third Lord Bellew of Duleek in the peerage
of Ireland, and their one son, John, who became the fourth
Lord Bellew, was born in 1702. In 1705 she was described
as 'a woman of much business and manages all her Lord's
affairs and law-suits'.[2] Her Lord died on 22 March 1714/15.
Sir Thomas Smyth, about a decade earlier appointed Chief
Ranger of Ireland, was, so King implies, her third husband,
though the marriage was never publicly acknowledged. She
never actually called herself Lady Smyth; to her death she
seems to have preferred the title Countess of Newburgh. In
English literary history she is generally referred to as Myra or
Mira.

Not long after the death of her second husband, Myra had,
through her extravagance, reduced Sir Thomas to a state of
penury, and had also made him responsible for the support of
her son. The Chief Ranger of Ireland was driven to such
extremes as selling his horses to pay Myra's gambling debts,
and borrowing sums of money—which he was later unable to
repay—using the Bellew estates and the emoluments from his
public office as part of his security. Constantly harassed by
creditors, he appealed to his nephew in Oxford, who dutifully
arrived in Dublin in 1723. He found Sir Thomas in a state of
genteel destitution, his house in Phoenix Park mortgaged for
almost as much as it was worth, and the mortgagee about to
foreclose. With imprudent generosity King immediately supplied his uncle with £500, discharged the debt on his house,
lent him £1,000 and then repaid another debt of £400. Exactly
how much money was handed over *in toto* is impossible to determine: in one place King gives the figure of 16,000 rix-dollars[3]
and in another £3,000. When it became clear that his loans
would not be repaid without coercion, King felt himself justified
in resorting to legal processes.

At this point Sir Thomas, Myra, the young Lord Bellew, and

[1] Further information on Myra's daughter is provided in Sir James Paul: *The Scots Peerage* (Edinburgh, 1904–14), Vol. 6, pp. 453f.

[2] Historical Manuscripts Commission: *Calendar of the Manuscripts of the Marquess of Ormonde, K.P.*, New Series, Vol. VIII, p. 193.

[3] The rix-dollar was a coin worth about four shillings and sixpence, or a little less, used in Sweden at the time King was writing.

several lawyers retained by them determined on a policy of defrauding King of his right to repayment. Myra attempted to dispose of Sir Thomas' nephew altogether by hiring three rogues to assassinate him, on the assumption that he was a complete stranger to Dublin, and that no lengthy enquiries would be made about his death. Infelicitously for Myra, one of these ruffians was struck with remorse, and confessed the plot to King, thereby enabling him to escape. Myra then turned to an attorney by the name of Dillon, who was engaged to draw a bill to prove that King's payments of money had been made 'in trust for another'. Supporting Dillon's side was Captain John Pratt, Constable of Dublin Castle and Deputy Vice-Treasurer of Ireland, along with several false witnesses. The case dragged on for years, during which time Myra managed to influence, directly or indirectly, such legal personages as Robert Jocelyn, the Attorney General; John Bowes, the Solicitor General; and Dr. Trotter, Judge of the Prerogative Court.

In addition to his other tribulations, King was subjected to at least one act of violence.[1] On this occasion one of Myra's friends, Sir Edward Pearce, apparently led a troop of banditti armed with carbines, pistols, hatchets, and other weapons to force possession of King's residence at Chapelizod, a village close to Phoenix Park. An amusing mock congratulatory ode on this exploit, supposedly written by a young student of Trinity College, in imitation of Horace, Book I, Ode 6, appears in the Appendix to *The Toast*. When King complained about this incident to the Court of Chancery, Sir Edward evidently made an affidavit that he used no force. He argued that the quiet possession of the house was delivered to him by King's servants, and swore in addition that King had assured him that he 'did not desire the Posssession of his own House.'

On 20 June 1732 Sir Thomas Smyth died, and the executors of his will were appointed: Sir Edward Pearce, and another of Myra's supporters, Sir Edward Crofton. Probably Myra forced Sir Thomas to sign the will when he was in no condition to resist; as King put the matter, 'the old sorceress conducted his mind, though she did not conduct his hand.' The will

---

[1] The first allusion to this incident is in the note to verse 17, Book III, of *The Toast*.

disregarded all obligations to King, but its mere existence created a new set of legal problems. Sir Edward Pearce died shortly after the battle had been rejoined, and his death was followed by that of Myra herself in 1735/6.[1] After Myra's demise Sir Edward Crofton and Lady Allen, wife of Viscount Allen of Stillorgan,[2] pressed the young Lord Bellew to continue the prosecution of the suit. Eventually, after much further wrangling, King won the case, but had to agree on a financial compromise by which he received only a portion of the sum awarded him by the court. His expenses throughout the entire period of litigation amounted to far more than the amount of money which he received.

He wrote his last and presumably most considered summary of the whole affair in a lengthy footnote embedded in the final version of his Latin epic, *Templum Libertatis*. There he complains about the evil effects of the legal system brought to the British Isles by the Normans, and continues:

Mihi olim haereditas luculenta, ut videbatur, a propinquo in Hibernia venit. Ut venit, litem iniquissimam intendunt nobiles quidam et potentes istius regionis incolae. Quae tum meae curae, labores, aerumnae! quae itiones crebrae, et odiosae mansiones in Hibernia! quae pericula maris adeunda! quanta a conductis sicariis metuenda! porro autem, quae adversariorum meorum convitia, injuriae, insidiae, fraudes! quae falsimonia ac manifesta testium perjuria! quae advocatorum praevaricationes et argutiae! quae procrastinationes, prolationes, cognitionum iterationes! Tandem post vicesimum annum, quum pars improbissimorum horum hominum ad Acheruntica loca abiissent, reliqui a lite cesserunt, et haereditas mihi adjudicata fuit et decreta: quam tamen (o gentis opprobrium!) lis immensa et onerosissima prope totam contriverat. Etenim, cum octo millia librarum ex ea debuissem percipere, jam expensi et accepti confectis rationibus, tricentenae tantummodo mihi salvae erant. Sed hujus sceleris historiam et adversariorum meorum facin-

---

[1] There is some doubt about the exact date. *The Complete Peerage*, Vol. II, p. 102, gives the date of Lady Bellew's death as 23 February 1735/6; the Burial Register of St. Audoen's Church, Dublin, indicates her burial as taking place on 4 January 1735/6. Obviously these two dates are irreconcilable. Since the latter is a contemporary, local record, it has a strong claim to *prima facie* credibility. There is no monument to her in St. Audoen's, which is at the time of writing in a half-ruined state. She is buried in the Molyneux vault.

[2] Viscount Allen was satirized as 'Traulus' by Swift.

ora sermone patrio accurate explicavi, et versu quidem, si incondito, haud tamen tristi et injucundo sum persecutus.[1]

A fragmentary background to these judicial proceedings is provided by the evidences surviving in the Registry of Deeds in King's Inns, Dublin, the Public Record Office of Ireland in Dublin, and the Public Record Office of Northern Ireland in Belfast. The principal collections of records containing information bearing on the proceedings described in *The Toast* are:

(1) In the Registry of Deeds: *Memorialls of Deeds, Conveyances and Wills*.[2]
(2) In the Public Record Office of Ireland: the *Chancery Bill Books*, the *Chancery Order Books*, and the *Repertories to Chancery Decree Rolls and Enrolled Decrees*.[3]

In addition, the Public Record Office of Northern Ireland possesses a relevant Indenture Tripartite made on 13 July 1730, of which William King is one of the signatories.[4]

---

[1] *Opera Guilielmi King*, p. 92. This note was in all likelihood composed during the early 1750s.

[2] The relevant memorials are principally:

Vol. 1: p. 249, No. 153.
Vol. 13: p. 387, No. 6079; p. 388, No. 6085.
Vol. 14: p. 207, No. 6078; p. 208, No. 6080; p. 210, No. 6084.
Vol. 15: p. 383, No. 7855; p. 384, No. 7856.
Vol. 40: p. 206, No. 25085.
Vol. 46: p. 175, No. 28180; p. 272, No. 28633.
Vol. 47: p. 505, No. 31667.
Vol. 52: p. 252, No. 34462.
Vol. 53: p. 36, No. 34304.

[3] The relevant references are principally:

Chancery Bill Books (in unnumbered volumes):

Volume for 1724–1726, p. 264
            1727–1729, p. 98
            1729–1731, p. 390
            1731–1733, p. 242
            1740–1742, p. 52

Chancery Order Books:

Vol. 50, pp. 12, 55, 60, 101, 138, 210, 290, 297.
Vol. 51, pp. 117, 144.

Repertories to Chancery Decree Rolls and Enrolled Decrees:

Vol. 4 (1709–1779), pp. 146, 179.

[4] Public Record Office of Northern Ireland, D207/2/1.

The *Memorialls* do not constitute a complete collection of the Irish deeds, conveyances and wills of the period. The registration of these legal instruments was a matter of choice for the parties concerned; consequently, it is impossible to estimate the number of unregistered legal documents of comparable significance affecting the litigation alluded to in *The Toast*. The information in the Public Record Office of Ireland is lacunose. The *Chancery Order Books* Vols. 53–103 (*c.* 1727–46) did not survive the partial destruction of the building during the Civil War of 1922. The *Chancery Bill Books* do not contain the texts of the bills, so that it is now impossible to identify the 'four long Chancery Bills' referred to by O'Donald in 'The Translator's Preface'. Virtually all of the relevant archives in the Public Record Office of Ireland are of a concise, formal nature, and imply documentary information which is no longer obtainable.

It would have been most illuminating to have available the will of Sir Thomas Smyth. It is listed in Sir Arthur Vicars's *Index to the Prerogative Wills of Ireland* (*1536–1897*), but perished in 1922 along with most of the original Irish prerogative and consistorial wills of the eighteenth century. There now survives only a brief entry in Sir William Betham's unpublished *Genealogical Abstracts*, a collection of 241 holographic volumes compiled partly from documents that were extant in the Public Record Office of Ireland before the Civil War. In Volume 62, page 59, there occurs this note:

> 144. Smith, Sir Thomas of Dublin, Baronet dated
> 17 Feb. 1731—pd [i.e. proved] 1732.
> Nephew Charles Withers, Esq., deceased.

And that is all that remains.

But despite their hiated nature, these records provide undeniable witness of the chronic indebtedness of Richard Lord Bellew and, after his death, of Sir Thomas Smyth. In deeds registered as early as 8 November 1708, Myra's second husband is described as selling lands and premises, mainly in the County of Dublin, for £500, and in a deed of 13 March 1713/14 (memorial 6079) a long list of his debts and creditors is supplied. Some of these debts are specifically described as 'drawn by Lady Newburgh'. Memorial 6085 refers to an Act of Parliament entitled 'An Act for Enabling Richard Lord Bellew Baron of Duleek to sell part of his Estate for discharge of Debts and Incumbrances affecting the same and for settling the residue thereof on himself for Life with Remainder to his protestant Issue subject to the Enlargement of the Joynture already settled on the Rt. Honble the Countess of Newburgh his wife.' By the deed recorded in the same memorial Lord Bellew leased a number of 'towns and lands' in the County of Kildare to Sir Thomas Smyth in recognition of an earlier loan from Sir Thomas of £2,250; later, when Sir Thomas became financially embarrassed, the same lands figured again in litigation with William King. The last set of documents to be registered by Lord Bellew was signed on 12 March 1714/15. One of these instruments, referred to in memorial 6084, indicates that the securities previously provided by Lord Bellew were insufficient, and that Sir Thomas Smyth had become bound in terms of security for him to several persons and in several sums of money. As a result, more lands were leased to Sir Thomas in the counties of Kildare and Louth for sixty years, the rent to be 'one pepper corn yearly if the same should be demanded'. Richard Lord Bellew, it may reasonably be assumed, never received even one peppercorn, for ten days later he was dead.

The relevant memorials that follow bear sombre witness to the steadily deteriorating financial position of Sir Thomas Smyth. In the memorial of a tripartite indenture dated 31 July 1716, he is described as 'Guardian of the Rt. Honble John Lord Bellew Baron of Duleek', and in later memorials is ordered to 'grant, assign and make over' a considerable number of properties to meet what must have been steadily worsening debts.[1] William King's name appears first in memorial 25085, relating to a tripartite deed of assignment of 19 October 1723; by the terms of this instrument King received, in legal theory, most of Sir Thomas' official emoluments. This document may have been connected with the 'reversional grant' which King mentions in

---

[1] Connected with these is the Humble Petition of John Lord Bellew and others for a bill to settle the estates of the late Richard Lord Bellew, in the British Museum, Stowe MSS. 354, folio 231. This document is undated, but should be assigned to 1723. Among the signatures appear those of the Countess of Newburgh and Sir Thomas Smyth.

The Toast as being security for his loans. In a subsequent tripartite deed dated 21 April 1725, and signed by the Countess
of Newburgh, Sir Thomas Smyth, William King, and Captain
John Pratt, it is directed that the Countess and Sir Thomas must
pay King a number of outstanding arrears. From an 'article or
instrument of agreement' registered on 21 April 1727, it is clear
that King had not yet received any of the monies that he was
legally entitled to collect from his impecunious uncle. It is not
until 13 July 1730 that the surviving documents show the
Principal of St. Mary Hall as the recipient of at least a portion
of what was owing to him.

For the following eleven years documentary evidence bearing on King's case is extremely sparse. A final bill dated 25
April 1741 was amended again and again, the last amendment
being dated in 1746. The decree that resulted is dated 15 July
1746,[1] and indicates that the plaintiff, King, should be awarded
two sums of £600 and £1800. These monies, by his own intimation, he never received in full.

Disappointing though his experiences must have been, the
persons whom he encountered during these years, unknown to
themselves, made him a poet. He made this fact plain in the
Epistola ad Cadenum, which appears in the beginning of the quarto
editions of *The Toast*:

> Non indigna cano. Debentur maxima MIRAE;
> Maxima monstriferi, studium quos cogere PAMMO,
> Taurorum, & tribadum, furumque, Deumque malorum
> Me coetus poscunt: & *me fecere poetam.*

His first poetical work, and probably his first published work of
any kind, appeared when he was forty-five years of age, in 1730.
Presumably written to relieve his own lacerated feelings, this
brief *Ode to Mira* was first published in Dublin as an anonymous half-sheet ballad, and was reprinted shortly afterwards
in London.[2] In it, the bard promised to sing Myra's praises,
despite the shortcomings of his subject:

---

[1] *Repertories to Chancery Decree Rolls and Enrolled Decrees*, Vol. 4 (1709–79), p. 179.
[2] A copy of the half-sheet edition is in the British Museum, C.121.g.8 (179). The
same text was reprinted in London—also in 1730—together with *Myra's Answer* in
the form of a twelve-page pamphlet. I do not know of any perfect copy of this

> I will form thee all Divine;
> And no Muse shall lie like mine.

Though Lady Newburgh's name was not mentioned, there could be little doubt that she was the poet's inspiration:

> I'll unbend the Work of Time,
> I'll restore thee to thy Prime,
> Feign, that now thou art as young,
> As when am'rous *G——ville* sung.

King never actually fulfilled this intention. By the time that he had started to write *The Toast*, the first edition of which appeared in Dublin in 1732, he had abandoned his original plan of presenting Myra as 'all Divine'.

King's early conception of what later was published as *The Toast* may have undergone modifications in other respects. At the end of the pamphlet of 1730 the following advertisement appeared:

Speedily will be Published,

THE HERMAPHRODITE.

A POEM in Four CANTO'S

By Mr. DONALD.

With the

LIFE OF *MYRA* THE *SORCERESS*,

By Mr. BUTLER.

The full implications of this advertisement cannot now be stated precisely. At one time King had intended to call his projected work *The Hermaphrodite*, but later changed the title to *The Toast*. However, of Mr. Butler and his projected book we know nothing. It is conceivable that King intended at first to write two separate works, under different pseudonyms, and finally decided to put all his material into one poem.

---

pamphlet which survives; two imperfect copies are still in existence: Bodleian Library, G. Pamph. 1286 (14), and the University Library, Cambridge, Hib. 7.732.24. In the half-sheet edition King used the spelling 'Mira'; afterwards, it appears generally as 'Myra'.

Only the first two books of *The Toast* appeared in the edition
of 1732. This was a poorly produced octavo volume, quite
unimpressive in comparison to the imposing quarto volume
which appeared in 1736. There are two forms of the first edition: the second is similar to the first, though it is shorter by
twelve pages. In addition to the text of the first two books of
The Toast, this second form contains a slightly revised text of
the *Ode to Myra* and *Myra's Answer*, the latter being an ode which
King may not have written, for he did not reprint it in the 1736
edition and never acknowledged it. It is possible that this
second form of the first edition was pirated. The collation of
these two versions is different: that of the first form is

8vo

[A]^2, B–G^8; pp. [iv]+96;

that of the second is

8vo

A–L^4; pp. 88.

The history of the writing of the final two books is obscure. A
short time before his death King wrote: 'I began *The Toast* in
anger, but I finished it in good humour. When I had concluded
the second book, I laid aside the work, and I did not take it up
again till some years after, at the pressing instances of Dr.
Swift.'[1] This statement seems to be contradicted by the contemporary evidence. First, there are the clear statements of
impending publication in a twenty-page booklet, *A Letter from
Mr. Lewis ONeil to Peregrine ODonald, Esq; with Mr. ODonald's
Answer*, published in Dublin in 1734 and reprinted in the
Appendix to the 1736 edition of *The Toast*.[2] Mr. O'Neil's
letter, dated 'Dublin, Feb. 9. 1733/4', written, of course, by
King, commences: 'According to your Desire, I have directed
Mr. *C.* to advertise the new Edition of the TOAST in all our

---

[1] *Political and Literary Anecdotes* (2nd edn., 1819), p. 97.

[2] There are only a few surviving copies of the 1734 text. Two are in the University Library, Cambridge: Hib.7.732.24^2 and the Williams Collection copy,
which is at present without a class mark. Another copy is in the Indiana University Library, PR 3539.K75L6. Mr. O'Neil's letter is essentially the same as in the
reprint, except that the date in the later version has been changed to 'Feb. 9,
1734/5'.

News Papers. Several ingenious Gentlemen, who apprehended,
that the third and fourth Books would never be published, have
since been with me, and express much impatience for a sight of
this compleat Translation.' The writer then requests Mr.
O'Donald to send sketches or descriptions of the copper plates
promised in an earlier advertisement. In a note added to the
1736 reprint O'Donald explains: 'The Copper Plates will not
be finished till next Winter.[1] For several reasons I could not
defer the Publication of my Book till that Time. . . .' and in his
answer to Mr. O'Neil he writes: 'I have indeed received so
many pressing Letters to hasten the publication of this Work,
that I cannot any longer disappoint the expectations of the
Town.' Finally, there is a letter which King himself wrote to
Swift on 20 September 1735, in which he explained that the
work was 'in such forwardness' that he hoped to have it
'finished in six weeks at the farthest'.[2] This letter could not
have been written more than three years after the publication
of the first two books. King must have been working on the
text of the final two books for some time before composing this
letter, since it would have been impossible to produce them,
together with their highly intricate notes in Latin and English,
in any very short space of time. The weight of evidence seems
to indicate that he could not have 'laid aside the work', after
the conclusion of the second book 'till some years after', and
that his memory, when he wrote the *Anecdotes*, may well have
been failing him.

The actual printing of the complete text of *The Toast* must
have taken place between September and December, 1736. The
third and fourth books appear still to have been in holographic
form in September 1736.[3] The complete text seems to have been
in print by the beginning of December, a date that may, I
believe, reasonably be claimed on three grounds:

(1) Some of the quarto copies bear the date 1736.[4]

---

[1] It is evident from this booklet that King intended to provide copper plate
engravings to illustrate the text of *The Toast*; in actuality only one, the frontispiece,
ever appeared.

[2] Harold Williams (ed.), *The Correspondence of Jonathan Swift* (5 vols.; Oxford:
at the Clarendon Press, 1963–5), Vol. IV, p. 395.

[3] Ibid., p. 530.

[4] For example, Bodleian Library, G.G.43, Art. and Mason Q. 159; British

(2) A few quarto copies contain a leaf headed *Advertisement by the London Bookseller* dated 'London, Decemb. the 1st, 1736'.[1]

(3) This edition appears in the register of books of *The Gentleman's Magazine* for January, 1737.

That King had intended to publish the finished work is demonstrated unquestionably by the advertisement which appeared in six consecutive issues of *The Grub Street Journal* between 27 January and 3 March 1736.[2]

Speedily will be publish'd,

In One Volume in Quarto,

THE TOAST: An Heroic POEM, in Four Books, written originally in Latin by FREDERICK SCHEFFER: Now *done* into English, and illustrated with Notes and Observations, by PEREGRINE ODONALD, Esq. . . .

Printed for Lawton Gilliver and J. Clarke, at Homer's Head in Fleet Street; and at their Shop in Westminster Hall.

The title page of the 1736 version of *The Toast* contains no reference to the printers and no proper colophon. The work was very probably done by Gilliver and Clarke, but the reasons for their remaining nameless are not far to seek.

Another indication of intention to publish is contained in the *Advertisement by the London Bookseller* of 1 December 1736. It reads in part:

I do not expect this Performance should be as well received in LONDON as it was in DUBLIN, where the Scene of Action lies,

---

Museum, 1466.k.21; Library of Congress, PA8540.K55.1754; Folger Shakespeare Library, PR.3539.K7.AI; Harvard College Library, 15491.11*, Columbia University Library, B824K583.X.1736; Henry E. Huntington Library, San Marino, 359398; Miami University Library, 826.K59; Newberry Library, Chicago, Y682.K582. Of the three copies of *The Toast* in the Sir John Gilbert Collection, at present housed in the Pearse Street Public Library, Dublin, two bear the date MDCCXXXVI.

[1] For example, British Museum, 1466.k.21; Folger Shakespeare Library, PR. 3539.K7.T7. In the former case the *Advertisement* is printed; in the latter, it is written by hand and tipped in.

[2] *The Grub Street Journal*, Nos. 370 to 375.

where the Characters are all known, and where every little Incident and Allusion in the private History are well understood. However, as there is some Humour in the Work, I imagine it will not be disagreeable to an *English* Reader, and therefore I hope to find my Account in Reprinting it here.

There is no reason for doubting that King wrote this Advertisement, and that he still hoped, towards the close of 1736, to obtain some return for his outlay in the form of royalties. This fact is made clear in *The Translator's Preface*, where it is explained that the 'Original' was entitled *Phoebus Noctivagator, seu Hermaphroditus*, but that the title was changed '. . . because I thought it too long to be adapted to the Voice of the *Dublin* Hawkers, on whose Address I must in some Measure depend for the Sale of my Book'.

There are at least three pieces of evidence that the 1736 edition was never actually published, in the usually accepted sense of the word. One is a paragraph in a letter which King wrote to Mrs. Whiteway from St. Mary Hall on 24 June 1737. The relevant passage reads:

You can't imagine how greatly I am vexed and disappointed that I have been so long obliged to keep back my conversation piece [i.e. *The Toast*]. I have in this respect, wholly complied with the reasoning, or rather with the humours, of some of my friends. They are willing to try their skill in accommodating my *Irish* affairs; in which, after all, I believe they will be disappointed as much as I have been: for the adversaries I have to deal with, proceed on a principle that will hear no reason, and do no good, not even to themselves, if others are at the same time to receive any benefit by the bargain. However, since you seem so earnestly to desire a second view of this work, I will send you a book by Mr. *Swift* [i.e. Deane Swift], who intends to go from hence about ten days or a fortnight hence. You will be so kind as to keep it in your own hands until the publication.[1]

The second indication occurs in King's *Political and Literary Anecdotes*. There he wrote:

. . . although it [*The Toast*] has been printed more than thirty years, yet it has never been published: I have, indeed, presented a

---

[1] Harold Williams (ed.), op. cit. ult., Vol. V, p. 52.

few copies to some friends, on giving me their honour that they would not suffer the books to go out of their hands without my consent.[1]

This passage, taken literally, leads to insuperable difficulties. The only edition that could have been printed 'more than thirty years' was that of 1732, and it was published in Dublin in two versions. The best explanation of the inconsistency is that, since King was writing, as he explains in the Preface, 'confined by the infirmities which are incident to old age', he was careless in his statement of the exact number of years, and that the 1736 edition was really intended.

Thirdly, there is a letter written by Charles Godwyn, Fellow of Balliol College, to John Hutchins, the historian of Dorsetshire, dated 2 April 1764, a little over three months after King's death. Referring to King, Godwyn remarked:

He printed, some years ago, a poem in four books, called 'The Toast'. That edition was never published, but some copies of it given to his friends. The rest of the impression lay in his lodgings, and is now ordered to be burnt. It was a dirty subject, and it did not become the Doctor to spend so much time as he did in raking into it.[2]

One other piece of evidence is perhaps worth mentioning. A copy of *The Toast* given to Martin Folkes, the President of the Royal Society, very likely by King himself, appeared in the sale catalogue of his library in 1756, two years before he died. However, King interposed before the sale and retrieved the copy from Folkes' executors, indicating that it was 'never purposed to be sold'.[3]

On the basis of the information which survives, one can only assume that King intended late in 1736 to publish the volume in the normal manner, but changed his mind and never actually did so. The explicit reason for this reversal of intention was intimated to Deane Swift in a letter which King wrote on 15 March 1737/8, probably addressed to him at the family home of the Swifts, Goodrich, in Herefordshire: 'I must beg the favour of you to leave behind you the copy of the *Toast*, at least

---

[1] *Political and Literary Anecdotes* (2nd edn., 1819), p. 99.

[2] John Nichols, op. cit., Vol. VIII, p. 241.

[3] See *A Catalogue of the Entire and Valuable Library of Martin Folkes, Esq. . . . which will be sold by auction by Samuel Baker etc.* (London, 1756), Item no. 5080.

to show it to nobody in *Ireland*: for as I am on the point of accommodating my suit, the publication of the book would greatly prejudice my affairs at this juncture.'[1] Evidently Deane Swift took this injunction to heart, for in his next surviving letter, dated 25 April 1738, King wrote: 'I thank you for the promise you make me concerning the *Toast*.'[2]

The unpublished 1736 edition is a handsome piece of book production, probably paid for by King himself. The sprinkled calf skin tooled in gold, thick boards, marbled end sheets, heavy leading, and wide margins must have sent the author's expenses soaring. There is also an elaborate copperplate frontispiece designed by Hubert Gravelot and engraved by Baron. The title-page is in two colours—red and black. Prefixed to this edition is the *Epistola ad Cadenum*, under the name of Frederick Scheffer, and followed by fifteen pages of *notae*, suppositiously written by O'Donald: in the *notae* it is explained that Cadenus is Jonathan Swift, to whom the work is inscribed. Neither the *Epistola* nor the *notae* is translated. Furthermore, Book I is lengthened by sixteen lines and Book II by fifty-two lines, and there is a long Appendix extending to thirty-seven pages.

Some bibliographers[3] have mentioned another quarto edition in 1747, though the version produced in that year could hardly be regarded as an edition in the customary sense. King had continued to make minor changes in the text, and had incorporated these changes in some, at least, of the copies of the text which he probably stored in his rooms in Oxford. Some of these altered copies have the date changed, very neatly in ink, from MDCCXXXVI to MDCCXLVII. Of the copies bearing the later date, a few have the errata, which originally appeared on a fly-leaf in the 1736 edition, neatly corrected in full, both in

---

[1] Harold Williams (ed.), op. cit. ult., Vol. V, p. 100. On page 99 the date appears as 'March 13th, 1737-8'. This would seem to be a misprint; the original source, Deane Swift's *Letters Written by the Late Jonathan Swift, D.D.*, 1768, gives the date as March 15, and thus it also appears in the List of Letters in Volume I of Sir Harold's collection.

[2] Ibid., p. 107. The date given in the List of Letters in Volume I is April 28; April 25 appears in the original source, Deane Swift's *Letters*.

[3] For example, William Davis, *A Second Journey Round the Library of a Bibliomaniac* (London, 1825); John Martin, *A Bibliographical Catalogue of Privately Printed Books* (London, 1834); William Lowndes, *The Bibliographer's Manual of English Literature* (London, 1834). Lowndes ascribes *The Toast* to the wrong author.

the text and the notes. These alterations of the date and of the errata give every impression of being in King's own handwriting.[1] In the copies dated 1747 the original M4 is cancelled by *M followed by eight additional leaves *M–*O1, pages *89–*104, which, to judge by the evidence of the notes, should be assigned to 1746 and 1747. There are also, in both the 1736 and 1747 versions, three additional *Q leaves, pages *113–*118, inserted between pages 118 and 119, and a different setting of these leaves for each of the two versions. In all the surviving copies which I have been able to trace bearing either date, leaf N2 is missigned M2. The collation of the 1736 version is as follows:

4to
A⁴, a–g⁴, h², B–P⁴, Q⁴ (Q3 + (*Q⁴(–*Q4))), R–Z⁴, Aa–Gg⁴, χ¹; pp. lxvi, [ii], 1–118, *113–*118, 119–232, [2].

The collation of the 1747 version is as follows:

4to
A⁴, a–g⁴, h², B–L⁴, M⁴ (–M4), *M⁴–*N⁴, *O¹, N–P⁴, Q⁴ (Q3 + (*Q⁴(–*Q4))), R–Z⁴, Aa–Gg⁴, χ¹; pp. lxvi, [ii], 1–88, *89–*104, 89–118, *113–*118, 119–232, [2].

The frontispiece, which includes eight half-lines of engraved text, is not included in these collations. The wording of the frontispiece differs in some copies: Mason Q.159 in the Bodleian Library, for example, has the original text covered by two slip *cancellantes*. Leaf Cc2 is sometimes a *cancellans*, as in the case of British Museum copy 1466.k.21, and sometimes not, as in the case of British Museum copy 642.l.5. Incidentally, the former of these two copies contains the autograph signature of Deane Swift inside the front cover; this may be the copy which he received from King himself, with the request that it not be taken to Ireland for fear of prejudicing the law-suit. Some copies of the poem dated 1736 contain the 1747 leaves; in these cases King presumably neglected to alter the date. Generally

---

[1] The following copies, for example, are fully or partly corrected by hand: Bodleian Library, Vet.A4.d.280; University Library, Cambridge, Syn.4.75.2⁵; British Museum, 642.l.5 and 441.f.15; Trinity College, Dublin, V.g.43; Sir John Gilbert Collection, Dublin, 14c/452; Victoria and Albert Museum, Forster Collection, 4835; Folger Shakespeare Library, PR.3539.K7.AI.

the 1747 leaves are included in the *Opera Guilielmi King*, the various portions of which seem to have been ready for binding in 1760. The discussion of *The Toast* that follows is based on the text of 1747, as representing King's most considered version.

The first element of the work, the *Epistola ad Cadenum*, extends over nine pages and is written entirely in Latin dactylic hexameter. Quite apart from its importance in the corpus of King's writings, it contains some of the most elegant tributes ever paid to Swift. None of the standard works on Swift makes reference to it, and to the best of my knowledge no English translation of it has appeared. Some idea of the admiration which King felt towards Swift may be gained from a perusal of the first eight lines of the *Epistola*:

> Semper culte mihi, semper, CADENE, colende;
> O decus & patriae tutamen! Crimina, curas,
> Atque hominum mores, & quicquid pulpita damnant,
> Seu nunc tu melius tractas irrisor acerbus,
> Seu Phoebi stimulis ignescens fundis Iambos,
> Aut STELLAE laudes recitas & amabile carmen:
> Si locus est interpellandi, en barbarus audet
> Ire salutatum, veniamque exposcere nugis! . . .

The first of the *notae* amplifies King's sentiments:

CADENUS. J. SWIFT D.D. D.S.P.D. sui saeculi deliciae, nec tam patriae, quam humani generis decus. Si virtutes illius contemplemur, nemini secundus; si divinum mentis ingenium, omnibus major. Cujus humanitatem, eloquentiam & eruditionem merito colebat SCHEFFERUS noster. Tales enim erant, quales sub Augusto principes viri, & ipsi in omni liberali doctrina politissimi, in suis literatis diligenter coluerant. Linguam Anglicanam usque ad fastigium venustatis provexit; & felicissimis numeris lusit poeta. Quippe CADENI spiritum, vim, & carminum suavitatem vel Flacci curiosa ambitio sibi adoptaret. Sale facetiisque Attico lepore tinctis facile superabat omnes. Sed & in scriptis suis utile dulci semper permiscuit; nec placere magis instituit, quam patriae prodesse. Hanc coloniam semel interumque in libertatem vindicavit, in aeternum vindicaturus, bona si sua norint coloni.[1]

---

[1] King took the name 'Cadenus' from Swift's *Cadenus and Vanessa*, published in London by Roberts in 1726. It comes from *Decanus* by metathesis.

King (under the name of Scheffer) then explains the purpose and background of the poem, alluding mysteriously in the *notae* to a Latin comedy, *Venefica sive Testamentum Mortis* from which the author is supposed to have derived some of his inspiration. Short extracts only are provided, but they exhibit King's abilities in the field of humorous Latin writing. In Act 1, Scene 2, Mira (described in the *Dramatis Personae* as '*Saga et Androgyne*') sings a ludicrous Latin ditty addressed to a *Bombardomachides* (a Grenadier Guard), to which King, on the last page of the work, thoughtfully provides the music.

The *Epistola ad Cadenum* is followed by 'The Translator's Preface', in which O'Donald provides in English a brief biography of Scheffer, and discusses some criticisms of his poem, here referred to as a 'Gothic performance'. After a brief 'Author's Preface', supposititiously translated from Scheffer's Latin, and three lesser items, there is a ΠΕΡΙΟΧΗ of the poem. The text proper commences on the recto of leaf B1.

The complete significance of *The Toast* is unassessable without a key to the characters. At least four keys have so far appeared in print,[1] and some copies of the text contain manuscript keys copied by previous owners. The differences among these keys are largely matters of amplitude; they appear to contain no significant contradictions, apart from a few immaterial mistakes. The following key to the principal onomastic analogues is compiled largely from those already in existence, with additional biographical information.

1. *Myra, Friga:* Frances Brudenell, alias the Countess of Newburgh and Lady Bellew.
2. *Volcan, Vol, Black Hero:* Captain John Pratt, Deputy Vice-Treasurer of Ireland and Constable of Dublin Castle. He was on friendly terms with Swift for a number of years, and is mentioned in the *Journal to Stella*. In 1725 he was accused of serious illegalities, tried, and found

---

[1] William Davis, op. cit., pp. 106–9; John Martin, op. cit., pp. 41–3; Pisanus Fraxi [i.e. H. S. Ashbee], *Centuria Librorum Absconditorum* (London: Privately Printed, 1879), pp. 320–2; Harold Williams, *The Toast, A Paper Read at the Four Hundred and Sixty Fourth Meeting of Ye Sette of Odd Volumes Held at Ye Savoy Hotel on Tuesday the 26th day of January MCMXXXII*, Imprinted for Ye Author at Ye Crozier Press and To be Had of No Booksellers (London?, 1932), pp. 36–44. Some copies of the text also contain a printed key which has been tipped in later.

guilty. Afterwards he engaged in coal mining and glass manufacture in Ireland.

3. *Mars:* Sir Thomas Smyth, King's Uncle.

4. *B——w:* John Bellew of Gafny, who once cudgelled Sir Thomas.

5. *Mrs. D.:* Mrs. Denton, a married woman with whom Sir Thomas had an intrigue for which he was tried and according to O'Donald (i.e. King) was 'mulcted in the sum of £5,000'.

6. *Lord John, Lord C***:* Lord Carteret, Lord Lieutenant of Ireland, 1724–30.

7. *Hor, Hortensius, B. H., Lord Pam, H——t:* Josiah Hort (1674?–1751), Bishop of Kilmore and Ardagh, and later Archbishop of Tuam. Satirized by Swift in *The Storm* and elsewhere.

8. *Milo:* Butler, a lieutenant of the Yeoman of the Guard.

9. *Clara:* Lady Louth.

10. *D of O:* Duke of Ormonde, patron of Sir Thomas Smyth and Captain John Pratt.

11. *Elrington:* Thomas Elrington (1688–1732), Deputy Master of the Revels, Steward of the King's Inns, and chief of His Majesty's company of comedians in Ireland.

12. *Lord A:* Joshua, second Viscount Allen (1685–1742). In 1707 he married Margaret Du Pass, who became Lady Allen. King maintained that she had tricked him into the marriage.

13. *Ali, Frow, The Imp:* Lady Allen. King describes her as *Judaea, ex Batavorum gente oriunda.* According to *The Complete Peerage*, she was born in St. James's Rectory, Piccadilly.

14. *Ottor:* Dr. Trotter, a Master in Chancery and Judge of the Prerogative Court.

15. *Sir Piercy, P——ce:* Sir Edward Lovet Pearce (d. 1733), Surveyor General of Ireland.

16. *The Prime:* Henry Singleton (1682–1759), Irish lawyer. Called to the Irish Bar in 1707, he became Prime Serjeant in 1726, and eventually Lord Chief Justice.

17. *George G——n——lle, G——ville:* George Granville, Lord Lansdown.

18. *D. of D.:* Lionel Cranfield Sackville, first Duke of Dorset. Lord Lieutenant of Ireland, 1730–37 and 1750–5.

19. *A——p:* Thomas Herring, Bishop of Bangor, 1738; Archbishop of York, 1743. He raised £40,000 to oppose the Jacobite invasion of 1745.

20. *H——:* Sir Richard Hoare, elected Lord Mayor of London in 1745.

21. *G——n:* Sampson Gideon, the Jewish financier consulted by Walpole.

22. *Laelius:* John Boyle (1707–62), fifth Earl of Orrery. He was a friend of Swift, and author of *Remarks on the Life and Writings of Dr. Jonathan Swift* (*1751; dated 1752*).

23. *M——:* Matthias Mawson (1683–1770). Bishop of Llandaff, 1739; Chichester, 1740; Ely, 1754.

24. *L——:* Samuel Lisle (1683–1749). Bishop of St. Asaph, 1744; Norwich, 1747.

25. *Aristo:* Forrester, an 'eminent Lawyer'.

26. *Iocco:* Robert Jocelyn (1688–1756). Attorney General, 1730; Lord Chancellor of Ireland, 1739; Baron Newport, 1743, Viscount Jocelyn, 1755.

27. *B——s, Bocca:* John Bowes. Solicitor General of Ireland, 1730; Chief Baron of the Exchequer, 1741; Lord Chancellor of Ireland, 1757; Baron Bowes of Clonlyon, 1758.

28. *Old Chum:* Dr. Monro, King's physician.

29. *Maccar:* McCarty, a footman of Myra, and hired witness against King.

30. *Cacus:* Sir Edward Crofton. Executor with Sir Edward Pearce of Sir Thomas Smyth's will, and suspected, by King, of having forged it.

31. *Curculio:* Captain Cugley, one of Lord Allen's officers.

32. *R——sse:* Lady Rosse.

33. *Miracides:* John Lord Bellew, Myra's son; not to be confused with John Bellew of Gafny.

34. *P——r D——:* Peter Daly, an Irish lawyer.

35. *W——st:* Richard West, Lord Chancellor of Ireland, 1725.

36. *Clio, Cadenus:* Dean Jonathan Swift.
37. *C.C.:* Colley Cibber.
38. *Dom Fuscus:* Ward, a Judge of the Common Pleas.

Book One of *The Toast* is entitled 'The Night Ramble of the Sun'. It opens with a conventional introduction in the Homeric manner:

Sing, O Muse, Phoebus' Wrath! say what Cause could persuade
So polite a young God his own Toast to degrade.
In a Matron say how a new Furor began;
Who extended her Figure and strech'd it to Man.

The Latin text, written in trochaic tetrameter, is provided by O'Donald (King, of course) in the notes and observations. O'Donald comments that, though Scheffer commences the poem in imitation of Homer, he does not show Homer's simplicity, for he proposes the arguments of the whole work in the invocation:

> Iram Phoebi, Musa, cane,
> Et quae plane scias, plane   .
> Dic: Ἄειδε Θεὰ ur-
> bane, quidnam causae, cur . . .
> Quur ex Vetula impura
> Furor novus & figura:
> Quis ex *Mira* finxit mirum;
> Ex Matrona Semivirum?

Already the reader is introduced to Myra, the heroine of the poem. Having made reference to the 'low pun' which Scheffer made on the name of Myra, O'Donald gives the reader some further information about her, briefly tracing her progress from hoyden to harridan. She was descended from a good family among the *Coritani*, a people of Northamptonshire, and was a woman of extraordinary stature, and of vigour and strength of body superior to most of her contemporaries. In her old age she so artfully repaired the damages of time that even Apollo was deceived. Apollo's deception and the incidents which follow upon it constitute the chief matter of the poem.

The story proper commences when Phoebus Apollo arrives

at night from the Atlantic Ocean in the form of a toupee-beau, in order to discover how mortals supply the absence of sunlight. He comes to Dublin, surveys the lights in the street, goes to court at Dublin Castle, and admires the splendour of the place. A glittering description of the Vice-Queen's circle follows. Apollo then catches sight of Cupid shooting arrows at random from the eyes of Clara (i.e. Lady Louth). Not wishing to be struck by an arrow, for he remembers his unhappy experience with Daphne, Apollo retires as the ball starts, with the intention of visiting Trinity College. While leaving the Castle he jostles Mars (i.e. Sir Thomas Smyth) and Volcan (i.e. Vol or Captain John Pratt) in the guard room. Mars and Volcan were the gods who, according to O'Donald, had been exiled from Olympus for repeated offences, and condemned to remain on earth for a period embodied as mortals. They invite Apollo to supper in Vol's Hole, which according to the notes was a little obscure tavern in Dublin to which Vol, while Superintendent of the Finances, used to retire to relax his mind and to seek solace with the mud nymphs of the River Liffey. The three sit down to eat in the tavern, and after some conversation Vol fills a bumper and calls for a toast.

The second book, entitled 'The Marriage of Mars and Myra', commences with the poet's address to Ottor (i.e. Dr. Trotter) and Iocco (i.e. Robert Jocelyn), and then describes the several orders of toasts: the household of Jove; the greater goddesses, among whom Venus is particularly distinguished; Thetis and her nereids or sea nymphs; the naiads or water nymphs; the hamadryads or wood nymphs; the silphs; the muses and graces with their maids of honour; and finally mere mortals. At last Phoebus proposes the toast of Myra, to the great amusement of Vol and Mars. The latter then expounds the story of his marriage to Myra and of her dissipation of his fortune on paramours, while denying her husband a subsistence. Apollo recants his toast with the comment: 'I confess, I was dup'd by George G—n—lle's report.' A new round of toasts is then drunk, and the book concludes as Mars and Vol become inebriated, and Phoebus returns to Parnassus.

Book Three is entitled 'The Acts of Myra and her Imp'. The poet addresses himself first to Piercy (i.e. Sir Edward

Pearce) and Lord Pam (i.e. Bishop Hort), and then offers an invocation to Phoebus. The sun god himself is meanwhile ruminating on his previous night's adventure in Dublin. He doubts the truth of Mars' story, and resolves to take a look at Myra. With the dawn he returns to Dublin, stops over Myra's house on Usher's Quay, and peeps into the window of her bed-chamber as she is getting out of bed. Here follow some extra-ordinarily repulsive descriptions of the apolaustic heroine, of her relations with her lovers, and of her imp (i.e. Lady Allen). Revolted, Phoebus issues an edict restraining Myra from all commerce with men.

Towards the close of the third book the author introduces the Episode of the Gridiron. It is not strictly relevant to the main story, and is mainly an opportunity for a more prolonged attack on Vol, his ambition and riches. He purchases a gridiron, conveys it to the treasury chamber, and proceeds to count the public money in it. The author uses this episode to cast aspersions on what he considered the unsatisfactory state of the Irish Treasury at the time. The episode concludes with some general reflections made by Mercury and Thetis.

The poet inscribes the fourth book, 'The Combat of Mars and the Hermaphrodite', to Cacus (i.e. Sir Edward Crofton). O'Donald notes that Scheffer had originally intended to address the fourth book to Sir Mars, but that before the work was finished Mars disappeared, 'or according to the general Opinion, he died; having first appointed Sir Piercy and Cacus his Successors, and the Executors of his Vengeance'. A good deal of the early part of this book is devoted to a description of an assembly of the gods on Olympus. Jupiter reviews his vice-gerents while Momus drolls on the absence of Vol and Mars. Juno is angry and demands their recall, but Jupiter refuses to grant her request. A serious quarrel is averted by the mediation of Momus, and a reconciliation is effected. No sooner has this crisis been allayed than Venus appears, affronted by the recent edict of Phoebus. She cannot rescind his decree, it being a 'standing order of the fates' that one god may not undo the acts of another. But she feels obligations towards Myra, and judges, as O'Donald puts it, 'that the loss of such an indefatigable Servant, so thoroughly experienced in all venereal rites and ceremonies, would be very prejudicial to the affairs of her Empire.' So she transforms Myra into a hermaphrodite, 'transferring at the same time to her new being all that vigour and vivacity which she was wont to exert in her Womanhood, with all other privileges and advantages usually annexed to the male Sex.' At the same time Venus gives Myra the name of Friga the Great. Fame, disguised as a dwarf, then flies to Phoenix Park, Dublin, and informs Mars, now referred to as 'her quondam Husband', of all that has passed above. Mars is rampageous and determines to do battle with the hermaphrodite. He arms himself in grand mock-heroic manner with *couteau de chasse*, muff ('which no other cou'd wield'), and, what turns out to be his most effective weapon, a full-bottomed peruke:

> So enormous the Bulk, and so pond'rous the Hair;
> Such a Cov'ring no Head, that was mortal, could bear . . .

He then drives 'as furious as Jehu' from his residence in Phoenix Park to Myra's mansion on Usher's Quay. Ignoring a treble voice that thrice repeats, 'Sir, my Lady's at Prayers', he makes his way up to her room, and there discovers the hermaphrodite with her tribade imp 'In a Posture—the Muse must not venture to shew!' A ludicrous combat ensues between Mars and Myra. In the end the epicene matron is blinded when her adversary throws his enormous powdered wig into her face with his whole might, and forces her to abandon her very unmilitary weapons. Jupiter, in his golden scales, meanwhile weighs the fates of the combatants in the approved Homeric manner. Mars trips up the now visionless Myra, and binds her hand and foot while she lies in a swoon. As soon as she revives, he offers her conditions of ransom, which at first she rejects with indignation, but at length, in danger of being eunuchated, she supplicates the conqueror and submits:

> 'Me an Eunuch!' she cries; and with suppliant Hands,
> Yet indignant submits to the Victor's demands.

With these lines, the 'translation' comes to a rather sudden conclusion.

At the end of his notes and observations, O'Donald adds an

epexegesis of thirteen lines in conventional dactylic hexameters which, he says, were transcribed from Scheffer's manuscript by Tir-Oen, a commentator of Cork. They give King a final opportunity to castigate his enemies and to demonstrate the difficulties under which the poem was written. At the same time they show that their author was capable of a certain kind of humility; he disarmingly describes at least the Latin parts of *The Toast* as *puerilia carmina*, despite the fact that they were written when he was *senior*:

Haec ego jam senior puerilia carmina lusi,
Haec, cum Scheffer eram: macerat dum febris; iniqui
Dum me causidici vexant; dum nigra lacessit
Dente malo TRAULI conjux; dum toxica miscet,
Accenditque virum cantu, ferrumque dolosque
ANDROGYNE molitur atrox; dum denegat audax
Depositum, haud uno contentus crimine, MAVORS
Hospitium violans, & avitas VATIS amici
Res moriens lacerat; dum PERSEUS pejerat omnes
Conceptis Divos verbis; dum raucus IOCCO
Bacchatur, VOLLUSque fremit; CACUSque, nefandos
Improbus ipse juvans PERSEI MIRAEque labores,
Dat venum mea regna, *abjuratasque rapinas*.

The Appendix which follows the poem proper contains a number of miscellaneous items, including a set of supplemental notes and observations, and the complete text of the *Ode to Myra* which had previously appeared on the Dublin streets in 1730. To it are added some extra notes, including one to the effect that Scheffer had taken some useful hints from this Ode, but had much improved on it in *The Toast*.

Perhaps the most powerful general impression which the poem makes on the reader is one of acrid, and at times ferocious defamation. Even Swift, in such poems as *A Beautiful Young Nymph Going to Bed*, *The Lady's Dressing Room*, and *Strephon and Chloe*, did not exceed the unsavouriness and mordancy of King's description of what Apollo saw when he peeped through the window of Myra's chamber as she rose from her bed:[1]

---

[1] The following three extracts are taken from *The Toast*, pp. 96–105.

There he saw the huge Mass tumble out of her Bed;
Like Bellona's her Stature, the Gorgon's her Head;
Hollow eyes with a Glare, like the Eyn of an Ox;
And a Forehead deep furrow'd and matted grey Locks;
With a toothless wide Mouth, and a Beard on her Chin,
And a yellow rough Hide in the place of a Skin;
Brawny Shoulders up-rais'd; Cow-udders; Imp's Teat;
And a Pair of bow'd Legs, which were set on Splay Feet.

However, after a certain amount of titivating with red and
white, Myra managed to make herself look fair and blooming,
despite her sixty years. Here the poet pauses in his account to
pass another sardonic comment:

Thus you see an old Hulk, many years Weatherbeaten,
All the Timbers grown rotten, the Plank all Worm-eaten;
Which the Owners, who doom her to make one more Trip,
Scrape and calk, tar and paint, till she seems a new Ship.

Myra's day starts with a series of curses instead of prayers:

Such the Morning Oraisons she us'd to repeat,
Since the Bead-roll of *Aves* were grown obsolete.
She began with great *Jove*, whom she curs'd for his Spleen,
Here to fix her Abode, and not make her Vice-Queen;
And she curs'd him again for his Meanness of Spirit,
Who assign'd her a Pension far short of her Merit.
Then, because at Threescore she was out of her Prime,
And her Tresses were hoary, she curs'd Father *Time*.
Ought her Head, like Mount Aetna's, be cover'd with Snow,
While she feels the fierce Flames, which consume her below?
Then she curs'd her next Kin, who refus'd to *adjure*,
And the useless old Matrons, untaught to *procure*.
All the Bankers she curs'd;—for they weigh foreign Gold:
And she curs'd the poor Players;—for their House is too old.[1]
Then she curs'd from her Soul, since her Luck was so ill,
Ace of Hearts, and Groom Porter, and odious Quadrille;

---

[1] O'Donald's note to this line reads: 'At that Time the old Theatre was standing.
But a new Play-House hath since been built in Dublin under the Direction of that
wise and honest Architect, who built the new Parliament-House. In the latter you
cannot hear, and in the new Theatre you can neither hear nor see.'

All the Duns, who want Manners, or Patience to wait;
All the Rich, who pass by, and the Poor at her Gate;
Little Priests, and great Prelates, who fix the Church-Pales,
From the Red-Hats of *Rome* to the Fidlers of *Wales*;
All the Belles of this Isle, who abhor the *French* Mode,
And the Bards, who address an old Witch in an Ode.
Next the *Morning* she curs'd, 'twas so hot and so light;
(If the Sun had been set, she had then curs'd the Night)
Little thinking Don *Phoebus* that Instant was near her,
That the God, whom she thus was blaspheming, could hear
her.

The eventual blinding of Myra is described with particular virulence:

Pointed Atoms of Powder in *Friga's* [i.e. Mira's] red Orbs
Deep infix'd, unresisting the Fluid absorbs:
And a Torrent of Tears, while she bellows and raves,
Now impetuous descending, the Salt-Water Waves
Roll a dreery wide Waste all adown her broad Cheeks;
And of all the fine Red only leave a few Streaks.[1]

Pungent though the verisimilar translation is, the author demonstrates his particular kind of expertise to the fullest in the notes and observations.[2] King has reproduced with great fidelity the manner and format generally used by editors and translators of Latin classics in the eighteenth century. So full are these notes that on some pages the text nearly disappears altogether. Long extracts are given from the pretended Latin original. Sometimes verses are given only in Latin in the notes, and for obvious reasons are not translated. From time to time, notably in Book III, Scheffer is made to put verses of his original poem into Greek, some of which do not appear in the English translation. In his rhyming Latin—and Greek—verses King shows remarkable sophistication, and maintains their quality

[1] *The Toast*, pp. 185–6.
[2] In *Political and Literary Anecdotes* (pp. 97–8) King later wrote: 'He [Swift] was chiefly pleased with the Notes, and expressed his surprise that I had attained such a facility in writing the burlesque Latin. The motives which induced me to form the Notes in that manner, was [*sic*] the judgment I had made on those of Mr. Pope's *Dunciad*. That Poem, it must be allowed, is an excellent Satire; but there is little wit or humor in the Notes, although there is a great affectation of both.'

through almost two hundred quarto pages. Furthermore, the notes contain many historically interesting allusions to contemporary personages. For example, John Bowes, who was later raised to the peerage as Baron Bowes of Clonlyon, is thus described: 'An illiterate Pleader. He was educated in a Cheesemonger's Shop near Billingsgate, where he learned his Oratory, and collected all those Flowers of Rhetorick which he occasionally throws out at the *Irish* Bar, to supply the Want of Law and Argument.' Dillon is given this description:

Dill . . . was a tall fat Lawyer, who without any kind of Learning or Skill in his Profession, had cunning enough to create Suits in all Places, where he was admitted, and to turn them to his own Profit. He advised the Method of cheating Mr. *Scheffer*, and drew that infamous Bill, by which it was pretended our Author's Purchase was in Trust for another. To support the Allegations of this Bill, he suggested to *Vol* and *Myra* all the Matter, out of which they framed their Depositions: And to second this Evidence, he chose for their Associate the greatest villain in the Kingdom; a Fellow who had formerly been Myra's Footman, and was suspected to conduct the Assassins, who were hired to murder our Author.

The notes and observations are replete with King's particular kind of humour. At no time is he in better form than when he is deliberately writing nonsense verse, either in Latin or in English. On page 78, for example, O'Donald tells his readers that Sir Mars was a great braggadocio, even when sober, but when a little mellow, which happened generally once a day, he was outrageous in his conversation, and would exalt himself by rodomontade far above all other gods or men. O'Donald then writes:

And since I began this Translation, I have seen the First Book of a Poem composed by our Knight in praise of himself, which he calls the *Martiad*. I remember the first six verses, as follow:

I will praise the great God Mars, for of all Gods he's most worthy to be prais'd.
And I'll sing Deeds so mighty, as shall cause ev'ry Reader to stand amaz'd.
I'll relate how he was much stouter than Horsa, who first landed in Kent;

And how he made better Speeches than any Member of
Parliament.

How that he could have a Countess or twain, when his
Honour inclined to kiss:

And that he could write better Verses than Homer: for he
himself wrote This.

And on page *115 O'Donald provides an extract from Scheffer's original, demonstrating Bocca's tautological manner of
speaking, and also providing an example of the frequently
untranslatable feats that King could perform with the Latin
language:

> Verbo, magne custos (tu no-
> tasti omnia) dicam uno.
> Nequid inest pol *Schefferi*
> Actis, factis, pactis, veri.
> Ne quid actis, factis, pactis;
> Ne quid factis, pactis, actis;
> Ne quid pactis, actis, factis.

Sometimes in his notes and observations O'Donald temporarily leaves the course of the story to provide additional
information on the background of his characters. Thus the
reader learns about such matters as John Pratt's forge, colliery,
and glass factory; Myra's influence in the composition and
signing of Sir Thomas Smyth's will; and, on page 65, Sir
Thomas's sciamachies with his chair:

It was a Custom inviolably observed by Sir *Mars*, after he had
been cudgelled by Mr. *Bellew* to kill that Gentleman MENTALLY,
once at least, every Day. The gallant Action was performed in the
following manner. The Knight, after a plentiful Dinner, being well
heated with Wine, his Guests departed, and Servants dismissed,
carefully locked his Parlour Door: Then supposing his Adversary
to stand before him in the Form of his great Chair, he devoted him
Diis inferis, and drawing a *Toledo*, which he kept for this Purpose, he
advanced with a seeming Intrepidity; and pushed with such Skill
and Violence, that generally, by the first or second Thrust, the Chair
was run quite through the Body. He then wiped his Blade, and
sheathed it with great Complacency; sung an *Io Triumphe* sitting
upon his Enemy, whom he had thus mortally wounded, and fell
fast asleep.

6—W.K.

This description is followed by a list of 681 persons 'MEN-TALLY killed by Sir *Mars*, from the Year 1708 to the Year 1728; faithfully extracted from the *Encomium Martis*, or *Killing no Murder*'.

In more serious vein, there are in the notes to Book III significant allusions to Jonathan Swift, who 'attended in the Court, while Mr. *Scheffer's* Cause was pleading, to keep a Stranger in Countenance; and perhaps, to give a publick Testimony of the Friendship, with which he honoured our Author.' The Dean is amused by the mediocre quality of the harangues which he hears in court:

> Ridet orationis genus
> Amicissimus CADENUS . . .

O'Donald adds that Swift's mere presence awed all the Irish pleaders—with the exception of Bocca—into such a decency of behaviour as the authority of the Lord Chancellor could never before oblige them to observe.

The fact that King represented the Latin original as having been written by a Swede may well reflect the interest which he took in the history and contemporary problems of that country. During the so-called 'Swedish Plot' of 1716 and the following year, the English Jacobites had received offers of help from Sweden, and some negotiations had taken place: King was in all likelihood aware of what was going on.[1] To broaden his knowledge, he had probably read the *Lapponia* and some of the other works of the Swedish Latin writer Joannes Schefferus: the coincidence of the surnames could scarcely be accidental. He must have been aware of the visit which the Duke of Ormonde had paid in 1717 to Peter the Great during the course of the Great Northern War, and of that Czar's desire to seek out Jacobites who would be willing to enter the service of Russia.[2] In this conflict, King's sympathy would almost certainly have been with the Swedes: he rarely wrote of the Russians with any

---

[1] The relationship between England and Sweden at this time has been discussed in several articles by J. F. Chance: see *The English Historical Review*, Vol. 16 (1901), pp. 676ff.; Vol. 18 (1903), pp. 81ff. and 676ff.; Vol. 19 (1904), pp. 55ff.

[2] On these matters see Maurice Bruce, 'Jacobite Relations with Peter the Great', *The Slavonic Review*, Vol. 14 (1935-6), pp. 343-62.

degree of affection. In any case, the Duke's mission was a failure, and Jacobite sympathies towards Sweden seem to have increased as a result. There is also some testimony that King was concerned about his own reputation in Sweden in one of the anecdotes collected by Joseph Spence:

'Quid dices de me quando reverteris in patriam tuam?' Dr. King, to a Swede who had resided in Oxford some time for his studies, (with a high air of expecting much).
'Dicam, Insignissime vir, te esse magnum grammaticum' (and the vast fall in Dr. King's look, upon it).[1]

In view of the paucity of printed copies of *The Toast* and the recherché nature of its contents, it is not surprising that there are very few allusions to it in the works of contemporary eighteenth-century writers. The first reference occurs in a letter written by Swift to Charles Ford, on 14 October 1732:

There is a most bitter Satyr against Sr Tho. Smyth, L^{dy} Newburg, and Capt Prat. I take it to have been writ in Oxford, by the means of one Dr King the Head of a Hall there who was Nephew and Heir to Sr Thomas and thought himself wronged by L^{dy} Newburg, and I presume employd some young Oxonians to write it. A printer brought it to me, and said a hundred of them were sent to him from England to give about; the Verses are rough, but it is very malicious, and worth reading. It is called *the Toast*.[2]

It is doubtful whether Swift and King knew one another at this time. Probably they met for the first time in the winter of 1734, when King was compelled on account of his lawsuit to remain in Ireland until the summer of 1735. As may be judged from King's subsequent reminiscences,[3] their acquaintance ripened gradually into friendship, as a token of which the Dean entrusted King with his holographs of *Four Last Years of the Queen* and *Verses on the Death of Dr. Swift*. Later corroboration of their amity is provided in a copy of John Macky's *Memoirs of the Secret Services*

[1] Joseph Spence, *Anecdotes, Observations, and Characters, of Books and Men*, ed. James M. Osborn (2 vols.; Oxford: at the Clarendon Press, 1966), Vol. I, p. 348.
[2] Harold Williams, op. cit., Vol. IV, pp. 76f.
[3] In King's *Anecdotes* (2nd edn., pp. 97–8), he quotes a few lines from the last letter which he received from Swift. The original letter has not survived. King also relates in the same place that Swift perused the manuscript of *The Toast* and commented to a lady relative that 'if he had read the TOAST when he was only twenty years of age, he never would have wrote a satire.'

of John Macky, Esq., with transcriptions of Swift's marginalia, presented to King by Robert Thorp in 1759. Thorp, a Dublin gentleman who studied at St Mary Hall and was afterwards called to the English Bar, wrote this inscription in the book:

The gift of Robert Thorp, Esq. to Doctor Willm. King, Principal of St Mary Hall; as a token of respect and esteem, as well as acknowledgement for the many favours conferred by Docr King on Mr. Thorp during his residence at Oxford: and which is only rendered of any value, as it may recall to Dr King's mind the many agreeable hours he had spent with that great genius the Revd Doct Jonathan Swift, Dean of St Patrick's in Ireland, author of the several observations and remarks contained in these trifling memoirs. Oxford, April ye 10th, 1759.[1]

Incidentally, Swift's dictum that 'the verses are rough' seems a trifle too severe as applied to the English version. King handles his anapaestic tetrametre measure generally with success. He justified his rather unusual metre by referring to the work of James I published at Edinburgh in 1584, and nowadays usually called *Essays of a Prentice in the Divine Art of Poetry.* O'Donald writes in 'The Translator's Preface' (page xlvii): 'I have therefore chose the Verse of twelve Syllables in Deference to the Judgment and Authority of one of our own Kings, who in his Art of Poetry (which perhaps he understood as well as the Art of Government) calls it *Rouncefallis* or *Tumbling* Verse, and which he assures us is the only proper Measure for Poems of this Kind.'

References to *The Toast* in English literature subsequent to the death of Swift are sparse and relatively unimportant. Prior to the work of Sir Harold Williams, only one journal article on the poem was published: that appeared in 1857 in *Bentley's Miscellany*.[2] In generally denouncing King's work, the author, Archdeacon Arthur Rowan,[3] pronounces an astringent con-

[1] W. F. Trench and K. B. Garratt, *On Swift's Marginalia in a copy of Macky's Memoirs* (London: The Bibliographical Society, 1938), p. 360. King's copy of Macky's *Memoirs* was later acquired by Charles Butler, brother of Alban Butler, the compiler of *Lives of the Saints.*

[2] 'The History of an Unreadable Book,' *Bentley's Miscellany*, June 1857, pp. 616–625.

[3] The article is unsigned, but the authorship has been established by reference to a letter in the Forster Collection. See F. E. Ball (ed.), *The Correspondence of Jonathan Swift, D.D.* (London: G. Bell and Sons, Ltd., 1913), Vol. V, Appendix XII, p. 458.

demnation: '. . . this handsomely "got-up" volume is so "farced" with impurity and grossness, that a man seems to forfeit his own manliness and self-respect while looking through the contents of the unreadable production.' Later he refers to 'the almost insane indecency of its contents', 'this foul production', and its 'overlying filth'. He concludes that King's submission of the book to Mrs. Martha Whiteway was 'in keeping with the tone and standard of propriety in a day when *Clarissa Harlowe* was a book recommended to the study of young ladies with as much freedom as *Madame Chapone's Letters* or *Hannah Moore's Moral Strictures* would be at present.'

Rowan appears to have overlooked the brilliance of King's whimsicality, but his criticisms do manifest one reason why *The Toast* has never been well known. The imagery is indeed gross, as Rowan indicates. The satire is, in places, obscene, and in this respect, the poem constitutes a kind of *ne plus ultra*. It is difficult to imagine how any other author could supersede King in this peculiar kind of learned impudicity. Furthermore, King's quarrel was a private one, and only a comparatively small number of persons, even in his own day, could have been expected to take any interest in it. Even if the poem had been published, it would never have attracted more than a tiny proportion of the poetry-reading public. Nevertheless, it calls for assessorial comment: some further observations on it are therefore included in Chapter IX.

III

Early Political Satire

THE extent to which King aided Jacobite activities will always be enigmatic. A large proportion of his correspondence has been lost, and what witness remains is often far from explicit. In 1735 he is listed 'to be Agent to the States of Holland',[1] but the nature of his duties and the extent to which he fulfilled them remain unexplained. Among the Stuart Papers at Windsor Castle there survives a letter penned by King from 'Ferrara' (i.e. Paris) on 24 November 1736 to James Edgar, Confidential Clerk to King James III, the Old Chevalier.[2] This letter is written partly in cipher, and can be interpreted only with the aid of the key which is included, in another hand, on the note-paper itself. Some examples of deciphered words are as follows:

Mr. Drake	:	King James III
Cambray	:	Ireland
Dijon	:	The Hague
little nursery	:	Affairs
Mr. Farquar	:	The King's Service
Gumley	:	The King's friends in Scotland
571	:	Scotland
Garth	:	The King's friends
Mercer	:	The Whigs
500	:	The Elector of Hanover (i.e. George II)
503	:	Walpole
473	:	The King's restoration
Ferrara	:	Paris
Mr. Gibson	:	Colonel Daniel O'Brien
Hatton	:	Col. William Cecil

[1] Marquis of Ruvigny and Raineval, *The Jacobite Peerage* (Edinburgh: T. C. and E. C. Jack, 1904), p. 234.

[2] The Royal Library, Windsor Castle, Stuart Papers 191/168. An account of how these papers reached their present home is told in Henrietta Taylor, *The Stuart Papers at Windsor* (London: John Murray, 1939). See also the Introduction to

King commences: 'I hope Mr. Drake will excuse me, that I have not sooner answered his last kind letter', a statement that confirms the suspicions of several historians that the Old Chevalier and the Principal of St. Mary Hall corresponded with one another. He continues:

The same affair which carried me to Cambray last summer, obliged me to repair thither again this year much against my will . . . It will be impossible for me to attempt a journey to Dijon, till my little nursery is settled. I am in great hopes, this delay hath not yet been in any respect prejudicial to Mr. Farquar, for whom I must ever retain ye greatest respect.

Gumley is grown very rich. I saw him lately: for I made 571 my way from Cambray.

I could heartily wish some proper steps were taken to unite Garth and Mercer in ye same interest, which I conceive would not be at all difficult to be effected at this juncture. I mean the same Mercer, who is such a professed enemy to all the measures of 500 and 503. I cannot help intimating this, because I am fully persuaded 473 in a great measure depends on that union.

He concludes in a postscript: 'I have not seen Mr. Gibson. I had nothing to say to him from Hatton.' The letter is signed by King in his own codename: A. Ingram.

King saw clearly what some Jacobites did not, namely that any resurgence of the Stuart monarchy would require the aid of the anti-Walpolean Whigs. In a reply from James Edgar[1] the writer expresses a desire that 'you were at Douay', together with another wish for 'the Union and agreement you mention between Messrs. Garth & Mercer, for I see the advantages. . . .' But nothing decisive came of these proposals to court the extreme Whigs. Walpole for his part strove to divide the Jacobites from his Whig enemies, principally by assuring them of his own feelings of good will toward the Pretender. James III, to thwart this ruse, warned '. . . 'tis fit my friends should know that I have not the least reason to think that Walpole or any other of the present Ministers are anyways favourably disposed towards

---

Volume I of the Historical Manuscript Commission's *Stuart Papers* (1902–23). The majority of the Stuart Papers after 1718 are still unpublished.

[1] The Royal Library, Windsor Castle, Stuart Papers 193/83. The letter is endorsed on the back: 'Copy to Dr. King. Jany. 16 1739'. This last figure is almost certainly a mistake for 1737.

me.'[1] Colonel William Cecil, to whom this admonition was addressed, did not benefit from the advice therein. According to King, he 'had a weak judgment, and was very illiterate . . . I believe he was a man of honour, and yet he betrayed his master.' This betrayal on Cecil's part was unintentional, King intimated:

For he suffered himself to be cajoled and duped by Sir ROBERT WALPOLE to such a degree, as to be fully persuaded that Sir ROBERT had formed a design to restore the House of STUART. For this reason he communicated to Sir ROBERT all his despatches, and there was not a scheme which the CHEVALIER's [i.e. James III's] court or the Jacobites in *England* had projected during Sir ROBERT'S long administration, of which that minister was not early informed, and was therefore able to defeat it without any noise or expense.[2]

In September 1737 King was in France and paid a visit on the Archbishop of Auch, Cardinal Melchior de Polignac. The Cardinal died in 1742, but throughout the remainder of his life King seems to have cherished the memory of this cultured French prelate who for a long time concerned himself in Stuart affairs and had once desired to makes James II King of Poland. King calls him 'a fine gentleman, as well as an elegant and polite scholar', who had 'a most engaging affability, and a peculiar art and manner of obliging every man, who was introduced to him, to lay aside all restraint.' King took the opportunity to compliment the Archbishop on a portion of his refutation of Lucretius in Latin verse, *Anti-Lucretius, sive de Deo et Natura*. The full text of this work appeared according to the author's wish, posthumously, in 1747, but an extract of about a hundred and fifty verses had already been published by Jean Le Clerc, the French protestant theologian. The manner in which these verses were printed is explained by King: the Cardinal, to gratify Le Clerc's curiosity, repeated them to him *once*, but even though he was then seventy years old, he was able to carry them away in his memory. King adds: 'I should have

[1] Letter of King James III to Colonel William Cecil, The Royal Library, Windsor Castle, Stuart Papers 140/195.

[2] *Political and Literary Anecdotes* (2nd edn., 1819), p. 37. Cecil made a fool of himself in other ways; see, for example, George H. Jones, *The Main Stream of Jacobitism* (Cambridge, Mass.: Harvard University Press, 1954), p. 218.

inclined to believe that the Cardinal had been deceived, and that LE CLERC had by some means got at the M.S. if I had not known in my own family a most amazing instance of the strength of memory.'[1] To which of his relations he was here referring will, barring some unlikely discovery, always remain a mystery.

For a period during the 1730s King attended the meetings of the Red Herring Club in Oxford, an organization founded in 1694, which, to judge from the names in its surviving records, contained a certain proportion of Jacobite members. *The Book of the Red Herring Club, 1694 to 1761*[2] includes a collection of Articles agreed to on 29 June 1714, e.g. 'that the Club shall be held every Tuesday night at one another's Chambers; and that it shall begin at Seven a Clock and continue till Tom tolls . . . that every Member who absents himself upon a Club-night when in Town shall forfeit Sixpence . . . that every Member that is not at the Club at eight o'clock by Tom (when in town) shall forfeit Sixpence . . .' King was fined on a number of days under the terms of these Articles, but though these petty amounts have gone on record, there is no indication of the topics that were discussed.

King's first strictly political satire appeared in print in 1737 in the form of an article in the periodical *Common Sense or The Englishman's Journal*. This publication had begun its career on February 5 of that year, founded from abroad by James III as a paper which he could use for his own purposes, but which would not be overtly Jacobitical.[3] A former contributor to *Fog's Journal*, Charles Molloy, became the editor, and for almost two years this curiously non-committal periodical appeared regularly. The term 'common sense' was much in use at this time: Fielding's *Pasquin*, first produced in 1736, contains a rehearsal of a tragedy entitled 'The Life and Death of

---

[1] *Political and Literary Anecdotes* (2nd edn., 1819), p. 11.

[2] Bodleian Library MS. Top. Oxon. f. 49. A presumably complete list of members' names appears at the beginning of the second volume, MS. Top. Oxon. e. 281. King seems to have been admitted a member in 1731 or before.

[3] The surviving correspondence regarding the inauguration of *Common Sense* is among the Stuart Papers at Windsor Castle: 189/80, 193/133A, and 194/10 B are especially significant. See also George H. Jones, op. cit., p. 197f. and his note in *The Review of English Studies*, Vol. IV, No. 14 (April 1953), p. 144.

Common-Sense', and Lady Mary Wortley Montagu's book *The Nonsense of Common-Sense* appeared a year or so later, to mention only two of the better known instances. But though the title had a fashionable ring, this paper was scarcely a success for the Chevalier de St. George. Molloy could indeed boast of such contributors as the Earl of Chesterfield and George Lyttleton, but the only known Jacobite writer was William King, and no more than one piece by him can be authenticated. It is perhaps significant that Pope, in a letter to John Brinsden of 15 December 1739, confided that he did not wish to have a set of verses on the *Essay on Man* printed in it.

The article in question appeared on 28 May 1737.[1] A copy of this issue was sent to Swift together with a letter written by King, but both were intercepted by the postal authorities. According to Deane Swift, the article was 'written by Dr. King himself'.[2] The argument of this essay will appear again in King's Latin poem *Antonietti Epistola ad Corsos*, which was published in 1744 as a folio pamphlet, and reset with slight variations in the collected *Opera*. The principal proposal put forward was that the people of Corsica (by which King meant Great Britain) should plan a new government for the future, headed by a king fashioned of oak, 'well shaped, and finely painted; with a Diadem on his Head, a Royal Mantle on his Shoulders, and a Scepter in his Right Hand.' This kind of monarchy would be superior to the governmental system of Plato's *Republic* or Sir Thomas More's *Utopia*, 'which sound well in Theory, but can never be reduced to Practice'. This king should not be a tyrant; he should be incapable of committing any acts of violence, and should be free from pride, avarice, and ambition:

He should neither injure himself, or his Subjects, through the Heat and Intemperance of Youth, or the Folly and Dotage of old Age. Love, which has made one King a Fool, and another mad, should never perplex his Head, or hurt his Constitution. His Manners

---

[1] This is the date proposed by Harold Williams in 'The Old Trumpeter of Liberty Hall', *The Book Collector's Quarterly*, Vol. I, No. 4 (1931), p. 36. The other date which has occasionally been suggested, 16 April 1737, is a palpable blunder.

[2] Harold Williams (ed.), *The Correspondence of Jonathan Swift* (5 vols.; Oxford: at the Clarendon Press, 1963–5), Vol. V, p. 53. A note on this letter by Deane Swift is to be found in his *Letters Written by the Late Jonathan Swift, D.D.* (Dublin, 1768), Vol. III, p. 113.

should be without Blemish. And his greatest Enemies (if undeservedly he must have Enemies) should not be able to impute to him any Impurity of Mind, or unfriendly Disposition, or Unevenness of Temper. In a Word, I would have such a King as *Jupiter* first gave to the Frogs; who, by the Way, possessed his Empire by Divine Right. . . .

The person of the king should be sacred and inviolable. His subjects of all degrees should approach him with the greatest reverence, and those introduced to him for a confirmation of their privileges and employments should be obliged to prostrate themselves and kiss the hem of his garment. He should be placed under a rich canopy and seated on a magnificent throne. A guard of a hundred halberdeers should be appointed to attend him, not so much for the security of his person as to serve for pomp and show at audiences of ambassadors. This guard should be the only standing army in Corsica, for there should be no use for soldiers except to defend the country in the event of an invasion. In that case, every man should be a soldier. New laws should be of no force until receiving his majesty's approbation, which should always be signified by his silence. To indicate his disapproval, the monarch should pronounce the word *veto* three times with an audible voice. (The author does not explain how a wooden monarch could speak.) The existence of a spouse for this ligneous ruler should be determined by the senate; King is not enthusiastic on this matter, commenting: "I can prove from ancient History, that a Wooden Queen hath sometimes done as much Mischief as a Wooden Horse, and overturned mighty Kingdoms.' But with or without a consort, such a king could do no wrong: 'A Succession of such Princes would not be less Glorious for themselves, than Beneficial to their Country: They would be universally esteemed during Their Reigns, and their Memories sweet and precious. Happy had it been for the World, if the long Catalogue of *Roman* Emperors (three or four only excepted) had been of the Wooden Species!' The not immediately obvious moral, with its subtle innuendos, concludes the article: 'Reason, which is the distinguishing Excellence of Human Nature, can only prove a Blessing to those, whether Princes or private Persons, who are Men of Honour and Virtue.'

The principal characteristic of this piece is the delicacy and indirectness of its irony. To a reader not acquainted with the political background against which King was writing, it would seem to be divorced of any but the most general significance. Indeed, as was undoubtedly the case with *Gulliver's Travels*, which had been published only a little more than a decade earlier, many readers could have digested the whole work and remained completely unaware of any subversive intention on the part of the writer. Slight though it is, it constitutes a good example of King's ability to simulate one point of view, while actually arguing for another. He was to use this device again on several occasions in the future.

This article also provides further illustration of the unique influence which the works of Swift exercised over its author. The irony is certainly Swiftian in nature, but created with a polished elegance which the Dean himself never achieved. That King read most, if not all, of Swift's published work there can be no reasonable doubt, but it is of special significance that the Principal of St. Mary Hall was chosen to supervise personally the publishing of *Four Last Years of the Queen* and the *Verses on the Death of Dr. Swift*. These two cases deserve discussion in some degree of detail.

The singular pre-publication history of Swift's *Four Last Years of the Queen*, which was composed mainly between September 1712 and May 1713 but issued only in 1758, has been recounted, in its main outlines, in several places.[1] However, it is still possible to add a few extra details to the accepted version of what happened. Briefly, Swift set aside the manuscript after its completion, and for twenty-three years gave it little attention. In 1722 he mentioned the manuscript in a letter to Pope, hinting that he occasionally spent some time on it, and he may have taken it to England with him in 1727 with a view to publication. After Swift and King had become acquainted in Dublin the question of printing the manuscript was discussed again:

---

[1] Notably Harold Williams, 'Jonathan Swift and the Four Last Years of the Queen', *The Library*, 4th Series, Vol. XVI (1935), pp. 61–90, and the same author's Introduction to Volume VII of *The Prose Works of Jonathan Swift*, edited by Herbert Davis (Oxford: Basil Blackwell, 1951). *The Library* is sometimes catalogued under the title *Transactions of the Bibliographical Society*: in this case the reference is 2nd Series, Vol. XVI (1935), pp. 61–90.

Swift was anxious to see his work in print, and according to Mrs. Whiteway he hoped to profit financially from it. King presumably undertook to make arrangements in London for publication: in a letter written from Paris to Mrs. Whiteway on 9 November 1736, he explained that after his return to London about November 20 he would 'put the little MS. to the press, and oblige the whole *English* nation.'[1] In fact King did not secure possession of the manuscript until about eight months later when it was brought to him from Ireland by Lord Orrery. The exact date of delivery is not known; the closest date is 2 July 1737, when Swift wrote to His Lordship, 'I have corrected the inclosed . . . please to deliver it, with Your own Hand, to Doctor King, at his Chambers in the Temple.'[2]

It is not clear what publication plans King had in mind. It is reasonable to assume that he had suggested the printing of the work by subscription, and that some of Swift's other friends were opposed to this idea: that is the implication of two sentences in his letter to Mrs. Whiteway of 24 June 1737: 'I don't know why the Dean's friends should think it derogatory, either to his station or character, to print the History by subscription, considering how the money arising by the sale of it is to be applied. I am not for selling the copy to a bookseller: for, unless a sufficient caution be taken, the bookseller, when he is master of the copy, will certainly print it by subscription, and so have all the benefit which the Dean refuses.'[3] The manuscript was certainly in King's hands by July 23,[4] but about the same time Lord Oxford and Erasmus Lewis were both deprecating publication. Lord Oxford had seen the manuscript in 1727, when it had been lent to him while Swift was in England; he still held opinions about it more than a decade later, for on 8 April 1738 Lewis wrote to Swift giving him a detailed *critique* of his work, incorporating the views of 'Lord O——d, and two or three more.'[5] The principal criticisms involved Swift's version of the

[1] Harold Williams (ed.), *The Correspondence of Jonathan Swift* (5 vols.; Oxford: at the Clarendon Press, 1963–5), Vol. IV, p. 542.

[2] Ibid., Vol. V, p. 59.   [3] Ibid., pp. 51f.

[4] Ibid., p. 65. The relevant letter is also printed in George Sherburn (ed.), *The Correspondence of Alexander Pope* (5 vols.; Oxford: at the Clarendon Press, 1956), Vol. IV, pp. 81f.

[5] Harold Williams, ed., op. cit. ult., p. 104. See also the letter of Erasmus Lewis of 4 August 1737, pp. 65f.

founding of the South Sea Company, and the accuracy of some
other specific matters such as the transactions with the Dutch
envoy to England, Monsieur de Buys, Marlborough's personal
courage, Prince Eugene's supposed hint that Harley might be
removed by chance assassination, and the author's claim that
'the present ministers' adhered to republican principles.

It is probable that King soon became of one mind with Lewis
and Lord Oxford, at least in the matter of postponing publication. He wrote to the Dean on the subject of 'some difficulties
I was under in respect of ye publication', but his letters were
intercepted, and never reached Dublin.[1] On 25 April 1738 he
wrote to Deane Swift with regard to the fact that his letters concerning the publication of the history had not reached the
author. 'I have not yet had any answer,' he lamented, 'and till
I receive one, I can do nothing more.' Definite dangers were
involved:

. . . I might have talked over with you all the affair of the History,
about which I have been so much condemned: and no wonder,
since the Dean has continually expressed his dissatisfaction that I
have so long delayed the publication of it. However, I have been in
no fault: on the contrary, I have consulted the Dean's honour, and
the safety of his person. In a word, the publication of this work,
as excellent as it is, would involve the printer, author, and every
one concerned, in the greatest difficulties, if not in certain ruin;
and therefore it will be absolutely necessary to omit some of the
characters.[2]

Here King frankly confesses that it was he who had delayed the
publication. The reason that Swift's *Four Last Years of the Queen*
was not published in his lifetime was simply that King refused
to arrange for the printing of the author's text.

One should add that King's intentions seem to have been the
highest. In an unpublished letter written by King to Lord
Orrery from London on 8 July 1738, he commented:

As to the Hist[ory of the Four Last Years of the Queen] I leave it to
Your Lordship to do as you shall judge proper. Only I wish, if it be

---

[1] Ibid., pp. 93f. The letters to which King refers in his letter to Mrs. Whiteway of
2 March 1737/8, have not survived. See also the letter to Deane Swift of 15 March
1737/8, pp. 99f. The date given on page 99, March 13, is erroneous, as was noted in
Chapter II.
[2] Ibid., p. 107.

redemanded from me, it may be put into your hands or Mr Popes, that if hereafter it should be mangled or published with many interpolations, which I do not think impossible, since you know there is another copy, the D^s friends in that case may have an opportunity of vindicating his memory.[1]

This piece of correspondence, which seems to have gone so far unnoticed by Swift's commentators, is of some importance, since it clearly indicates King's hopes that the authentic text would be preserved. His delaying tactics were apparently based on no motive more sinister than that of protection for all concerned.

In the meantime Swift, having suspected that King was procrastinating, proposed that an edition should be printed in Dublin by George Faulkner. But no success came of this plan either. Faulkner wrote two letters on the subject to Lord Orrery, which were shown to King, but the principal result was that His Lordship also became convinced that the publication of the work should be postponed.[2] After failing to persuade Faulkner to print his *Four Last Years of the Queen*, Swift seems to have let the matter rest for good.

The later history of the manuscript of this work is told by Faulkner in his pamphlet *An Appeal to the Public*,[3] the veracity of which may be generally substantiated from what little extrinsic evidence exists. Only the connection of King with the manuscript is of relevance for the present purpose. He was in possession of the holograph in 1740, as is clear from a letter written to Pope by Mrs. Whiteway on May 16 of that year: 'The history of the four last years of queen *Anne's* reign I suppose you have seen with Dr. *King*, to whom he sent it some time ago, and, if I am rightly informed, is the only piece of his (except *Gulliver*) which he ever proposed making money by, and was given to Dr. *King* with that design, if it might be printed: I mention this to you, lest the Doctor should die, and

---

[1] Bodleian Library, MS. Eng. hist. d. 103, pp. 3f.

[2] Harold Williams, ed., op. cit. ult., pp. 101f. Orrery's letters to Faulkner and Mrs. Whiteway are both relevant.

[3] George Faulkner, *An Appeal to the Public* (Dublin, 1758). This pamphlet is extremely rare: there are copies in the National Library of Ireland, Dublin (Swift Collection 32; half title only); and Harvard College Library (16422.58*). I do not know of any others.

his heirs imagine they have a right to dispose of it.' In his reply from Twickenham of June 18, Pope commented: 'I dare say nothing of ill consequence can happen from the commission given Dr. *King*.'[1] In 1741 Swift furnished Faulkner with a written order commissioning him to retrieve the manuscript from King. Faulkner travelled from Dublin to Oxford in September 1741, only to discover that King was at Bath, and so proceeded on his journey to London. Thence he wrote to King, who mentioned this piece of correspondence in his next letter to Lord Orrery, written on the following October 3:

By the last post I had a letter from Faulkner to tell me, that he has a letter for me from ye Dean requiring me to deliver the History to his Honour Faulkner. He says he had been at Oxford for that purpose. I am truly sorry he missed me: for I wish to be rid of the M.S. I have desired Faulkner to send me the Dean's letter, that I may have an authority for what I do; and I have promised to send Mr. Dean's papers to him by some safe hand. For Faulkner it seems, is just returning to Ireland.[2]

On October 5 King conveyed his thoughts to Faulkner:

I shall always be ready to receive the Dean's Commands. But the Manuscript is locked up in my Study at *Oxford*: And as you will be gone for *Ireland* before I can leave this Place, I will find out some safe Hand, immediately after my Return to *Oxford*, by which I may send the Papers to the Dean. But pray be so kind as to send me his Letter, that I may have Authority for what I do.—I write with great Difficulty by Reason of a Contraction in all my Fingers, for which I am using the Waters of this Place.[3]

Faulkner answered this letter; the text has not been preserved. On October 12 King wrote again from Bath:

. . . I am sorry I was not at *Oxford*, when you called there, that you might have taken the Papers with you. If you scruple to send the Dean's Letter by Post for fear of an Accident, leave it for me at any Friend of yours in *London*, or with Mr. *Bathurst* the Bookseller, whom I think you know.

---

[1] George Sherburn (ed.), op. cit., Vol. IV, pp. 240, 248.

[2] Bodleian Library, MS. Eng. hist. d. 103, p. 42.

[3] This, the following quotation, and those in the two subsequent paragraphs are drawn from Faulkner's pamphlet.

Having received this last communication, Faulkner again wrote to King, this time enclosing the Dean's letter and informing him that, since there was business in Dublin that required his immediate presence, he could not stay much longer in London. He requested King to leave the manuscript with Lord Orrery. By coincidence King arrived in London the day before Faulkner had arranged to leave for Ireland. Somehow Faulkner learnt the news of his arrival, and that evening 'went to the Doctor's Chambers in the Temple, where he was most politely received, according to the usual Custom, by that Gentleman, where that Affair of the Dean's Manuscript was talked over. The Doctor said, he was very sorry, that he did not know, that he, *Faulkner*, would be in *London* at his Return; if he had, he would have brought the Papers from *Ofxord* [*sic*], and delivered them to him; but was glad he was desired to deliver the Papers to Lord *Orrery*, from whom he got them.' Faulkner assured his readers that the Doctor kept his word and handed over the manuscript to His Lordship, 'who had it some Years in his Custody, without its being called for.' To be more precise Lord Orrery had the manuscript in his possession for about a decade, until in 1751 he surrendered it to Faulkner, who handed it over to the Archbishop of Dublin. Thence it was delivered to Lord Chief Justice Singleton. The tangled history of its subsequent publication is enlarged upon by Faulkner, and independent confirmation of his account has more recently been provided by Sir Harold Williams.

Part of the unique value of Faulkner's pamphlet consists in the fact that he supports his argument with morsels of information which, were it not for his mentioning them, would have been irretrievably lost. He explains, for example, that Swift had asked him to make the publication arrangements for the *Four Last Years of the Queen* with a London bookseller, when King, 'remarkable for his great Genius and Learning', persuaded the Dean to let him have the manuscript with the promise that he would raise him a Sum of some thousand Pounds by a voluntary Subscription in *England*, to endow his intended Hospital for Idiots and Lunatics.' King, it may be assumed, did not keep this promise, probably on the grounds that he was dissuaded from publishing the manuscript; Faulkner specifically mentions that he 'neglected the Publication of Proposals for Printing that Work by Subscription.' Faulkner adds graciously that he felt towards King 'the highest Honour and Esteem, having seen him at Dr. *Swift's* House in *Dublin*, and at other different Places in that City.'

The other work of the Dean of St. Patrick's with which King was intimately connected, *Verses on the Death of Dr. Swift*, was written in the period between approximately November 1731 and May 1732, and the manuscript handed over to King some six years later, during the early months of 1738. While it was in his hands, King took considerable liberties with the copy, perhaps surprisingly in view of the anxiety which he had shown to preserve the authentic text of the *Four Last Years of the Queen*. On the suggestion of Pope and others he made a number of excisions to the extent of about a third of the whole, and then proceeded to farce the other two thirds with an extract over sixty lines long from *The Life and Genuine Character of Doctor Swift*, which had been published in both London and Dublin in 1733. The wording of the interpolation was altered in a few places to make the patchwork less obvious. King also omitted all Swift's notes. The result, despite the adventitious material, was a shorter piece than the author had intended: Swift's original poem, in all likelihood, consisted of 484 lines; King's version, published by Charles Bathurst in January 1738/9, contains 381.[1]

The earliest surviving intimation that the *Verses on the Death of Dr. Swift* was about to appear in print is contained in King's letter to Lord Orrery of 8 July 1738; it shows that King at one time intended to have the poem published in September or October of 1738: 'Roch is in the press, and shall certainly be published in September or the beginning of the next Term. I believe I mentioned to you the accidents which had retarded

[1] The differences between the two versions have been discussed in Herbert Davis, 'Verses on the Death of Dr. Swift', *The Book Collector's Quarterly*, Vol. I, No. 2 (1931), pp. 67–71; and Sir Harold Williams (ed.), *The Poems of Jonathan Swift* (3 vols.; Oxford: at the Clarendon Press, 1958), Vol. II, pp. 551–3. The date of composition is given as 'November, 1731' on the title page of the version published in Dublin by George Faulkner, but Sir Harold Williams has shown that parts of the poem and its notes were completed later.

the publication of this work so long, when I had the honour of seeing you last.'[1] For some unknown reason publication was delayed: perhaps King already suspected that his emendations would incur Swift's displeasure. There is no doubt about his suspicions in his letter to the Dean of 5 January 1738/9:

At length I have put *Rochefaucault* to the press, and about ten or twelve days hence it will be published. But I am in great fear lest you should dislike the liberties I have taken. Although I have done nothing without the advice and approbation of those among your friends in this country, who love and esteem you most, and zealously interest themselves in every thing that concerns your character. As they are much better judges of mankind than I am, I very readily submitted to their opinion. . . .[2]

In subsequent correspondence King defended his decisions in some detail. Writing to Swift on the following January 23 he explained: '. . . I may urge the approbation of the public as some kind of apology for myself, if I shall find you are dissatisfied with the form in which this poem now appears.'[3] In his letters to Mrs. Whiteway of 30 January and 6 March 1738/9, he expatiated further: '. . . I am in some pain about *Rochefoucauld* [*sic*], and doubt much whether he will be satisfied with the manner in which he finds it published; to which I consented in deference to Mr. *Pope's* judgment, and the opinion of others of the Dean's friends in this country, who, I am sure, love and honour him. . . .' Specific reasons are given for some particular omissions, for example:

The last two lines,

> That kingdom he hath left his debtor,
> I wish it soon may have a better—

I omitted because I did not well understand them; a *better* what?— There seems to be what the grammarians call an *antecedent* wanting for that word; for neither *kingdom* or *debtor* will do, so as to make it

---

[1] Bodleian Library, MS. Eng. hist. d. 103, p. 4. 'Roch' stands for Rochefoucault; it occurs in the first couplet of the poem:

> As *Rochefoucault* his Maxims drew
> From Nature, I believe 'em true. . . .

[2] Harold Williams (ed.), *The Correspondence of Jonathan Swift* (5 vols.; Oxford: at the Clarendon Press, 1963–5), Vol. V, p. 133.

[3] Ibid., p. 135. The two following quotations are drawn from pp. 136f., 140.

sense, and there is no other antecedent. The Dean is, I think, without exception, the best and most correct writer of *English* that hath ever yet appeared as an author; I was therefore unwilling any thing should be cavilled at as ungrammatical.

As King had suspected, Swift was indeed displeased, and with some justice, at the maimed version of his poem published in London. The Dean again approached George Faulkner, this time with more success than in the roughly comparable case of the *Four Last Years of the Queen*. Faulkner published the poem in Dublin, without cuts but with many blanks, under the title *Verses on the Death of Dr. S——, D.S.P.D.* Copies of this edition were soon reaching London. King's reactions to this development, as he explained them on 6 March 1738/9, are understandable:

I was not a little mortified yesterday, when the bookseller brought me the *Dublin* edition, and at the same time put into my hands a letter he had received from *Faulkner*, by which I perceive the Dean is much dissatisfied with our manner of publication, and that so many lines have been omitted. . . . *Faulkner* hath sent over several other copies to other booksellers; so that I take it for granted this poem will soon be reprinted here from the *Dublin* edition. . . .[1]

King's prediction was not fulfilled: the poem was reprinted in London by Bathurst on several subsequent occasions, but not from the Dublin edition.[2] After the affair of the *Four Last Years of the Queen* there is no evidence of further intercourse between King and Swift. The former's letter of 23 January 1738/9 was the last surviving piece of correspondence to pass between them.

The editing of these two manuscripts of Swift could not have taken a great deal of time. Much of King's energy in the literary field during this period must have been spent on the composition of his early political satires in Latin verse. The first of these, *Miltonis Epistola ad Pollionem*, appeared in two separate folio editions in 1738. A free translation into English verse under

---

[1] Ibid., p. 139.

[2] Four editions of the *Four Last Years of the Queen* were published by Bathurst in 1739. The second edition is in two folio printings differently set; the third also appeared in folio. Another unnumbered edition appeared in octavo. In 1741 a second octavo edition was issued. The *complete* text of the poem was in fact not printed with accuracy until Sir Harold Williams' edition of 1958.

the title *Milton's Epistle to Pollio* was published in 1740; it may or may not have been made by King. The Latin text was revised and reset for the *Opera*. There are thus three separate Latin texts of the poem, and one version in English.

This poem purports to be a work of John Milton which, in the versions of 1738, has been edited and illustrated with notes by F. S. Cantabrigiensis, a pseudonym which is not used later. Milton is here supposed to be addressing Pollio, whose Latin name represents that of Sir Patrick Hume, first Earl of Marchmont and Baron Polwarth (1641–1724). A Scottish Presbyterian, he became, after a turbulent early career, a steadfast supporter of William III and a staunch anti-Jacobite. Sir Harold Williams has suggested that King's use of Milton's name may have been determined by the fact that a Patrick Hume, who edited an edition of *Paradise Lost* for Jacob Tonson, is said to have been a member of the family of Hume of Polwarth.[1] It could also have been prompted by the contemporary popularity of Milton's works: they were widely read and discussed, while a lengthy controversy on his prose writings had been waged in the summer months of 1738 in *The Gentleman's Magazine*, stirred up by the appearance of Thomas Birch's edition in March of that year. At about the same time John Dalton's revised acting version of *Comus*, set to music by Dr. Thomas Arne, was being well received by large audiences. In Westminster Abbey a bust of Milton had been erected in 1737, and was now an object of considerable attention. Furthermore the practice had developed in English schools of setting portions of Milton's works for translation into Latin: King was doubtless fully aware of the poet's usefulness to schoolmasters.[2]

Even so, the fact that so convinced a Jacobite as King should associate himself sympathetically with the name of England's principal republican poet, popular though he was, may seem surprising. This paradox is best explained as being a result of

[1] Harold Williams, 'The Old Trumpeter of Liberty Hall', *The Book Collector's Quarterly*, Vol. I, No. 4 (1931), p. 37.

[2] On the general subject of translations of Milton's poetry into Latin verse, see John W. Good, 'Studies in the Milton Tradition', *University of Illinois Studies in Language and Literature*, Vol. I (1915), pp. 41–3; and *Notes and Queries*, New Series, Vol. 12, No. 4 (April 1965), p. 144.

the political conditions of the time. Jacobites saw themselves as the victims of Whig tyranny, and in that respect could associate themselves with the puritans of the previous century, whose position under the Stuart monarchs was in some respects comparable to their own position under the Hanoverians. The Tories had produced no poet of the calibre of Milton, so in the exigencies of the political situation he was 'adopted' by some of them for the sake of his teachings on liberty. Furthermore, King quite possibly saw in Lord Polwarth an individual whose disposition towards the Stuarts was, *mutatis mutandis*, strikingly similar to his own attitude towards the Whigs. His admiration for this militant Scottish peer was probably stimulated by his friendship for Lord Polwarth's son, the second Earl of Marchmont, who, towards the end of his life, became a Tory, and to whom King dedicated his *Sermo Pedestris*.

The *Miltonis Epistola ad Pollionem* would be a more meaningful work if we knew the specific personal allusions intended in the names which King liberally scattered throughout the poem. Their significance was realized in his own day, as King explains in his letter to Swift of 23 January 1738/9: '. . . although that piece has escaped the state inquisition, by being written in a language that is not at present very well understood at court, and might perhaps puzzle the attorney-general to explain, yet the scope of the poem and principal characters being well understood, the author must hereafter expect no mercy, if he gives his enemies any grounds or colour to attack him.'[1] Cadenus is Dean Swift; Pollio, Lord Polwarth; and Pallas, Sir Robert Walpole; but beyond these allusions it is difficult at this distance in time to be specific. In the notes King provides deliberately vague or misleading explanations of most of these names; he gives little or no clue to any particular individual. An incomplete key in an eighteenth-century hand has been written into the margins of the copy in the University Library, Cambridge, *Editio Altera*, Syn. 4.73.5[1], but it is not consistently reliable, and is in places illegible. In the absence of an authoritative key to this work, inevitably some of its significance is now lost. The fact that contemporaries of the author were intended

---

[1] Harold Williams (ed.), *The Correspondence of Jonathan Swift* (5 vols.; Oxford: at the Clarendon Press, 1963–5), Vol. V, pp. 135f.

even though the poem was supposed to have been written by Milton does not present any insuperable problem: King's text *taken literally* does not contain anachronisms except in the matter of the conventional use of classical names. In any case, the attribution of authorship to John Milton is so diaphanous that few readers with any degree of perception could have been deluded; when King included the second recension of this work in the *Opera*, he *ipso facto* abandoned all extrinsic attempt to disown its authorship.

In comparing the separate versions of this poem, one notices certain significant differences. The two editions of 1738 both carry a two-page Dedication in Latin to Alexander Pope in which the pseudonymous editor indicates that the love of liberty which permeates the poem is a strong reason for ascribing it to Milton: '*Bene compertum est mihi, scriptam fuisse hanc epistolam a MILTONE nostro; quo anno incertum. . . .*' This Dedication is not prefixed to the translation of 1740 or to the version in the *Opera*. The 1738 editions extend to 209 lines; that of the *Opera* contains 222 and an additional prose postscript which incorporates the substance of the dedication without any mention of Pope's name. The elimination of all reference to Pope is not surprising; it is clear from King's *Anecdotes* that their relationship was not always one of mutual admiration.

The two editions of 1738 are distinctly different settings, though there are no significant textual changes. In the *Opera* the text has been reset with a rather large number of textual changes. Many of these matters of style and phraseology, some are amplifications, and others seem to have no special importance beyond the author's personal caprice. A few inexplicable changes may well have been made for good reason, but the thinking that motivated them is now obscure. For example, the first sentence of the poem in the 1738 versions reads:

Si vis ingenii, mihi si concessa potestas
Carminis, aut tibi qualis inest facundia, dignas,
CADENO quas ante meo, tibi dicere laudes
Inciperem, & Phoebum spirans, & plenus amico,
POLLIO, magna tuae facerem praeconia vitae.

The corresponding sentence in the *Opera* reads:

> Si vis ingenii, mihi si concessa potestas
> Carminis, aut, qualis Cadeno, spiritus esset,
> Dum canit uxorem, aut patriam defendere doctus
> Aggreditur vates, meritas tibi dicere laudes
> Inciperem; & Phoebum spirans, & plenus amico,
> POLLIO, magna tuae facerem praeconia vitae.

Is any significance to be attributed to the fact that King's final recension, prepared after Swift's death, contains an obvious reference to Stella as the Dean's wife?

There is no story in this poem; narrative was in any case not King's forte. The *Miltonis Epistola* is essentially a collection of escharotic laments on the corruption of the Whig government, and the venality of the times in general. After the invocation to Pollio, Milton is made to say:

> O si tam superis cordi populique patrumque,
> Quam tibi, jura forent!

The evils of the time are roundly attributed to Sir Robert Walpole:

> Pallanti quid non licitum est? Venalia cuncta,
> Pax, bellum, leges, divi, monimenta parentum,
> *Et nati natorum, & qui nascentur ab illis.*

Some of the qualities of the ideal monarch are related:

> Rex erit ille mihi, quo nomine cunque vocatur,
> Rex erit, arte sua qui publica commoda juvit,
> Sobrius, & sapiens, civis bonus, utilis agris,
> Felicis cultor pacis, fortissimus idem,
> Libertas moriens si quando accendit ad arma.

Monarchs in general are exhorted to consult their people's good, and, in a footnote, the Emperor of China is held up as a model: '*Sinarum Rex est tanquam paterfamilias, sic populum curans & fovens, ut si omnes ex seipso nati essent; sic in omnium oculis vivens & imperans, ut si patriae, non sibi ipse natus esset.*' In the text is quoted the law on which, King says, all Chinese welfare depends:

Summa SALLUS POPULI *lex esto,* & *summa piorum*
Relligio, summa haec eadem quoque gloria regum.

In contradistinction the Spanish monarch is singled out for
special attack. Milton is represented as saying that if Philip of
Spain were to approach the Emperor of China with a view to a
federation of their domains, the '*pater Sinae*' would thus reply:

> Qui procul a nobis, semper procul este, latrones
> Crudeles, avidi, meditantes bella, rapinas,
> Atque virum strages, queis pacem et munera fertis!
> Cursatur terras omnes, maria omnia circum;
> Nempe unus regem vestrum non continet orbis,
> Nec locus est sceleri summo. Quid America vobis?
> Quid gemini fecisse juvat certamina mundi?
> An tanti sunt fulva metalla? Latere volentes
> Effodiuntur opes: operi deus instat Iberus
> Infando; utque unum valeat ditare tyrannum,
> En, terras populat late, insontesque Penates;
> Atque nefas suadet, quantum haud molitur Erinnys!

The Emperor of China then goes on to comment on Spenser's
Mother Hubberd's Tale, which, he explains, has a moral. It soon
becomes clear that the monkey is George II; the fox, Walpole;
and the lion, the Old Chevalier. The conclusion is thereupon
drawn:

> Ni deus intersit vindex, reducemque leonem
> Gratatus, miserae reddat sua gaudia genti.

In the notes it is further explained that the lion is also intended
as a symbol of liberty:

Insignia regia leonis, dum altum dormit, furatus est simius & clam
eripuit, quibus ornatus leonem simulavit, regnum occupavit, &
vulpi permisit. At tandem Deus aliquis leonem expergefacit, in-
crepat, reducit, & inducit in regnum suum. Sic in fabula. Recte an
perperam interpreter, existimes velim, mi lector, REDUCEM
LEONEM hieroglyphicum esse LIBERTATIS signum, quippe
nihil timet, neque suspicax est, neque limis spectat, neque ad dor-
miendum in loca remota & secreta secedit; quippe denique gratus
est, & memor accepti beneficii.

In a passage of considerable grandeur, Milton is made to comment that if any monarch could conquer the whole earth, he would still lust for greater power:

> Heu, quem non agitat, seu rex, seu Caesar habetur,
> Falsus honos, strepitusque armorum, & dira cupido
> Regnandi late! Si terrae vinceret orbem,
> Lunam affectaret; posset deducere lunam,
> Stultitia peteret coelos, sive Ossan Olympo
> Imponat, falso tonitru seu terreat urbem
> Salmoneus, magnique Jovis sibi vindicet aras.[1]

Towards the close of the poem, the question is raised whether any reference remains for Magna Carta:

> . . . An, quae cecidit (nam credimus omnes)
> E coelo, nulla est sacrae reverentia chartae?

No direct answer is provided, but the implication in the verses that follow is that liberty must constantly be striven for and guarded, and the reader is warned in capital letters:

CANDIDA LIBERTAS NUNQUAM RESPEXIT INERTES.

The poem concludes with an equivocal reference to a *pius vates*, said in the notes to be Dr. Donne, though King indubitably had someone else—perhaps Swift or Pope—in mind, who often

> Haec eadem cecinit, cum tendit Apollinis arcum,
> Cum patriae, cum diis violatis advenit ultor.

Thus ends King's first extended poem in Latin hexameter. The principal characteristics of his later political satires in the same language and metre are already present and well developed: the use of a generally impeccable classical diction and vocabulary, the undeniable indebtedness to the best poets of the Augustan age, the lucidity *splendidior vitro*, the highly polished technical sophistication, and the bitter disapproval of everything in the contemporary political scene which did not harmonize with his idealistic Tory and Jacobite principles.

---

[1] I assume that 'Caesar' here refers to the emperors of the earth, with the probable exception of the Emperor of China. In *Antonietti Epistola ad Corsos* of 1744 the name 'Caesar' is used specifically for Charles VII, Elector of Bavaria.

Some of his verses exhibit considerable power, especially when he adopts the genuine Miltonic technique of filling them with thundering epithets of condemnation:

> . . . latrones
> Crudeles, avidi, meditantes bella, rapinas,
> Atque virum strages, queis pacem et munera fertis!

Even though King is mordant in his vituperations, his tone is always lofty and formal. In the *Miltonis Epistola ad Pollionem* he amply demonstrated that the contemporary policies of the high Tories and the nobility of the classical hexameter were capable of a very fine degree of synthesis.

If one may believe King's later reminiscences, the *Miltonis Epistola ad Pollionem* enjoyed a wide readership: 'As this was a political satire, and nothing in the same manner had been published before in this country, it was universally read by those who either understood, or pretended to understand the language, and was frequently extolled or condemned according to the prejudice of party: there was not a courtier, or a creature of the prime minister's, who did not set himself up as a profound critic, and censured the style of a composition which perhaps he could not read.'[1] King's comment that nothing in the manner of this work had been published before in England was perfectly justified: there had been any amount of political satire in English, but the *Miltonis Epistola* had no real predecessor. Prior to the end of the seventeenth century the principal topic of satire among British writers of Latin had been religion: George Buchanan's *Franciscanus* and Henry Oxinden's *Religionis Funus* constitute examples of this type of literature. King was the first Anglo-Latin satirist to choose the contemporary political scene as his principal subject.

For some time after King's death the *Miltonis Epistola ad Pollionem* continued to be popular among readers of Latin, and was reprinted by Edward Popham in Volume I of his *Selecta Poemata Anglorum Latina*, published at Bath in 1774. Together with King's text Popham also published a short ode entitled *Ad F.S. Epistolae Miltonianae Editorem*, composed by an anonymous author. It demonstrates the kind of adulatory

---

[1] *Political and Literary Anecdotes* (2nd edn., 1819), p. 151.

sentiments that King's work could on occasion elicit from his supporters:

> Numine tuo sacro bis terque afflavit Apollo;
>   Et tua musa placet.
> Anne faventis adhuc dubitas tu candida famae
>   Omnia? Pone metum.
> Multis spectatur Venusinae porta Corinthi,
>   Non ineunda tamen;
> Hunc ars destituit, natura benignior illum:
>   Attamen ipse ratem
> Impellit, felix et fidentissimus idem,
>   Saxa per aequorea;
> Perque procellosas syrtes, et per vada caeca,
>   Calliopea tibi
> Pandit iter liquidum.—Salve, doctissime vates;
>   Gloria gentis, ave!

It is also of some significance that the celebrated classicist and biographer Michael Maittaire became involved in the post-publication discussions on the purity of King's Latin style. Hume Campbell, the former Lord Register of Scotland, and Nathaniel Hooke, the author of the *Roman History from the Building of Rome to the Ruin of the Commonwealth*, decided to approach Maittaire on the subject. Having studied the poem, Maittaire marked eleven expressions as unclassical. Campbell and Hooke communicated these opinions to the author in Oxford. King thus explains how he dealt with these criticisms:

The same evening, by return of the post, I answered nine of MAITTAIRE'S exceptions, and produced all my authorities from *Virgil*, *Ovid*, and *Tibullus*; and by the post following I sent authorities for the other two. I could not help remarking that Maittaire, some little time before, had published new editions of those poets, from whence I drew my authorities, and had added a very copious index to every author: and in these indexes were to be found most of the phrases to which he had excepted in the MILTONIS EPISTOLA.[1]

King's relationship with Hooke has been the cause of some erroneous statements in the past, especially in the matter of the

---

[1] Ibid., pp. 152f.

latter's translation of *Les Voyages de Cyrus* from the French of Sir Andrew Ramsay. Gordon Goodwin, basing his statement on the *Literary Anecdotes* of John Nichols, indicates in the *Dictionary of National Biography* that in 1738 King met Hooke at Dr. Cheyne's house at Bath, and often acted as his amanuensis while he was engaged on the translation.[1] The difficulty about Goodwin's assertion is that it does not harmonize with the following facts:

(1) *Les Voyages de Cyrus* appeared in English in 1727, i.e. the same year as the publication of the first French edition in Paris.[2]

(2) Joseph Spence in his *Anecdotes, Observations, and Characters, of Books and Men* wrote thus: "Ramsay's Cyrus was translated by Mr. Hooke in twenty days. Mr. Hooke was then at Bath for his health; and Dr. Cheyne's brother was so good as to write for him." This comment is dated June 1729.[3]

(3) Nichols's statement contains no reference to the year 1738. It reads: "In 1739 he [Hooke] published a Translation of Ramsay's Travels of Cyrus, in 4to. Dr. King, the celebrated Principal of St. Mary Hall in Oxford, informed Dr. Warton that Hooke's Translation of the *Travels of Cyrus* was made at Dr. Cheyne's house at Bath, and that he himself had often been Hooke's amanuensis on the occasion, who dictated his Translation to him with uncommon facility and rapidity."

This problem is aggravated by the additional fact that in no edition of the English translation is reference made to any author or translator other than Ramsay himself; Spence lamented that the translation was 'generally mistaken for an original for a good while after it was published', and added: 'Almost everybody then, and many still imagine, that Ramsay himself had written it in English, as well as in French.'

As far as it is now possible to solve the problem, I suggest that Nichols made a mistake in the date, and that numbers of other writers following him have either repeated the same mistake or made others based on it. Hooke's translation was most likely made in 1727, and then revised for subsequent editions. Three editions in octavo had been issued by 1728, followed by the

[1] See the article on William King in the *Dictionary of National Biography* and John Nichols, *Literary Anecdotes of the Eighteenth Century* (9 vols.; printed for the author, 1812–15), Vol. II, pp. 607f.

[2] Chevalier Andrew Ramsay, *The Travels of Cyrus* (2 vols; London, 1727).

[3] Joseph Spence, op. cit., Vol. I, p. 455.

fourth edition and the 'fourth edition enlarged', both in quarto, in 1730. The sixth edition appeared in quarto in 1739. The changes and augmentations in the early English editions generally reflect those which Ramsay made in the successive revisions of the French text. Whether the translation was written by King or by Dr. Cheyne's brother is a more difficult problem, but Nichols' use of the word 'often' provides a useful clue. What probably occurred was that, when he was not in Oxford or Ireland in 1727, King was in a position to visit Hooke at Dr. Cheyne's house in Bath, and while there often acted as the amanuensis; at other times Dr. Cheyne's brother would have filled the same role, and could also have written the final copy for the printer. Though this solution is speculative, it does at least square with all the known facts.

There is no doubt that King was well acquainted with both Hooke and Ramsay. He wrote in his *Anecdotes* of his friendship with Hooke, the elder of whose two sons, Thomas, entered St. Mary Hall in 1742, where he is described in the Matriculation Register as the 'son of the Historian of Rome'. Ramsay, that remarkable son of a Scottish baker, who travelled over the continent, entered the Catholic Church under the guidance of François Fénelon, Archbishop of Cambrai, and for a little over a year acted as tutor in Rome to the two sons of the Old Chevalier, was admitted by King to St. Mary Hall in 1728, and awarded the degree of LL.D. by the University of Oxford in the same year. Fénelon's saying 'I love mankind better than my country', was recounted, together with a delightful story about the distinguished Archbishop, by Ramsay to King, who later included it in his *Anecdotes* with one of his most gracious compliments: 'Who amongst all the modern writers is to be more esteemed and admired than Monsieur FENELON, Archbishop of *Cambray*, and author of *Telemachus*; whose piety, politeness and humanity, were equal to his great learning?' Ramsay, in King's own words, 'hath ever made me reverence the memory of this excellent man.'[1]

The sequel to King's *Miltonis Epistola ad Pollionem* appeared in 1739 under the title *Sermo Pedestris*. Two folio editions were published in this year: each contains 308 lines with only very

---

[1] *Political and Literary Anecdotes* (2nd edn., 1819), pp. 19f.

minor differences between them. A third version appeared in the *Opera*: the text and notes are reset and to a certain extent rewritten, though there are no major changes. This second recension contains 307 lines. Edmund Curll at the end of the translation of King's *Scamnum, Ecloga*, which he published in 1744, perhaps subsequent to an earlier edition, promised a forthcoming translation of *Sermo Pedestris*; there is actually no evidence that any English version ever appeared. The two editions of 1739 are prefixed by a two-page dedication to A.H.C. which is omitted entirely from the final revision. As in the case of *Miltonis Epistola ad Pollionem*, the full significance of *Sermo Pedestris* is lost to modern readers by the lack of a reliable key. In the margins of the copy in the University Library, Cambridge, *Editio Altera*, Syn. 4.73.5², a key has been inserted by the same hand that wrote the key to *Miltonis Epistola*, but again its dependability is questionable.

The dedication is a stately piece of prose addressed to Alexander Hume-Campbell, second Earl of Marchmont, the eldest surviving son of the Lord Polwarth to whom the *Miltonis Epistola ad Pollionem* is addressed. Like King he was a lawyer, having studied at the University of Utrecht, and under the Hanoverians had held a number of responsible positions including those of Ambassador to the court of Copenhagen and Lord Clerk Register of Scotland. He had also been one of the British ambassadors to the Congress of Cambrai in 1722, a sworn member of the English Privy Council, and one of the Scottish representative peers. However, in 1733 he had opposed Walpole's excise scheme, partly in the hope that, by joining with the Prime Minister's opponents, he might assist in the weakening of Lord Islay's power in Scotland. The bill was dropped, but Walpole was not inclined to forgive those Whigs who had opposed him. Several were later deprived of their offices; in the process Lord Marchmont was dismissed from his appointment of Lord Clerk Register and was not re-elected in 1734 as a representative peer. He consequently played a part in the unsuccessful attempt to deprive the government of its power to intervene in the election of the Scottish peers, and soon afterwards joined the Tories.

The fact that both King and Lord Marchmont were actively

opposed to Walpole may well have brought them together in the first place. In the second half of the 1730s they met frequently; in this way King presumably made the acquaintance of his son Hugh, subsequently the third Earl of Marchmont and a trenchant critic of Walpole's administration. The second Earl died on 27 February 1739/40, but in a letter addressed to his successor and dated 29 February 1739/40, Pope enquires: 'What hour shall I meet Dr King tomorrow?', as if he expected the new Lord Marchmont to be conversant with King's movements. The same attitude is displayed again by Pope in a similar letter of 9 January 1740/41.[1] It is not clear whether the third Earl succeeded before the publication of *Sermo Pedestris*; if he did, the chances are likely that his father never set eyes on the completed text or on the dedication to himself.

The virtues of the second Lord Marchmont, now that he had abandoned Whiggery, are extolled by King in some detail. He is generally agreed by contemporary observers to have been a most capable parliamentary orator, an opinion which King corroborates in his Dedication: '*Amor patriae, & libertatis tuendae commune studium, quae senibus vires, arma & animos foeminis ministrant, te fecerunt oratorem, & me poetam.*' The historical logic of this statement is debatable. Lord Marchmont was certainly an orator in his Whig days when, according to the approved Jacobite rationale, he would have had little or no *libertatis tuendae studium*, but there is no record that King was ever called upon to explain this inconsistency. When the Dedication was being written, Marchmont seems to have been well-nigh faultless: '*Jam diu est, quod te diligere coepi, quia probus es, & doctus, & comis, & liberalis; jam nunc, quia optime de Republica meritus es, teque colere & venerari.*' In contradistinction to these excellencies, King is suitably humble about his own achievement in this poem: '*Nihil igitur hic reperies splendidum aut excelsum, sed tenuiora omnia*

---

[1] George Sherburn (ed.), op. cit., Vol. IV, pp. 228, 327. Both Alexander and Hugh Hume-Campbell were styled Lord Polwarth; Alexander from 1709 to 1724 and Hugh from 1724 to 1740. A conversation piece from a dinner given by Alexander Lord Marchmont is related in King's *Political and Literary Anecdotes* (2nd edn., 1819), pp. 48–50. An amusing story relating to Hugh and his twin brother Alexander during a visit to England by Chevalier Ramsay is told in *A Selection from the Papers of the Earls of Marchmont* (3 vols.; London: John Murray, 1831), Vol. I, p. xlv.

& leviora.' But at least the author was not writing for love of money or for personal glory: '*Neque ego, ut scis, lucri aliquid peto, cujus non indiget temperantia mea, neque gloriam ex libellis meis me capturum spero; nisi quae, praemium virtutis, bonis omnibus absque invidia deseratur: Qualem & pietas tua, & sociorum tuorum consilia vobis detulerunt.*' And the Dedication closes with a statement of King's general artistic intention: '*Hoc unum vero diligenter curavi, ut Musa mea & pudica & sani coloris, ut est, esse videatur, nullo delationi loco relicto, sed neque dubitationi.*'

Whether or not one considers King's muse to be *pudica et sani coloris* in this work, there is no doubt that this is a less forceful piece of writing than the *Miltonis Epistola*. It is almost a hundred lines longer than the earlier poem, and takes the form of a dialogue between F.S. (Frederick Scheffer or William King) and A.A., his imaginary opponent. F.S. commences the poem by stating that there are some to whom the *Miltonis Epistola* was displeasing, and in a note printed only in the *Opera* version adds a warning on the possible burning of this work: *Scilicet quo in viis publicis, curiae decreto, comburatur Miltonis epistola.* F.S. continues to lament the difficulty of finding an acceptable subject about which to write poetry:

> Quid faciam, si nec recitare poemata, doctus
> Quae cecinit vates, Carolo regnante; nec ausim
> Diis patriis, laticesque meis, sua dona, Camoenis
> Castalios libare, novumque intendere carmen?

A.A. tries to be helpful:

> At tibi Pindaricos numeros tentare licebit.
> Tale tuum fiat carmen . . .

He makes a number of suggestions for topics drawn from the scene of contemporary European politics; one proposal is to write about Caesar Germanicus, said in the notes to the *Opera* recension to be the Emperor, Charles VI:

> Rex regum, certus Romani nominis haeres;
> Induperatoris titulus cui ceditur uni.
> Hunc tu cantato; seu reddat jura Polonis,
> Seu jubeat pacem fusos exposcere Turcas.

Other tentative subjects follow.

8—W.K.

One is here impressed by the relative fullness of the notes in the *Opera* version. King was clearly not inclined to take undue risks in 1739 by being too specific in his references. Thus in the editions of that year A.A. makes the opaque exhortation to F.S.:

> Tum plectro majore canas Juvenemque, Senemque,

which could be variously interpreted in terms of the verses which follow. In the *Opera* it is explained that the young man is Louis XV and the old man Cardinal Fleury. King is, of course, using Swift's protective device of deliberate obscurity. He did not feel at liberty to abandon it completely even in the *Opera*; some of his notes are so vague as to be merely bewildering. Very likely some of King's readers knew whom the author meant by Horatius, but the uninformed could puzzle over the footnote interminably without reaching one undeniable solution:

Ne in hoc nomine, mi lector, erres, te monitum volo, Horatium hunc neque Romanum esse, neque poetam, neque Musis amicum, neque philosophum, neque divitiarum contemptorem, neque tumultibus urbanis alienum; sed foederum, induciarum, pacis & belli oratorem nervosum, volubilem, canorum, consummatum; aequalitatis, aequabilitatis, aequanimitatis, aequilibritatis judicem unicum.

F.S. is not impressed by A.A.'s proposals:

> EHEU, non nostrum est festum componere carmen;
> Nec fas Heroas cuivis celebrare poetae,
> Quales nunc aequus praefecit Jupiter orbi!

The use of *fas* is a clue to the message that is to follow: all the topics suggested by A.A. turn out to be unlawful. Pastorals in the manner of Vergil are proposed, and F.S. can only reply:

> HEU, quid formosi canerem pastoris amores?

He then goes on to make his own decision:

> Conabor tragicus decora alta inducere scenae ...

But this time it is A.A.'s turn to be pessimistic:

> Ah! vetitum aggrederis; nec fas intrare theatrum:
> Scilicet id curat camerarius.

King does not specifically say so, but I suspect that he intends *camerarius* to refer to the Lord Chamberlain. This interpretation harmonizes with the footnote in the *Opera* edition: '*Gravi jam senatus consulto scena histrionibus interdicitur, siquam novam fabulam acturi sunt; nisi hanc ipsam legat, & perlegat, & perpensam & exploratam habeat, & diplomate suo muniat magnus camerarius.*' These thoughts lead F.S. and A.A. to a lengthy discussion of official censorship. Both speakers nourish an antipathy towards it. In a note which appears only in the *Opera* version, it is manifested that the same kind of practice is not unknown in France:

Divinus ille vir, suae gentis gloria, ille *Fenelon* Cameracensis archiepiscopus, postquam immortale illud opus, Telemachi historiam, ediderat, calumniam & malignitatem aulicorum eludere non potuit; neque rex suus, Ludovicus XIV, liberam ejus vocem, aut vultum pati.

The general conclusion is that the only course of action which is not unlawful is to write in praise of the government. All manner of rewards will follow, even a bishopric. The sarcastic implication of the concluding lines is quite clear: prelacies go with political subservience.

Divitiis auctus nummos in foenore ponas:
Hortos, praedia emas: etiam coelestia tentes
Aemulus Ambrosii, titulisque ornatus & ostro
Incedas, divis vel par vel proximus ipsis.
Attonitus nec in hoc stupeas, dubitesve modestus,
Tale quod oblatum fuerit tibi munus inepto.
Quid mirum; si ultra cupiens fortuna jocari,
Quae modo plebeio fasces, magnumque tribunal
Infido scurrae permisit iniqua regendum;
Quae fabro donavit opes & rhetoris artem,
Pistori pallam, Cyclopi praemia scribae,
Et mimo lauros, tibi dicat, Episcopus esto?

The notes make reference to St. Ambrose, Bishop of Milan in the time of Theodosius and Honorius: *Nihil vero tam dissimilime, quam Ambrosius noster **** ensis, & ille alter Mediolanensis episcopus.* The author does not fill the gap: he could be referring to almost any of the contemporary Whig bishops.

It is questionable whether *Sermo Pedestris*, considered as a piece of poetry, is as successful as *Miltonis Epistola ad Pollionem*. What King published in 1739 was essentially a dialogic argument in verse: it is polished and carefully constructed, but the eristic subject is hardly one which lends itself naturally to poetical treatment. The reader is, in a sense, led from anticlimax to anti-climax: as he follows the course of the polemic from one speaker to the other he gradually realizes, perhaps with disappointment, that no *novum carmen* is going to follow. The discussion itself has no real depth: it is in general a collection of expressions of indignation against what King regarded as unjust restrictions on the freedom of the contemporary writer. *Sermo Pedestris* is not fully satisfactory either as poetry or as dialectic.

To determine whether King followed any particular archetype when he was composing *Sermo Pedestris* is difficult if not impossible. The form of the Latin hexameter dialogue is derived from the *Eclogues* of Vergil, but King's poem is not even superficially bucolic in nature, and its matter has no classical precedent. It does bear a certain resemblance to such contemporary vernacular dialogues as Pope's *Epistle to Dr. Arbuthnot*, which, since it was published in 1735, King had in all probability read. But *Sermo Pedestris* is academic in tone, and is clearly intended for a readership more limited than Pope's. Furthermore King, since he was writing in Latin, could not imitate the style of Pope or of any other writer in the indigenous tongue. It is more likely that he regarded *Sermo Pedestris* and his roughly comparable work *Monitor* of 1749 as being, at least partly, in the tradition of Latin dialogue satires, which the Oxford function of Encaenia had indirectly helped to sustain. One of the most successful of these was a satire on the South Sea Bubble in Latin verse entitled *Commercium ad Mare Australe*, written by Herbert Randolph, a Fellow of All Souls, and published in 1720, the year after King had been elected Principal of St. Mary Hall. This spirited poem contains a long discussion among three speakers—Marcellus, Crassus, and Eubulus—in which Crassus accuses Eubulus of being unpatriotic because he will not invest in the stock of the South Sea Company. In the end Marcellus, completely won over by the arguments of Crassus, departs for the Stock Exchange, paying no heed to

Eubulus's eloquent picture of the inevitable day of reckoning. *Sermo Pedestris* is much closer in spirit and formal structure to Randolph's dialogue than it is to any comparable poem in English.

Flattering though the dedication of this poem to the second Earl of Marchmont undoubtedly is, King's powers as a Latinist were not sufficient to prevent a later rift between himself and the third Earl. The resignation of Walpole in February 1742 removed one of the principal obstacles to agreement between Hugh Lord Marchmont and the Whig administration. He supported the government and the protestant succession during the rising of 1745, and, one may suppose, had less and less to do with his father's Jacobite admirer. On 24 March 1746/7 Lord Marchmont wrote to John, Earl of Westmorland: 'I have seen Dr. King. He is well and seems to expect us to continue with his (Jacobite) friends. I joking confirm'd our aversion to that cause and caution'd him against the folly.'[1] There is no subsequent evidence that King's relationship with the third Earl was further maintained.

While he was engaged in the publication of *Sermo Pedestris*, King was also contributing towards the cost of rebuilding the chancel of St. Mary's Church, Ealing. During the 1730s the fabric of the church had been allowed to fall into decay, and services were regularly held in a temporary timber structure erected by voluntary contributions. Towards the end of the decade work was started on the reconstruction of the church, an Act of Parliament was passed 'to enable the Parishioners of Ealing in the County of Middlesex, to raise money by Rates upon themselves for finishing the Church of the said Parish', and a Board of Trustees was appointed to supervise the arrangements. William King's name appears as one of the original trustees together with those of the Lord Bishop of London, Lord Hobart, Sir Richard Ellis, Sir Francis Child, Sir George Champion, Sir William Hatton, William Pulteney, William Melmoth, and some two dozen others including Dr. Thomas Mangey, the Vicar of the parish and Chancellor of the diocese. On King's

---

[1] Historical Manuscripts Commission, *Report on the Manuscripts of the Right Honourable Lord Polwarth . . . now in the Scottish Record Office, Edinburgh* (London: Her Majesty's Stationery Office, 1961), Vol. V, p. 228.

activities as Trustee only one tantalizingly incomplete piece of evidence survives, drawn from the *Minutes of Vestry for Ealing Church and Churchyard, 1739 to 1744*. Repeated searches have failed to trace this particular volume, but a short quotation from it, for 26 May 1739, is given in Edith Jackson's *Annals of Ealing*. On this day, at a meeting of the Trustees, we are told 'that Dr. King proposed to meet the Churchwardens to stake out the ground next week, and how far the chancel extends.' He also proposed 'to pay yearly such rate or tax equivalent with other persons proportionally to £180 per annum, in consideration of the Trustees finishing his chancel.'[1]

At least part of King's time in May 1739 was spent in London, if one may believe what the young John Cotton wrote in a letter to Sanderson Miller in that month from 'Gidding, Huntingdonshire':

. . . I saw Dr. King the night before and that was the first time we could meet, I had been twice at the Temple and twice at Tom's Coffee House to enquire for him . . . but without success, and they forgot my name at the Coffee House and only told the Dr. a young gentleman had been twice to enquire for him upon which he imagined that it might be Mr. [Deane] Swift whom he knew to be in town. . . .[2]

Cotton then laments the fact that he will have to travel northwards alone, suggesting that he should follow the Doctor's example in such circumstances: 'I must do like the Dr. and call to Guillot as he to Peter;—"Guillot, put up the Petronious [*sic*], will you have any more room?"—"Yes, Sir."—"Put in

---

[1] Edith Jackson, *Annals of Ealing* (London: Phillimore & Co., 1898), pp. 170f. This author claims that King was Rector of Ealing from 1739 to 1761. I believe that this information is wrong; even if he fulfilled some of the secular functions of the Rector, the evidence is that the Rector in legal theory remained the Chancellor of St. Paul's Cathedral, as long as the ultimate ownership of the property remained vested in the chancellorship. This matter is referred to again in Appendix IV. There is no doubt as to when the reconstruction was finished. A note in the *Register of Burials, 1765–1796* of St. Mary's Church reads: 'The New Parish Church of Ealing was opened for Divine Service on Trinity Sunday, 1740'.

[2] This and the following quotation are drawn from Lilian Dickins and Mary Stanton (eds.), op. cit., pp. 12f. The letter is dated only 'May, 1739'. Tom's Coffee House may be the establishment in Devereux Court near Temple Bar which Pope visited and in which Edmund Curll at one time had a controlling interest. Several other coffee houses of the same name were in existence in 1739; Bryant Lillywhite's *London Coffee Houses* provides descriptions, pp. 580–96.

Caesar and now try to get Sallust into that Corner, do not forget the Common Prayer Book."' It is not surprising to learn that, when the Principal of St. Mary Hall travelled, he was supplied with classical reading matter.

King also spent a certain amount of the same month—May 1739—with Pope as a guest of Lord Orrery at his country seat of Marston in Somerset. Pope mentioned the fact in a post-script to his letter to Swift of 17 May 1739: 'This I end at Lord Orrery's, in company with Dr. King. Where-ever I can find two or three that are yours, I adhere to them naturally, & by that Title they become mine.'[1] On the following July 2 King was back at St. Mary Hall, and, as he explained to Lord Orrery, preparing to see Marston again:

This fortnight past I have been on a journey of business and did not return to this place till last night, when I had the favour of your kind letter from Marston. Tho' I have scarce had time to look round our Hall, and tho' I find that riding but ill agrees with the present frame of my body, yet I am preparing for another journey. For I am determined to make you a visit before you leave Old England, as being in some doubt considering my age and the age you intend to be absent, whether I may ever have the good fortune to see you again.[2]

Already the infirmities of which King was to complain for the rest of his life were in evidence. Gout was the principal, a malady which, despite his several visits to Bath, he never overcame. His fingers were severely affected, as demonstrated by the signs of trembling in his penmanship which are observable with increasing frequency from about this time until the last letter which survives, written shortly before his death. His age when he indicated his determination to visit Lord Orrery

---

[1] George Sherburn (ed.), op. cit., Vol. IV, p. 180.

[2] Bodleian Library, MS. Eng. hist. d. 103, p. 5. The counterpart to this collection of forty-six of King's letters written between 1738 and 1745 is at the Houghton Library of Harvard University, MS. Eng. 218.2. By collating the letters in these two collections, one is able to acquire a fairly full though not complete conspectus of both sides of the correspondence. The group of letters in the Bodleian Library remains as a whole unpublished; a number of the letters of Lord Orrery now at Harvard University were published, some in truncated form, by the Countess of Cork and Orrery in 1903. The two folio and five quarto volumes in which Lord Orrery's letters are contained were acquired by Harvard University in 1923.

again was fifty-four years; he was often to comment on his senescence in the future.

King kept his word and visited Marston soon afterwards. A touching—though unabashedly rhetorical—tribute to him shortly after his departure was paid by Lord Orrery in a letter of 27 August 1739, written from Dublin:

When you was gone, my dear Doctor, Marston Bowers lost all their Charms. The Leaves wither'd, the Flowers droop'd, the House-dog grew sullen, the glow Worms died, and Melancholy diffused itself throughout the whole Parish. Our Curate had thoughts of turning Methodist, and the Esquire relaps'd into the Ague by drinking Water. Mr. Scott broke his Ruler, and Twitzer talk'd of planting Thistles and Crab trees. The Harpsicord prov'd out of Tune, Lady Orrery grew hoarse, and little Kate would squeal no more.[1]

Lord Orrery then brings up the matter, already broached at Marston, of his proposed translation of Pliny's epistles, the complete text of which appeared in two volumes, with observations and an essay on Pliny's life, in 1751, the same year as his more famous *Remarks on the Life and Writings of Dr. Jonathan Swift*. The translation was not to be literal. 'I would make Pliny an Englishman,' wrote Lord Orrery in the same letter, 'I would keep up his Sense and Spirit, but I would endeavour to use such Expressions as He himself would have chose had He written in English.' He also requests the favour of sending parts of his work to King from time to time for his comments.

In his reply from St. Mary Hall of 23 September 1739, King showed himself to be enthusiastic about Orrery's forthcoming translation: 'I design you no compliment,' he wrote, 'when I add that you only are qualified for it. A Translation of Pliny's Epistles should not be attempted but by a polite Scholar and can never be well executed but by one, who very nearly resembles his author, and participates of the spirit and manners of that great Roman. . . . In a word Pliny is not to be translated but by one, who speaks, and writes, and thinks, and lives like Pliny.'[2] King further intimated that Lord Orrery could not send 'a more acceptable present' than parts of this work, and

---

[1] Countess of Cork and Orrery, *The Orrery Papers* (2 vols.; London: Duckworth, 1903), Vol. I, p. 264.

[2] Bodleian Library, MS. Eng. hist. d. 103, p. 8.

said that he would pass on the sheets to one or two colleagues. He would himself go over the translation also: 'I love you too well not to read it with a critic's eye' was his way of putting the matter.

It is impossible to gauge with any degree of precision the influence that King exerted over Orrery's *Pliny*. In his surviving letters to the translator, King certainly provided a plethora of sympathy and encouragement; such statements as 'I approve the whole manner in which you propose to conduct this noble work', 'I shall look on your Book as my favourite mistress', 'I am as certain of your success as I am that there will be another revolution of the Sun' are typical of many others in similar vein. There is no evidence that King ever actually rewrote any part of Orrery's scripts, nor was any acknowledgement paid to King in the published version. In his correspondence King offered assistance of a rather general nature, such as promises to make 'researches among the works of the Medalists and Antiquaries for the Heads of the principal persons to whom Pliny addressed his letters,' and to advise the author on head-pieces and tail-pieces. On one occasion he sent 'a leaf I took out of a Magazine, which by the date you see was published in 1738,' and on another suggested the use of decorations comparable to those employed in Conyers Middleton's biography, *The Life of Cicero*. King's contribution to Orrery's work was probably no more specific than these intimations imply. It would be as unfair to blame King for the shortcomings and infelicities that this version of Pliny's letters exhibits as it would be to praise him for its passages of undeniable elegance. The fact that it is in places a loose paraphrase rather than a translation is the inevitable result of its writer's avowed aim.

While Lord Orrery, with King's blessing, was making his translation of the letters of Pliny the Younger, King's son-in-law, William Melmoth, was also working on *his* English version of the same Latin work. Melmoth's translation appeared in print in 1746; it is generally conceded to be the superior of the two.[1] The existence of Melmoth's *Pliny* constitutes one reason why Orrery's *Pliny* has not been more widely known. It would

[1] The English translation used in the Loeb Classical Library edition of Pliny's *Letters* is a revised version of Melmoth's.

be interesting to know King's opinion of the relative merits of the two translations, since he must have been acquainted with both. Unfortunately no correspondence between him and his son-in-law has survived and King nowhere expressed his sentiments on the matter in print.

Most of the winter of 1739 to 1740 was spent by the Principal within his lodgings at St. Mary Hall. It was bitterly cold in Oxford. In his letter to Lord Orrery of 15 January 1739/40, he complains that his fingers are frozen and adds: 'Here is truly such a face of Nature as I have never yet seen, and the present Winter prospect is as fit a subject for poetry and painting as it is for the contemplation of philosophy.'[1] He continues with an allusion to his being a teetotaller: 'I have, however, the good fortune in a general scarcity to have my Cellar well stock'd, that is, my pump is not frozen. So that I have not only Water enough for my own drinking, but I am able to fill all ye Teakettles and Boilers in this neighbourhood. Some Wags of my acquaintance maintain that our Well is supply'd from Helicon.'

During this winter King wrote his third Latin political satire, *Scamnum, Ecloga*, which appeared in print probably in March 1740. A copy of it was enclosed with a letter which King wrote to Lord Orrery on 25 March 1740. Together with it was an 'English Thing' which is not now identifiable. Thus King describes his most recent Latin work:

In the Latin Eclogue I have attempted a new kind of Satire, which you may remember I mention'd to you at Marston, and which I wonder has never been practis'd by any of our modern poets: especially since Virgil hath shown us a plan for a work of this nature in most of his pastorals. One of my Shepherds you see hath ventur'd to address Your Lordship tho' without your consent in so plain a manner, that no one can mistake his meaning. To say the truth I could no longer resist the vanity of telling the World that Lord Orrery is my friend. Nay if you do not forbid it, I shall write that name at length, if this poem shall bear a second Impression.[2]

Scamnum never appeared in a second published impression. The work was revised and included in the *Opera*, but by the time

[1] Bodleian Library, MS. Eng. hist. d. 103, p. 9. The following quotation occurs on the same page.
[2] Ibid., p. 11.

King gathered his Latin works together for this collection, he seems to have forgotten his promise to Lord Orrery. Two English translations also appeared: one in 1741, published by Josiah Graham, and the other in 1744, published by Edmund Curll. Both of these vernacular versions are anonymous. Curll may have issued an earlier edition of his translation; if he did, no known copy has survived.

Except for some changes in proper names, there are no important differences between the two Latin texts. However, there are numerous minor variations. The 1740 version contains 205 lines, the *Opera* recension 204. The dedication to G.K.S.M. (Georgio Keith Scotiae Mareschallo), covering two folio pages, is omitted in the recension. This particular dedication provides a certain amount of flattering information about George Keith, but is more in the nature of an explanatory preface to the poem.

The eclogue, as a poetical form, has been variously cast at different times. The Greek root of the word, ἐκλογή, is not especially helpful: it means simply a 'selection'. The term is generally taken to mean a pastoral dialogue, but it cannot be defined more specifically than that. Of the thirty *Idylls* attributed to Theocritus—some are not genuine—eleven may be categorized as true pastorals. They were the product of the Alexandrian age, when civilization had become complex to the extent that some readers of poetry turned to the lives and conversation of Greek Sicilian shepherds by way of artistic respite. Theocritus wrote his eclogues in a literary adaptation of the native rustic speech of the Dorian Greeks of Sicily. The effects that he achieved were roughly comparable to those which Burns was later to accomplish by adapting the Scottish dialect for literary purposes. These Greek eclogues were not literal reproductions of native songs, but they were based on a genuine stratum of reality. The characters are real shepherds of flesh and blood engaged in singing contests or improvisations such as used to take place at Sicilian village festivals. The eclogues of Vergil and Spenser, on the other hand, idealize reality, and in doing so produce an atmosphere which is for the most part artificial. The Vergilian and Spenserian shepherds are not really shepherds at all: they are masqueraders set against a background of stylized rusticity. They may represent real persons, sometimes in political life, or may be embodiments of ideas which the poet prefers not to hint at too openly.[1] King's eclogue is in the tradition of Vergil and Spenser, but is even more artificial than theirs. The shepherds of these artists are quite transparent, but they do speak their native language. King's English shepherds, by speaking in Latin, are one stage further removed from reality.

King was by no means the first English writer to produce a Neo-Latin eclogue. His numerous predecessors included Thomas Watson, Giles Fletcher, Phineas Fletcher, William Gager, Richard Latewar, and William Hawkins. Nor was he the first poet to compose a satirical eclogue in Latin, for this genre had been written since the time of Mantuan.[2] What is original about *Scamnum* is the fact that the subject under discussion is party politics, treated in a manner which is only incidentally bucolic. The form of this poem is indeed that of the classical eclogue, but its spirit, in general, is that of the Tories-in-opposition.

King, in his Dedication, makes the character of his shepherds plain when he writes: '*Ecce tibi Pastores meos, non quidem de infima plebe, sed urbanioris notae homines; qui norunt sane, quid segetes, quid arbores agant, quid oves & boves: sed & bene hercle norunt, quae sint civium studia, procerum mores, regum consilia.*' He explains that it is not alien to bucolic poetry to inveigh against *malos, indoctos, invidos*, pointing out that '*Pastorum ille & poetarum princeps, dum Phyllida amat, dumque Pollioni blanditur, Bavio & Maevio ignominiae notam inussit per omnia secula indelebilem.*' The *princeps* is, of course, Vergil, and the reference is to the third eclogue, where Menalcas is at pains to explain, '*Phyllida amo ante alias*'. It is not King's fault that many modern classical scholars do not adhere to the view that Menalcas in this poem represents Vergil and that he personally loved Phyllis—whoever she was.

[1] I am not convinced by the theory of Léon Herrman advanced in *Les Masques et les Visages dans les Bucoliques de Virgile* that every name in Vergil's *Eclogues* always represents one and the same *person*.

[2] Of the ten eclogues of Mantuan, four are satirical (4, 5, 6, and 9). They appear in Giambattista Spagnuoli, *Opera Omnia* (2 vols.; Antwerp, 1576) and are reprinted in the edition of W. P. Mustard, *The Eclogues of Baptista Mantuanus* (Baltimore: The Johns Hopkins University Press, 1911). None is political, though the ninth, *Falco*, on the Roman Curia, influenced Spenser (in the *September Aeglogue*), Milton, and perhaps King.

But matters of identification apart, the author's contention is quite justifiable: Pollio is indeed complimented and the contemporary poets Bavius and Mevius are stigmatized during the course of Vergil's eclogue.

King continues with the question: '*Ecquis autem de Ecloga nostra merito irascatur?*' Without providing a direct answer, he proceeds to justify his method of composing *Scamnum*:

Lusimus sub umbra, agresti calamo, fictis nominibus. Ac tale temperamentum, necesse est, teneat, quisquis Latinos versus scribere aut cantare parat, sive quid acerbius meditetur, sive quid jucundius. Gothicorum enim & Barbarorum nominum conditione efficitur, quo minus & illi, quos aperte odimus, vel colimus maxime, in carminibus nostris ponantur.

Some lofty tributes are paid to George Keith: '. . . *eximia tua virtute, pietate, fide, probitate morum, suavitate ingenii, & fraterno amore toto jam notus es in orbe, & magnis regibus dilectus, & magnis Diis . . .*' and so on. At the opposite extreme are King's enemies, '*qui in curuli sella sedentes, aut solio fulti SCAMNUM meum prorsus contemnunt.*' To these enemies must be added some friends whom King is ashamed to own as such, who admire themselves for their own performances, and complain because his verses have no force or elegance, or, if they do, are obscure: '*Obscurus scilicet, ni plane dicam palamque, quis sit Mopsus, quis sit Iulus, quis sit Mavors, quis sit Typhoeus, &c. Quid si dicam? aut in ultimam occidentis insulam relegandus, aut piratarum jussu cum Ecloga mea in mare projiciendus.*'

In the case of *Scamnum* there is the same difficulty that occurs in all the author's other Latin political satires: no reliable key exists, and so the allusions, with very few exceptions, remain without precise identification. What can be said with confidence is that King did intend most, if not all, of the individuals named in the eclogue to correspond to real persons, and that their characters were, in his opinion, presented with impartiality. He himself enlarged on this matter in his letter to Lord Orrery of 25 March 1740: '. . . both in Panegyric and Satire I have drawn my characters by my personal knowledge of the men, their virtues and their vices. And as I have never been directed by any interested views, so I have no where that I

know exceeded the truth.'[1] He corroborates his own opinion of
his disinterestedness by adding: 'I have lived long enough to be
thoroughly convinced that there is but little virtue in any of our
parties; in the Heads and Managers none at all.'

Scamnum starts with a description of the author, sitting on a
bench near the bank of the River Isis. Like the Tityrus of Vergil's first eclogue, he is *sub tegmine fagi*:

> Dum fagus (namque aestus erat) me protegit umbra,
> Isidis ad ripas scamno jam forte sedebam:
> Scamno, frugiferi dominus quod fecerat agri
> Ruricolis sacrum, Musisque dicaverat Alcon.
> Laeve, ut marmor, erat, latumque: altare putares.

Though as smooth as marble, this bench is made of oak
descended from the same parents as those beams which, sweeping the sea, now

> Hispanos terrent, & mittunt fulmina ponto.

The mention of *Hispanos* is a reference to the conflict between
England and Spain which started in 1739, generally referred to
as the War of Jenkins' Ear. King was opposed to the hostilities,
which he regarded as unnecessary, implying that oak trees
could be put to better uses than the building of warships.

The author then returns to the bench and the river which
runs beside it:

> Nam facit, ut melius rus contemplemur amoenum,
> Gratior & qui fit, dum praeterlabitur, amnis.
> Otia dat pigris; praebet solatia fessis,
> Et senibus somnum, & mensam messoribus aptam;
> Atque suburbanis, si fama est nuntia veri,
> Praebet dura nimis, sed grata cubilia Nymphis.

The countryside outside Oxford is described in a highly
stylized manner, and the author contemplates the scene,

> . . . volucrum dulcedine captus,
> Floribus aut pascens oculos, fluvialia regna,
> Et genus arboreum meditans, annique meatus,
> Coelumque, & solis radios . . .

---

[1] Bodleian Library, MS. Eng. hist. d. 103, p. 12. The following quotation occurs
on page 13.

Meanwhile two shepherds, Lacon and Tityrus, approach, and King calls on the muse Calliope:

> Est aliquid voluisse imitari carmina divum,
> Quin age, Calliope, si unquam coluere Britanni
> Numina vestra, adsis; & quercu cincta capillos
> Pastorum alternos (nec te meminisse pigebit;
> Et potes haec meminisse) mihi refer ordine versus.

The two shepherds then proceed to sing verses of praise to the Goddess Liberty in an artificial amoebaean manner: how artificial may best be judged by comparing King's work to Vergil's third eclogue, in which the Roman poet comes closer than anywhere else to the spirit of Theocritus. In *Scamnum* the shepherds indulge in no preliminary backchat, and, when they sing alternately, the thrust and parry of Vergil's rather ungenial shepherds, Damoetus and Menalcas, are conspicuously absent. The verses of King's Lacon and Tityrus are in the nature of formal antiphonal incantations: while they lack all trace of realism, they do exhibit an impressive degree of stateliness and dignity. The nearest classical prototypes of King's shepherds are Corydon and Thyrsis in Vergil's seventh eclogue, but whereas they sing four lines apiece alternately for less than fifty lines, Lacon and Tityrus keep up their contest for more than a hundred and fifty.

Lacon commences the duologue by thus addressing the goddess Liberty:

> Libertas, o si qua dea es, nunc annue vati:
> En, tibi surgit opus, si quid mea carmina possunt.
> Munera pauperibus tu das, mentemque beatis;
> Tu das pascere oves; tu das cantare sub umbra.

To this lofty opening Tityrus replies:

> O dea Libertas certe! tibi ponimus aras:
> Hac vitula, mox & niveo donabere tauro,
> Nil mirum, si, regis opus, stas fictilis: at si
> Legibus emendes res nostras, aurea fies.

The promise of Tityrus to erect a golden statue in honour of the

goddess Liberty is immediately reminiscent of the similar promise of Vergil's Thyrsis to the god Priapus:

at tu,
Si fetura gregem suppleverit, aureus esto.

More invocations to the goddess follow; factitious though they
are, their mellifluous beauty is undeniable:

LACON

Hei mihi, quod pavidae fugiunt sua tecta columbae!
Obscoenas accepit aves nam candida turris.
Si venias, mea Clara; tuo jam numine tutae,
(Sic Venerem ore refers) volucres ad tecta redibunt.

TITYRUS

O formosa veni; nec rustica munera sperne:
Hic cerasi dulces, & mollia fraga leguntur.
Si mea rura colas, habitabunt dii mea rura;
Ipse, nec invitus, sit rursus pastor Apollo.

A perhaps rather jarring reference to Lady Allen, the *conjux
barbara Trauli*, and Myra, the *saga*, indicates that the events
described in *The Toast* were not far from King's mind when he
was writing *Scamnum*: possibly he was already engaged on his
revision of the text of 1736. A number of veiled allusions follow,
but not even the notes in the recension are enlightening. Thus
when Tityrus sings about *infelix Pholoe*, the entirety of the
information which King provides on who she was and why she
was unfortunate is this:

Fuit haec puella formosissima e Scotorum gente; quam veneno
tollere, aut saltem ei formam eripere Delia ista conata est, semel
iterumque puellae insidias molita. Notior haec est fabula aulicis
viris, populo vero obscurior.

Having vituperated against an unidentified Mopsus—he
could be King's son-in-law, William Melmoth—Lacon announces that this is the birthday of Iulus:

Huc ades, O Lenaee. Mei est natalis Iuli.
Vos lauro juvenem victrici ornate, Quirites.
Si tamen has silvas, haec si sua rura reviset,
Bina tibi, Fortuna redux, altaria fument.

Tityrus, not to be outdone, suggests further manifestations of rejoicing:

> Ecce ferunt violas, & candida lilia nymphae,
> Et, mea dona, rosas inscriptas nomen Iuli.
> Jam tandem o nostris puerum dii reddite votis!
> Aurea templa Jovi statuemus, & aurea Phoebo.

Then in striking contrast Lacon goes on to lament the *barbara gens* at Cambridge, by which he presumably means the large number of Whigs and their sympathizers:

> Musarum sedes, Cami quas alluit unda,
> En petiit, Geniumque loci divasque fugavit,
> Barbara gens. Ah! quo te mutas numine, Granta?
> Nec tamen ille tuus frustra regnavit Apollo.

Some of the following verses are today quite obscure on account of the vagueness of the allusions. But a brief survey of the contemporary European scene leads Tityrus to gloomy moralization:

> Nullus adest hostis: Martis tamen omnia plena.
> Nullus adest (at quid melius speravimus?) hostis.
> Sic sibi nunc compti promittat militis ardor,
> Atque ducis plumatus apex, sine clade triumphos.

Lacon now broaches another subject, and praises Lord Orrery under the name of Laelius. In the *Opera* version Laelius is replaced by Carolus, an appellation that is not definitely identifiable:

> Carole, quae nuper, Phoebo modulante canebas,
> Carmina mitte mihi. Sic dent laeta omnia Musae,
> Ne tibi quid desit: si quid tibi defuit, ex quo
> Dii fortem optatam pulchramque dedere Sabinam.

Tityrus is still more flattering:

> Carole, noster amor, gentis quoque gloria nostrae,
> Magni cura Jovis; qui fecit pectus honestum,
> Pectus amicitiae tibi, Carole: quo neque possit
> Quid melius, nec quid majus generatur in orbe.

The eclogue comes to an end with Lacon's lamenting that it is unlawful to relate things worthy of the country's divinities, and

9—W.K.

with the barely disguised hopes expressed by Tityrus for a
golden age in the future under the restored House of Stuart:

LACON

Haec lusi: neque adhuc pastoria cernere sacra
Aut datur, aut patriis diis fas est digna referre.
Si tamen ipse meum potui servare tenorem,
Pierides, caussam vatis defendite vestri.

TITYRUS

Nos quoque, conati Latias revocare Camoenas,
Hic fagos inter parvum pro tempore carmen
Fecimus: at quanta o, & quae, Saturnia mundo
Secula si redeant, & jusserit Ipse, canemus!

Perhaps it is not too much to say that *Scamnum* is one of the
most impressive examples in European literature of the grand
eclogue: in its way grander than any of Vergil's own. True the
topics sung about by the shepherds in *Scamnum* do not always
follow one another with logical consistency: the whole exhibits
a certain disjointed quality. But this characteristic is derived
from the conditions of the original amoebaean contests. The
singer who started could broach a new topic whenever he
wished, and his rival had to invent an equal number of verses
on the same theme—or one deliberately contrasted—designed
to improve upon the utterance of the first singer. In the matter
of adhering to the rules of the singing match, King is most
punctilious. He cannot maintain Vergil's peculiar quality
described by Horace as *molle atque facetum*; there is too much
evidence of personal spite towards his political enemies. For
this reason he lacks Vergil's tenderness and his universality.
But if one is going to use the eclogue for the rather unnatural
purpose of disseminating party political propaganda, it is difficult to see how King's general method of handling his allegorical
medium could be improved upon.[1]

[1] The most exhaustive discussion of the Neo-Latin eclogue is provided in W.
Leonard Grant, *Neo-Latin Literature and the Pastoral* (Chapel Hill: University of
North Carolina Press, 1965). Grant's many divisions of the eclogue are, I think,
somewhat arbitrary, but as a work of reference this book is of value with regard to
the continental poets. The development of the eclogue in England and Scotland
is treated best in Leicester Bradner, *Musae Anglicanae* (London: Oxford University
Press, 1940). See also the same author's '*Musae Anglicanae*: A Supplemental List',
The Library, 5th Series, Vol. XXII, No. 2 (1967), pp. 93–101.

IV

Templum Libertatis

IN THE summer of 1740 King suffered an attack of what he described as a violent fever. Writing to Lord Orrery in a not entirely steady hand on 5 August 1740, he lamented his illness:

wch for some time deprived me of all my faculties, and I fear you will perceive they are now but very imperfectly restored to me. This is the first day I have sat down to write, since I got out of my bed; and tho I handle my pen very awkwardly, yet I am resolved to say as much as my strength will permit me. . . . My hand begins now to tremble, so that I must finish my letter as fast as I can. . . .[1]

On the following October 28 he was again ailing:

I have been a month in London and for more than 3 weeks I have been confined to my chamber by the Gout, or what ye Physicians call a Rheumatick Gout. The worst has been that ye violence of the distemper has fallen into my right hand; and till this day I have not been able to hold my pen, and that I now handle very awkwardly, my hand being still wrapt up in flannel, and in great pain.[2]

In this same letter occurs the first mention in King's writings of *Templum Libertatis*: 'The times are grown so hard, that I am now preparing a work for ye press in full expectation of getting some money by it. Which is a thing I never aimed at before, tho' I have in ye course of my Life blotted some Reams of paper. What I intend is a Latin poem in 3 Books . . . .' The writing becomes more and more difficult to read, but it is clear that King intended each book to have a frontispiece, head-piece and tail-piece, making nine copper plates in all, 'so that my sub-scribers (if I publish it by subscription) may be sure of some-thing for their money.'

Perhaps King dictated *Templum Libertatis* to an amanuensis,

---

[1] Bodleian Library, MS. Eng. hist. d. 103, pp. 15ff.
[2] Ibid., p. 17. The following quotation is drawn from page 19.

but if he wrote the text himself, it must have been under considerable difficulties. His illness continued throughout the winter of 1740–1, witness, for example, Pope's intimation to Lord Orrery on 10 December 1740: 'I am unwilling to add to your Concern, by telling how dangerously ill Dr King is still.'[1] King's letters to Lord Orrery during this period contain frequent complaints about the continuing gout in his fingers, and on one occasion—20 May 1741—he makes an obscure allusion to a device for overcoming his ailment: 'You have been so good to me, that I am resolved to try if I can thank you without my fingers. For that purpose I have invented a wooden instrument, by ye help of wch I seem to perform tolerably well, and to be able to write so plainly, that any Clerk in the post-office may read my Letter without calling for a Decypherer.'[2] From time to time King's condition temporarily improved, as towards the end of the month, when Lord Orrery paid him a visit. In his letter of May 29, written to Lady Orrery 'from Dr. King's Study at St. Mary Hall,' His Lordship remarked: 'He is gaining ground very fast, not so fast as we wish but as fast as the perverseness of his Distemper will admit of.'[3] But until his death the gout in his fingers was always liable to return, especially in cold weather. Hence on 1 January 1741/2 he complained, '. . . my hand is so lame that I can scarce hold my pen,' and on the second page of his letter to Lord Orrery of 29 December 1742, he wrote in a kind of scrawl:

My Hand will not serve me beyond this page. I have lately had 2 or 3 severe strokes of my old Rheumatism in my hands only—so that I am forced to use them at present with great tenderness. For I would willingly preserve my writing fingers, as long as I keep my senses—that I may be on all occasions able to boast of ye friendship, with which your Lordship and Lady Orrery have honoured ye old Monk of St. Mary Hall.[4]

The principal problem concerning *Templum Libertatis* is that,

[1] George Sherburn (ed.), op. cit., Vol. IV, p. 304.
[2] Bodleian Library, MS. Eng. hist. d. 103, p. 21.
[3] Countess of Cork and Orrery (ed.), op. cit., Vol. II, p. 165.
[4] Bodleian Library, MS. Eng. hist. d. 103, pp. 48, 63. The Lady Orrery referred to here is His Lordship's second wife, the former Margaret Hamilton, daughter and sole heir of John Hamilton of Caledon, Co. Tyrone. Their marriage had taken place on 30 June 1738. His first wife, Henrietta, had died on 22 August 1732.

though King and later his publishers, Charles Bathurst and George Hawkins, spoke of three books, in fact only two ever appeared in print. The problem of the missing third book is aggravated by the difficulty of discovering when the other two were finished. The evidence, taken literally, involves contradictions. Thus on 4 September 1741 King informed Lord Orrery that the work was 'finished':

My Temple is just finished, and I intend shall make it's appearance in November. If you do me the favour to come to Bath, you shall see the dress it is now in. It has passed thro' the hands of two of my Critical friends. The oftener I look on this piece, the more I am confirmed in my opinion, that it will quite ruin my Character. But see the obstinacy of an old Author, that knowing this I send it abroad.[1]

In view of his later statements, King could not have been referring to the finished work: he must have intended the first book to be understood. On 10 November 1741 he wrote to Orrery, agreeing with His Lordship's opinion that the *whole* of *Templum Libertatis* should appear 'at once'.[2] Again, only Book One is presumably intended, for when King later refers to Book Two, he describes it as 'my second Temple'. It is impossible to ascertain with any degree of precision the dates within which the second book was written, but it was probably finished, except for corrections and minor changes, by the end of the following December. On 1 January 1741/2 he remarked: '. . . my spirits are so good, that I have begun my 3ᵈ Book. And if the evil Genius of Britain be not again triumphant and consequently oblige me to alter my plan, I shall have finished the whole work before next winter.'[3]

Volume I of *Templum Libertatis* was published in 1742, very probably in early January, with the imprint

LONDINI:

Apud C. Bathurst, & G. Hawkins, in *Fleet Street*.

It is listed in the Register of Books of *The Gentleman's Magazine* for January 1742. On October 31 of the same year King wrote

[1] Bodleian Library, MS. Eng. hist. d. 103, pp. 32f.
[2] Ibid., p. 47.   [3] Ibid., p. 49.

to Lord Orrery from Oxford: 'I am printing my second T. which goes slowly, because of the distance I am from yᵉ press. However I must stay till I can finish it.'[1] On the following January 5 King sent a copy of the second book of the poem to Lord Orrery with an admonition and a promise of another copy to follow: 'Your Lordship must not part with yᵉ Templum till it be published. But let any body read it, who pleases. Don't imagine I design this blue-covered thing for yᵉ authors presents. No. You shall certainly have a fine one—marbled and guilded —Believe me . . .'[2] This second book, which bears the publication date of 1743, and is listed in the Register of Books of *The Gentleman's Magazine* for January of that year, must have appeared in the bookshops by 21 January 1742/3, for on that day King wrote: 'I have not heard a Word about my Templum from any of my great friends in London, since it was published. So that I do not know their opinion of this performance. However I am little solicitous about it.'[3] And a little later in the same letter he remarks that the third book is still unfinished: 'You have certainly encouraged me to proceed. And I hope I shall be able to finish yᵉ Work according to my present plan, as soon as Don Phoebus will give me leave. For, without a Metaphor, it is only the genial heat of the Sun, which can inspire me.' These words constitute the final witness on the third book. Whether it was ever finished and, if so, why it was never published are both unsolved enigmas. But as a result of its absence, King's most important serious work and one of the most forceful Latin poems of its time remains incomplete.

There must have been frequent interruptions in the composition of *Templum Libertatis*. King's letters to Orrery reveal that the Principal of St. Mary Hall was often called upon to provide entertainment for visitors: Lord Orrery himself, Pope, Lord Chesterfield, and various university officials among them. The weather during the autumn and winter of 1741 seems to have been severe: King's correspondence at this period is sprinkled with such *obiter dicta* as 'It rains—and blows—and thunders', 'I am writing this by the fire-side', 'It rains hard— my Head is muddy', and so on. In September of 1741 he journeyed to Bath, even though he felt reservations about the

---

[1] Ibid., p. 61.   [2] Ibid., p. 66.   [3] Ibid., p. 69.

efficacy of the waters. 'The truth is,' he explained to Orrery on 9 September 1741, 'I doubt much whether ye Bath-Water will do me any service, but I am so earnestly exhorted to try it, that I must give up my own opinion to the Sages of Physic.'[1] Having reached Bath a little over a week later, he explained that he had been trying the pump for his hands, adding: 'I wish I may have any reason to boast of ye virtues of ye Bath Water.'[2] In fact he benefited little from the waters of Bath. On 6 October 1741 he wrote: 'I have been pumping and pumping to no purpose. And I begin to think that all ye Waters of Bath will not relax my joints. So obstinate they are . . . I believe I shall return to my Monastery sooner than I intended, tho' I must go by ye way of London to look after my Legacy.'[3]

The legacy to which King here refers must be that which he inherited with his two surviving brothers, Thomas and John, on the death in 1741 of his second cousin, Sir William Smyth of Warden, Bedfordshire. This bequest deserves some comment. At the time King was writing, it consisted of a number of pieces of property including Akeley manor in Buckinghamshire with its accompanying lands. In 1647 this parcel had been compounded for by King's maternal grandfather, Sir William Smyth of Radclive, Buckinghamshire. In his will it was assigned to Sir Thomas Smyth, who reassigned it, as security on his nephew's loans, by deed of 17 November 1724.[4] The reassignation is confirmed in the will of Sir William Smyth of Warden, Bedfordshire, though most of his estate, as he was a bachelor and died without issue, seems to have gone to King's brother John and his family. Because no records of the matter survive in the Buckingham County Record Office, the details of the administration of the legacy are obscure, but the suggestion has been made that the brothers alienated the property.[5] There is no indisputable evidence to indicate that William maintained any further direction connection with Akeley manor. A record does survive of litigation over another piece of land at Aspley Guise in Bedforshire, which was inherited by John King's son

---

[1] Ibid., p. 33.   [2] Ibid., p. 37.   [3] Ibid., p. 42.
[4] The original deed does not appear to have survived, but it is referred to in the Registry of Deeds, King's Inns, Dublin, *Memorialls of Deeds, Conveyances and Wills*, Vol. 52, p. 252, No. 34462.
[5] See *The Victoria History of the County of Buckingham*, Vol. IV, p. 145.

William Smyth-King, in a Chancery Proceeeding *King* v. *How* of 5 February 1763.[1] Though the action mentions both Sir William Smyth of Radclive and Sir William Smyth of Warden, the plaintiff's celebrated uncle seems not to have been involved. It is certain, however, that King was involved in the probate proceedings in London in connection with the will of Sir William Smyth of Warden, the verified copy of which, with its accompanying certificates and documents, was handed to the executors on 2 November 1741. King gives an indication of what the legacy was worth to him in a letter to Lord Orrery of 18 August 1742: 'I have been in Buckinghamshire to view a Legacy which was left me about a year ago, and which I find will bring me annually clear of all taxes & charges £60, a very good addition to an old Monk's commons.'[2]

While King was writing *Templum Libertatis*, he had, of course, to carry out the various official duties that were incumbent on him as head of St. Mary Hall. In addition, he took upon himself a number of other administrative tasks, one of which was the attempt to induce the authorities to confer the degree of D.D. on William Warburton so that Pope would be persuaded to accept the degree of D.C.L. King played a significant though ultimately unsuccessful role in this odd affair, the main outlines of which are fairly clear. During 1741 Pope and William Warburton, later to become Bishop of Gloucester, visited Oxford together. While they were there, the then Vice-Chancellor, Dr. Theophilus Leigh, Master of Balliol, offered the degree of D.C.L. to Pope and that of D.D. to Warburton. The proposal in Warburton's case was especially unfortunate, because when the circumstances of the offer became known, the resistance of some of the clergy successfully prevented the granting of the degree. Pope refused to be 'doctored' unless Warburton were also given the D.D. The Chancellor, the Earl of Arran, refused to implement Dr. Leigh's proposal against the wishes of the opposition and, after prolonged discussions, the tentative plans for both degrees were dropped.

King seems to have done what he could to support Pope on behalf of Warburton. On 17 June 1741 Lord Orrery wrote:

'Mr. Pope is at Oxfd with Dr. King', and on the following August 12, Pope, now back at Twickenham, confided to Warburton that he was chagrined by the delay over the promised D.D., but added: 'Dr King tells me it will prove no more.'[1] King's efforts were, however, unavailing, and on 13 January 1742/3 Pope communicated with Lord Orrery on the matter: 'You are not to be now told, that the Vice Chancellor Dr Leigh & several Heads of Houses sent & offerd Mr Warburton the degree of a Dr of Divinity, when he had no such Expectation, after which it was monstrously refused by the unaccountable Dissent of 2 or 3. Dr King either has, or will acquaint you of the particulars.'[2]

Pope's intimation was fulfilled on the following January 31, when King wrote to Orrery on the subject of the refusal. According to this letter, Warburton's orthodoxy had been impugned by Dr. De Blosshier Tovey, Principal of New Inn Hall, and Warburton's enemies had taken advantage of this attack to have the affair of the degree postponed *sine die*. King was furious; he thus describes Tovey to His Lordship: 'In short, he is a man, who never speaks a serious truth, unless it be sometimes in ye pulpit, when he can't well avoid it; but even there he buffoons with it in such a manner, as to make ye most sacred mysteries appear ridiculous. Judge you, whether any regard ought to have been had to such a man.'[3] This indictment is followed by an exhortation to Orrery to communicate directly with the Vice-Chancellor: 'I really believe, if in this interim you would give your self the trouble to write a strong letter to the Vice chancellor in favour of Mr Warburton, nothing would have a better effect. For ye Vice in his conversation with me professed ye highest esteem for your Lordship. . . .'[4] Lord Orrery complied with this request and on 16 February 1742/3 wrote to the Vice-Chancellor. On the same day he wrote again to King, hoping that there would still be a method of solving the

[1] Countess of Cork and Orrerey (ed.), op. cit., Vol. II, p. 168; and George Sherburn (ed.), op. cit., Vol. IV, p. 357.

[2] George Sherburn (ed.), op. cit., Vol. IV, pp. 436f. Dr. Leigh, shortly after making his offer, had been succeeded in the Vice-Chancellorship by Dr. Walter Hodges, Provost of Oriel, who was opposed to Warburton's receiving the award.

[3] Bodleian Library, MS. Eng. hist. d. 103, p. 69.

[4] Ibid.

matter satisfactorily and conferring on Warburton the doctorate in Divinity.[1] But all this effort was ultimately of no avail. In his letter to Orrery written on Ash Wednesday 1742/3 King was forced to admit, 'I now perceive that Mr W. has more enemies among our Governors than I imagined.'[2] The following September Pope visited Oxford for the third time since the question of the degree was initiated, being, as he wrote later, '. . . in full assurance of finding Dr King, but he was gone the day before to London; however I took possession of his lodging, & got away the next morning, un-doctor'd, the third time: *Sic me servavit Apollo.*'[3] Pope, Orrery and King were together again on 8 February 1743/4, at Burlington House, when King was entertained 'with all the elegance, civility, openness and noble qualities that Ld Burl^n can show.'[4] But by this time the possibility that the degrees might be awarded had in all likelihood been abandoned. The proposal was never revived.

The two published books of *Templum Libertatis* were incorporated by King, with small variations, in the *Opera*. Despite occasional published notices of a forthcoming translation, no English version of the work is known to have appeared. The 1742 version of Book One contains an introductory note *Bibliopola Lectori* and a prose preface *Divae Libertatis Cultoribus*, both of which are omitted in the recension. The date given at the end of this preface is *Calend. Dec.* MDCCXLI. The original text of the first book contains 575 lines; the revision, 617. Book Two was expanded from 612 to 614 lines. In the original folio versions of both books, the notes are inserted at the end of the text; in the *Opera* they are placed at the foot of the page. In view of the fact that King spent both time and labour in revising the text and notes already published, his decision to leave the final version of the work unfinished is especially puzzling.

Templum Libertatis is an allegorical epic in dactylic hexameter, and among the last of its kind to be composed in Latin. W.

---

[1] The Houghton Library, Harvard University, MS. Eng. 218.2 (v. 4), pp. 349ff.
[2] Bodleian Library, MS. Eng. hist. d. 103, p. 70.
[3] George Sherburn (ed.), op. cit., Vol. IV, p. 472.
[4] Countess of Cork and Orrery (ed.), op. cit., Vol. II, p. 183.

Leonard Grant has described the epic as the 'least successful of all forms of neo-Latin poetry',[1] and he is undoubtedly correct. The history of the neo-Latin epic is strewn with artistic failures, some of monstrous proportions (such as Basinio de' Basini's *Hesperis* in thirteen books), some merely fragments. Even Petrarch felt misgivings about his own epic, *Africa*, but no reasonable critic would deny that portions of it do exhibit literary merit. A few other neo-Latin epics are still worth reading for their poetical qualities; among them should be mentioned Giacopo Sannazaro's *De Partu Virginis*, Marco Vida's *Christiad*, Phineas Fletcher's *Locustae*, and the *Sarcotis* of Jacobus Masenius, all of which contain passages of genuine artistry. The latter two productions appear to have influenced Milton, and were probably known to King. Since Book Two of *Templum Libertatis* is avowedly influenced by *Paradise Lost*, it is highly probable that King was also well acquainted with Milton's *In Quintum Novembris*, the supernatural machinery of which anticipates in some respects that of both *Paradise Lost* and *Templum Libertatis*. It is possible too that King was conversant with Andrew Ramsay's *Poemata Sacra*: it also was known to Milton, and exhibits a vigorous Latinity comparable in power to that of King.[2] *Templum Libertatis* may thus be regarded as the product of a long if not particularly successful tradition; truncated though this epic is, it is of greater interest than many of the other works in its own category.

As is the case with so many of King's Latin works, the text is edited by the author himself, and the notes constitute an important part of the artistic whole. Both books were originally published anonymously, but the writer's identity was no doubt known to a good proportion of the readers. The *Bibliopola Lectori* is deliberately evasive in expression:

Carmen hoc, quale vides, imperfectum edidit Poeta ex consilio meo. Quippe quum tres Libros simul publicare cogitaret, ego hominem dehortatus sum, ne id faceret. Jamdiu enim opera Latina, qualiacunque sunt, paucos inveniunt Lectores, patronos vero

---

[1] W. Leonard Grant, op. cit., p. 44.

[2] The Scottish divine and poet Andrew Ramsay (1574–1659) should not, of course, be confused with the author of *Les Voyages de Cyrus*, whose dates were 1686 to 1743.

paucissimos. Et quicquid hic noster magnificentius est praefatus de pulchritudine materiae, ac Diva sua; satis hercle scio, quod hujuscemodi scripta sola brevitas excuset: & ne vix haec quidem. Usque adeo senuerunt literae!

Here again King employs one of his favourite literary practices: he writes under the guise of another with a view to confusing his enemies.

In the Preface *Divae Libertatis Cultoribus* the author explains his motivation in composing the work:

LIBER ILLE SPIRITUS, quo adjutore opera omnia mea composui, Epistolas, Sermones, Eclogas (res tenues quidem & tenuiter aestimandas) nunc incitatius fertur, *per ambages, Deorumque ministeria praecipitandus.* . . . Non enim mala ambitione adductus carmen hoc in publicum dedi, quod laureolam mihi expectem, vel quod aliquid aut alma matre nostra, aut auribus vestris dignum proferre videar; verum ut quoquo modo satisfacerem amori patriae, & laudibus LIBERTATIS.[1]

He then suggests a transmutation of an old paradox:

Ciceronianum istud, seu Stoicum Paradoxon, NISI SAPIENTEM LIBERUM ESSE NEMINEM, sic immutari volo, NISI LIBERUM SAPIENTEM ESSE NEMINEM.

From this position, King is led to speculate on the vice of conformism under tyranny:

Saepenumero igitur mirari soleo ignavum istud hominum genus, immo pecus ignavissimum, qui de communi sententia deserunt communem salutem, et aequo animo et patienti ferunt spectantque tyrannorum potentiam, praefectos, stupra, rapinas, caedes, parricidia.

He returns briefly to his old theme expounded in *Common Sense*: if gods can be fabricated out of wood or clay, why not kings also? But he dismisses the facetious suggestion immediately with the comment *absint saevi et illiberales joci*, and enlarges, in a passage of considerable rhetorical power, on the kind of rulers who are needed:

Cives meos monitos volo . . . ut in principes Reipublicae nobis eligamus viros sapientes, justos, temperatos, fortes, firmos: ut Libertatis

---

[1] The italicized quotation is from Petronius.

numen, quasi Palladium nostrum tueamur et conservemus; quasi Solem ipsum suspiciamus et veneremur; cujus sine auxilio nec serere nec metere datur, nec arbores, nec oves, nec liberi nostri nobis crescunt. Noster hic sit labor, haec meditatio, hoc negotium, hoc otium.

He warns that citizens should be prepared to defend freedom with financial contributions and military intervention:

Et semper parati simus, siquid Respublica detrimenti ceperit, non modo consiliis eam adjuvare, sed opibus, sed armis.

King's final thoughts in the Preface represent the development of what he has already expressed. He admonishes his readers against despair, however trying the circumstances:

Si tamen, aut bonorum infirmitate, aut iniquitate temporum, aut temeritate fortunae hostis aliquis externus, aut nostrorum civium vir sceleratissimus tyrannidem occuparit, ne tum quidem turpiter desperemus, necquid relinquamus intentatum, quo dignitas patriae et Libertas recuperetur.

In conclusion he urges that it is preferable to die a thousand times than to be a slave:

Satius est mori, mori millies, quam servire.

A brief summary in Latin of the argument of the first book precedes the text of the poem proper. The work commences with an invocation to the goddess Liberty:

Diva potens, coeli proles pulcherrima, cujus
Nomen dulce sonat, semper mihi dulce sonabit,
LIBERTAS, fas sit tandem pia pandere sacra,
Et sedes reserare tuas: tua splendida facta
Fas mihi nota loqui, Musis indicta Latinis.

In a passage exhibiting an ostentatious use of extended anaphora, the poet next calls upon the companions of the goddess:

Et vos, O Divae comites, clarissima gentis
Nomina Patriciae, rerum columenque decusque,
Qui LIBERTATIS sanctas defenditis aras,
(Muneris hoc vestri est) Divae defendite vatem;
Si mihi quid dirum minitetur foeda Celaeno,

Sive truces regum vultus, & ferrea jura.
Sin teneras aures offendunt verba Latina;
Seu nimius videor; sive est minus utilis armis,
Seu minus apta jocis, sive est mea fabula verax;
Dicite, somnus erat: ni sit quoque crimen in illo.
Nam venia quandoque carent vel somnia vatum.

A note in the recension supplies further information on the *Divae comites*: '*Viri primarii, & ii, qui vere sunt, non qui se esse simulant, patriae parentes. Novum enim est apud nos hominum genus, qui, cum patriae & libero populo insidias maxime cogitant, id agunt, ut cives optimi videantur.*'

A verbal picture of the island of Great Britain now follows:

Est locus ante alios felix, placidissima sedes,
Insula magna, ferax; cujus fundamina rector
Oceani, aeternum ut maneant, solidissima jecit,
Mercedem pactus nullam pretiumve laboris.
Anne igitur mirum, quum sit penetrabile missum,
Et majus fulmen, polus & concussus uterque
Seu nutu, seu voce Jovis, (seu causa malorum
Est alia atque alia: haud etenim cognoscere possis,
Unde tremor terris;) quum erumpant undique venti
Ignesque & fluvii, rigidique cacumina montis,
Et silvae, & rupes laxis compagibus altae,
Et loca mille labent, terrae loca mille dehiscant;
An mirum, si tanto haec insula numine freta,
Sacra mari si immota sedet; spectantque Penates
(Sed longe spectant) aliena pericula, luctusque,
Eversasque urbes, magnasque impune ruinas?

The disjunctive interrogation at the end of the last sentence is intended primarily as a rhetorical device; it is followed immediately by the author's observations on the development of the British Empire:

Quin fovet & populos Neptunus, (nec genus usquam
Acrius est hominum) queis & sua jura, suique
Imperium pelagi late dedit: omnia velis
Aequora nam currunt, quae Sol collustrat ab ortu,
Queis cupit occiduus tingi, quibus imperat Arctos,
Sidere quaeque tuo, Capricorne, inimica premuntur.

The general fertility and opulence of the island are presented as worthy of the gods who have found a home here: among them Ceres commands huge harvests while Pan cares for the flocks of sheep and grazes the herds of cattle.

The glowing description of Britain culminates in a grand encomium of Oxford, which is referred to by a Latinized form of what was then supposed to be the city's ancient Celtic name, Rhedychen.[1] The University of Oxford is described in laudatory manner as *novae Athenae*. Here the Camenae may be seen:

> Huc quoque posthabitis tandem venere Camoenae
> Fonte sacro Pindique jugis: vidi ipse sorores
> Ad Tamesis ripas, Phoebo comitante, sedentes;
> Moxque tuis spatiari hortis, divine poeta.

A note explains that the address *divine poeta* refers to Alexander Pope: '. . . *cujus horti jacent ad Tamesim fluvium amoenissimi quidem et cultissimi: ubi antrum e longinquo aspicias celeberrimum, bellissime quippe situm, & gemmis radians, Musarum & Apollinis opus: quod tamen naturae opus esse credideris.*' It is typical of the fairly large number of small revisions that King made in the *Opera* version of the text that the unequivocal ascription of Pope's grotto to the work of Apollo and the Muses is later modified by the injection of *fortasse: Musarum fortasse & Apollinis opus*. Is this a sign of disenchantment on King's part?

One of King's grandiloquent climaxes is approaching; he prepares it well:

> Saepe etiam laetas vidi, citharasque tenentes
> Auratas, magnum Rhedycinae intrare theatrum;
> Agnovique Deas, & publica vota precesque,
> Atque meis auxi plausus.

Thus the author leads into one of the most superb passages in Anglo-Latin poetry, his unrestrained but completely ingenuous apostrophe to Oxford:

---

[1] This name is now generally conceded to be an invention of Geoffrey of Monmouth. See Thomas Parker, *The Early History of Oxford* (Oxford: at the Clarendon Press, 1885), pp. 17ff., 310. Orthographic variants have been numerous: *Rhydychen, Ridocen, Ridichen,* etc.

O, divitis aulae
Pierides luxum fugiant, ac limina regum![1]
Et tibi semper eant comites, dulcissima mater,
O decus, O tutela meae, Rhedycina, juventae!
O decus, O requiesque meae, Rhedycina, senectae!
Ingenii est in me siquid; si noster Apollo,
Et Latiae annuerunt mihi mollia carmina Musae;
Si patriae cecini laudes; inimica tyrannis
Si mens non potuit flecti vel Caesaris auro,
Pallantisve minis aut blanda voce nefandi;
Si lare contentus tenui, si vivere parvo
Et didici, & didicisse juvat; cantamina turpis
Canidiae, & lites, & quae nova vulnera sensi,
Frangere si nequeunt vires, aut rumpere somnos;
Cuncta tibi fateor deberi. Cuncta fatebor,
Quae vatem recte moneas, praecepta Deorum.
Ergo te memorem semper; persolvere grates
Si possim dignas, famamque augere tuorum.

Having sung the praises of Oxford, King proceeds, in a less
personal but hardly less exalted manner, to pay his respects to
London:

Haec est, haec urbs est fama notissima, terrae
Haec patriae caput est, (absitque superbia dictis)
Haec caput est orbis. Neque enim Europaeque Asiaeque,
Gens habet ulla parem; magnis ni ex urbibus istis
Aemula siqua foret, sibi quas extruxerat olim
Confuci ingenium, & regum pulcherrimus ordo:
Si forte est usquam regum pulcherrimus ordo.

From the sting in the last line the reader is quickly taken to an
assembly of the gods, where Jupiter announces that he is sending the goddess Liberty to the people of Britain:

[1] In the recension this line is expanded into two:
          Luxum ultro (neque enim locus est sceleratior ullus)
          Pierides fugiant, invisaque limina regum!
An anonymous translation of the entire section into English verse appears in *The
Gentleman's Magazine*, October 1743, p. 547.

LIBER ERIT: Plausu resonant longa atria coeli,
LIBER ERIT: Nutu firmat pia dicta verendo
Rex hominum Divumque, olim majora daturus.[1]

The goddess duly descends and is received by the people of
Britain *laeto clamore*. The tutelary deities of the nation, Ceres,
Vertumnus, Pan and Tamesis, pay homage to Liberty and
bring gifts with flattering compliments.

This part of *Templum Libertatis* contains several elegant
speeches and some descriptive lines of considerable artistry.
Ceres is first depicted:

Spicea serta ferens, fruges, & adorea liba,
Et quaecunque suo fundit bona Copia cornu.

She eulogizes Liberty with sonorous declamation:

O Dea, grata tuis, semper gratissima terrae!
Pectoris humani (tu scis tamen hoc oriundum
Semine coelesti) tantum tibi laetor inesse.
Atque o semper ames vultus coetusque viriles,
Et tibi non unquam sit terrae cura pudori!

Now that you are present as a witness, she continues, brutes
will not devastate the cultivated fields, nor will any victor command his abominable soldiery. Other horrors need not be
feared:

Virgo nulla dolos metuet raptoris avari;
Nec mater natam, aut nutrix plorabit alumnam.

She concludes her speech with an appropriate reference to her
daughter:

Hei mihi! Persephonae si tu comes una fuisses,
Cum Siculos legeret flores; conjuncta marito
Non tali nunc illa foret, non praeda tyranni.

---

[1] In the recension this line is revised, and two others added:

Rex hominum divumque; olim quoque cuncta daturus,
Quae studia atque artes, quas mercatura parare
Divitias & opes poterit, vel bellica virtus.

Then Vertumnus comes forward:

> Dat plenis poma canistris;
> Dat modo quae pulchrae mollissima vina pararat
> Pomonae potanda, & adhuc in conjuge felix;
> Felix illa viro.[1]

The god declaims blandishingly to the goddess. He assures her that everything will flourish under her protection, while at the same time he commands evils to disappear. At the end of his speech, King provides a pleasant aside:

> Haec dederat pia dicta: probant hominesque Deique:
> Dumque probant, Zephyri veniunt, atque evocat Auster
> Irriguas herbas, & laetum nunciat annum.

Next to appear is *Pan corniger*, surrounded by a host of goat-footed divinities. He also brings presents, such as a bowl of milk, eggs, dewy honey water (*roscida mella*), and a huge cheese:

> . . . opes & culti gloria ruris;
> Quem duo vix Satyri possunt cervice subire,
> Quem vix sex homines; tanto circundatur orbe
> Immanis moles.

Pan is followed by Tamesis attended by a hundred water nymphs. He is resonant in his praise of the goddess:

> Salve, O LIBERTAS! (iterabant Naiades omnes
> Salve, O LIBERTAS!) Divum placidissima salve!

His laudations indicate that he is well acquainted with the fourteenth book of the *Iliad*:

> Tecum se comparet uxor
> Ipsa Jovis, vel (si majori nomine gaudet)
> Stelliferi regina poli, dum spirat amores,
> Blandum cincta, potens alieno numine, ceston,
> Et quaerit captare Jovem; me judice victa,
> Se dicet victam; & cedet tibi regia conjux.

She had her place in Roman history, according to Tamesis:

> Tu certe illa dea es, cui consulis annua jura,
> Et, quos nunc frustra poscit sibi, Fabriciosque
> Debuit, & Brutos, & duros Roma Catones.

---

[1] The *vina* here refers to cider.

In the matter of the Roman invasion of Britain, Tamesis has nothing complimentary to say about Julius Caesar:

O quam te memini pictos monuisse Britannos,
Et servasse diu, cum urbes invadere nostras
Auderet Caesar, cessura sibi omnia sperans:
Sed vidit tantum, referens inglorius arma.

In the matter of the history of England during the Norman conquest, King's political sympathies, put into the mouth of Tamesis, are clearly on the side of the Anglo-Saxons in contradistinction to the invaders. Thus when speaking of the descendants of Hengist, the river-god addresses Liberty in these words:

O quam te memini Hengisti juvisse nepotes!
Juvisti merito. Nostro nil aequius usquam
Saxone: nec proceres, nec plebs tentare quid ausi
Te sine, nec, secum quos portavere, Penates.

King's tendency to interpret portions of human history in terms of broad and unprovable generalizations, when it suited his argument, is even better illustrated in his long note on Norman law which he inserted in the *Opera* version of the text. Tamesis explains that it was not rightful that he or his nymphs should serve the Norman tyrant, William the Conqueror, and adds:

Omnia qui rapuit, qui primus jurgia, lites
Intulit, atque feris rabidum jus saevius armis.

The note amplifies the author's views: '*Normannorum legibus, quibus in Anglia et Hibernia utimur, revera sunt pestes reipublicae: et haud fere quidquam gravius unquam excogitatum fuit, non dico in liberis civitatibus, sed in exteris iis gentibus, ubi reges principesque pro arbitrio suo omnia gubernant rapiuntque.*' From what follows it appears that King's unusual attitude was based on his own unhappy experiences during his Irish litigation: another instance of his proclivity for allowing his personal misfortunes to warp his judgement. Tamesis, for his part, is made to comment to Liberty:

O sit cura, precor, tales tibi pellere pestes!
Sit, cum tempus erit. Neque sunt haec verba dolentis:

Nam mihi nunc oblita mala omnia, servitiumque,
Et labor, & populi clades, & nomina regum.
Te veniente, iterum faustos sperabimus annos.

Perhaps King sincerely believed that favourable prospects of peace in the future were impossible as long as the laws inherited from the Normans remained on the statute books.

Tamesis continues appositely to comment on the flourishing commercial activities carried on in the port of London. There are ships bearing fragrant wines from the vine covered hills of France, Persian garments, coffee, incense, and merchandise from Turkey. He offers the goddess presents:

Africa mittit ebur, tibi gemmas Indus & aurum,
Felix Sina team.

In the *Opera* text, she receives a gift of Jamaican sugar:

Nostri sub sole jacentes
Ardenti, succos dulces (nec Hymettia mella,
Nec divum hos superat nectar) quos canna quotannis
Jamaicae fundit, sua maxima dona, coloni
Ecce ferunt.

The god concludes with a magnanimous flourish:

Quin cuncta tibi sunt denique parta,
Quae mare, quae tellus, vel quae mea numina praebent.

At the close of the speech of Tamesis, the assembled concourse commences to sing:

Vulgus, proceresque patresque
Circumstant omnes, incondita vota canentes,
Laetitiae pia signa suae.

The goddess Liberty is now to be installed in the *templum Libertatis*, a building especially erected for her. A long, solemn procession is formed; she is led inside and enthroned. Here King takes the opportunity to provide his readers with a gorgeous description of the building and its *décor*. In terms of opulence, Solomon himself would not have been ashamed of this temple:

Aerea erant tecta, atque aereis innixa columnis:
Aureum erat Divae solium; radiantiaque auro
Delubra, & gemmis arae: de marmore factus
Interior paries, & sectile vermiculatumque
Arte pavimentum mira: longa atria, & ingens
Circuitus, populique capax. Quodcunque videres
Artificis summum posset jactare laborem.

Tapestries show the defeat of the Spanish Armada:

Servitio assuetos populos, & castra Philippi
Cernere erat, portumque Tagi, saevumque tyrannum,
Et formidatam, innumeris armisque virisque
Instructam, classem. Quid? fertur Iberia tota
Navibus. Addunt se socios, & foedera jungunt,
Degeneres quoscunque tuos, O Roma, nepotes
Vana superstitio traxit.

King's reference to the approval of the Roman Church towards
the Armada is further developed in his allusion to Pope Sixtus
V, whom he calls *Jovis ipse sacerdos*, and his wicked exhortations
to violence:

Rex idem regum, diademate tempora cinctus
Turrigero, verbis altis hortatur ad arma.

There follows an adumbrative survey of the course of the
Spanish defeat, during which King avers that the divinities
were on the English side. Perhaps the South Wind was most
influential:

Insula chara Deis! tibi fortis militat Auster,
Et ruit in classem. Tu gaudens surgere cernis,
Instar montis, aquas: fuerat nec justior unquam
Ira maris. Tu, coelo & vastis freta procellis,
Arma virum, pictosque Deos, magnasque carinas
Huc agis atque illuc diversas. Naufraga saevis
Pars haeret scopulis, & mox lethalibus undis
Obruiter. Pars en, fugiens, quos spreverat, hostes,
Turpiter, amissis sociis opibusque, redire
Jam tentat retro, pelagi ludibria nostri.[1]

---

[1] In his revised version in the *Opera*, King repunctuated this passage in two
sentences.

This digression made, the author returns to the enthronement of Liberty. As the goddess is seated, Jove provides an auspicious omen with a peal of thunder. The goddess Victory thereupon descends from the sky and flies round the temple nine times. Liberty appoints men of all ranks of society to be the guardians of her shrine, and admonishes them to be vigilant night and day. She also selects a number of nobles as her ministers, men of impeccable reputation:

> His amor est patriae nulla mutabilis arte;
> His amor est patriae nullo violabilis auro:
> Est pudor, & probitas, generosum & pectus honestum,
> Propositique tenax, & semper vivida virtus:
> Fallere quae nescit mens est, et nescia falli.

Among those chosen, four are mentioned specifically and singled out for praise under the names of Laelius, Maximus, Memmius, and Varus; in the recension these names appear as Cadenus, Maximus, Memmius, and Priscus.

The identity of these men and the reason for King's changes are matters which have in the past aroused discussion. In the notes to the initial text of *Templum Libertatis* King cited the four original names, and provided this enigmatic note: '*Ne quis forsitan de hisce nominibus male erret, quanquam in re tam clara vix errori locus est, horum nobilium virorum, & clarissimorum civium, cum ad calcem operis mei perveniam, vera adjiciam nomina.*' In fact, he never arrived *ad calcem operis*, and so there has always been ample opportunity for conjecture. According to Leicester Bradner the names in the text of 1742 refer to the Lords Orrery, Gower, Chesterfield, and Cobham; the same identifications are made in the footnotes to an anonymous letter dated 25 January 1741/2, and published in *The London Magazine* for February 1742.[1] It is impossible to ascertain how much authority the writer of this letter carries. Different readers must have held different views even in King's own time, as he indicates in the rewritten notes to the recension. Laelius disappears altogether in the later version and is replaced by Cadenus, who is obviously Swift. The suggestion that Laelius represented Orrery is cor-

[1] Leicester Bradner, op. cit., p. 261, and *The London Magazine*, February 1742, pp. 95f. For *Varus* Bradner reads *Varius*.

rect; his replacement may well indicate that His Lordship later lost favour in King's eyes.[1] Maximus, according to King's notes in the *Opera*, does not represent Gower, even though this may have been the author's original intention, but the Earl of Oxford:

De hoc nomine, postquam editum est hoc carmen, prope errarunt omnes, id attribuendo homini, cui tum quidem minime conveniebat; et cujus moribus nunc mehercule nihil est tam contrarium, quam hoc elogium. Sed, ut dubitatio omnis jam tollatur, hic agnoscas, quaeso, mi lector, illustrissimi ac primarii illius viri, EDVARDI HARLEY, comitis de OXFORD et MORTIMER, imaginem, quam hisce carminibus effingere, et proferre conatus sum.

King's attitude towards Lord Gower is clearly expressed in the *Political and Literary Anecdotes*. He had originally been a member of the Old Interest, with whom King had lived 'in some degree of intimacy' for many years; his later defection to the Whigs 'was a great blow to the Tory party, and a singular disappointment to all his friends . . . he bartered a most respectable character, and sacrificed his honour and his country.'[2] No note is provided in the recension on Memmius, though it is entirely possible that he does represent Lord Chesterfield, who is mentioned specifically as one of the 'Heroes of your Temple' in a letter which Orrery wrote to King on 9 September 1741.[3] Varus is undeniably an analogue of Lord Cobham. In the *Opera*, part of the address to Varus is reassigned to Priscus, who is identified in the notes as John Fane, Earl of Westmoreland.

That King at one time intended to publish a key to the original edition, which would presumably have provided information on the original identifications, is clear from the author's letter to Lord Orrery of 5 January 1742/3:

. . . as, for my own part, I am not altogether inattentive to some threatening expressions, wch have been thrown out, I am providing

---

[1] The identification of Orrery with Laelius is confirmed in King's letter of 19 January 1742/3, Bodleian Library, MS. Eng. hist. d. 103, p. 66, and again in the footnote to page 25 of his *Tres Oratiunculae Habitae in Domo Convocationis Oxon.* of 1743. The possibility of a rupture of King's friendship with Orrery is discussed further in Chapter VII.

[2] *Political and Literary Anecdotes* (2nd edn., 1819), pp. 45–8.

[3] The Houghton Library, Harvard University, MS. Eng. 218.2 (v. 4), pp. 241f.

myself with a Key, wch I intend to publish in a week or 10 days after ye publication of ye poem, especially if it be attacked by any old or new ministerial writers. In ye mean time I have given those gentlemen a short admonition wch you read at ye end of my Notes.[1]

Whether the Key which King mentions was ever published or not is doubtful; if it ever did appear, no copy has survived to the present day. The 'short admonition' to which the author refers is no doubt that which occurs at the end of the notes to Book Two. It is no substitute for the non-existent key:

Nunc autem abesto, quisquis es malignus interpres. Neque foedum fac poetae convitium, neque suspicione mala ad te rape, quod est alterius, fortasse nullius, fortasse omnium. Meum enim propositum & vim hujus fabulae haud quisquam sentiet, nisi Latiis sit Musis amicus, idemque Libertatis acerrimus vindex, ac sine labe cultor. Talis viri, etiamsi inter aulicos reperiatur, neque judicium verear neque reprehensionem.

Part of the difficulty of settling these problems of identity is that King more often than not couches his sentiments in the form of lofty generalizations; thus the same magnanimous comments could frequently be applied indifferently to several of those men with whose views he sympathized. Furthermore, the changes in identification in the recension were made with the minimum of disturbance to the text and, of course, had to be effected without unsettling the metre. That these mechanical revisions could be injected into the structure of the text without leaving any impression of patchwork is partly the result of King's own powers as a Latinist, and partly the result of the fact that he deliberately avoided unmistakably recognizable identifications. One example must suffice to illustrate King's revisions of this portion of the poem. In the 1742 text the author writes of the virtues of the ministers whom Liberty chooses (*amor patriae, pudor, probitas*, and so on), and then comments of those selected:

> His successores en sunt, quos novimus ipsi,
> Quos populus meritis veneratur laudibus omnes:
> Quos inter vidi (nec Divae gratior adsit)
> Te quoties, LAELI charissime?

[1] Bodleian Library, MS. Eng. hist. d. 103, p. 65.

In the recension the question is thus recast:

> Quos inter, Cadene, (deae quis gratior adsit)
> Te quoties, vidi, charissime?

Even though the name—and identity—of the figure under discussion have been changed, the passage that follows does not seem any less appropriate:

> . . . quem mihi junxit
> Foedere amicitiae studium commune, favorque
> Musarum Phoebique patris. Quae gratia Musis,
> Qui Phoebo debetur honos pro munere tali?
> Nam vult esse mihi vel quem sibi legit amicum:
> Dignum o, quem legeret. Sed enim nil dignius illo,
> Cui placidam mentem, mores Deus ipse pudicos,
> Cui dedit ingenii vires, & carminis artem.

A special difficulty arises in the case of the verses reassigned from Varus to Priscus. Varus represents Lord Cobham, whose estate at Stowe with its temples, gardens, towers, and other adornments is praised a little later in the poem.[1] However, King could not credit the Earl of Westmoreland with such possessions, so he changed the early part of the invocation to Varus to apply to Priscus (an easy revision since these names have metrically equivalent syllables) and then added some extra lines intended for Westmoreland. One feels grateful that the author provided a note on the subject, for the sentiments inserted in the revised version are quite generalized; for example,

> Dumque fovet, doctasque omnes complectitur artes,
> Dumque fidem, et mores patrios & jura tuetur,
> Magna illi cura est, ut sit sibi fama perennis,
> Sit salvus pietatis honos: neque praemia sanum
> Ulla suae poterint vitae mutare colorem.

The description of Stowe follows, for the most part as it is in the 1742 text, with greatly augmented notes. King here paints a verse picture in the grand manner, impressive in its stately beauty, and amplifying well the note which the author provides on Stowe. '. . . *cujus magnificentiam nunquam satis mirari*

---

[1] The identification of the estate is provided in the notes.

potes. Horti sunt amplissimi, templis, aris, statuis, tabulis, imaginibus, columnis &c. referti; qui magnitudine omnes alios superant, et etiam elegantia; nisi si aliquis fastidiosior contenderit hic nimia esse omnia.'
It is impossible to gain from a short extract any just concept of the magnificence which King evokes in this lengthy passage: it has to be read *in extenso*. But perhaps it is worth mentioning that King enhances the effect of the description by expressing his own astonishment at the grandeur of the place:

> Quid, quod & arboreos labyrinthos, antra, columnas,[1]
> Balneaque, & turres, & pastoralia tecta,
> Pyramidas, vatum tumulos, pontemque superbum,
> Heroas, priscosque Deos, & templa Deorum
> Daedaliae finxere manus? Vidi omnia, rebusque
> Attonitus tantis stupui.

The conclusion of the description of Stowe in its final form is an especially majestic piece of writing, incorporating a lengthy example of anaphora, and consisting syntactically of one single sentence:

> Digna loco Titan Vari praecordia fecit,
> Numine digna loci: Sic pergat dicere Musa,
> Vare, tuas laudes, modo si constanter ad actum
> Extremum perstes, nec splendida polluat arva
> Ambitio, nequeatque tuam vexare senectam:
> Si tibi, dum juvenes Sardos audire recusas,
> Crescat amor patriae, quantum horti gloria crescit:
> Si tibi vel quos ver, vel quos tibi blandior aestas
> Hic gratos spirat, sint Libertatis odores:
> Si domus omnis idem, si fontes, saxa, columnae,
> Si, possent arbusta loqui, tibi consona, Vare,
> LIBERTAS O MAGNA DEA EST, arbusta sonarent.

After a meditative digression on the part of the author, the scene returns to the temple:

> Jamque frequentatur templum; proceresque Britanni,
> Plebeiique senes, pueri teneraeque puellae,
> Et lauro ornati vates, auroque nitentes
> Magnanimi heroes festinant ad tua sacra,

---

[1] In the recension *columnas* is emended to *lacusque*.

Candida LIBERTAS, & te, Dea, rite precantur;
Festaque muneribus cumulant altaria dignis.

Solemn vows are paid to the goddess; cows, fat goats, and wild
beasts from the mountains are placed on the altars; sweet liquor
is presented as a libation. In a note written for the *Opera* King
explains that by *dulces liquores* he means *cerevisia* (beer), and
adds that Pliny was mistaken when he asserted that it was first
brewed in Gaul; for King, beer was indigenous to Britain. The
sacrifices are offered by a *vir bonus* from Wales: probably Sir
Watkin Williams Wynn is intended.[1] Then a Scotsman enters:

Deinde pruinosis commigrat Scotus ab oris
Gnarus militiae, frugique, & fortis amicus,
Bellica dona ferens: dumque hanc circumspicit aedem,
Et formam, & comites, Divaeque insignia, jactat,
Nomine communi gaudens, sese esse Britannum.

According to the anonymous writer already referred to in *The
London Magazine*, the *Scotus* represents either the Earl of Stair
or a general character of the Scots. Whatever his identity, his
presence augurs well. He promises honours for those citizens
who have merited them, peace for the farmers, and safe seas for
the sailors. Already the future of Scotland looks brighter:

Jamque Caledonii melius procedere Soles
Incipiunt, melius gelidi glacialia fulgent
Signa poli. Immites jam libertate fruuntur
Orcades, & messes sperant. Vix cognita coelo,
Nullius vel cura Dei, coelestia tandem
Numina sentit ovans, & adorat barbara Thule.[2]

Most of the remainder of the first book is devoted to a speech

---

[1] He was the most important of the Jacobites of North Wales, where he was known
as 'the Great Sir Watkin'. Jacobite gatherings were held at Wynnstay under each
successive Watkin Williams Wynn from 1710 until after 1850, and from these
developed the White Rose League, historically the principal English Jacobite
society. It was reorganized in 1886 as the Order of the White Rose by Lord Ash-
burnham and Henry Jenner. The presidency is held by each member in rotation,
hence the Order is sometimes referred to as the Cycle Club. It is a different organization from the Royal Stuart Society, founded by Henry Stuart Wheatly-Crowe
in 1926, of which the present Governor-General is Sir Compton MacKenzie.

[2] By *Thule* King means Shetland.

delivered by a *dux magnus* on the subject of liberty in general. The anonymous writer in *The London Magazine* posits that the speaker is the Duke of Argyle; King himself in the *Opera* states that he is the Duke of Ormonde. This last address in the *Liber Primus* must have enjoyed a certain popularity, for it was reprinted in full with an anonymous verse translation in *The Gentleman's Magazine* for March 1742.[1] The *dux magnus* eulogizes the goddess, and urges those present to be cognizant of their good fortune:

> Hic & vestra salus posita est, & gloria gentis,
> Census, opes, artes: hic tanti est muneris auctor.

In the recension the wording of the last line is changed, and two extra verses are added making the attribution to the Duke of Ormonde unmistakable:

> Census, opes, artes, pia quas nunc aula tuetur,
> Et quas lucrosas mercatura invenit urbi,
> Et docta ingenuas mea quas academia tradit.

The notes indicate that the *aula* is the *Aula Annae, piissimae reginae,* and that the *academia* is '. . . *Oxoniensis, cui dux ille Ormondus praefuit, bonarum omnium et liberalium artium nutrix et alumna, atque insulae hujus gloria et decus. Quam primarii et clarissimi cives fovent, amantque, quam exterae nationes summa observantia colunt.*' After several historical allusions, the speaker asks the rhetorical question

> At quid feliciter actas
> Res veteres Divae referam, sua commodat ultro
> Numina cum nobis praesens?

Liberty still controls the earth, he explains, and the leaders of the world, the poets, and even the gods themselves obey her summons. The oration concludes with a flourish inspired by Juvenal:

> Hoc orate Jovem: nostros doceantque nepotes
> Hoc unum, quod nos docuere, oracula prima,
> Annales prisci, & felicia tempora mundi,
> SI SIT LIBERTAS, NON ULLUM NUMEN ABESSE.

---

[1] *The Gentleman's Magazine*, March 1742, pp. 157f.

The final speech having been delivered, King thus ends Book One of *Templum Libertatis*:

> Haec ubi, conticuit. Dat prospera signa futuri,
> Dat certa; & patrum, & plebis Dea comprobat acta.
> Deinde jubet, votiva aris quaecunque ferantur,
> Illis dona dari, qui sunt modo vulnera passi
> Pro patria. Affulsit populo, dum talia mandat,
> Laetior, ambrosios & ab ore afflavit odores.

The author's last note in the *Opera* edition of this book could have been composed with the events of 1745 in mind:

> Quanquam, de seculi hujus heroibus, nunquam mehercule animum induxi, ut bene existimarem, quorum consilio bella suscepta sunt et inflammata, quum sit bellis nihil miserius; ii tamen, sive nobiles sive ignobiles, qui pro patria ac libertate publica fortiter pugnaverint, mea quidem sententia nunquam satis digne laudari, honoribus decorari, praemiis donari possunt. Quapropter praedicare soleo, et admirari gerontocomia ista, ubi veterani milites, et nautae grandaevi, jam belli laboribus fracti, benigne excipiuntur et aluntur, in hospitia perquam commode divisi.

This publication appears to have been well received. An anonymous letter published in *The Gentleman's Magazine* for February 1742 included two verbatim extracts from it, preceded by some remarks on 'modern Latin Poetry in general'.[1] According to this correspondent, *Templum Libertatis* is wholly free from the defects which he found in the work of other modern Latin poets, and contains besides 'a great Number of real Beauties'. The anonymous writer in *The London Magazine* whose exegetical efforts have already been mentioned included with his selection of extracts some flattering observations on the author:

> Among the *Roman* Historians, *Salust* is famous for the Characters he gives of some of the Persons mentioned in his History, but no such Thing was ever attempted, so far as I remember, by any of the *Roman* Poets; which certainly proceeded, either from the Difficulty of the Task, or from their not having a Patron, whose Character they could give with Justice and without Offence. Thank God! the present Age is more propitious to the Poets of this Country; and it must be

[1] *The Gentleman's Magazine*, February 1742, p. 98.

agreeable to every *True Briton*, to see this difficult Task attempted with Success by a *British* Bard, and in as pure *Latin* as was wrote by any of the Authors of the *Augustan* Age.[1]

No doubt the Latin-reading public was well prepared for the appearance of Book Two in the following January.

This second book opens on a more subdued note. Thus far, King writes, the Muses have sung only with happiness, but Jove often upsets pleasant conditions. The king of the gods now looks askance at the happy times being enjoyed in Britain. Hence proceed the miseries which, the author proclaims, now exist; he comments briefly on them in a three-verse sentence combining the rhetorical devices of asyndeton, anaphora, and isocolon:

> Hinc sine honore aras, hinc fraudes, bella, rapinas,
> Hinc late scelerum videas florere ministros,
> Hinc fortem ignavis populum servire tyrannis.

King wrote two notes on this last verse: one for the 1743 edition and one for the *Opera*. It is interesting to see how his thinking changed subtly between the two. The first reads: '*Ita quidem regnantur Europae gentes fere omnes trans fretum Britannicum. Britanniae vero Regnum legitimo & sacrato jure continetur: & Rex ipse ita est, ut Phoenix, avis magna, admiranda, unica.*' *Rex ipse* in this context refers to the Old Chevalier; there is no mention of him in the later note:

Quot, quales, quantas terrae regiones ita hodie regnari nobis constat? sed enimvero mira sunt, ni principes isti, qui in pueritia bonis artibus et disciplinis haud liberaliter fuerint instituti, in provectiore aetate vitiis obruantur; quique sola spe imperii fuerint educati, non modo injusta ea novam sibi dominationem comparandi, sed rerum omnium cupiditate incendantur.

There follows a further invocation to Liberty, during which reference is made to two of the principal characters in this book, Plutus, the god of riches, and one of his colleagues, Cyclops:

> At tu sancta fave, si nunc quoque rite vocaris,
> LIBERTAS: si me damni instrumenta recentis,
> Venalis populi mores procerumque notare

[1] *The London Magazine*, February 1742, p. 95.

Si delicta jubes, aptam superinjice nubem,
Aut, precor, arma tuo Vulcania porrige vati:
A PLUTO, a PLUTI sociis, coetuque CYCLOPUM
Quo nos, & cursus nostros, suetosque labores,
Otia quo praestes, quo praestes omnia tuta.

An invocation to Laelius—Lord Orrery—is altered in the recension to apply to Dean Swift under the name of Cadenus. Again, King's compliments are so generalized that he had only to change two half lines: everything else which he wrote about Orrery is allowed to stand, and in fact is equally appropriate to the Dean. In the *Opera* King added an extra note on the newly inserted vocative, *Cadene*:

Quo tempore hoc scribebam, in morbum incidit gravissimum et diuturnum, quem quidem, praesentiente animo, semper reformidabat Cadenus meus, et quo tandem extinctum fuit clarissimum illud ingenii et patriae lumen. Animi et ingenii vires, ut supra dixi, satis testantur Cadeni opera venustatis, salis, leporis, eruditionis et humanitatis plena.

However much King's opinions about other men may have shifted, he never lost his admiration for the quondam Dean of St. Patrick's Cathedral.

The reader is next taken down into Tartarus, where a messenger arrives to convey the news of Liberty's arrival in Britain. The infernal powers are furious. Dis quickly calls a conference to decide on a plan of action for getting rid of the goddess. King is here patently influenced by Milton's Satan; indeed, borrowings from *Paradise Lost* are evident throughout the remainder of the book. The assembly of the devils is vividly described:

Conveniunt Erebi proceres. Ingentior aequo
Exundat Phlegethon, volvitque incendia late
Irarum fluctus. Squalorem vultibus addunt
Terribilem Manes, & longa silentia rumpunt:
Atriaque insolitis implent clamoribus Umbrae.
Rex Stygius famulosque Deos, dirasque Sorores,
Harpyiasque, Hydrasque, & Gorgonas evocat omnes,
Monstraque, quae semper moesta versantur in aula.

Plutus rises and cuts an impressive figure. The assembly is silent as he prepares to speak:

> At nunc aula silet. Circumstant undique Manes
> Innumeri, & voces gaudent haurire nefandas
> Auribus attentis, dum PLUTUS talia fatur.

The address of Plutus extends to seventy-nine lines in the original version and eighty in the *Opera* text. An anonymous translation of it appeared in two consecutive issues of *The Gentleman's Magazine* in 1744.[1] It could be argued that this lengthy harangue is, at least in places, oratory in verse, but its tone compares well with that used in the speeches of Milton's devils. The basic reasoning of Plutus is that with money all things are possible. He insists that force is not a desirable policy, and demonstrates to the assembly their 'power, might, and arms' in the form of masses of gold. Greece and Rome, he argues with dubious historicity, were brought low by over-abundance of money, as were many other nations and peoples.

> O quantum profuit auri
> Majestas, Superum quod reddidit irrita dona;
> Quod sua Coelicolas oracula fallere jussit?
> Coelicolaeque iterum, ni me mea ludat imago,
> Deficiantque artes, loca nobis debita cedent.

The goddess Liberty, he continues, even though guarded from Olympus, cannot survive cupidity. He lays bare his plan:

> Nil moror excubias vigilum, qui limina templi,
> Qui servant aras; cum molles centuriones,
> Causidici, proceresque illis miscentur egeni,
> Et scribae, venale genus. Mihi dona ferenti
> Tota cohors aderit supplex, & foedera vestra,
> Quae modo calcavit, firmata mente reposcet.

Liberty herself will succumb:

> Ipsaque virgo dolis (ipsam tentare vel ausim)
> Succumbet nostris, pretio qua cuncta patebunt,
> Si posuit sedes. Quid? Foemina respuet aurum

---

[1] *The Gentleman's Magazine*, May 1744, p. 274, and June 1744, p. 330.

Haeccine, tantillum numen? parvosque Penates,
Et magno exiguam dubitabit vendere terram,
Si Deus est aliquis, qui coelum vendidit auro?

Plutus, who is well read in classical mythology, proceeds to give
his audience several examples of his previous victories, concluding with the case of Jove, who, being enamoured of Danae,
the beautiful daughter of Acrisius, succeeded in his quest only
with the aid of gold:

Ecce, tenet Danaen (vidistis) ahenea turris.
Jupiter hanc ardet. Sed nec pater invenit artem,
Tela nec, aeratos valeat queis frangere postes,
Fortia sufficiunt armamentaria coeli.
Poscit opem: ferimus. Mea gaudens induit ora,
Fitque aurum: & vincit, quod nulla potentia Divum,
Quod non vincit amor. Cunctis gratissimus hospes
Tecta subit, Danaenque petit, potiturque petitam.

With Jove thus safely in possession of Danae, Plutus concludes
his speech and is sympathetically applauded.

Dis is delighted with the proposal, and lends Plutus his
chariot and horses to make the journey to earth. The chariot,
we are assured, is the same as that in which Proserpine was
taken down to the underworld. The journey of Plutus is
described in some detail:

Per sedes Noctis opacas,
Perque informe Chaos, perque aspera viscera terrae
Fertur ovans; sequiturque viam, quam fecerat olim
Dux Erebi, ut gemino feralia foedera mundo,
Et facilis fieret superas ascensus ad auras.

The god of riches finally emerges into the daylight from the
Peak Cavern, near Castleton in Derbyshire, and send the steeds
and chariot of Dis back again to Tartarus. The place where
Plutus stands is quite desolate:

Omnis perit arbor, & omnis
Aret ager: squalent montes: nec vota, nec ulla
Ars revocare potest Cererem infelicibus arvis.

In the recension the author increases the verisimilitude by providing a note on the actual state of the countryside at this spot:
'*Ager, in quo sita est haec spelunca, et tota, quae circa est, terra informis, infoecunda, infructuosa est.*'

Before attempting to corrupt Britain, Plutus assumes the outward appearance of a man. He then betakes himself to the temple of Liberty. So far the information provided by King as to the geographical position of the temple has been quite vague; we learn a little more from a note in the *Opera* version: '*Atrium atque templum Libertatis, quod in libro superiore dicitur olim fuisse regia tyranni, cujusdam Rufi (puto) e Normannorum gente, jacet in occidentali urbis parte prope Tamesis ripam.*' This enigmatic sentence seems to imply that the goddess Liberty was enthroned in Westminster Hall. If so, the poet has created an insoluble inconsistency, for the earlier descriptions of the temple in the first book are not applicable to this building.

Plutus enters the temple, and soon acquires popularity with the assembled throng:

> Hanc intrat; plebique piae se immiscet, et audax
> Omnia respondet scitantibus, Unde? Quis esset?
> Utque habitus, gestusque viri mentitur, & ora;
> Sic patriam, & proavos, generosaque nomina fingit.
> Nec sua nunc aberat merces. Spectabilis auro
> Mille capit splendore oculos; primaque colentum
> Mille capit pietate animos, ex ordine cunctos
> Indigetes, magnumque loci dum numen adorat,
> Blanditiasque affert, arisque ingentia dona.
> Quaeque fidem verbis facerent, si pectora donis
> Tartareisve dolis possent coelestia falli.

He succeeds so well in winning friends that he is made the leader of the cohort to whom the task of guarding and maintaining the temple is entrusted. He prepares rich and regal gifts, and by his diabolical largess corrupts almost the entire nation: not only the poor, but also the leaders, the nobles, and the bishops. The native divinities and the *loci Genius* flee the country as almost everyone succumbs to luxury and inertia. King deals in particular with four specific cases of corruption under the names of Ambrosius, Curio, Rufus, and Lollius. He explains in the notes to the 1743 text: '*Nihil in toto hoc opere aut obscurum est aut ambiguum, ni forsitan de hisce nominibus dubitetur. Quapropter his etiam, quando mihi commodum erit, vera addam nomina. Nunc vero non est sane commodum.*' In fact, King never did provide the names of the actual persons represented—or misrepresented. Instead, in the recension he changed the first three names to Augustinus, Scaurus, and Bassus. Lollius was retained. Another personage, whose name is given only as R*FFENSIS, appears a little later in the original edition: in the recension he is named Cerealis. He is one of the few enemies of Plutus:

Praesul hic fuit, siquis alius, sanctus, praestanti ingenio, et altissima eruditione et doctrina: cui vero nemo homo Britannus ea tempestate par erat eloquentia. Semper quidem in senatu civis optimi functus est officio, omnia Pluti consilia acriter oppugnando, neque unquam desistendo, quibuscunque rebus posset rempublicam adjuvare. Ob eximias hasce virtutes Pluti astutiae et optimatum invidia excellentem hunc virum, iniquissimo senatus consulto damnatum, in exilium egere.

One other enemy of Plutus is alluded to under the name of Brutus: he had died an untimely death before King published in 1743, and his two sons did not emulate their father's virtues. His identity cannot be ascertained with certainty, but he was, Dante's implications in the *Inferno* notwithstanding, '*sicut ille Romanus, cultor ac socius . . . divae Libertatis, patriae parens, et in senatu facile princeps*'.

Part of the scheme of Plutus is to invite enemies of England into the country: they molest and plunder the Britons without punishment. Rejoicing in his success, the god of riches now sets about the accomplishment of his final ambition, the complete overthrow of the state. He secures the assistance of a rapacious colleague by the name of Cyclops, and with his aid establishes suzerainty over the country. Plutus is now '*domi praeses, ad exteros legatus, ad populum concionator*'. The state of the nation throughout this conquest by the god of riches is indeed appalling; King's poetry is at its strongest when composed in the form of jeremiads:

Furiosa libido
Quantum egit, monitis si non contraria Pluti!
Omnia sed monitis parent. Jacet obruta virtus.

> Fortia nostrorum ridentur facta parentum,
> Simplicitas & prisca fides: ridentur & omnes,
> Quos incendit amor patriae; populumque tuendi,
> Et quibus est studium firmandi fata nepotum.
> Ridentur, viles animae, qui praemia poscunt
> Ingenii, lauros fragiles, titulosque caducos:
> Scilicet haec sibi cuncta habeant, haec munera tantum.
> Odit enim PLUTUS divinas Palladis artes,
> Musarumque choros. . . .

No Latin poet living during the declining years of the Roman
Empire described the corruptions of his time with the disgust
and asperity with which King described the imaginary reign of
Plutus. Cyclops is the most revolting single character in the
poem: he has most of the vices of Plutus—on a smaller scale—
but none of his grandeur. Although this grasping, misshapen
fiend is laughed at by all to whom he is sent, he is exceedingly
useful to Plutus:

> . . . hostes
> Provocat innumeros: socialia foedera rumpit:
> Instituit censum: auget vectigalia, tristi
> Et quicquid vexet populum spolietve rapina.

Like his classical namesake he has a large number of relations,
the *perfida turba Cyclopum*, who accompany him in making
mischief.

Having seized power, Plutus imposes a system of taxes and
imposts, and by this means acquires a large sum of money for
himself. The citizens, in their state of corruption, are quite
helpless:

> Jamque, sua Plutus quod vix speraret ab arte,
> Victa malis cessat pietas, & ubique tacetur
> Libertatis amor.

The seers of Phoebus then chant a *lugubre carmen*: the performers
are thus identified in the *Opera*:

Qui iis temporibus laude ingenii praecipue floruerunt poetae, Swift,
Pope, Gay, reipublicae partibus, ac libertatis causae semper fave-
bant, et Archilochiis carminibus, quae quidem populo erant

jucundissima, distringebant Plutum et Plutonios omnes, praesules, senatores, milites, legatos, archimagiros, et totam Cyclopum familiam.

Their lamentations have an imprecatory quality:

> Di, quibus est terram, nunc siqua est, cura tuendi,
> Aspicite afflictas urbes, & squalida rura,
> Et maciem populi! Vestris si floruit unquam
> Albion auspiciis, si grata haec insula Phoebo,
> Grata fuit Cereri sedes: audite querelas,
> Et damnis miserae tandem succurrite gentis.

Swift, Pope, and Gay continue their lugubrious elegy in the same strain for another forty-seven verses, serving a dramatic function similar to that of a Greek chorus.

At the conclusion of this dirge, Plutus, completely confident of his own abilities, approaches the goddess Liberty herself, and supplicates her with feigned piety:

> Tum magnos montes, Divae blanditus, & omnes
> Quot Golconda parit gemmas, regumque favorem,
> Jura etiam, & veteres aris promittit honores;
> Si modo virgo suos comites (corrumpere quorum
> Ille animos tentat frustra) dimittat ab aede;
> Consiliumque uni credat studiumque CYCLOPI:
> Omnia si credat.[1]

When the promises of Plutus are ignored, he is moved to anger and orders the leaders of the people to leave the temple immediately. Now it is the turn of the goddess to be indignant, but she has only to touch Plutus with her sceptre, as Ithuriel touched Satan with his spear in *Paradise Lost*, and his real nature is made plain to the people:

> Tum PLUTUM sceptro feriens (sceptrumque gerebat
> Diva Jovis donum) speciem formamque removit
> Humanam; & Stygios vultus, & reddidit ora,
> Immanesque artus. Quin verum denique PLUTUM,

---

[1] King's note on Golconda reads thus: *Regnum Peninsulae Indiae intra Gangem, ubi unionum gemmarumque pretiosissimarum ingens est copia. Hodie pars magni Mogolis imperii.*

Dum loquor, exhibuit populo, monstrumque, crearat
Quale Chaos quantumque. Illum erubuisse Camoenae
Tum primum perhibent, propriamque odisse figuram.

On this note of diabolical revelation, the second and last surviving book of *Templum Libertatis* abruptly finishes.

This book, like the first, seems to have been well received.
Thus an epigram in *The Gentleman's Magazine* for March 1743
headed *Verses, occasion'd by reading the* TEMPLUM LIBER-
TATIS, though anonymous and not notably inspired, is
patently intended as a compliment to King:

> When *British* LIBERTY, with thoughtful eyes,
> Beheld her new-erected temple rise!
> Adorn'd with all the elegance and art
> Which truth could give—or learning could impart,
> The noble dome transported she survey'd,
> And thus to *Pallas*, sweetly-smiling, said;—
> 'This work, celestial sister!—must be thine,
> 'For thro' the whole I see thy wisdom shine!'[1]

One need not consider seriously King's claim in his letter to
Lord Orrery of 14 October 1741 that Lady Orrery, as he
wrote, 'has inspired me with all that is good in ye Temple of
Liberty (if there be any thing good) for I never drew one of my
Characters, but I thought of Lady Orrery's good sense, and
Wit, and sweetness of temper, and affection for her friends,
with all the train of her good and amiable qualities.'[2] Rather
obviously King's most significant source of inspiration for his
greatest Latin work was Milton's *Paradise Lost*. His indebtedness shows itself principally in the plot; since King was writing
in Latin he could not imitate the style of *Paradise Lost*. In
this respect King differs markedly from the other eighteenth-
century imitators of Milton, who, as a general rule, followed
his style without incorporating his matter.[3]

---

[1] *The Gentleman's Magazine*, March 1743, p. 156. In his letter to Lord Orrery of
9 April 1743, King indicates that he has seen the epigram (Bodleian Library, MS.
Eng. hist. d. 103, p. 72).

[2] Bodleian Library, MS. Eng. hist. d. 103, p. 45.

[3] On these Miltonic imitators, some of whom were anonymous, see R. D.
Havens, *The Influence of Milton on English Poetry* (Cambridge, Mass.: Harvard
University Press, 1922).

It is easy enough to point to defects in *Templum Libertatis* quite apart from the thinness of the plot. The action is slow moving and performed in a setting that is always artificial and contrived. The rationale is of questionable validity: there were numerous political commentators in the 1740s advancing the view that Englishmen were then enjoying unparalleled freedom. Above all, the poet's attitude reflects the sentiments of only one political pressure group to the complete exclusion of those of the opposition. Nevertheless, it is significant that King's satire in this poem is always of a general nature: he does not allow himself the luxury of indulging in *specific* Jacobite propaganda, and he never loses his ability to create an atmosphere of *hauteur* and amplitude. The diabolical loftiness of the second book is not greatly inferior to that of the comparable sections of *Paradise Lost*. The indictments against contemporary venality are written with a Swiftian force and with a conscious grandeur absent from those of the Dean. However, the author is sometimes led to make statements which, even when judged with sympathy, are somewhat exaggerated. To mention only one example, his depiction of the bishops of his time as being motivated by little except love of money and power is, to say the least, biased; one could demonstrate the evidence of many works of genuine piety, especially in the form of sermons, written by some of these prelates, quite apart from the role which a number of them played in furthering missionary activities and church building.[1]

King's greatest strength is his Latin style. The numerous tiny changes that he made in the *Opera* edition reveal the scrupulous care which he devoted to the construction and phraseology of every line in the poem. The result is a presentation which exhibits a marmoreal smoothness and a crystalline brilliance which few later Latin poets have managed to attain. And though King's Latinity has a pompous quality, *Templum Libertatis* lacks the lumbering character of so many uninspired neo-Latin epics. Despite all its shortcomings, it has no serious contemporary rival.

It is perhaps of incidental interest that this is the only poem by King that seems to have been imitated. Richard Powney in

---

[1] King's views on this subject were little changed when he was in his final sickness. See *Political and Literary Anecdotes* (2nd edn., 1819), pp. 183–8.

the *Templum Harmoniae* and Michael Clancy in the *Templum Veneris*, both published in 1745, were to some extent indebted to the author of *Templum Libertatis*. The influence of King is especially evident near the commencement of the third book of Powney's poem:

> At tu, carminibus pollens & numine Phoebi,
> Tu servare vices qui rhetoris atque poetae
> Idem ausus, summo comes huic succurre labori,
> Et faveas, precor; in melius dum fingere mores
> Corruptos acer satira moliris & urbem
> Venalem, ingenuus libertatisque patronus,
> Extruis en! reduci jam templa perennia Divae.
> Tuque tuae referes pretium haud ignobile famae,
> Seu vocet ad coenas te sermonesque Deorum
> *Pollio*, libertatis amans; cui maxima mentem
> Pieridum studiis & natam rebus agendis
> Ipsa olim undulsit Pallas: seu *Laelius* altum
> Poscat epos, nectatque modos & nobile carmen.[1]

Neither of these poems exhibits the vigour or the elevation of *Templum Libertatis*. In fact, neither is technically an epic: the sub-title of *Templum Harmoniae* is *Carmen Epicum* and that of *Templum Veneris* is *Amorum Rhapsodiae*. Though the Latin epic continued to be written for some time longer on the continent, *Templum Libertatis* was the last attempt at that *genre* by an English poet.

---

[1] Richardus Powney, *Templum Harmoniae* (London, 1745), pp. 29f.

V
Later Works of the 1740s

DURING the early months of 1743 King suffered from his usual hiemal attacks of gout. On Ash Wednesday he was lame in both hands and feet, but, as he explained on April 9, he did succeed in escaping from an attack of influenza that was raging at the time: 'The Epidemical cold, or which yᵉ physicans say is yᵉ Italian *Influenza* is got among us here and I think I am yᵉ only person in our Hall, who have [*sic*] escaped it hitherto, which I attribute to my temperance only.'[1] Notwithstanding the difficulties created by the inclemency of the weather, the Principal of St. Mary Hall was preparing the Latin speech which he delivered in Convocation on the following April 14, when James Hamilton, Duke of Hamilton and Brandon, was presented for the degree of D.C.L., *honoris causa*. On August 25 of the same year King delivered the Latin orations when George Henry Lee, Earl of Lichfield, and Lord Orrery were awarded the same degree. These three speeches were later published with a Latin preface dated 1 December 1743, under the title *Tres Oratiunculae Habitae in Domo Convocationis Oxon.* The published text of these orations may not correspond precisely to what King declaimed; in his letter to Lord Orrery of 9 September 1743, he intimates that he has been 'earnestly implored' for copies of the three speeches, and adds: 'I must (I believe) take a resolution to print them after having made some few additions.'[2]

The Duke of Hamilton was eighteen years of age when he received the honorary degree, having been a member of the university since 23 February 1740, when he had matriculated at St. Mary Hall. King refers to his youth with tact and delicacy, describing him as '. . . *optimae indolis adolescentem, et sui ordinis spectatissimum: adolescentem verecundia quidem, sed virum prudentia, sed senem gravitate.*' He cannot resist the temptation to imply that

[1] Bodleian Library, MS. Eng. hist. d. 103, p. 73.
[2] Bodleian Library, MS. Eng. hist. d. 103, p. 79.

such a youth is something of a rarity: '*Itaque gratulor reipublicae, et almae huic Academiae, et literis ipsis pro ingenio tali; quod in homine adolescente rarum est, in nobili vero rarissimum.*' The young Duke's family—the same as that of Lady Orrery—is described in glowing terms:

De splendore generis, et vetustate familiae HAMILTONIAE et DUGLASSIAE, unde Dux nobilissimus est oriundus, qua nihil clarius, ne quidem domus regia, (quippe in Gallia, in Germania, in Italia, in omnibus fere Europae gentibus sunt principes et primarii viri, qui ab hac stirpe originem suam se accepisse gloriantur) quot et quanta praedicarem, si mihi spatium esset dicendi?

He does not subscribe to the aristocratic vices so prevalent, according to King, at the time:

At vero quam dissimillimus est novis istis hominibus qui superbos titulos et ingentia nomina quaerentes (quae quidem salva et florente republica desperassent) non excellentia generis, aut majorum fama, sed flagitiis suis, sed perfidia summa fiunt nobiles: adeo ut de celsa illa et amplissima, in quam ascenderunt, dignitatis sede dignitatem jam pene omnem sustulisse videantur!

Here the speaker checks his own indignation: '*At non hic nostrum est cum iniquitate temporis pugnare. Suo jure utantur aulici: emant, vendant, corrumpant, corrumpantur.*' He concludes with an exhortation to his listeners to adhere to the principles of traditional morality, once again exhibiting his fondness for syntactical parallelism:

Vos autem, viri integerrimi, antiquum vestrum semper ita tenete morem, vestram tenete authoritatem philosophiae praesidiis, fide et firmitate animi, et liberali semper ita munitam custodia; ut hunc senatum, hanc venerabilem domum nulla unquam attingat infamia; ut neque judiciis, neque consiliis vestris nefariorum hominum interponatur potentia; ut denique Academici honores nemini deferantur, nisi qui sit dignissimus, et honoribus illis et majoribus suis.

King's magnificently rhetorical assessment of this young aristocrat is difficult to verify today, so little is known about his minority.[1] He came of a family of Jacobite Tories: no doubt his

[1] His career seems to have been uneventful. In 1752 he married Elizabeth Gunning of Castle Coote, Roscommon, one of the celebrated beauties of the day, and died at the age of thirty-four at Great Tew, Oxfordshire, as the result of a cold.

views were essentially those of his more famous father. Apart from the formal expressions proclaimed in his speech, King himself wrote little which has survived on the subject of the Duke. In a letter to Sanderson Miller from Bath, dated only 'April, 1743', King commented of his speech, '. . . in truth I intended it only as a Lesson for his Grace. I wish he may always consider it as such.'[1] And in his letter to Lord Orrery of 6 June 1743, he shews the newly created Doctor of Civil Law in a state of temporary indecision: 'You know I have engaged to attend his Grace of H. to some French Academy and see him settled. He talks of going ye beginning of August. But as he is at present a very uncertain young Gentleman, I think he will not go so soon. Nay, I think he will not go at all.'[2] Such pieces of evidence are too slender to support any definite conclusion with regard to the Duke, though one may assume that, in his public utterances, King would scarcely have laid himself open to a charge of disingenuousness for the sake of this *adulescens*. What is undeniable is that King used this occasion, as he did others similar, to extol what he regarded as Jacobite uprightness, and to attack, in heavily veiled language, the morality of the New Interest.

The Earl of Lichfield was somewhat older than the Duke—twenty-six to be precise—and was later to attain the highest honour of the university as Chancellor. King's eulogy for him is grandiloquent, but not unduly fulsome if one considers the oratorical canons of the time. The listeners are given ample assurance of His Lordship's virtues: '*Quicquid enim in viro nobili aut requirere, aut amare solemus, sive elegantiam ingenii, sive probitatem morum, sive, quod omnium est pulcherrimum, amorem patriae; in hoc spectatissimo juvene haec insunt omnia.*' The audience is reminded that Lord Lichfield has been an exemplary Member of Parliament, '. . . *qui pene puer senator factus nihil pueriliter dixit, nihil fecit; sed pulchra, sed honesta, sed praeclara omnia.*' He has always been *honest* (an epithet with special overtones for Jacobites) and has always held steadfastly in mind 'the most sacred name of liberty.' Nor is he deficient in private parts: '*Sed neque modo in curia et consiliis publicis, sed etiam in otio et privatis officiis ipse ita sibi*

---

[1] Dickins and Stanton, op. cit., p. 95.
[2] Bodleian Library, MS. Eng. hist. d. 103, p. 77.

cunctos devinxit humanitate sua et singulari comitate, ut gravissimi senes eum ament, probissimi juvenes admirentur, colant amici, observent propinqui, invideant pauci, oderit nemo.' King's extended panegyric leads him to a rhetorical climax: a kind of crescendo of exhortation in carefully elaborated parallel constructions: '*O! si sic semper curemus decernendos, civibus nimirum huic simillimis; non quia nobiles sunt, aut quia Academici, sed quia viri boni, et bonorum et doctorum amantissimi; non quia hosce petunt honores, sed quia merentur: quod quidem genere, et nobilitate, et cunctis nominibus, et cunctis honoribus est ornatius.*'

Of the speeches published in *Tres Oratiunculae* King liked the third best. 'You will see some little alterations and an addition of a line or two,' he wrote to Lord Orrery, but added, '*Lead* has made yᵉ publication of yᵉ whole necessary.'[1] By 'Lead' King means the Bishop of Llandaff, Dr. John Gilbert, who had apparently been maligning the Principal of St. Mary Hall on account of his speeches. Magnanimous though King had been to Lord Lichfield, the encomium for Lord Orrery manifests a much greater feeling of *camaraderie* and a degree of praise which one might consider to be unduly inflated were it not for the similar sentiments constantly expressed in the speaker's private correspondence, with apparently complete candour. Orrery is first presented as '*hunc nobilissimum virum, . . . hunc ornatissimum virum, hunc, in quo glorior, LAELIUM*[2] *meum: qui a puero mire studiosus, et avito praeditus ingenio, in almae nostrae Matris sermone ita fuit educatus, ut omni liberati doctrina, et Graecis literis et Latinis haud quisquam hodie sit eruditior.*' His ability in English is equal to his powers in Latin and Greek: '*Anglicani vero sermonis tanta ei est elegantia, tanta oris suavitas, tanta comitas cum gravitate judicii conjuncta et in dicendo et in scribendo, (Lyrica ejus opera testes, et disertissimae epistolae, et jucundissima convictio) ut saepissime arbitratus sim, Apollinem ipsum, ut ita dicam, si Anglice loqueretur, hunc quidem velle imitari.*' Compliments are piled on compliments: Orrery is *politissimus, paterfamilias prudens, maritus continens, amicus fidelis,*

---

[1] Bodleian Library, MS. Eng. hist. d. 103, p. 83.

[2] King provides footnotes setting forth references to LAELIUM in *Scamnum, Ecologa* and *Templum Libertatis*. These constitute the strongest proof that Laelius is to be taken as representing Orrery in the original editions of these works. As already indicated, the references to Laelius do not occur in the recensions contained in the *Opera*.

hospes liberalis, fautor et patronus literarum munificus, quo nihil humanius, modestius, sanctius. King's oratory rises to paeans more laudatory than he ever bestowed on any other individual, not excluding Swift:

Neque vero est mirum, quod in hoc clarissimo viro tot animi dotes, totque naturae bona, optimarum artium studiis exculta, reperiantur; quum haec omnia illi plane sunt gentilitia. Quam illustria enim sunt avorum ejus, proavorum, atavorum nomina apud nostros, apud exteros, apud eruditos omnes! Adeo ut hic unus fortasse de tot nobilibus sui temporis ab stirpe ipsius Philosophiae oriundus esse videatur.

He takes the opportunity to compare His Lordship with less worthy men in the land (the audience must have known which political interest the speaker had in mind) and vituperates against those

. . . qui se primos omnium esse contendunt, proceres, antistites, principes Reipublicae; qui tamen simulatione pietatis nihil non impie faciunt, et simulatione publicae utilitatis omnia (pro dolor!) sane apta esse vident suis commodis suoque imperio.

As he draws to his conclusion, he adopts an autobiographical tone:

At vos, si laudationibus meis faveatis, ignoscite, quaeso, meae indignationi; quae, siqua est, est honestissima; quum unum quidem hoc cogito non tantum in hac oratiuncula, sed in omnibus scriptis meis, et in omni vita; ut satisfaciam opinioni vestrae, et praestem eam, quam Reipublicae, quam Academiae, quam ingenio huic excellenti et summo meo amico debeo reverentiam.

King adds to the conventional conclusion of such presentation speeches the unusual comment to Convocation, *illustriorem sane legistis nunquam.*

In the months immediately prior to the publication of *Tres Oratiunculae*, King delivered some other speeches which he did not see through the press. Thus on 23 August 1744 he presented the Whig Sir Edward Turner for the degree of D.C.L. *honoris causa*, and made 'a very polite, tho' severe speech on modern patriotism and the times.'[1] On October 26 he spoke again in Convocation; Euseby Isham described the performance as

---

[1] *The London Evening Post*, No. 2625, 1–4 September 1744.

'one of yᵉ best Speeches in yᵉ finest and coolest manner I ever heard.'[1] The text of neither speech has been preserved.

The preface to the three published orations constituted the start of a peculiar literary 'controversy', all of which, with the possible exception of the final piece, was very probably written by King himself. Addressed *LECTORI*, the preface to *Tres Oratiunculae* implies that the author has been attacked by some anti-Jacobite canon and that other members of the New Interest are engaged in personal onslaughts against him. The canon in question is Dr. John Gilbert, Bishop of Llandaff, who, after his consecration, continued to hold the canonry at Christ Church which he had received from the crown *in commendam*.[2] He went so far as to call for the expulsion from Convocation of the Principal of St. Mary Hall, as is made manifest in King's letter to Lord Orrery headed 'Bagshot Oct. yᵉ 6th 1743':

Would you think (yes you would) that *Leaden Gil——t* has been pleased to criticize my speeches, wᶜʰ he did not hear, and to abuse me most outrageously in all places for he does not know what. . . . Among other things he says, that if he had been in the Convocation, he would have moved yᵉ House to expel me. To this I have answered, that altho' I am persuaded no person would *second* his motion, yet I will submit to be expell'd, if he can make it. You know he must make it in Latin.[3]

The bishop did not propose the motion to Convocation, and the Principal of St. Mary Hall remained unexpelled.

King's grievances against Bishop Gilbert are expounded at greater length in the preface to *Tres Oratiunculae*. He first makes it plain that he is publishing these speeches *ut obviam irem malevoli cujusdam CANONICI injuriis*, and continues:

Nam ex quo tempore libertatis & patriae laudes, & ingenuarum artium studia, & optimorum civium virtutes in senatu nostro celebrare aggressus sum; &, quod neutiquam a meo munere alienum esse arbitrabar, novorum hominum in rempublicam perfidiam &

---

[1] Northamptonshire Record Office, Isham (Lamport) Collection No. 2696.

[2] In 1749 he became Bishop of Salisbury and in 1757 Archbishop of York. *The Dictionary of National Biography* corroborates King's general contentions: 'Gilbert seems to have possessed few qualifications to justify his high promotion in the church. He was neither a scholar nor a theologian. Nor were these deficiencies compensated by graces of character.'

[3] Bodleian Library, MS. Eng. hist. d. 103, pp. 8of.

proditionem leviter notavi; ita rei novitate perculsus est vir iste magnificus, ut ultra modum intumuerit (quanquam semper intumescit notabiliter) meque in conviviis rodere, maledictis lacessere, & procacissima censura in odium & invidiam vocare vix usquam destiterit.

King regarded him, as he did the other Whig Clergy, as receiving unjustifiable political favours from the state:

En, hic ille est, qui modo dite sacerdotium arroganter recusavit: nempe cogitat (vide, quid avaritia impudenter cogitat!) ditissimum; quo scilicet erit contentus; & quo (eheu! ita est seculum) fortasse donandus. Nos autem nonne interea his ipsis praeclare admonemur, quid de re amplissima, de speciosis titulis de regum, quaecunque sunt, donis statuat deus optimus maximus; quanti faciat, et quam nolit ea esse virtutum praemia; quae talis vir, qui virtutibus plane omnibus caret, sine aut periculo, aut contentione, aut sumptu sibi potuit comparare?

He continues to allege further shortcomings on the part of Gilbert, especially that he is *literis vix mediocriter imbutus* despite the fact that he holds a canonry which is *ornatissimam et fructuosissimam*. The publication of these speeches, he indicates, is the result of the insolent and contemptuous threats which have been offered him.

Bishop Gilbert did not answer these charges, and so King wrote an answer instead. It takes the form of two short works: *Epistola Canonici Reverendi Admodum ad Archidiaconum Reverendum Admodum* and *Epistola Objurgatoria ad Guilielmum King, LL.D.*, which are nowadays only to be found together, in a single binding with consecutive page numbers.[1] The *Epistola Canonici* is the first of King's two satires in doggerel Latin prose, and is intended to be in imitation of Gilbert's Latin style. The archdeacon to whom it is addressed is not identifiable; he may have been only a literary device.

The total effect is ludicrous as for nine pages the supposed author rants in appalling Latin against '. . . *impudenti isti Doctori, qui locutus est tam multa contra me in sua praefatione*'. The

---

[1] There were two editions in 1744 of the combined publication: in the first, page 24 is misnumbered 23, and there is an *Erratum* at the foot of page 30; in the second, page 24 is numbered correctly and the *Erratum* is emended. Though these two pieces have their separate title pages in both editions, it is quite possible that they were never published singly.

Epistola Canonici and the comparable *Epistola Dedicatoria* to *Oratiuncula Habita in Domo Convocationis, Oxon. Die. Oct. 27, 1756* (which King wrote in the guise of Robert Jenner, the then Regius Professor of Civil Law) must constitute two of the worst pieces of continuous Latin prose ever to appear in print. Grammatical and syntactical blunders, stylistic monstrosities, and factual inaccuracies are crawling all over the pages. Gilbert is represented as a kind of prelatical nincompoop explaining to his *venerabilis frater*, the archdeacon, the causes of his antagonism towards the author of *Tres Oratiunculae:*

Ultima aestate ego eram ad prandium cum multis aliis generosis ad domum Domini H. cum unus vir, qui ibi erat una ad tabulam, dixit aliquid bonum de isto Doctore, et suis Oratiunculis; quod me fecit magis rubeum in facie, quam ego sum ordinarie, et magis iratum, quam unquam fui in tota mea vita. Tunc ego responsi: iste Doctor est magnus Jacobita, et non amat regem, et debet expelli ab Universitate pro suis Oratiunculis, quae sunt plenae seditionis, et abutuntur Episcopos et nobilitatem et omnes ordines virorum, ut ego audivi ab illis qui audiverunt istas Oratiunculas pronunciatas.

He continues to expatiate in the same jejune, Anglicized Latin on the subject of King's Preface, *in qua scandalizavit me, quantum est possible, ut videtis.* His lawyer, he writes, has told him that he does not have a good legal case against the author because the language of the preface is not sufficiently plain. This state of affairs seems to him to constitute a serious defect in the law, *cum omnes pueri in Universitate sciunt, quod ego certe intendor per istam praefationem.* However, he continues, he has a friend, a *magnus minister*, who has advised him to find someone who can write a reply to the preface in good Latin; thus he has commissioned a *mirabilis disputator et jocator* to write for him the *Epistola Objurgatoria.* He is delighted to have found such an individual '. . . *ponere ea omnia in bonam Latinitatem, quam ego quidem nunquam curavi, quia non est utilis in minimo ad promotiones et translationes in nostro ordine.* . . .' King is shortly to discover what a mistake he has himself made: '*Sed profecto quando haec ORJURGATORIA publicabitur, ille statim inveniet suum errorem, et me oderit, ut si essem unus diabolus; dum ego gloriose dico cum Apostolo, veni, vidi, vici.*' There is no signature, but the letter is dated *EX STUDIO MEO infra decimam & undecimam in mane post jentaculum. Jan. 30, 1744.*

One of the incidentally interesting aspects of this atrociously written letter is the indirect attack on the scholastic deductive logic that was still being taught at Oxford. Gilbert is represented as using it to argue that King was illogical when he accused him of lacking gravity while at the same time being 'leaden'. Like Lewis Carroll, King was a master at composing the facetious logical deduction: '... *quodcumque est plumbeum, id est grave, secundum quod communiter dicitur et proverbialiter; grave ut plumbum. Ergo, si plumbeitas mihi non deest, gravitas non deest; et e contra si gravitas mihi deest, plumbeitas deest.*' This is followed by a deliberately transparent syllogistic argument in which Gilbert assails with comic sincerity King's insinuation that he (a man) is lacking humanity:

Omnis homo est humanus, sed omnis humanus habet humanitatem, ergo omnis homo habet humanitatem: Qui habet humanitatem, ei humanitas non deest, sed homo habet humanitatem, ergo homini humanitas non deest. Et hoc est secundum istam infallibilem regulam, quam posuit unus magnus philosophus et bonus Theologus, (cujus nomen ego non memini nunc) qui dixit valde laudabiliter et logicaliter, *Homo sum: nihil humanum a me alienum puto.*[1]

Argumentation such as this, Bishop Gilbert is made to assert, '*non modo objurgabit, sed secabit istum Guilielmum frustillatim, et percutiet eum mutum in aeternum*'.

The *Epistola Objurgatoria* is dated *Pridie Calendas Februarias*, and purports to have been completed the day after Gilbert's letter. It is preceded by a short notice, BIBLIOPOLA LECTORI ERUDITO, in which the bookseller declares with a certain appropriateness: '*DONO mihi missa est haec Epistola plumbea pyxide inclusa, & mitrato capite obsignata. Si quaeris, Unde? Nescio.*' Consequently the author is presented as anonymous, but the bookseller has his own opinions on the book itself: '*Id sane venustum est, si ei viro, quem defendit facetus scriptor, totum displiceat: venustius, si tibi tuique simillimis satis placeat: verum hercle certe venustissimum, si mihi bono lucro fiet futurum.*'

There is no real argument in the sixteen pages over which

---

[1] This quotation (or misquotation) is from Terence. The original passage, said by Chremes to Menedemus in the *Heautontimorumenos*, usually reads in modern editions:

Homo sum: humani nil a me alienum puto.

this brief work extends: it is essentially a mock-serious presentation of Gilbert's imaginary case against King. The Whig to whom it is credited, a lawyer in the Middle Temple, writes better Latin than the bishop, but his case is just as banal. It would be tiresome to summarize this piece: its humour consists principally in the elaboration, at times *ad nauseam*, of the most trivial logomachies in purposely muddle headed fashion, filled out with numerous examples of unfounded personal abuse against King and equally unfounded praise of the 'leaden man'. A single example must serve to illustrate King's manipulation of this singular kind of satire and his ability to make amusing (at least from time to time) what is fundamentally nothing more than a tissue of twaddle.

One of the arguments used in favour of the episcopal Canon of Christ Church is that King's epithet *plumbeus*, far from detracting from his merit, is actually extremely appropriate:

Quod denique studes inclyto viro invidiam facere PLUMBEOS clamando (quorum mentionem, haud dubio, quin tecum putaris sane callide injectam esse, atque id verbum salsissime dictum) nihil profecto est ineptius, aut a re tua tam alienum. Quid enim? Quinam homines sunt vere plumbei? Praeclarissimi videlicet heroes, philosophi, et poetae veteres; quorum vultus in procerum aedibus, atriis, hortis usquequaque se ostendunt ex plumbo efficti. Quinetiam deos plumbeos, qui tamen coelitum sunt elegantissimi, et bonis literis favent, Apollinem et Mercurium, quoties ego contemplatus sum? quoties deas, catas, doctas, pulchras, Minervam Musasque Gratiasque ex eadem materia bellissime expressas?

This last piece of special pleading (if the term may be allowed) is corroborated by further evidence from nearer home in the form of a footnote to *Musasque*: '*Quae hodie praesunt Musae TYPOGRAPHEO CLARENDONIANO, in conspectu omnis populi stantes, eae quidem plumbeae sunt. Nonne?*' On these premisses the supposititious author reaches a triumphant conclusion: '*Plumbeos omnes, ii cujuscunque sunt ordinis, aut ubicumque sedes suas posuerunt, diligentius inspice, perspice explora; nusquam unquam invenies aut illepidum caput, aut invenustum; id nisi sit fortasse quiddam regium: quod nihilominus et dignitas personae et mos gentium excusarit satis, si parum cerebri habeat.*' At this stage the reader is presented with a *caveat* to the statement just made, and thence the idiotic polemic meanders on, proving nothing except King's competence in caricaturing a certain kind of inferior thinker. No evidence survives of Gilbert's own reaction to all this, but whatever he thought, it is unlikely that the Principal of St. Mary Hall was yet prepared to let the matter rest.

Epistola Objurgatoria was followed by *A Letter to a Friend Occasioned by Epistola Objurgatoria*, dated 23 March 1744. Almost certainly this brief pamphlet is the work of King himself, though on the title-page the author is given as S.P.Y.B. The usual explanation of these initials is that they stand for Samuel Parker, Yeoman Bedel. The nature of the relationship between King and Parker is now far from clear: Parker was a younger man who had matriculated at Magdalen College in 1730 and had been yeoman bedel of the university since 1731. Why King should have wished to impersonate *him* will probably never be determined, but it is equally unlikely that any other person is intended. He is represented here as complaining to some nameless friend that he has been erroneously attributed with the authorship of *Epistola Objurgatoria*: 'The Gentlemen tell me, I am the Author of it; but, as I have a Soul to be saved, I am as innocent of any hand in it as the Child unborn . . . I thought I wou'd write to you about it, and let you know I never did, nor ever will, trouble myself to write for or against any Man.' This contention is elaborated at some length and with an excessive use of cliché and proverbial quotation: very likely the superficial, periphrastic style is intended to mirror Parker's limited conversational powers. He is made to issue some naïve reactions to the false attribution of its authorship, being 'ready to go wild about it' and 'almost worried to death'. He regards *Epistola Objurgatoria* as a 'wicked Book' and declares his abhorrence of it. He complains because men who think he really is the author unkindly mutter scraps of Latin about him to one another. One, for example, cries: '*Invidus alterius rebus macrescit opimis.*' Parker's comment is: 'So, because I am thin and meagre, truly I must be envious; when all the World knows (the more's my Misfortune) my poor Visage is thus miserably reduced merely by the plaguy Tooth-ach.' A good deal of the force of this kind of writing is inevitably lost to readers who have never known S.P.Y.B. personally.

The last item in this strange series is entitled *A Chiding Letter to S.P.Y.B. in Defence of Epistola Objurgatoria*. No author's name is given, but this short pamphlet of nineteen pages is generally attributed to King. It takes the form of a letter, dated 4 May 1744, in answer to that of Samuel Parker. The anonymous writer claims to be indignant at Parker's letter and waxes strong against him: 'How durst you write that LETTER of the 23d of *March*? Was it for one of your mean Abilities to enter the Lists with a Man, not only of fine Parts and elevated Genius, but a *Wit* of the first Magnitude? Is he, think you, Sir, to be called to Account by every Blockhead that can get a Sheet of Paper to scribble on? . . .' This tone is maintained fairly consistently to the end: S.P.Y.B. is roundly condemned, and King is enthusiastically extolled together with *Epistola Objurgatoria*.

A Chiding Letter is indeed an oddity. If King really was the author, he was composing appreciably below his usual standard, and with a surprising poverty of sophistication. Furthermore, this piece lacks his customary clarity, especially in its use of pronouns without a definitely unambiguous antecedent. The amount written in an earnest—not mock-serious—tone in praise of King himself is proportionately much greater than is to be found in any work definitely known to be by him. In this publication it seems to be taken for granted that King really *is* the author of *Epistola Objurgatoria*, a fact which he had hitherto not admitted. On the other hand, the writer does not explicitly regard King as the author of *A Letter to a Friend* of March 23, and assumes throughout S.P.Y.B.'s authorship of it.

None of these considerations constitutes irrefutable evidence against King's authorship of *A Chiding Letter*. To one so capable of disguising his literary personality, a work with an unauthentic quality would not have been difficult to create. In the circumstances in which he was placed, King had good reason for wishing to envelop the entire controversy in a haze of confusion. But in the last analysis one can only regard the established bibliographical attribution to King with suspicion: especially in view of such heavy-handed and questionable compliments as these, which, if I interpret them in their context rightly, are intended to be taken literally, without ironic *innuendo*:

The Dr . . . is perfectly well satisfied of his own entire Merit, not-withstanding the small Value others sat on it. . . . The Doctor, far from regarding what such a *Tool* as you says of his more than *Attic* Performance, is for ever reading it, and for ever admiring it: And prithee, Fellow, if you will needs attempt to be witty, learn of him *the Difference between* Attic *Irony*, and *Elegance of Wit*; *and your intem-perate Scurrility, and illiberal Banter.* . . . He is Master of a *courtly* Stile, which he fails not to improve with Plenty of *Attic* Seasoning. . . . In one Word to attack the Doctor is to attack the united Elegance of *Rome* and *Athens.*

King *could* have penned these statements, but their expressions are not typical. If he did compose them, whom was he attempt-ing to impersonate? And why should he choose to defend him-self in so mediocre a manner against an attack which—in all probability—he had himself written? To such questions there are at present no precise answers.

At about the same time as he was engaged in this controversy, King was rebuilding the east range of St. Mary Hall with the aid of contributions furnished by old members. The style which he decided upon may be described as eighteenth-century Elizabethan: its simple rusticity was in all likelihood regarded as a pleasant anachronism. He also added a new room to the Principal's lodgings, which in those days were in the northwest corner of the Hall quadrangle. Though King's east wing still survives today, little remains of the lodgings which he occupied. The reconstruction of the west side of the Hall in 1826 and the addition of the Rhodes Building some eighty-five years later have now replaced the quarters used by successive Principals until the union with Oriel College in 1902.[1]

The spring of 1744 also saw the publication of another Latin work by King, *Antonietti, Ducis Corsorum, Epistola ad Corsos*, the argument of which had already appeared in 1737 in *Common Sense*. The later version which appeared in the *Opera* bears the title *Antonietti, Corsorum Ducis, Epistola ad Corsos*. There are other slight variations between the texts. The 1744 printing is pre-ceded by an introductory prose paragraph under the heading

[1] *The Oxford Almanack* for 1746 incorporates a large woodcut of St. Mary Hall: it is idealized and by no means precise in every detail. See also Antony Wood, *The History and Antiquities of the Colleges and Halls in the University of Oxford* (Oxford: at the Clarendon Press, 1786), p. 674.

Editor Lectori and by another more extended passage entitled *Antoniettus, Dux Corsorum, Clarissimo Pasquillo Romae Censori.* In the recension, the heading *Editor Lectori* is omitted, but the introductory paragraph is printed as a note beneath the beginning of the text of the poem. The substance of the second prose passage appears at the end of the work under the title *Antoniettus Clarissimo Pasquillo, Romano Censori.* There is a certain amount of rewording in the later version, and some topical references are added. The original text of the poem contains 229 lines; the *Opera* revision 228. The precise date of the first appearance of this work cannot now be determined, but it must have been shortly before April 24; on that date King wrote to Lord Orrery: 'I have just now published the Corsican Epistle. I think no party can be angry with it. And yet it may so happen, that as I have been formerly deemed a Jacobite, I may now be called a Republican. The Leaden Man, you may be sure, will criticize me with all his might—but not in Latin.'[1]

In the *Editor Lectori* the author praises the Corsicans and, in effect, indicates that they represent the British people: '*Quae sit bellicosissima illa Corsorum natio, jam norunt omnes; eique favent omnes, qui patriam amant, et colunt libertatem; omnes nimirum, qui sunt bonae ac sanae mentis. Si tu, Lector, es ex iis, si Britannus homo es, si vir es; totum hujus fabulae argumentum tibi satis placebit.*' The literary device of using the term *Corsi* for the British was not entirely inappropriate from the Jacobite point of view. The island of Corsica was then administered by the Genoese who, since 1729, had had to deal with a series of rebellions led by nationalist subversives. The Holy Roman Emperor, Charles VI, had patched up a temporary peace in 1732, but by 1734 the island had been declared independent by two of the principal seditionists, Luigi Giafferi and Giacinto Paoli. Corsica had its counterpart to the Old Chevalier: Theodore Stephen, Baron von Neuhof, a German aristocrat who persuaded the illegal Corsican leaders to crown him king at Cervione, as Theodore I, in 1736. Running short of money, he was forced to leave the island later in the year. With French help the authorities in Genoa had re-established order by 1740. Giafferi and Paoli

---

[1] Bodleian Library, MS. Eng. hist. d. 103, pp. 87f.

were driven into exile, and though Theodore returned on a British ship in 1743, he was given only a lukewarm welcome before again departing. The analogy between the Corsican rebels and the Jacobites is, of course, far from exact, a truth which King must have realized, but the fact that the British government was aiding both the rebels and Charles Emmanuel III, King of Sardinia, against Genoa about the time that King was actually writing presumably helped to give the *Antonietti Epistola ad Corsos* an extra immediacy.

In discussing the poem itself, I am assuming that the text in the *Opera* is the author's final version, and that when he had finished with the text, he wished the prose letter to Pasquillus to *follow* the verse letter to the *Corsi*. The first page of the *Opera* version contains two copperplate engravings. Their messages are reasonably plain, but to avoid any doubt there is printed, on the facing *verso*, an *Aenearum Tabularum Explicatio*. The first engraving is thus explained: '*In hac tabula regem ligneum conspiciatis in regali suo solio sive loculamento collocatum, et auro et purpura regifice ornatum; infra autem Corsorum concilium magnum de summa reipublicae deliberans.*' The second engraving is a historiated initial capital N, the ornamentation of which is elucidated in these words: '*In hac litera initiali faber lignarius Corsorum regem fabricatur buxum artificiose sculpendo, et tornando.*' From these two visual aids the general import of the poem is already clear.

The introductory sentence plunges the reader into the hostilities of the War of the Austrian Succession, with Caesar representing Charles VII, the Elector of Bavaria, and Philip V of Spain introduced under his own name:

> Nobile si carmen mihi Musae, quale Maroni,
> Annuerent; aut, quae sibi poscunt, grandia vates
> Moliti, ingenii vires centenaque Phoebus
> Ora arguta daret; non magni Caesaris arma,
> Aut quae Boiorum nudarunt praelia campos,
> Gallorumque acies, ingenti aperire ruinae
> Quae loca cuncta parant; sed nec victricia signa,
> Austriacosque duces, vicinaque castra Philippi,
> Magnaque per pelagum vecturos bella Britannos
> Jam canere inciperem; sed facta et fata meorum.

King then addresses the Corsicans directly:

> Vosque pii cives, vos, fortia pectora, Corsi,
> Servitiumque pati indociles, fidosque Penates
> Certe equidem laudarem ultro; puerosque senesque,
> Qui nunc pro patria pugnant, galeisque cucullos
> Mutantes monachos.

A note is provided on the last two lines: '*Tantum erat libertatis conservandae studium, ut monachi etiam arma caperent, et milites in aciem excirent. Valde suspicor Antoniettum meum monachum fuisse,*' A little later King commemorates the former king of Corsica, Theodore I, who, he explains, has abdicated the throne *nescio quo malo fato*, and passes on to the subject of a monarch for the future:

> Dum dubitatis enim, quoniam Theodorus in oras
> Ignotas abiit, quis debeat esse futurus,
> Et qualis rector Cyrnaeus;[1] si mea vota
> Dictaque quid valeant, gentis de more vetusto
> Rex erit; at sancta rex majestate verendus.
> Qui Veneri imbelles noctes donare recuset,
> Ignavosque dies Baccho: qui extendere fines
> Imperii nolit, bellum meditatus iniquum.

The future king will be *antiqua stirpe creatus*, but a warning is provided that he should not be made from the same stock that produced the golden bough which Aeneas plucked for the Sibyl:

> Vos porro a rege cavete
> Iligno, ne stirpe genus deducat ab ista,
> Trojano Aeneae quae ramum detulit auri.
> Olli semper enim vis certe antiqua manebit:
> Et quamvis sit truncus iners, se vestiet auro,
> Corsorum spoliis. Nonne hoc Germania tota,
> Gallorumque urbes, et nudus plorat Iberus?

When the new king has been fabricated, he should be given a

---

[1] *Cyrnos* was the Greek name for Corsica; *Cyrnaeus* is the Latinized adjective corresponding to *Corsus*.

sceptre and throne of the same material as himself—oak. He should also be clothed in purple:

Ipse sedebit
Purpuream indutus pallam; sed tempora cinget
Aut edera aut laurus, doctorum praemia vatum,
Et veterum heroum, frugique aptissima regi.
Quem nisi perjuri cives, nisi fulminis ictus,
Aut subitae tulerint flammae, decor integer illi
Gloriaque, et solidae stabunt per saecula vires.

King now demonstrates again his skill in the use of extended anaphora:

Jamque viri pietate graves, queis publica cordi
Commoda sunt, proceres centum patresque legantur.
His populi credenda salus; his templa deorum:
Hos penes arbitrium sit belli et pacis: iniquos
Hi pellant Ligurum socios:[1] responsa superbis
Hi dent legatis; dent nobis jura: ministros
Hos, plebi fidos, hos solos noverit aula;
Hosce magistratus urbes; hos castra tribunos.

The change in person that follows makes for an effective rhetorical contrast:

Vos, tamen in medium quoties, proceresque patresque,
Consulitis; felix vobis rex buxeus adsit:
Praeside quo rerum, quo fiant omnia coram.

The analogy of the wooden monarch to the king which Jupiter gave to the frogs, already touched upon in the earlier article in *Common Sense*, is here expanded at some length. The poem concludes with a reference to the vain prayer of the chiefs of the frogs:

... frustra, rex ut sibi ligneus adsit,
Nunc optant, orantque Jovem. ...

and Jove's reply:

... Coelesti indigna favore,
Humanae similis, gens vana, et nescia reges
Ferre bonos, discat jam saevos ferre tyrannos.

---

[1] King's note on *Ligurum socios* reads: '*Germanos, Gallos, Hispanos, aut quicumque cum Liguribus sive Genuensibus faciunt contra Corsos*'.

There follows the letter of Antoniettus to Pasquillus, who is described as a Roman Censor. The author makes clear in a note that Pasquillus is no ordinary example of his kind:

Pasquillus, seu Pasquinus, Italice Pasquino, nomen statuae mutilatae in urbe Roma, cui affigi solent versus atellanici, satirae breves, epigrammata et dicteria procaciora in pontifices, reges, principes, cardinales et magistratus, quorum vita et mores odio et opprobriis sunt digna; digna et quae stigmate quodam notentur. Haec statua nomen sumit a cerdone quodam Romano, viro lepidissimo et cive optimo; qui in eodem vico olim habitabat. Felix Pasquille! Cujus memoriam cives tui conservant, consecrant, immortalem reddunt, cum tot Caesares, totque pontifices suos malint quidem oblivisci.

Antoniettus explains to Pasquillus that he is seeking

. . . uti me, et carmen hoc meum tibi commendatissimum habeas, simul et dignitatem eximii illius regis, quem belle quidem ac diligenter hodie excogitavi ad usum civium meorum.

The writer indicates that this king is wooden, but toys with the possibility that Pasquillus might prefer a monarch of gold or marble. The disadvantages of both possibilities are outlined, and wood is found to be preferable. Antoniettus continues:

Proin tu, censor lepidissime, qui apte et praeclare potes omnia eloqui cum omnibus, benevole elabora, et tua opera vel eblandiendo effice, vel minitando, ut summo pontifici rex Corsorum sit probatissimus, et imperatoriis titulis et filiatione perhonorifica augeatur. Haud fere quisquam ex beatissimi patris filiis reperietur, (hoc fide mea spondeo) sive reges sunt, sive reguli, seu quicunque basilicum hodie tenent statum, qui eum magis lubenter omni obsequio et observantia colat, quam hic ligneus noster; quem quidem spero, et confido post centum annos canonizandum fore; si tum canonizari eos oportebit, qui bene et recte vixerint, labe omni carentes.

The letter closes with some more sentiments in favour of a wooden king, who is all that is necessary to maintain peace and preserve freedom.

On these two letters there is little that need be added to the comments already made on the article in *Common Sense*. The substance of what King published in 1744 is clearly based on his thinking of some seven years earlier; the later version is much expanded, but represents no fundamental advance in content. One of King's reasons for reworking his English article was probably to give it a greater permanency: he hoped that at least some copies of the *Opera* would survive, but very likely had doubts about an issue of a journal which had already been defunct for some years. He presumably also regarded his Latin version as having a dignity far surpassing what could be achieved in the ephemeral pages of a vernacular periodical. Above all, in an age when so much philosophical and political speculation was expressed in the form of verse, King must have judged that his Latin hexameters would have a literary value over and above that of his English prose.

One other publication warrants some discussion among the events of 1744. In that year Charles Bathurst, who seven years previously had published the first six volumes of the complete version of Dr. Robert South's *Sermons Preached Upon Several Occasions*, issued the last five, edited, according to John Nichols, by William King.[1] No editor's name appears in the five volumes of 1744, but in the 'new edition' of the entire work, published at the Clarendon Press in 1823, Nichols's statement is referred to without contradiction.[2] It seems to me quite incredible that King performed any editorial function in connection with Bathurst's badly produced volumes of 1744. The anonymous Advertisement to the 1823 edition has this to say of the homilies supposed to have been edited by King: 'These Sermons do not appear to have been prepared or even intended for the press by the author, from whose rough drafts they were evidently printed in so careless and incorrect a manner, as in many passages to be absolutely unintelligible.'[3] It is further explained that, in the preparation of this edition, recourse had been made to a copy bequeathed to the Bodleian Library by Charles Godwyn, in which many of the errors were corrected by Godwyn himself. Lists of emended words and passages are annexed to the relevant

---

[1] John Nichols, op. cit., Vol. II, p. 608. On page xiii of King's *Political and Literary Anecdotes* (2nd edn., 1819), Philip Bury Duncan, quoting Chalmers, intimates that King edited the *first* five volumes. The assertion of Nichols is repeated correctly by Daniel Lysons in *The Environs of London*.

[2] Robert South, D.D., *Sermons Preached Upon Several Occasions* (7 vols.; Oxford: at the Clarendon Press, 1823), Vol. V, p. iii.

[3] Ibid.

volumes, which in the 1823 edition are three in number. There is no satisfactory explanation for the often deplorable textual state of the sermons collectively published in 1744. No competent editor could have seen them through the press. Their author, who lived from 1634 to 1716, had taken the oath of allegiance to the House of Hanover, a fact which would not have endeared him to King. Indeed, the Principal of St. Mary Hall is not known to have had any interest whatever in South or in his sermons. Admittedly, the two men had some characteristics in common: both were known for their independence of outlook and for their forthright manner in condemning the vices of their age. From time to time South's sermons reveal a pleasant, underlying sense of humour, of a kind which King could have appreciated. But these correspondences are far too slender in themselves to support any editorial hypothesis in relation to King. Nichols made numerous errors, as his later lists of corrections indicate. Many slips, however, were left unemended: his attribution of homiletical editorship to the Principal of St. Mary Hall appears to be yet another of these.

King published nothing in 1745. His four surviving letters of that year—three to Lord Orrery and one to Sanderson Miller—deal mainly with personal or obscure political matters.[1] Some kind compliments are paid on the subject of Lord Orrery's eldest son, who matriculated at St. Mary Hall on 23 May 1745, forecasts are made of bad news from the West Indies and specifically Jamaica, and an informal cipher is provided for possible use in the future: 'If I have occasion to mention ye D. of B, in a post letter, I will call him Mr. *Stephens*, and ye intended presentation speech, the *Manuscripts*, and Ld A. *John Dory*.' His letter to Miller constitutes a reply to a social invitation: '. . . I am become so stout I can travel in any manner. Three days ago I walk'd five miles to dinner, so that you need not be concerned about providing a vehicle for me. But after all my boasting I may think it best to accept of your offer.'

One of the most serious *lacunae* in the extant documents on King's life occurs between July 1745 and 10 April 1746, the

[1] Bodleian Library, MS. Eng. hist. d. 103, pp. 88–93; Lilian Dickins and Mary Stanton, op. cit., p. 114. In its printed version the letter to Sanderson Miller is abbreviated; the original is in the County Record Office, Shire Hall, Warwick, Miller Collection CR 125 B/159.

very time when the rising led by the Young Chevalier was taking place. Charles Edward landed in Scotland in July—though news of his unwelcome arrival did not reach London until the second week of August—and seized power in Edinburgh on September 17, at Prestonpans on September 21 after a battle lasting little more than five minutes, in Carlisle on November 17, and in Derby on December 4. His suzerainty there lasted almost three days—until Black Friday, December 6. Thence his long drawn out retreat to the Scottish highlands continued until the battle of Fort Augustus in March 1746, and the final defeat at Culloden on April 16 of the same year. What part, if any, did King play in the rising? What were his reactions to the initial victories and the later defeats? Alas, there is no documentation to answer either of these questions. All that is known for sure is that on 8 July 1745 his spirits were low, as he explained to Lord Orrery: 'As to publick affairs, My Dear Lord, this is a dreadful Crisis. We have bad news from all quarters with a stinging political lie here and there intermixed in order to prevent universal panic. To what place the Genius of England is retired, I know not; but that he is departed from us is most certain.'[1] With the letter of this day the Bodleian collection of King's correspondence to Lord Orrery comes to an end. Any other letters that King wrote to Lord Orrery during the period of the rising may well have been confiscated by the postal authorities, who were certainly aware of the author's political sympathies. When the silence is broken by King in his letter to Lord Orrery of April 10, there is no reference to the activities of Prince Charles, and when a month later Lady Orrery writes to her husband, then a guest at St. Mary Hall, all is sweetness and light: 'Pray let Dr. King know that I thank him for his Letter . . . Desire the Dr. if he has any business to be done at Law, that he will employ no other Solicitor than myself. . . .'[2]

King produced one Latin work in 1746, *Hydra*, which appeared in print only in the *Opera*. A note on the title page

[1] Bodleian Library, MS. Eng. hist. d. 103, pp. 92f.
[2] Countess of Cork and Orrery (ed.), op. cit., Vol. I, pp. 312f., Vol. II, p. 214. King's letter is headed *St. Mary Hall, April 10th, 1746-/7*, which is an impossible date. But it refers to a 'new paper' called *The National Journal*, which first appeared on 22 March 1746, and was suppressed in the following June. The letter must therefore have been written in 1746.

reads: 'SCRIPTA EST HAEC SATIRA ANNO MDCCXLVI, ANTEHAC NUNQUAM EDITA.' The government was especially alert to the activities of known Jacobites for some years after 1745: King was wise not to publish this production as soon as it was written. The hydra, it is explained in the *Aenearum Tabularum Explicatio*, represents '. . . *nocentissimos civium nostrorum mores, numerosas ac detestabiles eas reipublicae pestes, quae quidem, quicquid conatur, et suis mandat Britannia omnino prosterni, vix mehercule paulisper reprimi nequeunt. Quippe alio Hydrae capite, id est, alio malo exciso, aliud continuo renascitur.*' Several variations on this vituperative theme are elaborated during the course of the 214 dactylic hexameter verses of this poem, to say nothing of the lengthy notes which accompany the text.

King commences *Hydra* with interrogations:

> Semper ego satirae scriptor? Sic omina nostros
> Significant nondum pacatos laeva Penates?
> Praeparat et terris infaustum Jupiter annum?
> Queis agimur fatis? Cum pulsum dedecus omne,
> Ac priscas patriae vires rediisse putabam;
> En, male sancitum rumpit discordia foedus,
> Mensque hominum perversa iterum fert omnia retro.

In a note to the first question, he provides a general justification for again adopting the role of satirist:

Quicunque artibus ingenuis est instructus, et in civitate libera diu vixit, sane hercle ei grave est et difficile satiram non scribere, quum adeo sunt civium corrupti mores, ut optimas hasce artes brevi perituras, et libertatem ipsam jam evertendam arbitretur. Quinimo talem scriptorem, animumque talem boni omnes debent amplecti, cum hujuscemodi scripta sint, necesse est, pietatis indicia et admonitiones officii.

The rest of the work consists mainly of the author's reflections on contemporary wickedness in general, and on a number of odious individuals in particular who are identified only by classical pseudonyms. A small amount of space is devoted to the praise of a handful of men for whom King felt a special sympathy.

The favoured few may be disposed of briefly. None of their names is unexpected: all of them were those of stalwart Tories.

The Duke of Beaufort, the two Harleys (father and son) Earls of Oxford and Mortimer, the Earl of Sunderland, and the Earl of Arran are among them. The Chancellor of the University of Oxford is paid a touching tribute by his former Secretary for his prudence as an administrator:

... Cujus constantiam et pietatem, quum optime semper meritus est de republica, ecquis non amat? cujus amorem fraternum, et erga suos omnes liberalitatem summam ecquis non valde laudat? Qui, cum veritatis semper fuit amicus, bonos omnes sibi amicos faciat, necesse est: et, cum nihil eo comius, humanius, moderatius est, inimicum, credo, habeat neminem.

The other persons who feature in this poem constitute collectively a kind of rogue's gallery. The acerbity which the author infuses into his treatment of his enemies is, in its own way, as powerful and revolting as anything from the pen of Swift. Like the Dean, he sometimes mixes his satire with humour. Especially venomous are the verses devoted to an Irish prelate '... *qui porcellas, ut jucundissime saperent, et succi dulcioris essent plenae, lacte novo vescendas curabat, quo tempore homines permulti in ea regione, proximi et etiam vicini, propter summam suam inopiam, aut caeli intemperiem, fame laborabant.*' This pontiff, who was quite possibly Josiah Hort, Archbishop of Tuam since 1742, had a simple argument:

> At quid ridiculum magis est, quam pauper obesus,
> Et plebeia anima in nitida cute? Dedecus istud
> Propulsant urbani homines; nec pascere vulgus
> Muneris est nostri: nobis nos nascimur omnes.

Immediately afterwards, another prominent ecclesiastic is ridiculed: Samuel Squire, chaplain to the Duke of Newcastle, Fellow of St. John's College, Cambridge, and later Bishop of St. David's. If anyone in his presence praised Homer or Vergil, he would say:

> At nos
> Versificatores vanos hercle odimus omnes,
> Qui nunquam cessant mentiri. Scilicet ipsis
> Legimus his oculis, ut quidam, nomine Ulysses,
> Ligneo equo invectus Trojanam everterit urbem,

> Et cunctos cives clava mactaverit una.
> Somnia quae, et tricae! cum non fuit ullus Ulysses,
> Ullus equus: sed nec de ligno animalia fiunt.

And so on. This piece of bathos is unlike any other example of the author's burlesque Latin. Generally King used prose or some non-classical verse metre for his doggerel effects, but here he showed that the hexameter itself could be used to produce results just as jocose. At the end of this absurd tyrade the speaker is given an opportunity to proclaim his unique version of the defeat of Troy:

> Fratrum par nobile quondam
> (Nam pulchre memini) fuit Hector et Hannibal: olli
> De regno certant: cadit Hector, et Hannibal urbem
> Vi potitur; monachasque rapi ad stuprum, monachosque
> Imperat occidi: namque hos bonus Hannibal omnes
> Ex *Jacobitis* natos cognovit, et ipsos
> Tam patribus similes, quam lac lacti, ut Polycarpus
> Testatur recte.

The note to *Jacobitis* reads:

Unum hoc verbum plurimum quidem, etiam mirum quiddam valet, atque iis, qui admirabiliter rempublicam et civitates nostras hodie administrant, non solum utile est, sed maxime necessarium; ut quod tributa et vectigalia facile augeat, milites alat, classem instruat, denique clamores, iras, plausus, risus, metus, motus excitet pro re nata, vel ad principum virorum arbitrium.

Another subject of King's mockery is Diaulus; his identity is thus alluded to in the note on his name:

DIAULUS sive Tartuffius, Anglice et Gallice *Tartuffe*, quod cognomentum homini ex moribus datum est. Is vero quemadmodum sacris initiatus fuerit, dein in purpuratum creverit, dein, ad altissima animum adjiciens, sedes ornatissimas et lucrosissimum sacerdotium obtinuerit, et quales hodie sint ejus gestus, habitus, negotia, facinora, machinationes, cogitationes, ex comoedia celeberrima facile perspicias. Ubi enim poeta comicus Tartuffium suum suis civibus exhibet, omnes ejusdem generis veteratores, ii cujuscunque sint regionis incolae, sane commode depingit. Sane commode etiam et jocose satis sui et Diauli nostri munus et artificium designat hoc epigrammate Martialis:

> *Nuper erat medicus, nunc est vespillo Diaulus:*
> *Quod vespillo facit, fecerat et medicus.*

Neque ego quidem miror, quod medicus nullius nominis in vespillonem primarium se mutari concupierit, quippe qui quaestuosissimum fungendo munus, infinitum scilicet mortuorum numerum quotannis efferendo, et sepeliendo, magnam pecuniam aut imperaret, aut corrogaret.

The author pitilessly rakes up some choice morsels of scandal to support the appellation of *Tartuffius*; a riddle and answer which he provides in the notes will sufficiently indicate their tone:

> Cur toties intrat lenae Tartuffius aedes?
> Ut doceat vetulam, quid sit amare deum.

One final character—Pothinus—is intended by King to be generic. His name is applicable, we are told, to all those who are *inconstantes et venales*. They are, as King indicates in various places, a not inconsiderable number. The original Pothinus was the betrayer and murderer of Pompey; it is significant that his name rather than that of any other figure in Roman history is chosen to represent those whom King considered the enemies of Britain and freedom. The author's castigation of Pothinus is thorough:

> Corruptius aevum
> (Quis negat?) hoc dixi nullum. Verum ecce Pothinus,
> Patricios opibus magnis qui adjunxit honores,
> Crimine perfidiae meritus, dum cuncta gubernat
> Ceu Plutus, ceu rex, aliis dans commoda vitae,
> Divitias, titulos; quam sunt sua vitrea fracta!
> Quam subito praeceps agitur! non fulmine coeli
> Percussus rapido, non passus principis iram,
> Non legum, amissis opibus, vel rebus ademptis.
> Temnitur. Hinc hominem luctus cruce saevior omni
> Nunc angit. Quid enim? nemo hercule, nemo salutat,
> Aut illi assurgit. Vitant juvenesque senesque
> Matronaeque nurusque omnes.

13—W.K.

These thoughts are developed and lead, two pages later, to the ending of the poem:

Quorsum haec? ne ignores, quam turpis distet honesto,
Laudato infamis, (quicquid male suadeat aula
Serviles animas) fas ut sit dicere, necdum
Omnis honos abiit, nec virtus nomen inane est.

Having digested the entire work, one is forced to the conclusion that *Hydra*, apart from its burlesque elements, is not dissimilar in character to its author's other satires in hexameter.

Most of the year 1747 seems to have been comparatively uneventful in King's life, but during a good deal of the following twelvemonth he was again in the heat of controversy. To start with, Richard Blacow, Master of Arts of Brasenose College and later Canon of Windsor, was convinced that the Principal of St. Mary Hall was responsible for what he called the 'treasonable riot' of 23 February 1747/8, the birthday of the Old Chevalier's son Prince Henry, Duke of York. Blacow eventually published his version of what happened in *A Letter to William King*, which appeared in 1755.[1] According to this account, Blacow was in a private room at Winter's Coffee House near the High Street at about seven o'clock on the evening of 23 February 1748 when he heard several gownsmen at the door shouting, 'King James for ever,' 'Prince Charles', and other treasonable words. 'Upon which,' wrote Blacow, 'I thought myself doubly bound to take notice of the Treason: Because I had taken the Oath of Abjuration, and had been invested by the University with the authority of an Officer in that particular

---

[1] Richard Blacow, *A Letter to William King, LL.D., Principal of St. Mary Hall in Oxford; containing a Particular Account of the Treasonable Riot at Oxford, in February 1747* (London, 1755). Three editions appeared in that year; the third was reprinted at Liverpool in 1813. The dates in this pamphlet are given in Old Style: hence the attribution of these events to 1747. The same disturbance is touched upon in Tobias Smollett, *The History of England from the Revolution to the Death of George the Second* (London, 1790), Vol. III, pp. 257f.; and Samuel Hulton, *Rixae Oxonienses* (Oxford: B. H. Blackwell, 1892), pp. 152ff. The substance of about half of Blacow's pamphlet appears in *The Gentleman's Magazine*, Vol. XXV (April 1755), pp. 168–70. A brief report of the disciplinary meeting of the Vice-Chancellor, heads of houses, and proctors on 11 April 1748 is printed in Vol. XVIII (May 1748), p. 214. One of the preventive measures here suggested is that all those in residence should 'attend in the common hall at the usual hours of dinner and supper'.

street.' He thereupon followed the rioters down the High Street and into Saint Mary Hall Lane, where he was forced to take refuge in Oriel College. Blacow indicates that one of the leaders of the disorder was from King's institution, and quotes his own words to prove the point: 'I am a man who dare say, God bless King James the Third; and tell you my name is DAWES of St. MARY HALL. I am a man of independent Fortune, and therefore afraid of no man.' A Mr. Knox, Gentleman Commoner of Christ Church, was one of those who later confirmed the treasonable expressions; he had been resident at St. Mary Hall, but had left 'because he was heartily tired of the Principles of the Place.'

It is extremely doubtful whether King had any direct connection with this disturbance. Blacow provides no evidence apart from vague insinuations. It is quite possible that the Principal was not even in residence; Thomas Carew, writing from Lincoln's Inn Fields to Lord Orrery on 27 February 1747/8, describes King as being 'in town' at the time.[1] A rebuttal to Blacow's pamphlet by 'A Student of Oxford' provides answers to several of his charges, as well as raising such fresh questions as '. . . what has Dr. *King* said against you which all Men do not agree in the Truth of?'[2] Quite apart from the Jacobite issue, it is certain that Blacow, by the time he was writing *A Letter to William King*, had read *The Toast*, and had not felt endeared to the author by its contents. King explains that he had

presented a few copies to some friends, on giving me their honour that they would not suffer the books to go out of their hands without my consent. One of these persons, however, forfeited his honour in the basest manner, by putting his copy into the hands of BLACOW, and the rest of the Oxford informers; but as they had no key to the work, and did not understand or know how to apply the characters, they were content to call it an execrable book, and throw dirt at the author. . . .[3]

King's controversy with Edward Bentham, tutor of Oriel

[1] Countess of Cork and Orrery (ed.), op. cit., Vol. II, p. 17.
[2] A Student of Oxford, *An Answer to Mr. Blacow's Apology* (London, 1755), p. 30. The author is unidentifiable.
[3] *Political and Literary Anecdotes* (2nd edn., 1819), pp. 99f.

College, which started a little later in 1748, helped to fan the flames of the controversy between the court party and the anti-Hanoverians in Oxford. Bentham, when he was an undergraduate at Corpus Christi College, had studied under the supervision of his cousin—and another of King's enemies—John Burton. In 1743 he had been collated to a prebendal stall in Hereford Cathedral, a promotion which was, at least in part, a reward for his known loyalty to the government. His booklet of 1748 entitled *A Letter to a Young Gentleman of Oxford* constitutes an indictment of Oxford Jacobitism: in the initial Advertisement the author emphasises that 'the Occasion of putting together these Reflexions . . . was entirely distinct from the late treasonable Disturbance in Oxford', but adds that they will provide 'some Antidote for the Use of his Pupils, whenever an Attempt should be made to tamper with their Principles, and withdraw them from their Obedience to the Laws of the Land.' The young gentlemen to whom this work is addressed are exhorted to ponder the words of the oaths of allegiance and abjuration, both of which are printed in full, and to reverence kings, even though they are but men. 'Their Province has Difficulties of a peculiar Kind,' the author avers with confidence. He praises the Revolution of 1688 and comments that those in favour of the principle of indefeasible hereditary right founded in lineal succession ought to search for evidence to support their opinions among the records of the Saxons and the natives of Wales and Cornwall, the 'original Proprietors of this our Soil.' He discouragingly adds, '. . . this Enquiry is beyond the Reach of Your Abilities.' Towards the conclusion of his argument, the writer returns again to the subject of the troubles of the previous February:

It is to be hoped, that the late Treasonable Disturbance will at least have this good Effect, that it will excite those Persons, whose only Ambition it hath been hitherto to mind the proper Business of their private Stations and be quiet, to answer the loud Demands, and earnest Expectations of the World; and wipe off, from themselves at least, that Scandal of Disaffection to his Majesty's Person and Government, which at present indiscriminately affects the whole University. . . .

The first version of *A Letter to a Young Gentleman of Oxford* seems to have been privately issued. In a letter of 27 May 1748, addressed from Oriel College, Bentham refers to his pamphlet written 'under a sense of duty both to the Government and to the University', and provides the information that 200 copies had been printed.[1] In a subsequent letter to Lord Hardwicke, Visitor of Oriel College and Lord Chancellor, dated 24 June 1748, he writes: 'The Bishop of Oxford having done me the honour to lay before Your Lordship the *Letter to a Young Gentleman* as I had printed it off for private use, I beg leave to present my Duty to Your Lordship with a copy of it as it is now revised and published.'[2] King presumably started composing his first reply shortly after acquiring a copy of the booklet. He was possibly engaged on this task when Lord Orrery wrote to Alexander Forrester on June 13: 'I have not heard from our friend [Dr. King] these many months. I have scarce heard of him, so that I can only guess he is in his Cell. I imagine his thoughts are taken up in preparations for the troublesome consequences that are likely to attend the late uproars and misconduct at Oxford.'[3] Among the consequences was a rash of attacks by anti-Jacobite scribes on those guilty of 'disloyalty'. One of these, under the *nom de plume* of 'Loyal Oxonian', argued that Oxford had since the time of Wycliffe been in the forefront of reform, and that

when some of the junior students shall be better informed, when his EMINENCE *the very learned C[ardina]l KING, the CICERO of the present age, shall have published his eloquent orations in defence of the Protestant Royal Family: and his Phillipicks* (divinae famae) *against a Popish pretender* . . . that learned Society will make full amends for the temerity and indiscretion of some of their rash and inconsiderate members, and no longer suffer themselves to be misled by some persons of *anti-revolutional* and *anti-constitutional principles.*[4]

As far as is known King did not answer this polite attack; instead, he published at some time in the latter half of 1748 *A Proposal for Publishing a Poetical Translation, Both in Latin and English, of the Reverend Mr. Tutor Bentham's Letter to a Young*

[1] British Museum, Add. MSS. 39311, fo. 58.
[2] British Museum, Add. MSS. 35590, fo. 75.
[3] Countess of Cork and Orrery (ed.), op. cit., Vol. II, p. 33.
[4] *An Epistolary Conference between a Reverend Non-juror and a Loyal Oxonian* (London, n.d.).

Gentleman of Oxford. A second edition appeared in 1749; there are only minor variations between the two.[1] This brief work is in the nature of a prodrome to King's second reply to Bentham, *A Poetical Abridgement, Both in Latin and English, of the Reverend Mr. Tutor Bentham's Letter to a Young Gentleman of Oxford,* of which two editions appeared in 1749. The author's original intention was to issue the poetical abridgement 'in six or seven numbers'; he changed his mind before publishing and put the entire work of sixty-one pages between two covers.[2] A knowledge of King's initial intention explains the fact that this latter book is actually a collection of several separate elements.

A Proposal, like its sequel, is tart and waspish, but amusing in a rather malicious manner. King announces that he intends to put Bentham's *Letter* into Latin and English poetry, and suggests, with stinging irony, that these two versions 'will sufficiently dilucidate my AUTHOR'S Meaning in those Places, where he seems most obscure.' In addition, he promises,

. . . I shall illustrate the whole Work with critical Notes and Observations, reconcile many seeming Contradictions, and answer all those impertinent Objections, which have been offered against Mr. B's Style, and Manner of Expression. For, (would you believe it?) notwithstanding our AUTHOR may justly claim a Rank among the *English* Classics, yet some of his Adversaries have been so foolish and impudent as to give out, that in this his incomparable Discourse there is scarce one Page of Sense. . . .

King insinuates that several satirical pieces relating to Bentham's *Letter* were circulating when he was writing: the following (probably composed by himself) is one of two examples which he provides of these 'childish things':

The political Letter, which lately you sent me,
Give me leave, Sir, to say, doth in no wise content me.
But alas! would you send such a Piece to the Printer?
You, my Tutor! who did so much better last Winter.

---

[1] The page numbering of the second edition jumps from 24 to 33, and all subsequent page numbers are erroneous.

[2] The private library of the Warden of All Souls College contains a copy of *A Poetical Abridgement* with the usual sixty-one pages, together with an added list of subscribers' names bound in but unpaginated.

Better? How? For last Winter I publish'd no Letter.
Very true, my good Sir, and there-fore you did better.

To illustrate his intentions, King provides two versified specimens of the initial part of Bentham's *Advertisement*; the Latin
version, he indicates, may be sung to the tune of *An Old Woman
Cloathed in Grey*, or the first song in *The Beggar's Opera*, and, as
to the English version, 'I will speak to my Friend HAYES to
set it to Music.' The first two stanzas will manifest the consciously banal quality of the writing:

1.

Men of *Oxford*, I tell you, (and faith! it is true)
Not a Page of this Work did I write with a View
To inflame our great Folk, or to hurt one of you.

2.

But howe'er, to cajole my good Friends at *Whitehall*,[1]
And to find out the Way to some pretty neat Stall,
Let me loudly declare, *Ye are* JACOBITES *all!*

The same stanzas in Latin appear thus:

1.

Non haec exaravi per fidem,
    Ut principes hos inflammarem;
At nec, ACADEMICI, quidem
    Ut pueros hos pessundarem;

2.

Sed aulicos viros & nurus
    Benevolos reddat ut quis mi.
Ut sim praebendarius futurus,
    Incusem vos JACOBITISMI.

A comparable level of doggerel rhyme, but expanded to
greater length, is to be found in *A Poetical Abridgement*:

---

[1] King provides a note to this line: 'The Reverend Mr. B. is one of the *Whitehall*
Preachers.'

LITTLE B——, who writes (and who doubts his Ability?)
Latin, English, and *Greek,* all with equal Facility,
Now collects his whole Force on a weighty Occasion,
And bestows on our ALMA a quaint Dissertation:
Reprimands the hot Youth, who so wilful is grown,
That surveying all Parties he sticks to his own;
Unreclaimed by his Tutor's Advise, is so steady,
That he fancies his Father, as honest as NEDDY.[1]

The Latin version is headed: 'EPISTOLAE BENTHAMI-
CAE SUMMARIUM, POETICUM, RHYTHMICUM,
MONACHICUM.' The stanzas corresponding to the eight
English lines just quoted read:

> GRAECE loqui, & Latine,
> Angliceque sine fine,
> Aeque calles, (quis est, qui ne-
>   sciat tete?) EDOARDE:

> Utque, qui vir nunc sis, data
> Occasione insperata,
> Constet; das consilia cata
>   ALMAE nostrae, EDOARDE.

> Culpas puerum, qui morum
> Imitator haud tuorum
> Doctus, amat meliorum
>   Partium esse, EDOARDE.

> Nec te audiens, pervicax est,
> Et propositi tenax est.
> Quid? quod probior te evax! est
>   Pater ejus, EDOARDE.

The versified forms of Bentham's *Letter,* together with the promised notes and observations, are followed by a further collection of Latin doggerel stanzas under the title *Monitor Monitori.*
This lampoon take the form of counsel offered to Bentham by
an anonymous junior:

[1] King's note to this line reads: 'Our Author through his whole Discourse
insinuates, that the young Gentleman's Principles are hereditary, and derived from
the Prejudices of his Family.'

Hac mente, BENTHAME,
Oportuit qua me,
Epistolam tuam legisse,
Nae mihi pergratum'st;
Et sat tibi datum'st,
Hanc talem pol me perpendisse.

Sed seriam, amabo,
Quam tibi narrabo,
Vicissim nunc tu audito rem:
Ni tibi sit places,
Ut mihi non vaces,
Nec feras me si juniorem.

The advice that ensues, like the verse in which it is couched, is nugatory, though it may have had some ephemeral influence as satire. An English translation of *Monitor Monitori* follows immediately afterwards, during the course of which Bentham is described as

Half a Casuist, half Lawyer, half Courtier, half Cit,
Half a Tory, half Whig (may I add, half a Wit?)

The next ten pages are devoted to a postscript on the subject of Bentham's *Letter to a Fellow of a College*, which presumably appeared while King was working on the earlier part of *A Poetical Abridgement*. This second *Letter* is dated 24 October 1748; the date that appears on the title page is 1749. It would be wearisome to analyse this rather pedestrian disquisition which is drawn out to seventy-two pages: it is an apology for the court party, laboriously compiled and well integrated, but exhibiting no particular originality. King's rebuttals are in places amusing, but have no more value than the arguments which they are intended to demolish. They lead to 'an approved RECEIPT, for composing a truly-loyal-political-rhetorical Discourse' in the manner of Bentham. From a list of ninety-eight nouns, the would-be writer is urged to take ten or a dozen handfuls, 'fairly written on square or oblong Pieces of white Paper,' and then to add

. . . a proportionable Quantity of VERBS and ADJECTIVES, selected from the best *English* Classics, and among the latter as many COMPOUNDS and DECOMPOUNDS, as you can possibly procure. Then throw in your PRONOUNS and PARTICLES, about two Ounces and a half. Let the whole be well mixed, and shaken together in a large green Bag (such as is usually carried after our great Lawyers) and then let each Paper be drawn out, only one at a Time, by any handy Servant. . . . Be very careful to write down every Word in the exact Order, in which it comes forth. And as soon as your Work is finished, send it to the Press, and serve it up to the Public.

King provided a similar recipe later for writing Greek in the style of John Burton: this second—and better—piece, which appears in the *Elogium Famae* of 1750, is obviously modelled on the original 'receipt'.

The last element in *A Poetical Abridgement* is a Latin prose paragraph headed *Academiae Oxoniensi*. Here King is serious again: '*Ignosce mihi, VENERANDA MATER, quod causam tuam hic jocosius leviusque agere institui, quam aut studiis meis, aut adversissimo tuo tempori conveniat; quum & ipse philosophus haberi velim, & tota tua domus fama ac fortunis suis jam periclitetur.*' He laments once more the activities of those whom he considers are damaging the university's reputation, commenting '. . . *audivimus iterum iterumque, (quod cum meminerim, horreo animo) DELENDA EST OXONIA.*' And the conclusion is devoted to a further indirect attack on those whom he considered the enemies of Oxford: '. . . *Neque ego quenquam hominem tibi inimicum cognovi, nisi qui bonis artibus & religioni Christianae sit inimicissimus; nisi qui exterminandam velit non dico hanc rempublicam, sed florentissimas civitates, sed universam libertatem, sed humanum genus.*'

One other humorous diatribe against Bentham remains to be mentioned, *A Certain Proposal of a Certain Little Tutor for Making Certain Reformations in a Certain Method of Education Most Certainly Practis'd in a Certain University*. It bears no author's name and no date. However, it is possibly by King and seems to have been issued about the same time as *A Poetical Abridgement* or shortly afterwards.[1] One reason for not pressing the claim of King's authorship too hard is that the syntax is loose

---

[1] The ascription of the authorship of this pamphlet to Bentham in Halkett and Laing's *Dictionary of Anonymous and Pseudonymous English Literature* is certainly mistaken.

in places: in all of King's known works, even when they are
written in burlesque style, the constructions are, as a rule,
trim and precise. There is also, by comparison with the
authenticated poems, an unusually high proportion of imperfect rhymes (e.g. that—educate; moon—known; good—
allow'd), though these could have been introduced deliberately. *A Certain Proposal* is *supposed* to be by Bentham himself, but
he was not such a fool as to write this kind of verse:

> What all concerns I advertise,
> Whether they foolish are or wise;
> All Fathers, Mothers, Guardians that
> Have Sons or Wards to educate:
> I. *E.B.*, long since known
> A *mighty Tutor* in the Town
> Hight [Oxford] and in [Oriel College],
> Expose to Sale a Stock of Knowledge
> Of ev'ry Kind and ev'ry Price,
> Each Chap to please, however nice:
> And all is good, I will be bold
> To say, and new as e'er was sold.

Among the subjects for sale are Logic, Rhetoric, Ethics, Civil
Law, and Theology. Part of the tuition in Theology, according
to the author, consists of instruction in praying to the monarch:

> For [George] I teach my Lads to pray,
> And *to him* likewise,—that's the Way—
> To pray to *him*, sure there's no Harm in't,
> From whom we hope to get Preferment.
> And, as the Catholics, they say,
> Ten times unto the Virgin pray
> For once they pray unto their God,—
> (The Thing indeed is somewhat odd)
> So we ten Pray'rs to [George] direct,
> For once to God we pay Respect.

The intimation at the end of the poem is that respect for the
House of Hanover is a matter of religious faith:

> In this Religion I agree
> T'instruct your Sons, if send to me;

A Tutor qualify'd for any
Or all of these Points, besides many
Others, which I could eas'ly mention,
Did not you plain see my Intention:
Viz. To declare, how much I'd do,
That I might serve myself and you.

Whether or not the Principal of St. Mary Hall wrote this stuff, it does express his known feelings towards the much maligned Bentham. But soon King's controversy with the court party was to increase in scope, the *casus belli* being his celebrated speech in the Sheldonian Theatre at the opening of the Radcliffe Camera.

VI

The Radclivian Oration of 1749 and its Aftermath

Ten years were needed for the erection of the Radcliffe Camera, named after its principal benefactor, Dr. John Radcliffe, who had died in 1714. After much initial discussion, the design of James Gibbs was decided upon, being preferred to that of Nicholas Hawkesmoor, and the building was begun in 1737. It was completed in 1747 and formally dedicated on 13 April 1749.[1] The fullest accounts of the ceremonies are provided in a pair of letters written shortly after the event by two Whigs of Exeter College: Benjamin Kennicott, the distinguished Hebrew scholar, and Thomas Bray, who later became Rector.[2] One gains the impression from both letters that King intended this to be his last oration, though in fact it was certainly not. Bray explains that the audience at the opening solemnities in the Sheldonian Theatre was anxious to hear King declaim even during the previous speaker's oration:

. . . Dr Lewis from one of the Rostroms made an Incomparable Speech in praise of Dr Radcliffe of half an Hour long during which time the Audience grew tired not through any defect of the Orator but out of Impatience to hear Dr King. When Dr Lewis ended a fine

---

[1] Some comments on the preliminary activities are provided in a letter written, with obvious haste, to Lady Newdigate, almost certainly by Sir Roger Newdigate, now in the County Record Office, Shire Hall, Warwick (Newdigate Letters, MS. B. 1999).

[2] Both letters are transcribed in full in 'The Opening of the Radcliffe Library in 1749', *Bodleian Quarterly Record*, Vol. I, No. 6 (Second Quarter, 1915), pp. 165–72. Kennicott's letter is also printed in S. G. Gillam, *The Building Accounts of the Radcliffe Camera* (Oxford: at the Clarendon Press, 1958), pp. xxii–xxv. Both letters indicate that King was in favour of awarding the degree of Doctor of Physick to the three Scottish doctors Pitcairne, Conyers, and Kennedy, whereas Thomas Taylor of All Souls was opposed. King's point of view prevailed, and the degrees were granted.

piece of Musick was play'd off. Dr King arose in all the Majesty of
Ancient Eloquence. Bless'd the Day in which he had the Honour to
Speak before that Illustrious Assembly. Blessed himself that neither
ye Infirmities of Age nor an ill state of Health deprived him of that
opportunity of taking his final Leave of the Publick as an Orator. . . .
Upon the whole the Speech was very inflaming. . . .[1]

Kennicott's description is in some respects less flattering but not
fundamentally different:

. . . amidst the Thunder of the [Sheldonian] Theatre, rose the great
Oxford Orator, & Patriot, Dr King, to deliver, as he said, his last
Speech to the University. He spoke near an hour, seemingly
Memoraliter, but, tis said his Son sat behind him to prompt him, &
to hold his Lemon. Strangers and Oxonians all agreed to give the
Doctor the greatest of Characters, as an orator for his manner, but
the Matter of his Oration was not so universally agreeable. 'Tis said,
that the Doctor had been previously desired to be decent in his
political Reflections. But—he was resolved to go off gloriously, &
to speak, this once, with all the Spirit of a Dying Patriot.[2]

Of all King's Latin speeches, this made the strongest impression. A model of periodic, neo-classical Latinity, it may be
compared favourably with the most mature orations of such
continental Latinists as the two Pieter Burmans, Jacopo
Facciolati, and Johann Ernesti. In it King adheres, consciously
or not, to the general principles of classical *compositio* and *decla-
matio* laid down by Quintilian in his *Institutio Oratoria*. In only a
very few respects does King fall short of Quintilian's standards,
for example in his disregard for the injunction *Male etiam dicitur,
quod in plures convenit, si aut nationes totae incessantur aut ordines aut
condicio aut studia multorum*.[3] This matter is referred to again in
the critical assessment of King's works which is attempted in
Chapter IX.

King commenced his oration in the Sheldonian Theatre on
a disarming note, describing himself in the opening sentences
as an 'infirm and forgetful old man, and already exceeding the
climacteric year' (i.e. 63):

Delegatum hoc mihi officium quum minime suscipiendum esse

---

[1] *Bodleian Quarterly Record*, Vol. I, No. 6 (Second Quarter, 1915), pp. 166f.
[2] *Ibid.*, p. 170. There is no authentic evidence that King was in any way prompted
during his speech.
[3] Quintilian, *Institutio Oratoria*, Book VI, iii, 34.

putarem, quippe verebar infirmus et obliviosus senex, et climactericum jam excedens annum, ut quid dignum aut judicio vestro, ACADEMICI, aut elegantia illustrissimi hujus coetus proferrem; sane quidem adductus sum ea, qua vos me semper prosequuti estis benevolentia, et amplissimorum virorum et optimorum civium admonitu, qui semper mihi pro ratione sufficiet, ut nequa hodie aut valetudinis aut aetatis meae excusatione vellem uti.

Special praise was then lavished on John Radcliffe, the celebrated physician, most of whose funds, after his death, were left to the University. Describing his liberality and piety King proclaimed, although without demographic justification: '. . . *vir qualis semel anno centesimo nascitur: et, si privatus esse debeat, semel sexcentesimo.*' The lofty grandeur of King's eulogies of Radcliffe may be fairly estimated from the elaborate construction and even flow of the following single sentence, written in a polished style reminiscent of that of Cicero, and consistently rising in tension, with striking use of syncrisis, to a climax in the words *deo auctori consecratam esse voluerunt*:

Quinetiam hanc, et alias omnes RADCLIVIANAS donationes ideo vobis gratiores fore existimo, quod pecunia omnis, quae erogata est (erogata est autem non temere, aut impetu quodam, sed optimo animi judicio) in istas sumptuosas aedes, in collegium Universitatis, in alimenta Academicorum, qui quinquennium in nobili peregrinatione consumere jubentur, haud quidem constructa et coacervata fuerat furtis et dolis, aut turpissimis venditionibus, aut iniquissimo foenore, aut haeredipetarum artificiis, nedum rapinis, et bello piratico; sed bene et honeste parta, laboribus et vigiliis, virtute et doctrina, et ea gloriosa arte exercenda, quae morbis et incommodis hominum medetur, et quam propter beneficium et excellentiam omnes gentes, reges, nationes deo auctori consecratam esse voluerunt.

Further encomiastic compliments were paid to *Radclivius noster*, until King offered Radcliffe the supreme and certainly exaggerated compliment of placing his fame above that of all other British doctors of both the past, the present, and the future: '. . . *quanquam in Britannia nostra semper floruerunt, et nunc florent medici peritissimi doctissimique, concessum tamen ab omnibus arbitror, neminem quemquam ad RADCLIVII famam olim processisse, aut posthaec processurum.*'[1] Briefer commendations were then accorded to the Trustees '*qui res RADCLIVIANAS nunc administrant, et RADCLIVIANAM bibliothecam exaedificandam, atque hodie dedicandam curarunt*'. They were all men close to King's heart: the Duke of Beaufort, the Earl of Oxford and Mortimer, Sir Walter Wagstaff Bagot, Bart., Sir Watkin Williams Wynn, Bart., and Edward Smyth.[2] 'I dare not, while they are present at my speech, offend their modesty by repeating their surpassing virtues before them', proclaimed the speaker, and then continued:

Pertinet autem ad exemplum dicere; siqui, praestantissimis hisce viris similes, excellentem animum omni liberali doctrina excoluerint, cui etiam accesserit summa vitae integritas et elegantia, mira comitas suavitasque morum, et, quod caput est omnium, singularis in patriam amor, et perpetua in hanc Academiam benevolentia; ii sibi concilient necesse est eam dignitatem, quae est maxime expetenda, gratiamque bonorum omnium, non modo civium suorum eorumque, quibuscum necessitudinem conjunxerint, sed quibus nomine et fama noti fuerint.

The one criticism that King made of Radcliffe related to the great benefactor's decision not to allow the Trustees to choose the Librarian:

MIRUM est igitur, ni indoluerint Academici nostri, prudentissimis hisce et integerrimis RADCLIVIANI testamenti curatoribus haud concedi potestatem eligendi bibliothecarium suum. De hac re aut male judicasse, aut plane errasse videtur RADCLIVIUS noster. Quid enim? Quibus tot possessiones, tanta pecunia ac tota haereditas credebatur, nonne iis alia omnia essent concredenda?

King did not answer his own question, and intimated that he would not say a word more on so invidious a subject.

---

[1] If one were to take King at his word, Radcliffe might well appear to be a second Hippocrates. But, as Munk remarks in the *Roll of the College of Physicians*, it is difficult to form a correct estimate of Radcliffe's skill as a doctor. He was not strictly a scholar, but he was 'an acute observer of symptoms, and in many cases was peculiarly happy in the treatment of disease.'

[2] Before King had prepared the text of his oration for the printer, Sir Watkin Williams-Wynn had been killed. An ornate Latin tribute to his memory appears in the published version in the form of a long footnote. King's letters to Sir Watkin no longer survive: they were possibly destroyed, together with other Jacobite records, during the fire of 1858 at Wynnstay, the ancestral home of the family. The remaining papers of the third baronet are in the National Library of Wales, Aberystwyth.

The designer of the Camera, James Gibbs, was then lauded for the 'superb and splendid library' which he had provided in Oxford, and also for his other sumptuous edifices in London, Cambridge, and other parts of Great Britain. King's declamations were no mere impersonal flattery, for he was intimately acquainted with the greatest architect that eighteenth-century England produced: '*Ego vero, sicut meretur, hominem amo veterem meum hospitem, quem humanissimum et amicissimum cognovi, et non modo architecturae, sed omnis vetustatis et multarum rerum bene peritum.*' Further gratitude was bestowed on the learned and munificent men of the past who had spent so much labour and money in founding universities and building libraries. King pointed out that one of these ancients was Asinius Pollio, who dedicated the first public library among the Romans. It was built in the porch of the temple of Liberty, and dedicated on the Ides of April, the same day on which the Radcliffe Library was formally opened.

From personalities King turned to the troubles besetting contemporary society. He inveighed with especial vehemence against those 'who delight in the slaughter of men and the destruction of cities, and cruelly contrive the ruin of those they govern as well as of others.' No doubt he was thinking of the miseries of the recently concluded War of the Austrian Succession, but he proceeded to establish a general maxim:

Qui primus invenit, quo artificio fingatur olla fictilis, aut texatur qualus vimineus, eum multo melius meruisse de omnibus gentibus, quam omnes duces (nisi qui pro patria pugnaverint, quales sunt nostri; et quos id propterea libenter secerno) quam omnes, inquam, duces, imperatores, etiam victores, qui nunc sunt, quique fuerunt. Porro autem mecum reputanti, quid vox veneranda, quid lex coelestis domini nostri Jesu Christi praeceperit, sane mihi videntur hi bellicosissimi heroes terrarumque domini nihil dilexisse praeter semetipsos, omnia metuisse praeter deum.

Like most of the contemporary Tories, King looked back wistfully to the days of Queen Anne: '*Et saepissime mihi gratulor me vixisse illis temporibus, quum neminem hominem Britannum puderet seculi; quum curia patrum esset sanctissima, et summa auctoritate praedita, et non tam publicum gentis concilium, quam tutela et salus.*' There

14—W.K.

had been a time, he informed his audience, when Britons had retained their ancient frugality and strictness of manners, together with a glowing zeal for the support of liberty. Their representatives had been chosen with the utmost care and foresight. No candidate could then be elected who was susceptible to bribery or the threats of ministers. But now everything was changed! The people had grown completely corrupt. They showed no signs of shame or sense of their pristine majesty. Their voting practices were especially deplorable: they set up their votes for sale in as public and open a manner as the vendors of meat or fish in a market. There was only one cause for the national degeneracy: '*Si quaeritis, quid sit causae, quamobrem plebs nostra ita turpiter se inverterit, usque adeo degeneraverit ab institutis et gloria majorum, uno verbo respondeam, LUXURIES. . . .*'

Further comments followed on the *politica calliditas* of the time, including some sharp criticisms of the Whig informers within the university. For withstanding the pressures of the Whig dons, the Vice-Chancellor, Dr. John Purnell of New College, was accorded particular praise: '*Videtur enim fortuna hunc excellentem hominem ab initio tot malis exercuisse, ut virtutes ejus spectatiores forent. Si quae enim res aliae, certe equidem adversae virum magnum faciunt, ostenduntque.*' A promise was given that the speaker's political enemies would be dealt with at greater length in forthcoming books which would vindicate the university. In the meantime, it was indicated, the position was so serious that only God could rescue the nation from the calamity and ruin to come. The orator therefore said that he would end his discourse with prayers.

There were five prayers altogether, each opening with the word *REDEAT*, in obvious reference to the King over the Water, though he was not mentioned by name. Some idea of the magniloquence of this part of the speech may be gained from the second *Redeat* paragraph, spoilt though it perhaps is by the personal antipathy against the Whig delators and informers implied in the phrase *infames delatores*: '*REDEAT simul magnus ille Genius Britanniae, (sive is sit nuncius, sive sit ipse spiritus dei) firmissimum libertatis et relligionis praesidium; amandetque procul (o procul!) a civibus nostris grassationes, caedes, rapinas, pestilentes annos, superbas dominationes, infames delatores, et mala omnia!*' The final prayer constituted a kind of litany of supplications, that the young men of Oxford might be modest, frugal, and studious; that the old men might be learned, grave, and honest; that neither young nor old might be corrupted by false tenets or the love of riches or honours and so on. The concluding petition was *' Ut nequis denique ambiat, aut assequatur Academicos honores, nisi qui fidem, disciplinam, liberalitatem, literas et literatos diligentissime colat; nisi qui, cum optime consulat, navetque operam reipublicae, tum prae-cipue Oxoniam nostram officiis et beneficiis omnibus augere, et ornare studeat!'* And with these words the orator resumed his seat amidst ovations of applause.

Shortly after its delivery, King's oration was printed under the title *Oratio in Theatro Sheldoniano Habita Idibus Aprilibus, MDCCXLIX. Die Dedicationis Bibliothecae Radclivianae.* On 24 April 1750 King wrote to Lord Orrery that his political adversaries had 'sold off (for I will attribute nothing to the merit of the Performance) the whole impression of my Speech, tho' it was the largest of any Latin Work which has ever been printed in England: and next week I shall publish a 2d Edition.'[1] He must here be referring to the *editio altera* which appeared towards the end of April 1750. There are no differences of any great significance between the two editions: some pages are reset in the later version, and there are a few extra notes. King gave away a number of copies of the first edition as presents to fellow-Jacobites; one of the best preserved of these is at present in the private collection of the Warden of All Souls College. The recipient, Sir Edward O'Brien, Bart., has thus inscribed it:

> This Oration was a Present from the Author
> My old Worthy Friend; the Great and Good
> Doct^r Wm King; Head of St Mary Hall Oxford:
> to his Admirer and Faithfull Humble Servt
> Edwd O: Brien

Near the front of both editions there appears the following admonition in block capital letters: 'SPERO ME IMPE-TRARE POSSE AB ERUDITORUM OMNIUM AEQUI-TATE, UT NEQUIS, ME INVITO, HANC ORATIONEM

---

[1] The Houghton Library, Harvard University, MS. Eng. 218.2 (v. 4), p. 71.

IN SERMONEM PATRIUM VERTAT.' Despite this warn-
ing, two English versions of the speech were in fact published,
neither written by King or issued with his approval. The first
appeared in 1750 under the title of *A Translation of a Late
Celebrated Oration*,[1] and the second in 1755 entitled *A Satire Upon
Physicians*. In addition, a short extract appeared in English in
The Monthly Review for November 1749. These renderings will
be discussed later.

King's speech gave rise to both praise and protest for a considerable time to come. Thomas Warton, in his poem *The
Triumph of Isis*, thus eulogizes King's oratorical powers:

> But lo! at once the pealing concerts cease,
> And crowded theatres are hush'd in peace.
> See, on yon Sage how all attentive stand,
> To catch his darting eye, and waving hand.
> Hark! he begins, with all a Tully's art,
> To pour the dictates of a Cato's heart:
> Skill'd to pronounce what noblest thoughts inspire,
> He blends the speaker's with the patriot's fire;
> Bold to conceive, nor timorous to conceal,
> What Britons dare to think, he dares to tell.
> Tis his alike the ear and eye to charm,
> To win with action, and with a sense to warm;
> Untaught in flowery periods to dispense
> The lulling sounds of sweet impertinence!
> In frowns or smiles he gains an equal prize,
> Nor meanly fears to fall, nor creeps to rise;
> Bids happier days to Albion be restored,
> Bids ancient Justice rear her radiant sword;
> From me, as from my country, claims applause,
> And makes an Oxford's, a Britannia's cause.[2]

---

[1] In the *Cambridge Bibliography of English Literature*, Vol. II, p. 320, Sir Harold
Williams wrote that the Radclivian oration was 'Englished, not by King' in the
translation of 1750. The Bodleian Library possesses three copies of this translation:
G. Pamph. 204 (8), Gough Oxf. 120 (1), and a variant, G. A. Oxon. 8°. 63 (3).

[2] Thomas Warton, *The Poems on Various Subjects* (London: Printed for G. G. J.
and J. Robinson, 1791), pp. 7f. This poem was written in the author's twenty-first
year. Richard Mant, in his 'Memoirs of the Life and Writings of Thomas Warton'
prefixed to the fifth edition of *The Poetical Works of the Late Thomas Warton, B.D.*
(1802), relates an anecdote told by Mr. Prince, the Oxford bookseller: '. . . Dr.

Another bard, calling himself simply DEVANUS, produced a poem in a similar strain entitled *To Dr. King*.[1] If the internal evidence is reliable, it was written in gratitude for a printed version of the speech sent to the author. It is certainly no masterpiece, but since only one copy of it seems to have survived, there is perhaps justification for reproducing the first—and the best—stanza:

> Accept, O KING! an humble Muse's Lay,
> Nor scorn the Tribute which she seeks to pay;
> Her slender Strains, tho' unadorn'd with Art,
> Convey the Dictates of a grateful Heart,
> And say, that all respectful Thanks are meant,
> For that most perfect Piece you lately sent;
> What nervous Sense in each pathetick Line!
> How the Whole glows with Energy divine!
> Soon may thine ev'ry REDEAT-Wish prevail,
> And Right and Justice hold again the Scale!

William Lord Shelburne wrote that, on King's introductions of the word *Redeat*, 'the most unbounded applause shook the theatre, which was filled with a vast body of Peers, members of Parliament, and men of property.'[2] Lord Orrery, in his letter from his Irish estate of Caledon of 2 May 1749, remarked: 'Your new acquisitions of Fame may please me, they cannot surprize me. Fame, if a shadow, must naturally follow such a Sun.'[3] When he acquired a copy of the printed text, he was particularly impressed with the tribute to the memory of Sir Watkin Williams Wynn. 'It is a felicity to dye esteemed, regreted, and sung by Dr. King,' he observed, 'because it argues

---

King came into his shop soon after the publication, and having enquired whether five guineas would be of any service to the young man, who was the author of the poem, desired Prince to give him that sum'.

[1] Bodleian Library, MS. Rawl. J. 4°.5.460.

[2] Lord Fitzmaurice, *Life of William, Earl of Shelburne* (2nd edn.; London: Macmillan, 1912), Vol. I, p. 27. Though the quoted observation, which occurs in an imperfect autobiographical fragment left by Lord Shelburne, is essentially accurate, as can be corroborated from other sources, His Lordship's information is sometimes erroneous. Thus he gives the date of this speech of King as 1754 and intimates that King introduced the word *Redeat* three times only. These lapses are undoubtedly due to what Lord Fitzmaurice, in his Preface, calls 'a complete absence of all revision'.

[3] Countess of Cork and Orrery (ed.), op. cit., Vol. II, p. 54.

the honour and happiness of having enjoyed his friendship *durante vita.*' The published speech itself he described as a learned present which must prove an honour to any Library where it is placed.'[1] John Cleland, writing in *The Monthly Review*, commented on the beauties of King's Latinity, 'beauties which, even were we abler than we presume to be, are incommunicable in our language.'[2]

Other commentators were less kind. On the day following King's speech, Henry Brooke, Fellow of All Souls and Regius Professor of Civil Law, offered his sincerely expressed sympathies to Convocation, saying, according to Benjamin Kennicott, that he hoped

that such a Concourse of Venerable persons had been now assembled, not *from a political principle but the Love of Learning*, & therefore was sorry their Ears had been so abused with Reflections on the Misery of the Nation—That the Man who endeavour'd to rouse the Spirit of Discontent by Insinuations against the Peace of his Country, (& by the Country must be meant the Laws, the Constitution & the King of it) took the ready way to undermine those Laws and that Constitution, which alone coud support both the University and Great Britain. And as he woudn't scruple to pronounce such a Man the greatest Enemy to his Country, & to the University, so his Prayer shou'd be, Absit ut Tempora sint iniqua Academiae, vel Academia Temporibus.[3]

Horace Walpole, writing from Strawberry Hill to Horace Mann on 3 May 1749, indicated obscurely that the prevailingly Whig government of Henry Pelham intended for a short time to discipline the Oxford opposition: 'We were to have had some chastisement for Oxford, where, besides the late riots, the famous Dr. King, the Pretender's great agent, made a most violent speech at the opening of the Ratcliffe Library. The ministry denounced judgement, but, in their old style, have grown frightened and dropped it.'[4] And even as late as the 1760s, the

---

[1] Ibid., pp. 65f.

[2] *The Monthly Review*, Vol. II (November 1749), p. 69. The authorship of this anonymous article has been assigned by Benjamin Nangle in *The Monthly Review, First Series, 1749–1789, Indexes of Contributors and Articles* (Oxford: at the Clarendon Press, 1934).

[3] *Bodleian Quarterly Record*, Vol. I, No. 6 (Second Quarter, 1915), p. 171.

[4] W. S. Lewis (ed.), *Horace Walpole's Correspondence* (Oxford: Oxford University Press, 1937–67), Vol. 20, p. 50.

echoes of King's speech were still ringing in the ears of John Wilkes when he was engaged in criticizing the University of Oxford:

Methinks I still hear the seditious shouts of applause given to the pestilent harangue of the late Dr. King, when he vilified our great deliverer, the Duke of Cumberland, and repeated with such energy the treasonable *redeat*. Was the conduct of the University at the opening of the Radcliffe Library, by their behaviour to the known enemies of the Brunswick line, and their approbation of every thing hateful to liberty and her friends, *worthy of imitation*?[1]

True it was that King had not mentioned the Duke of Cumberland by name, but many Whigs had always felt sure that he had been implied. Thus Bray, without indicating which of King's words he had in mind, wrote that the speaker 'Drew yᵉ character of military Hero's & without mentioning the Duke of Cumberland, cast Reflections that without any Violence might be apply'd to him.'[2]

Several of King's critics rushed into print, for the most part under pseudonyms. One writer, calling himself 'a Lover of Honest Men' produced a booklet, which ran into three editions before the end of 1749, entitled *Oxford Honesty: or, A Case of Conscience*. King's name is nowhere mentioned, but the title page clearly indicates that this performance was 'Occasioned by the *Oxford* SPEECH, and *Oxford* BEHAVIOUR, at the Opening of *Radcliff's* LIBRARY, 13 *April* 1749.' It is addressed to the 'Club of Patriots Meeting at the Cocoa-Tree,' a designation which carried political significance. The Coco or Cocoa Tree Chocolate House had been established in Pall Mall probably in the 1690s, but about 1745 had been converted into a private club for the use of its members, most of whom were Jacobites or their sympathizers. During the rebellion of 1745 it had apparently been regarded as the headquarters of the Jacobites.[3] The 'Lover of Honest Men'—in all likelihood a Whig of Exeter College—refers unmistakably to King under the appellation of Cataline, with his '*mighty Rumble*', and

[1] John Richard Green and George Robertson, *Studies in Oxford History chiefly in the Eighteenth Century* (Oxford: at the Clarendon Press, 1901), pp. 300f. For similar sentiments see *The North Briton*, No. XXXII, 8 January 1763.

[2] *Bodleian Quarterly Record*, Vol. I, No. 6 (Second Quarter, 1915), p. 166.

[3] For corroboration see Bryant Lillywhite's *London Coffee Houses*, p. 164.

'*sonorous Nothings*': '. . . an Assembly is called to *dedicate* the *Temple* of *Vanity*; at which Assembly *Cataline* harangues, and was *so* approved, *that* the *Speech* of *one* became the *Act* of *all*, and was as much as if they had said, one by one, "So we believe, and so we teach."' The author paints a rather unflattering picture of the orator who caused the 'horrid Din', noting his 'daring Eye', '*perilous* Look', 'Gestures fierce', 'mad Demeanour', and 'big Voice'. With what any impartial critic would regard as excessive harshness, he inveighs against King's Latinity: 'His Prose would *Cicero* be *amazed* at, as he would at the *Ease* where-with he *gabbles* it: And *Latin Verse* (for Verses does he make as well as Speeches) is so *peculiarly* his *own*, that he writes it *prohibente Musa, invita Minerva, Apolline nullo.*' In a subsequent note the *Templum Libertatis* is described as '*A String* of *Latin* Verses, which the Speech-maker's self did *spin*, and eke did *weave*, without the help of *Pallas.*'

Another unsympathetic observer, in *An Epistle to Florio at Oxford*, published in London in 1749, made a captious reference in verse to King under the name of Mezentius, the tyrant whom Vergil in the *Aeneid* referred to as *asper Mezentius, contemptor divum*, and in the form of several other uncomplimentary epithets. *An Epistle to Florio at Oxford* is generally attributed (for no good reason) to the nineteen-year-old Thomas Tyrwhitt, though King himself indicated in 1750 that he had 'some reason to believe' that this piece was written by a certain Sir Fitz, who was formerly a lawyer's clerk.[1] 'Sir Fitz' was King's appellation for William Melmoth the Younger: he could indeed have been the author. King provides in his *Elogium Famae* two characters of Sir Fitz, one in Latin and the other in English: they both clearly reflect King's conception of Melmoth's character. But whoever the author was, certain connections between his work and Warton's *The Triumph of Isis* will be immediately obvious. The author of *An Epistle to Florio at Oxford* tells his readers that foul faction knows how to play the part of a patriot, often to win the brave, unwary heart, and then continues:

[1] See King's *Elogium Famae*, pp. 44 and 56ff. *An Epistle to Florio at Oxford* was re-printed as the work of Thomas Tyrwhitt in *The Gentleman's Magazine*, Vol. IV, New Series (December 1835), pp. 595–600. According to Lord FitzMaurice, op. cit., p. 15, King was first given the name of Mezentius by William Melmoth the Younger.

'Tis thus *Mezentius*, haughty, bold, and loud,
With stoic raptures awes the admiring crowd.
Virtue and *Britain* are his pompous themes,—
Revenge, just Jove! the violated names.
What? was it virtue arm'd thy daring hand,
To deal rebellious slander through the land?
Was it thy boasted zeal for Britain's cause,
Reviled her monarch and despised her laws?
In tender minds perverted growing truth,
And fill'd her prisons with corrupted youth?
If such thy merit, who can grudge thee praise?
Go on, vain man, thy empty trophies raise:
Still in a schoolboy's labours waste thine age,
In fulsome flattery or in pointless rage.
Still talk of virtue which you never knew,
Still slander all to her and Freedom true—
Though crowded Theatres with Iös shook,
And shouting Faction hail'd her Hero's Joke,
Who but must scorn Applause, which K—— receives?
Who but must laugh at Praise, which *Oxford* gives?

Applied to King, as the author quite clearly intended them to
be, many of these verses are quite unjust. There is no evidence
that King's words had filled British prisons with corrupted
youth, and to regard the preparation of Latin speeches as
'schoolboy's labours' was paying scant respect to the long
tradition of academic oratory, to which, at Oxford, both Whig
and Tory dons had contributed. It was certainly unfair to suggest that the Principal of St. Mary Hall had never known virtue.
The Mezentius of *An Epistle to Florio at Oxford* is as much a
caricature of King as the Mezentius of *Letters on Several Subjects*,
written by Melmoth under the pseudonym of Sir Thomas
Fitzosborne. This Mezentius will be discussed in Chapter IX.
    Especially hostile to the Radclivian oration was the author
of *A Letter to the Oxford Tories*, who calls himself simply 'an
Englishman' and signs his *Letter* 'MIDDLE-TEMPLE, *Jan.* 1.
1750'. He is usually assumed to be Henry Brooke, who had
already taken verbal issue with King. He remarks that he has
recently read the published version of King's speech, and adds,

I have, I say, afforded a due Attention to this Astonishing Performance; am vain enough to think Myself Master of the *whole*
Purport of every Period in the Composition; of every reported *Pause*
in the *Action*, and cannot withold an Intimation of my Concern that
Prevalent Parts and masterly Talents should, at any Time, or on any
Occasion, be disgraced by the Society [i.e. the University of Oxford]
of *Slander, Obloquy, Faction, Sedition*; and that a Head, well-instructed,
is not always attended by a benevolent Heart.

The author comments that spleen and malevolence in an able
writer and an admired speaker are to be lamented as a public
misfortune. He then cautions any future translator of King's
speech with the words *Caveat Interpres*, and implies that such an
individual could lay himself open to prosecution for libel.

Of the several *censeurs* who assailed King's speech in print, one
alone made no attempt to disguise his authorship. He was John
Burton, Fellow of Corpus Christi College and Eton College, in
addition to being Vicar of Mapledurham. Burton was influential in Oxford both as a theologian and classical scholar and as
the protagonist of the move to introduce the study of Locke's
philosophy into the curriculum.[1] As the cousin and patron of
Edward Bentham, he naturally felt indignant at King's attacks
of 1748 and gave expression to his wrath in his Latin work
Epistola ad Edw. Bentham, S.T.P.[2] At the conclusion the date is
given as 28 September 1749, though the title page contains
MDCCL as part of the imprint. Burton's *Epistola* is a spirited
and acrimonious piece of denigration, exhibiting a constantly
dyslogistic tone towards King and devoid of any tincture of

---

[1] As well as helping to inaugurate the S.P.C.K. and the Society for the Propa-
gation of the Gospel in Foreign Parts, Burton is also regarded as one of the founders
of the state of Georgia. See H. B. Fant, 'John Burton, D.D., one of the Founders of
the Colony of Georgia', *Oxoniensia*, Vol. VI (1941), pp. 70–83. This article includes
the fullest available bibliography of Burton's works, though a few listings are
erroneous. Fant comments, 'In his career Burton fell just short of real greatness', an
opinion which would have amused King. See also Edward Bentham, *De Vita et
Moribus J. Burton, S.T.P., Etonensis* (Oxford, 1771) and A. H. Cooke, *The Early
History of Mapledurham* (Oxford: Oxfordshire Record Society, 1925), pp. 172ff.

[2] The *Epistola ad Edw. Bentham, S.T.P.* is always found bound with two other of
Burton's works: *Epistola Critica Graece Conscripta ad Joh. Gul. Thomson, Dialogi
Platonis, qui Parmenides Inscribitur, Editorem* and *Eulogium Memoriae Sacrum Joh. Rogers,
S.T.P.* A review devoted mainly to the *Epistola ad Edw. Bentham, S.T.P.* appears in
The Monthly Review, Vol. II (February 1750), pp. 342–344. Benjamin Nangle (op.
cit.) assigns this anonymous article to William Rose.

impartiality. In it, the Principal of St. Mary Hall is referred to as *civis factiosus, gnaviter impudens, praevaricans, levis et malignus, senex querulus et iracundus, intemperans, audax, fraudulentus, petulans, licentiosus, temerarius, seditiosus, ineptus,* and by a score of similar descriptions.

Towards the middle of this work, shortly after commenting, *Arrogantiam hominis intolerabilem!*, Burton provides a prosopopoeia supposedly spoken by *Alma Mater.* It is preceded by this explanation: '*Quoniam vero ille Almam matrem* Academiam *non importune minus quam familiariter compellare solet, nunc vicissim ea quae non vult, audiat quae vicissim respondeat Mater illa, sic cum sene filio injuriam hanc expostulans.*' She spumes for almost the next eleven pages at her objectionable and unruly sexagenarian son, exhibiting, for a mother figure, a repulsively dyspeptic kind of maternalism:

Nae tu nimium tibi arrogas, qui injussus causae meae defensionem suscipis, levis et iracundus orator. Quid tibi nomen praetendis meum, quod factis dedecoras tuis? quid, libidines profundens tuas, ad mea provocas judicia? Ego, illa ingenuarum artium, verecundiae, severitatis & decori nutrix, Egon'ut sim petulantiae fautrix atque adjutrix tuae?

She finds him quite unfit for the company of the orators of Greece and Rome; in fact, he is comparable only to the worthless monks of the middle ages:

Sed heus! quid *tu* tibi tantum arrogas, *tu*, in republica literaria *novus* homo, cujus ego ne nomen quidem ante paucos annos audieram. . . . *Tu*, nullius inter literatos notae, nisi forte illos sequioris aevi Monachos, homines ingenio sterili misere abusos: horum nempe tu famae invides, pseudo-rhythmorum consarcinator, eadem pariter experturus fata, brevis aevi scriptor; cujus laus omnis cum ipso risu plausuque, quem forsan ad tempus excitare potueris, illico extinguitur.

She keeps up this matriarchal bluster to her last indignant warning:

Scias igitur me pro amicis meis atque defensoribus habere, non illos, qui aetatem consumunt ignaviae aut luxui dediti, aut qui male officiosi rebus politicis se ingerunt, & dum factiones, nescio quas, fovent, se rerum omnium primos esse volunt: sed Illos, qui quicquid habent ingenii & industriae rebus impendunt meis, qui omni opera Religionis & literarum studia promovent praeceptionibus, autoritate, exemplo, pristinae illius meae disciplinae saluberrimae vindices, in qua unice incolumitatem meam atque gloriam contineri sentio.

At the end of the *Epistola*, Burton appends a postscript on the subject of the printed version of King's speech at the opening of the Radcliffe Camera. 'Do you ask what I feel about it?' Burton questions. He indicates that he recognizes the elegance of the type, the neat appearance of the pages, the art of the engraver, and everything that embellishes the work—except the natural capacities and the Latinity of the author. In this vein he comments:

Quod ad monitionem praefixam attinet—miror sane hominis magnificentiam, & de re tantilla tantam sollicitudinem. Postulationi tam modestae ultro favebit *eruditi* cujuscunque Lectoris sive *Aequitas* sive Prudentia; neminem enim arbitror ita opera abusurum sua. Ipse sibi hanc laudem integram sine invidia servet, idem Scriptor & Interpres: ea sane quae *sermone patrio* potius quam *Romano* prius cogitata fuerint, forsan & scripta, ea facili negotio in eundem relabi haud invita docebit ille mirus styli artifex. Quod si porro me Autore uti velit, admoneo, ut id ipsum, quod a plerisque desideratur, effectum reddat, orationem illam suam, colore & veste donatam nova, reddat *Latinam*.

One can only wonder on what evidence Burton based this assumption: the existence of an original version *sermone patrio*, either in King's mind or on paper, is not demonstrable from the Latin text. But without providing any corroboration, he thus concludes the work:

Video equidem quam periculosum sit expectationem magnam excitare, cum tam difficile fuerit eandem cum dignitate sustinere. Lubenter profiteor nunquam me de Oratore isto Oxoniensi magnifice sensisse: atque adeo, si suorum vota & spem fefellerit, at meam certe opinionem adeo non fefellit, ut etiam judicia confirmaverit.

In his *Anecdotes* King described his earlier treatment at Burton's hands as 'rude and dirty'. Determined to avenge himself, he produced three separate publications, all intended to reply to the *Epistola ad Edw. Bentham S.T.P.* Chronologically the first of these answers was a broadsheet, probably produced in the early months of 1750, entitled *The Wonder of Wonders or Fresh Intelligence from Eton*. Two enlarged editions were soon afterwards issued under the title *An Answer to Dr. King's Speech: By the Rev. Mr. John Burton, Batchelor in Divinity, and Fellow of Eton College*, and essentially the same material was reprinted as an appendix to King's third reply, *Elogium Famae Inserviens Jacci Etonensis, sive Gigantis*. The third edition of the broadsheet is the fullest. In it King translated freely the abusive names which Burton had previously called him in the *Epistola ad Edw. Bentham, S.T.P.*, and also the flattering appellations which its author had used to describe himself. In the *Anecdotes* King subsequently wrote:

> . . . I printed the whole catalogue on a large sheet of coarse paper, such as Grub-street ballads are printed on, and delivered the impression, which was a very large one, to a scavenger, to be cried about the streets of Oxford, Windsor, and Eton. And, in truth, this is the only proper answer that can be made to a work of this kind; for foul language and hard names, when a man does not deserve them, like an overcharged gun, will always recoil on the author.[1]

It is questionable whether this sardonic and vindictive production does King any justice. The satire is strained and unsubtle. On the left side of the sheet King provides free translations of the Latin descriptions that Burton used of him, formulated in such a way as to make Burton look ridiculous. Some examples will indicate how King translated his adversary's insults:

Spurcus: 'A filthy, sorry, rascally, bloody dishonest Fellow.'
Nullius inter literatos notae: 'A Man of no Note among *us* learned.'
Rabula: 'A wrangling Pettyfogger and Glutton.'
Assecla: 'A Spunger, Hanger-on or Footman.'
Ardelio: 'An impertinent Medler or Busy-Body.'

An *Errata* at the foot of the sheet relating to these last two descriptions reads: 'Not applied to Dr. King, but to the Vice-Chancellor, the Radcliffe Trustees, many others of the Nobility and Gentry, and nine-tenths of the University.' The phrase *Et adolescentes ex stultis insanos facit* is followed by the italicized words *This Sneer I borrow'd from Terence* and is translated 'And Dr.

---

[1] *Political and Literary Anecdotes* (2nd edn., 1819), p. 156.

King endeavours to make all the young Gentlemen of the University MAD, who, between Friends, are FOOLS already.'

On the right side of the sheet King provides equally free translations of the descriptions which Burton used of himself, preceded by the capitalized words 'I JOHN BURTON AM.' For example:

Ingenuus & benignus: 'A Man of good Extraction, ingenuous, honest, courteous and good natured.'

Judex vere Romanus: 'The only true Judge of the Latin Tongue.'

Vir sapiens atque cordatus: 'Judicious, prudent, discreet, and full of Wisdom.'

In the version of Burton's supposed *Answer* which appears as an appendix to King's *Elogium Famae Inserviens Jacci Etonensis, sive Gigantis,* King translates Burton's words *apta responsio!* as 'What a pat, clever answer's this to the old Doctor's speech!' Reading these 'translations', one may reasonably question how many readers would have been deceived by the ascription to Burton, and how much King helped his own cause by making his opponent's phraseology bear far more innuendo than the original Latin will support.

King's next answer to Burton took the form of a translation of *Alma Mater's* speech in the *Epistola ad Edw. Bentham S.T.P.* published under the title *The Old Lady in her Tantarums: or Mother Oxford Ranting at her Eldest Son K—ng.* Eighteen appendices are annexed to the translation. Only one edition of this work ever appeared: copies are now very scarce. The translator, indicated on the title-page as 'a school-boy at Eton', first provides a brief *Advertisement* which is transparently apologetic. He quite misleadingly represents his work as a very close translation, and adds: 'As it is but a *School-Boy's* Attempt it will be worth no *Man's* while to play the Critick with it. If it yields the Reader *no* Edification, he may thank the Author of the *Latin*; if the *Translation* gives him any Mirth, the Tribute then I claim as my *Own*.' The *Advertisement* is dated Eton, 1 February 1750.

This version makes Mother Oxford appear at least as rumbustious as she was in Burton's Latin original. A comparison between an extract from the Latin text and King's free translation of it—in places more like a loose paraphrase—will illustrate how the bravura of the original is preserved, while at the same time the speaker, *Alma Mater*, is made to look like a haranguing termagant. First, here is a portion of the maternal diatribe as Burton composed it:

Quid ergo tu quieta turbas? quid suspiciones, odia, & dissidii materiem foves? quid abalienare cupis animos, quos utilitatum communium cognatione oportet esse conjunctissimos? Siccine vero me defendis, ut Defensoribus meis invisam me, vel suspectam reddas?

King's translation reads:

Pray let me ask you one civil Question, what is the Meaning that you are always disturbing and breaking in upon the Quiet of *me* and my Family? Why are you ever raising Jealousies, and, by blowing up the Coals of Contention, bringing an Odium upon us? I am amazed that you should endeavour to make young Men run resty, whose Minds ought to be firmly ty'd together *by the Cognation of common Utilities*. A very pretty Manner indeed of defending Me, exposing me to the Hatred and Suspicion of Those who would be my Friends!

In the second appendix the translator provides an observation on the phrase *Cognation of common utilities*: 'A most uncommon Thought, dish'd out in as uncommon Expression. I don't remember it either in *Tully* or any Author of Credit but B —— n. However the Translation is litteral, lest I should lose one Grain of it's Beauty by Deviation.' The liberal number of interjections (e.g. *vah, heus*) with which *Alma Mater's* expostulations are sprinkled are variously translated 'Marry Muss', 'O, fye upon it', 'Upon my soul', 'Come, hang it', and by other such expletives. The general effect is so raucous that one is not surprised to find the translator commenting in the third appendix:

... I am afraid Scolding and Ranting are no recommending Qualities. If I had been *Fellow* of *E-on*, as I am only a *School Boy*, I would not have painted *Alma Mater* in such a filthy, *Billingsgate* Dress, but instead of an old scolding *Vixen*, I would have reduced her into a more mild *Mood* and *Figure*, and represented her as pitying her Children's Weakness, instead of whipping their Posteriors or boxing their Ears.

Nor does one feel inclined to criticize the appropriateness of the quotation from Proverbs XXV, 24, which is printed on the title page: 'It is better to dwell in a Corner of the House Top, than with a brawling Woman in a wide House'.

The *Elogium Famae Inserviens Jacci Etonensis, sive Gigantis* constituted King's final reprise against Burton's *Epistola ad Edw. Bentham S.T.P.*, of which it was intended, in the author's own words, to be a 'faithful abstract'. It is actually a piece of defamatory, macaronic persiflage, mainly in doggerel verse. On its title page, the 'praises of Jack of Eton, commonly called Jack the Giant' are described as being 'collected into *Latin* and *English* Metre, after the manner of THOMAS STERNHOLD, JOHN HOPKINS, JOHN BURTON, and Others', but no author's or editor's name appears. The book is indicated only as being 'By a Master of Arts'. According to the note to stanza VI of the Prologue, it was written in December 1750.

The first element of this production is an *Advertisement* which covers some eight pages. It is largely devoted to a mock-panegyric of the titanic characteristics of Dr. John Burton. He is called Jack the Giant 'not on account of his Stature or the Bulk of his Body, but in Consideration of his great Talents and the extraordinary Endowments of his Mind.' He is the best Greek and Latin Scholar that ever flourished in any age of the world, a most able divine and a profound philosopher, a most eloquent orator, an excellent poet, a most elegant writer of letters, memoirs, and travels, and a judicious and skilful critic in all parts of polite literature. The author explains that this is not his own judgement, but the opinion of the Giant himself, 'whose Testimony, as he seems to be sufficiently acquainted with his own Abilities, and fully conscious of his great Merit, is certainly superior to all others'. Not surprisingly, the Giant has constituted himself 'the Censor General and sole Judge of all *Latin* Compositions', and promptly took offence when King made the Radclivian oration in the Sheldonian Theatre without paying proper regard to his censorial dignity. King thus explains the steps taken by the Giant after the oration:

He immediately composed a Counter-Speech, as it was called, full of Fire and *Attic* Salt; which was read in the same Theatre by a learned P——, and with the best grace imaginable. And yet it so happened, that it was not well understood; and consequently had not that

Effect on the Audience, which might reasonably have been expected from so much Wit and Eloquence. Our GIANT, thus disappointed, was not however discouraged. He resolved to atchieve a nobler Work, and advance into the Public with greater Abilities, than he had ever yet discovered.

This nobler work was the *Epistola ad Edw. Bentham S.T.P.* The purpose of *Elogium Famae* is to give a 'faithful abstract' of the *Epistola.*

The main part of *Elogium Famae* follows: the style is deliberately jejune and banausic throughout the thirty-six stanzas of the Prologue, the forty-five stanzas of the main body of the work, and the two postscripts. At the end of the text properly so-called, the anonymous editor of the poem (King himself) provides fifteen pages of Notes and Observations, written mostly in English. These are followed by an essay in four chapters entitled 'A Dissertation on the Burtonic Style' and an appendix containing the substance of the earlier broadsheet.

The verses of the poem are written in both English and Latin: the English text appears on the verso and the Latin on the recto. In the first stanza of the Prologue, King invokes the spirit of Thomas Sternhold, the early sixteenth-century versifier of the Psalms:

> SPIRIT of STERNHOLD me inspire,
>   And hither deign to bring
> Not *David's*, but thy own sweet Lyre,
>   While GIANT JACK I sing!

The stanzas that follow are consciously trite and mercilessly derisive. The sarcasm as a whole is too drawn out and patronizing to be wholly effective: if Burton's mind were really as pigmy as King suggests, it would be inexplicable that so many of his voluminous writings were published *E Typographeo Clarendoniano*, and that he was awarded the degree of Doctor of Divinity only two years later. Furthermore, it is difficult to know which work or works King is satirizing. Most of Burton's verse, including his *Sacerdos Paroecialis Rusticus* and the selections in the better known *Opuscula Miscellanea Metrico-Prosaica* were published later than 1750. Perhaps King had in mind either a lost work or one of Burton's early publications, *Sacrae Scripturae*

15—W.K.

Locorum Quorundam Versio Metrica, which had appeared in
1736.

Whether King had a specific model or not, the *Elogium Famae*
has significance of a peculiar kind in that it is the only example
in English literature of a diglot satire in which the subject is
made to look ridiculous by having his own purported style
imitated in both Latin and English *pari passu.* It is somewhat
different in aim from *A Proposal* of 1748 and *A Poetical Abridgement* of the following year: these works, though macaronic like
Elogium Famae and intended to pillory one particular individual,
were not intended to be written in the *style* of Edward Bentham.
Two not untypical examples will indicate both King's satiric
method in *Elogium Famae,* and the inane, jingling character of
both the Latin and English versions. Stanza 6 of the main body
of the work, which represents Burton as addressing Edward
Bentham, reads in Latin:

> *Praestans ceteris incedis.*
> *Quur non quoque tu mitratus?*
> *Nam cum literas tot edis,*
> *Sane vir es literatus.*

The English version reads:

> Thus—Neddy you deserve a Mitre
> Much better than your Betters:
> For, since you are a LETTER-WRITER,
> You are a Man of LETTERS.

In stanza 3 of the first postscript King puts into verse one of
Burton's arguments against the Latinity of the Radclivian
oration:

> *Quod* Latinum *videatur*
> *Opus, juro (doctus qui no-*
> *vi meliora castigator)*
> *Esse* Anglicum *omnino.*

This stanza appears in a more brutal form on the verso:

> Next, tho' to some he doth appear
> To use a *Latin* style;

> The Blockhead writes, as I can swear,
> In *English* all the while.

Though John Burton is the main object of King's satire, a few other persons are criticized incidentally. Of these perhaps the most unexpected is the learned printer William Bowyer the Younger, who sympathized in his quiet way with Tory political aspirations and fostered in his heart a qualified admiration for King's achievements. It appears that Bowyer had in good faith passed some comments on the Doctor's Latinity, after the Radclivian oration, which had put King on the defensive. His lines in *Elogium Famae* referring to the incident were composed with considerable animus:

> Some, loudly as the Nightbird's screech,
> Profess Dislike; some hint it;
> Ev'n little Bowyer damns the Speech,
> Because he did not print it.

It is a credit to Bowyer that he accepted this jibe with comparative equanimity. In a letter quoted by John Nichols he wrote: 'Be it known that, for having hesitated in private conversation, and with the greatest deference, some doubt concerning the Latinity of an eminent Orator and Poet, I have felt the effects of his double talent of fiction and colouring, and have been thus figured and disfigured by his magisterial hand. . . .'[1] If Bowyer's words are true, King's criticisms of him would appear to be both unduly harsh and unjustifiably hyperbolic.

The Notes and Observations which follow the poem contain a number of miscellaneous references to corresponding passages in Burton's *Epistola*, together with some observations on William Melmoth under the name of Sir Fitz. King intimates, with reference to the *Letters on Several Subjects*, that Melmoth's allusions to him were obscure even to contemporary readers: '. . . because his several Descriptions of the DOCTOR (all under feigned Names) might, with as much Truth and Propriety, be applied to any other Man in *England*, his Bookseller

---

[1] John Nichols, *Literary Anecdotes of the Eighteenth Century* (9 vols.; printed for the author, 1812–15), Vol. II, p. 224.

was instructed, in a Whisper to his Customers, to decypher the Libel and explain the Characters.' Other droll comments are included, such as that of some of Burton's friends, that he should light his pipe with his *Epistola*. This advice, we are informed, lessened the regard that Burton had for their judgement, but not the high opinion which he entertained of his own performance. Rather more ironic in conception is 'A Dissertation on the Burtonic Style', which follows the Notes and Observations. It is divided into four chapters which are entitled 'An Excellent Greek Mixture to be Used upon Any Occasion', 'How to Make the Best Sort of Latin', 'How to Make an English Ode in the Burtonic Sublime', and 'Of the Burtonic Style in Satire'.

In the first chapter, King utilizes the 'recipe' method of satire which he had already employed against Bentham in *A Poetical Abridgement*.

Take as many Verses as you please out of *Homer*. Turn them into Prose by changing the Order of the Words: And be particularly careful, that none of your Sentences conclude with a Dactyl and Spondee; for this neglect may betray your Plagiarism. Then select a large Quantity of Phrases from *Lucian*, and a few sentences from St. *Paul's* Epistles; shake them well together, and mix them with your *Homerican* Prose. This MIXTURE will serve you for any Subject you think proper to handle. . . .

Similar advice is provided in the following chapter on the writing of Latin in the Burtonic style. Here King expatiates in some detail on the kind of Latin vocabulary to be employed.

Thus our HERO, perceiving that the Classic Authors had no one Word to express GRATITUDE, and that *Cicero* always used GRATUS ANIMUS (an unpardonable *Periphrasis!*) hath boldly introduced GRATITUDO in the Dedication of his *Latin* Sermon to Dr. GODOLPHIN, *omni honoris &* GRADITUDINIS *officio devinctissimus*. . . . Moreover, after the Example of this illustrious Modern in his Epistle to EDW. BENTHAM, you may freely use any barbarous Words, that are sonorous and give a Grace to your Periods, such as DERISIONES, CONSARCINATOR, FAMIGERATISSIMA, SUBSANNATIO, &c. provided always, that in the same Discourse you exclaim vehemently against all Writers of impure and barbarous *Latin*.

In order to illustrate his directions to the would-be writer of an English ode in the 'Burtonic Sublime', King suggests that he should be well read in Sternhold and Hopkins, and have studied their version of the psalms with as much application as a parish clerk. Some examples from Burton's *Sacrae Scripturae Locorum Quorundam Versio Metrica* are used to corroborate his proposals. King's comments on the poetry of the Vicar of Mapledurham can be withering. Thus he quotes two verses from Burton's English version of Psalm 137:

> *In* Babylon, *near proud* Euphrates *Stream,*
> *Silent in melancholy Thought we sat;*
> *And there with many a Tear bewail'd thy Fate,*
> *Lovely, unfortunate* Jerusalem!
>
> *Musick, farewel! our* HARPS *no longer please:*
> *They, like our heavy* HEARTS, *untun'd, unstrung,*
> *Motionless, useless, on the neighbouring Trees,*
> *In mournful sympathetick Silence, hung.*

King describes these stanzas as 'inimitable' and far excelling the Latin translation of Buchanan. He continues:

But what I chiefly here admire is a Discovery made by our great AUTHOR, which had escaped the Observation of all former Translators, Commentators, &c. For it seems, the *Jews*, during their *Babylonish* Captivity, were used to hang their HEARTS upon the neighbouring Trees, as well as their HARPS. 'Tis no wonder, after such a painful Operation, if the poor Men sate in mournful Silence.

A Dissertation on the Burtonic Style concludes with a chapter of observations on the steps to be taken if one wishes to be a satirist in the manner of Burton, for example: 'make a large Collection of Ribaldry, and of all the scurrilous Terms and Appellations, which are in daily use among the lowest of the People, when they are well heated with Gin and begin to quarrel'; 'converse, for at least six Months together, with Tinkers, and Coblers, and Barge-men, and Car-men, and Herb-women, and Oyster-women, and Cinder-women, &c.'; and 'preface your Satire with a pompous Declaration and strong Protest against all kind of Invective.'

Before leaving the subject of *Elogium Famae*, I think it is germane to suggest the influence of Swift on the composition of the vernacular stanzas. In a copy of Dr. James Gibbs's *The First Fifteen Psalms of David Translated into Lyric Verse*, which was published in 1701, Swift wrote some parodies of the author's efforts which are remarkably similar in tone and form to King's English verses in *Elogium Famae*.[1] Thus wrote the Dean:

> Poor David never could acquit
> A criminal like thee,
> Against his Psalms who couldst commit
> Such wicked poetry.

and

> 'Tis wonderful that Providence
> Should save thee from the halter,
> Who hast in numbers without sense
> Burlesqued the holy Psalter.

These marginalia were unpublished in King's own day, but it is possible that, through his acquaintance with Swift in Dublin, he knew of these parodies and allowed himself to be influenced by them. It would not be justifiable to put the case more strongly than that.

One other hostile pamphleteer should be noticed in the post-oration babel: his *non de plume* was Phileleutherus Londinensis; his treatise was entitled *Remarks on Dr. K's—— Speech*. Published early in January 1749/50, it constitutes a paragraph by paragraph critique of the published version of King's speech together with some slanted observations of a more general nature. During the course of this vitriolic publication the Principal of St. Mary Hall is accused, rather unjustly, of indecency, scurrility, insincerity, lack of good sense, madness, and a host of other shortcomings. In the past this work has usually been credited to John Burton, an attribution which was first

---

[1] On the rather obscure history of the text of these marginalia see Temple Scott (ed.), *The Prose Works of Jonathan Swift, D.D.* (12 vols.; London: George Bell and Sons, 1907–8), Vol. IV, p. 232 and Harold Williams, *Dean Swift's Library* (Cambridge: Cambridge University Press, 1932), pp. 41f. Both Scott and Sir Harold Williams indicate that a manuscript copy made in 1745 of these marginalia is in the library of Trinity College, Dublin. Several searches in recent years have not brought it to light.

made by John Nichols and seems to me to be quite erroneous.[1]
On the available evidence a far stronger case can be made that
the author was Samuel Squire of Cambridge.

The two most important pieces of witness in support of
Squire's authorship are from the pen of King himself. Perhaps
the more significant consists of his comments in the *Anecdotes*:

When I published the oration, which I pronounced at the opening of the Radcliffe library, I was immediately attacked by one
SQUIRE of *Cambridge*, who hath since been greatly promoted in the
church, and is, I think, Clerk of the Closet to the Prince of Wales.
He asserted that six or seven expressions in this speech are barbarous
Latin, though they are all to be found in the best Latin authors, as
Terence, Tully, Caesar, Sallust, &c. He was particularly so unfortunate
as to usher in his criticisms with condemning the phrase *fortiter &*
constanter sentire, and to spend three or four whole pages to prove that
this is neither Latin nor sense: that is, that CICERO could neither
write one nor the other; for this is CICERO'S Latin, and not mine.
See the third book of his *Tusculan Questions*, and his oration for
SULLA.[2]

And in *Elogium Famae* King, commenting on his critics, wrote:

See in this Train PHIL-LONDINENSIS!
Who proves by solid Reason,
Nor *Latin* in the SPEECH, nor Sense is,
And, if there be, 'tis Treason.

[1] See, for example, John Nichols, op. cit., Vol. II, p. 223, and *Illustrations of the Literary History of the Eighteenth Century* (8 vols.; London: Printed for the Author, 1817–58), Vol. I, p. 767; Gordon Goodwin's article on King and W. P. Courtney's on Burton in the *Dictionary of National Biography*; Halkett and Laing's *Dictionary of Anonymous and Pseudonymous English Literature*, Vol. V, p. 68; H. B. Fant, op. cit., p. 83; Harold Williams, 'The Old Trumpeter of Liberty Hall', *The Book-Collector's Quarterly*, Vol. I, No. 4 (1931), p. 40; and the British Museum's *General Catalogue of Printed Books*, Vol. 30 (1965), col. 806. A review of *Remarks on Dr. K——'s Speech* appeared in *The Monthly Review*, Vol. II (January 1750), pp. 229–35. Benjamin Nangle (op. cit.) has assigned this article to William Bewley and Ralph Griffiths. No suggestion is made by the reviewers as to the identity of Phileleutherus Lon-dinensis.

[2] *Political and Literary Anecdotes* (2nd edn., 1819), pp. 153–5. King was correct about Squire's appointment as Clerk of the Closet to the Prince of Wales: it dated from 1756. Much the same accusation is levelled more briefly against Squire—under the name of Samuel Squib—in Chapter IV of King's *A Key to the Fragment*, published in 1751.

His note to this section of the text indicates: 'This Gentleman, who calls himself PHILELEUTHERUS LONDINEN-
SIS, is the GIANT'S ARCH-SQUIRE. Soon after his
Master's *Latin* Work appeared, the SQUIRE published a
Volume in *English* replete with the same kind of Satire,
for which the *Burtonic* EPISTLE is so justly celebrated.' A sub-
note to the last sentence provides the information that this
volume was *Remarks on Dr. K——'s Speech*. There is no doubt
that King himself considered that Samuel Squire was the
author.

It is highly unlikely that King was mistaken. He knew personally several of the Cambridge dons who were in touch with
Squire. He expresses the attribution without doubt or qualifi-
cation. Nichols's attribution of *Remarks on Dr. K——'s Speech* to
Burton was not made until well over half a century later, and
then without evidence or corroboration. In any case, why
should Burton wish to conceal himself under a pseudonym,
when at about the same time not hesitating to expostulate with
greater vehemence against King under his own name? The
customary accreditation of *Remarks on Dr. K——'s Speech* to
Burton should surely be abandoned.

As regards the merits of the arguments presented by Phileleutherus Londinensis there is not much to be said. He lacks
Burton's sheer gusto and confines himself a good deal of the
time to quibbles over matters of phraseology. One of these was
King's use, alluded to in the *Anecdotes*, of the phrase *fortiter &*
constanter sentire. Cicero in the third book of the *Tusculanae Disputationes* had written '*Non et dicemus hoc melius, et constantius sentie-
mus?*' And in the *Oratio pro Sulla* he questioned '*Quis non de
communi salute fortissime, quis non constantissime sensit?*' And yet in
the *Remarks on Dr. K——'s Speech* we read:

. . . neither Poet, Orator, nor Historian, ever said *fortiter & constanter* SENTIRE. All these Kinds of Writers have said *fortiter &
constanter* AGERE, *fortiter & constanter* DICERE, and *fortiter &
constanter* DISPUTARE; but our *Speechmaker* is the first Writer I
have met with, who has dared to say, *fortiter & constanter* SENTIRE;
the first, who had not Discernment enough to see, that FORTITUDE
and CONSTANCY are attributes of the WILL, and not of the
UNDERSTANDING, and that whenever they are joined with any

Verb that is applicable to the *Will* and the *Understanding* (as in the *Verbs* DICERE and DISPUTARE) they necessarily restrain their Application to the Will only: Which cannot be done here in regard to the *Verb* SENTIRE, because that is only capable of being applied to the *Senses* or the *Understanding*, and can no more be *predicated* of the *Will*, than the ADVERBS *fortiter* and *constanter* can of the *Understanding*. The Blunder arose from our *Speechmaker's* not comprehending the Difference between *fortiter & constanter* SENTIRE, and SENTIRE *cum fortitudine & constantia*: The former of which Phrases ascribes *Fortitude* and *Constancy* to an Act of the *Understanding*; and the latter only expresses an Act of the *Understanding* accompanied with the Attributes of the *Will*, *Fortitude* and *Constancy*.

One may reasonably wonder whether arguments of this nature should not be allowed to pass into oblivion.

Remarks on Dr. K——'s Speech occasioned a letter to *The London Evening Post* which deserves mention. It was addressed from Westminster School on 12 January 1750. The author, signing himself Phileleutherus Westmonasteriensis and claiming to be a sixth-former, sharply criticized the strictures on King's Latinity which he had found in the work of Phileleutherus Londinensis. The pupilarity of the writer in *The London Evening Post* was almost certainly an epistolary disguise. The device of posing in print as a school-boy was sometimes used by literary gentlemen of the period: King himself claimed to be a school-boy in *The Old Lady in her Tantarums*. 'The REMARKER hath made several Criticisms on Dr. KING'S *Latin*,' the writer explains, 'in every one of which I will venture to say he is mistaken.' One particular example is selected

. . . on which the REMARKER lays the greatest Stress: for he says, 'That *Testamentum quo decessit*, is such *Latin* as would not save a School-Boy from Whipping': And I say, that the REMARKER ought to be whipp'd for not knowing that this is good *Latin*, and for being unacquainted with the elegant Writer who uses this Expression. If, therefore, the sagacious *Phileleutherus Londinensis* will not take it amiss to be instructed by a Boy in the sixth Form at *Westminster-School*, I refer him to *Pliny*, Book 5, Epist. 5, where he will find *Decessit veteri testamento*; and Book 7, Epist. 24, where he will find *Decessit honestissimo testamento*. The rest of the REMARKER'S Criticisms, and all his Translations . . . are of the same Kind, and shew his Skill in the *Latin* tongue to be equal to his Judgment in Politicks.[1]

This correspondent, whoever he is, propounds a perfectly valid counter-objection to one of the censures in the *Remarks*: indeed, quotations from the standard classical authors could be produced to invalidate most, if not all, of the author's trifling hermeneutics.

Very shortly after the publication of the work of Phileleutherus Londinensis, there appeared *A Translation of a Late Celebrated Oration*, occasioned, as the title-page indicates, 'by a Lible, entitled, *Remarks on Doctor K——g's Speech.*' Prefixed to the translation is a 'seasonable Introduction,' which is dated 15 January 1749/50. This publication must have been produced and circulated in a hurry; a brief notice regarding it appears in the issue of *The Monthly Review* for January 1750 immediately after the article on *Remarks on Doctor K——'s Speech.*[2] The identity of the translator remains unknown, but he gives every impression of being a wholehearted admirer of King. At the very end of his rendering, after having interpreted *REDEAT*, *efficiatque* in the three final paragraphs as 'Restore and prosper him', he adds a further aspiration of his own in the same vein: 'RESTORE and prosper him, that it may be no Crime to have translated this forbidden Oration; and that our great Author may have the Pleasure of forgiving his disobedient, yet honest, Translator.'

In his Introduction, the translator waxes with a certain eloquence on the general subject of freedom, and while doing so refers to King as 'the Favorite of the Muses, the Graces, the Virtues', and 'the Darling of Liberty, and all the Sons of Liberty'. He has no doubt that 'our great Orator' is a model of patriotism:

For while he hopes and pants for Freedom himself, he pours the same Spirit by his Eloquence into others; and whenever he makes a Friend to his Country, he makes a Friend to himself. If we admire

---

[1] *The London Evening Post*, No. 3464 (11–13 January 1750). Another letter relevant to *Remarks on Dr. K——'s Speech* on the matter of the Radcliffe librarianship appears in No. 3465 (13–16 January 1750). It is undated and signed simply 'A.B.'

[2] *The Monthly Review*, Vol. II (January 1750), p. 235.

the Knowledge of Books, accompanied with that of Men; the finest
Learning, adorned with the brightest Genius and perfect politeness;
if we admire any human Excellence, how shall we esteem the Man
who possesses them all? How shall we love the Man who devotes
them all to his Country? What an antient *Roman* in Sense, as well as
in Sound! What an antient *Briton*! What an *Oxonian*!

More thoughts follow in like manner; we are told that 'if Eloquence ever preserved a Nation; if *Tully* vanquished a *Cataline*;
if *Demosthenes* withstood the Power and Fortune of *Philip*; surely,
in these Times, our *British* Orator must be dear to every
Briton.' Only one fault is ascribed to him; namely, that of dis-
couraging unauthorized translations of his oration. 'In this our
great Patriot certainly judged wrong, or committed an Error,'
the writer observes. 'For why indeed should he refuse those any
thing, for whom only he bears to live, for whom he would dare
to die?' It is then pointed out that the great orator has many
enemies: '. . . every temporizing Dunce presumes to scribble at
him.' Amongst the works of King's adversaries is 'that doughty
Performance, entitled, *Remarks on Doctor K——g's Speech*, which
misrepresents every noble Paragraph, and degrades the Stile of
that excellent Oration, down to its own most wretched Dialect.' In order to offset this piece of misrepresentation, the
translator explains, this English version of the speech has been
published. Now every Briton may understand 'this noble
Defence of public Virtue, and may have the Satisfaction of
worshipping Liberty, in a known Tongue.' Ladies in general
should be especially grateful, he declares, 'since, in translating
Doctor *King*, I have gratified the reigning Passion of their Sex,
which is universally allowed to be *The Love of Oratory*.' The
Introduction concludes with a simile which is apologetic yet,
despite its imperfect expression, disarming: 'After all, it may,
perhaps, afford some Entertainment to take a View of Truth, as
she appears in a simple Dress, and unattended with the Blaze
and Lustre of *Roman* Oratory: As the Sun over-powers the Eye,
if we look at it in the Heavens, while its Image in a River may
be contemplated for ever.'

With the exception of a few lapses, this translation, though
stylistically inferior to the Latin original, gives a fairly faithful
reproduction of the speaker's meaning. The same cannot be

said of the English metrical version which appeared five years later under the title of *A Satire Upon Physicians*. This anonymous piece of doggerel is described as a 'heroic paraphrase': it bears as much relationship to King's oration as Henri de Picou's travesty *L'Odyssée d'Homère* does to the original which inspired it. King's words

... quippe verebar infirmus & obliviosus senex, & climactericum jam excedens annum. ...

appear as

> In me, ah! pity to behold!
> A Wretch quite wither'd, weak, and old;
> Who now has pass'd, by heaven's decree,
> The dangerous year of *Sixty-three*. ...

An example of his forgetfulness (not in the original) is gratuitously provided:

> My memory oft mistaking names,
> For G——RGE, I often thing of J—MES;
> Am grown so feeble frail a Thing,
> I scarce remember *who is King!*
> Th' imperial purple which does wear,
> A lawful or a lawless Heir!

It is only fair to add that *A Satire Upon Physicians*, considered as a piece of pure mockery, shows intermittently a certain cleverness. For example, King, in describing the virtues of Radcliffe as a physician, had proclaimed:

... tam simplici et aperto erat pectore, ut, abhorrens ab aliorum consuetudine, nihil simularet aut dissimularet, nihil aegrotantibus sycophantiose faceret, aut diceret, ad captandum favorem, ne regibus quidem; sed ex animo omnia, planissime verissimeque.

The version of 1755 reads (in part):

> Whene'er he took a patient's Fee,
> He chose the open way and free;
> (Unlike those Sycophants, who tell
> A gasping wretch, he'd soon be well)

Told rich and poor, both low and high,
That kings, like slaves, were born to die;
Nor whisper'd it, but spoke aloud—
'—Dear friend, prepare to buy your Shrowd! . . .
That Hectic Cough you'll quickly rue,
Which soon will split your lungs in two.
You sigh so deep, and heave and pant,
A coffin, Sir, is all you want.
Think on your Parson and your Text,
You'll want 'em both by *Sunday* next;
Your sins and failings, great and small,
E'er 'tis too late, repent of all;
No julep, potion, dose, or pill,
Could ever cure a man so ill;
Then send for wax, and sign your will.'

In his speech King had continued:

Ex quo illud assequebatur, ut fides sua et integritas esset specta-
tissima; utque ii, quibus remedia adhibebat, res familiares et
domesticas placide et ordinate disponerent; liberis, propinquis,
amicis bene consulerent; et sive convalescerent, sive mortem
obirent, summa gratia illustri medico haberetur.

In the 1755 version Dr. Radcliffe is made to continue his mock-
lugubrious advice to his patients:

And e'er you leave the world, provide
For your next heir, and weeping Bride;
Fixing what Portions you think due
To *Jack* and *Harry*, *Kate* and *Sue*.

The doctor's recommendations are followed, but the disjunct
sive convalescerent is quietly suppressed:

Such counsel, kindly thus exprest,
Was welcome to the patient's breast:
With whose advice the wretch complied,
Paid him his usual Fee—and died.

Perhaps the best method of demonstrating how the Anglicized
versions of King's speech differ from their original is to select
one portion from the Latin text and compare it to its English

counterparts. The third *REDEAT* paragraph, which consists of one sentence only, will serve well enough for this purpose:

REDEAT, efficiatque, ut revirescat respublica, revocetur fides, firmetur pax, sanciantur leges justae, honestae, salutares, utiles, quae deterreant improbos, coerceant milites, faveant doctis, ignoscant imprudentibus, sublevent egenos, delectent omnes; omnes nunc demum a periculis litium ita liberando, ut nequis omnino unquam civis ingenuus, innocens, indemnatus vexetur, multetur, spolietur.

Three English renderings of this paragraph were printed. The first appeared as part of John Cleland's article in *The Monthly Review* of November 1749 on the published text of King's *Oratio*. There we read:

RETURN, with effect return! that the national good may reflourish, faith be restored, peace confirmed; that just, honourable, salutary, useful laws may be enacted: Laws which may discourage the wicked, keep the military within due bounds, favour learning, forgive the imprudent, relieve the indigent, and give general satisfaction; especially in a general deliverance of all from the dangers of law-oppression, insomuch that no free-born subject, unattainted, and without legal condemnation, shall be harassed, fined, and plundered.[1]

The next English version to be offered to the public is to be found in the anonymous translation of 1750:

RESTORE and prosper him, that the Common-wealth may revive, Faith be recall'd, Peace established, Laws ordained, just, honest, salutary, useful Laws, to deter the Abandoned, restrain Armies, favour the Learned, spare the Imprudent, relieve the Poor, delight all; by delivering all at length from the Perils of Law, that no ingenuous Subject, innocent, uncondemned, may ever more be tormented, fined, plundered.

Already one of the effects of King's studied ambiguity is apparent. In the original Latin, the subject of *REDEAT* could be, if the text is taken literally, either *Astraea nostra, aut quocunque nomine malit vocari ipsa Justitia* (in the first paragraph of the peroration) or *magnus ille Genius Britanniae* (in the subsequent paragraph). In the 1749 translation the matter is left open; in that of 1750 the *Genius Britanniae* is implied. Both translations

---

[1] *The Monthly Review*, Vol. II (November 1749), p. 70.

allow for the innuendo which the audience understood, as evidenced by their applause. And even in that matter there is room for more than one interpretation: I assume that King's aspiration was the return of James III, though he *could* be referring to Prince Charles, who was by this time the individual in whom the Jacobites placed their greatest hopes. On the whole there is not a great deal to choose between these two Englished versions: both adhere closely to the form and structure of the original, while at the same time exhibiting small liberties in vocabulary and syntax. The metrical version of 1755, on the other hand, is nothing more than a free parody. Here the writer assumes that the subject of *REDEAT* is *Astraea*, but proceeds to call her a 'sacred goddess', despite the fact that the orator has already called her *Christianissima virgo*.

> Once more, *Astraea*! visit earth,
> A sacred goddess by thy birth!
> Thy antient seat once more regain,
> Preside in courts, in senates reign;
> Thou Goddess, thou, ah! clip the claws,
> Of all our cruel harpy laws;
> That people may enjoy their ease,
> And use their inkhorns, as they please;
> Let not the guiltless feel thy strokes,
> For a few harmless merry Jokes;
> Unheard their cause, be sent to jail,
> For healths, when overcome with ale;
> Who ne'er were known once to commit
> Such frolics in a sober fit;
> In every college, every hall,
> Good, loyal, serious subjects all:
> And zealous for the royal line,
> In none more zealous than in mine.
> To me who pay a just regard;
> Who often pray, and study hard;
> Fond of the precepts I instil,
> Nor ever act against my will.

It is worth remarking that during the period of literary contention immediately following the speech, Lord Orrery actively exerted his influence on King's side. On 23 January 1749/50 he wrote from Dublin to Theobald Russell:

His [i.e. King's] friendship to you is an instance of the excellence of his heart, which I have always observed to be entirely equal to the excellence of his head: each superior to the common run of mankind. He blooms and becomes splendid at a time of life when other men wither and grow dim. His lustre is the same if not greater in his evening than in the noontide of his day. Worship him, if you will oblige me. He desires, He expects, He will receive no other adoration than that of sincerity and honour.[1]

The spectacle of the controversy between King and his Whig antagonists seemed to Orrery comparable to an eagle against any army of frogs. He used the same simile nine days later in a letter to William Cowper. There he commented, with regard to a now unidentifiable publication:

A virulent paper or pamphlet against Dr. King has been shewn to me lately. I know not the Author, but he seems almost as severe upon Dr. Ratcliffe and the Trustees as upon Dr. King. He is very dull, and yet his scurrility is of a kind that ought to be answered. In the mean time the Doctor appears to me like a noble Eagle flying high in the air and basking himself in the Sun, while his enemies are like so many frogs croaking in a dirty pool, and constantly pelted, whenever they thrust up their heads thro' the scum of the water.[2]

And to King himself on the following April 7 he remarked:

When I find you engaged against low adversaries, and see you smiting every impertinent Insect that crawls upon your Skirts, you appear to me, like Hercules stooping to brush off flies. Victory must attend you every where; whether you think fit to combat with Giants, and Hydras, or amuse yourself, in destroying moths and woodlice.[3]

For Orrery's moral support, the Principal of St. Mary Hall was duly grateful:

... your approbation of my Speech has given me great pleasure, especially at this juncture, when I am attacked by all Orders and

[1] Countess of Cork and Orrery (ed.), op. cit., Vol. II, p. 66.
[2] Ibid., pp. 67f.
[3] The Houghton Library, Harvard University, MS. Eng. 218.2 (v. 5), p. 41.

Professions, by all Sects and religions and No-religions, by Giants and Knights, Squires and Dwarfs, Women and Children. These new Criticks will allow me no more learning than Melmoth will allow me morals. . . . But under all these persecutions. . . . I am conscious to myself that I have done my duty in that station in which I have been placed to the best of my skill and judgement.[1]

King produced one further work on the subject of the attacks made on his speech of 13 April 1749. This was an eristic dialogue in Latin verse entitled *Monitor*, which was never actually published. Nowadays it is to be found only in the *Opera*. According to the title-page, this work was written in 1749 (SCRIPTUS EST HOC DIALOGUS ANNO MDCCXLIX) and had not been in print before the final compilation of the *Opera* (NUMQUAM ANTEHAC EDITUS). Parts of the notes must have been written later than 1749 as their content clearly shows. Though it seems to have been generally unknown in King's own lifetime, this poem provides valuable insights into the trend of his thinking subsequent to his celebrated speech. Once again, the comprehension of the modern reader is hampered by the absence of a key: Aulus is clearly King and Aulicus is his opponent, but many of the other names cannot be attributed to particular individuals with any degree of certainty.

The occasion for writing *Monitor* is explained by King in his footnote to the first line of the poem:

Incredible est dictu, postquam orationem habui in theatro Sheldoniano, die dedicationis bibliothecae Radclivianae, quanta in offensa fuerim apud eos omnes, qui aulae deserviunt, consiliarios, milites, medicos, causidicos, lenones, mimos, parasitos, delatores, maxime vero sacerdotes purpuratos, et non purpuratos; qui quidem, quisque suo more ac tempore, me petebant, et maledictis insectabantur. Ex iis insigniores quosdam notavi, graviore fortassis animadversione posthac coercendos.

Monitor commences with an address by Aulicus to Aulus:

Vane senex, frustra contendis rhetor haberi,
Si laudare parum est, ni tu dicteria fundas,
Et regum offendas socios. Commendat amicum
Vir catus experiensque? haud dulcibus acria miscet,

[1] Countess of Cork and Orrery (ed.), op. cit., Vol. II, p. 68.

16—W.K.

> Auditorum animos irritans. Nesciat uti
> Fortuna rebusque suis, qui Tempora! clamat,
> Et procerum mores, propiusque inquirit in aulam.
> Nil te commoneat Libertas vincta catenis,
> Arcesque invisae, et rabidi perjuria Byrrhi,
> Et Taurus judex, comitumque exempla tuorum,
> Cum miser hic periit cruce, percussusque securi
> Ille jacet; dum quae nostro pars exulat orbe
> Miratur, quod sit tam mitis numinis ira?
> Sic quoque mireris! Neque enim veterisque sodalis,
> Officiique memor tibi quid violentius opto;
> Si modo desieris, monitusque HEROA, DUCEMQUE—[1]

At this point Aulicus is interrupted by Aulus who asks complainingly:

> Aulice, quo properas, horrenda, extrema minatus
> Indigno? quid enim peccavi, ut publica verba
> Sermonesque pios sceleris tu nomine damnes?

A good deal of the rest of the poem is an attempt by Aulicus to answer these questions. He argues that Aulus should stop praising liberty and attacking the court. Aulus naturally refuses to take this advice, implying that if he were to do so, men could write of him in the future (in capitals): VENDIDIT HIC AURO PATRIAM. Aulicus considers the arguments of Aulus to be worthless, and comments:

> > Ah! somnia narras,
> More senum.

Thence he enlarges on his objections for three and a half pages, to be answered by Aulus, who argues against his standpoint for another two. Aulicus then coolly tells Aulus, *Re tota errasti*. The dialogue ends in an impasse six pages later, without any definite conclusions having been reached on either side. Aulus, for his part, is unruffled, and the poem concludes on an autobiographical note with his saying:

---

[1] Byrrhus and Taurus are only two of the unidentifiable designations in this poem. A deliberately vague paragraph is provided on Byrrhus in the notes; of Taurus, King writes merely: *Ut tuto sim, de Tauri judicio, quisquis ille, et id qualecunque, tali tempore sileatur.*

Attamen aequo animo, non ullis rebus egenus,
Non inhonoratus vixi: neque gratius usquam
Dii munus dederunt, cui se favisse fatentur.

There is a certain stale quality about the argumentation in *Monitor*. The poet presents very few, if any, ideas which he had not already used or implied in his earlier works of the same decade. The principal value of this poem, apart from its Latinity, lies in the incidental light which it sheds on King himself and persons known to him. In this respect the notes, which are very full and detailed, are often more interesting than the 216 verses of the text. Thus one long footnote deals splenetically with GIGANTA, who can hardly be anyone other than John Burton. King explains that on the day of the Radcliffe oration, there was present by chance a certain *S.T.B. ex grammatistarum grege*. Scarcely had the oration finished,

. . . cum homo incenditur, furit, cursitat huc et illuc, me calumniatur, horribiles strages mihi minatur. Itaque postquam secessit, se ad scribendum comparat, librum conficit, orationi meae respondet, singula refutat; deinde librum, quem imprimendum curat, magnifice ostentat, ingenium suum venditat, se victorem appellat, triumphum canit.

The book in question can only be the *Epistola ad Edw. Bentham S.T.P.* As King intimated elsewhere, it was published against the advice of his friends, and only after some hesitation on the writer's part:

Dehortantibus vero amicis, ne librum edat, quum nulla ei a me orta fuisset injuria, primum repugnat; deinde labascit, mitescit, librum tandem indignatus abjicit, quasi facti ipsius eum puderet. Aliquot post menses iterum vehementissime commovetur grammatista noster, ne tum quidem aut verbo ullo, aut scripto a me violatus; disputat, clamat, latrat, in me bacchatur in circulis omnium, doctorum, indoctorum, bonorum, malorum, puerorum, puerarum. Quem abjecerat libellum, retrahit, recognoscit, emendat, auget, et, spretis demum amicorum consiliis, emittit.

The opinion that King here expresses on Burton's *Epistola* is what one would expect:

Qualem vero, dii boni, libellum! in quo nihil inest ingenii, aut doctrinae, ne quidem criticae, quam mehercule artem homo

opiniosissimus totam vult esse suam. Qualem vero! non modo sacer-
dote Christiano, sed homine ingenuo, sed quovis homine indignum:
quandoquidem nulla est hujus pars opusculi summae expers turpi-
tudinis, cum propter maledicta, quae ex trivio et miserae plebeculae
convitiis scriptor arripuit, mihique ultro ingessit, tum propter miras
sane et numerosas laudes, quae quum de uno nemine haberi possint,
eas sibi arrogat, et nomini suo libat gloriosus.

Later on, so King alleges, Burton underwent a softening of
heart, a condition which the author of *Monitor* associates with
mental sickness. Incidentally, he does not allude to this particular development in any other place:

Ex quo fit, ut, cum aliis ludibrio, aliis contemptui, aliis odio, suis
omnibus sit dedecori, magnam quidem mihi misericordiam com-
moveat. Quippe qui plane ea aegritudine et aegrotatione mentis,
in quam incidere solent invidi et malevoli omnes, usque adeo
opprimitur, ut indies ingravescente morbo, caput insanabile, vel
Hippocrate nostro judice, esse videatur.

When Aulus speaks of the *stolidi Armigeri convicia* he can be
referring only to Samuel Squire. In a note King refers his readers
to a verse in *Hydra* containing the phrase *Bellulus hic Abbas*. His
explanation of the phrase leaves no room for doubt concerning
the identity of the *Abbas*: 'In carminibus meis Gaurus, sive Armiger
appellatur; in scriptis suis Archimagirus, Archimimus, Phileleutherus,
aliisque polysyllabis titulis insignitur; a Cantabrigiensibus vero plane
rustice vocatur Fax, et Faex, quae quidem nomina ei addita sunt, et
imposita tum a vitae et generis conditione, tum a studiis et facinoribus
suis.' In *Monitor* King provides additional corroboration for this
identification. When writing of the Giant's Squire, he comments: '. . . si eum penitus perspicere velis, et cognoscere, qualis sit
criticus, sacerdos, philosophus, medicus, &c. consule Elogium [i.e.
Elogium Famae], et libellos eos jocosiores nuper editos, in quibus
academici Cantabrigienses de nova et ignominiosa dominatione cum
praefectis suis expostulant.' This note must have been written later
than the main part of the text. The *libellos jocosiores* here referred to are presumably *The Fragment* and *A Key to the Fragment*,
which were published in 1750 and 1751 respectively. It is only
in *Monitor* that King admits the relationship between his *Armiger*
and Dr. Squirt of the *Fragment* who becomes Samuel Squib in
the *Key*.

Another note refers to Ascalaphus, who is designated *B——delator insignis*. There is no reason for more than one interpretation of this description: nobody fits it better (from King's point of view) than Richard Blacow of Brasenose. He figures more prominently in King's writings during the period following the Oxfordshire county election of 1754, but had been mistrusted by the Principal of St. Mary Hall as a Whig informer long beforehand. King's opinions about Blacow are usually expressed in English—the language of the election controversy—but in *Monitor* King could make statements of a kind which would not have been suitable for popular consumption. Here Blacow is described as: '. . . *fraudum, calumniarum et machinarum omnium inventor, quae ad famam meam laedendam adhibebantur. Hic est iste delator, qui aditum habuit facillimum ad regni praefectos, et ipse perjurissimus, et cujusdam impurissimae lenae perjuriis adjustus, Academiam OXONIENSEM vehementer accusavit, et in odiosum laesae majestatis crimen vocare potuit.*'

Towards the end of *Monitor*, the author has composed what is, for him, an unusually apologetic footnote. Here he provides an intimate and almost naïve piece of self-justification which has no comparison in any of his previous Latin works:

Velim, mi lector, mihi ignoscas, quod in libris meis aliquid de meipso gloriari videor; atque hoc totum, quicquid est, ascribas, attribuasque malevolentissimis inimicorum meorum obtrectationibus, quos nisi quodammodo redarguissem te docendo, ipse qui sim, et quae vitae meae consuetudo, et ii cujusmodi, et omnino quales fuerint eorum mores, non modo me nimis patientem, sed plane inertem et infantissimum existimares; non modo non primariorum virorum et optimorum civium, sed neminis cujusquam hominis ingenui liberique amicitia me putares dignum.

This piece may have little value as explanation, but it manifests one of King's principal shortcomings, his tendency to blame others for real or imagined faults in himself. He never conquered this failing: it will appear again in the epitaph which he wrote for himself in the final years of his life.

VI

Controversies of the Early 1750s

THE fact that King arrived at a disinterested conclusion in
Monitor is significant. Perhaps he was already starting to lose
faith in the Jacobitism which he would formally abjure in
twelve years' time. Even if this was not the case, King's meeting
with Charles Edward, the Young Chevalier, in the following
year, definitely caused him to feel grave doubts as to the calibre
of the second Jacobite claimant to the throne. This encounter
is usually regarded as the *terminus a quo* of the Elibank Plot, the
last and most obscure attempt to restore the Stuarts to the
throne of Great Britain by means of a rising within the country.

The small amount of evidence on the subject has been presented most recently by Sir Charles Petrie, and there is now
little new to add to the existing knowledge of the purely military aspects of the plot.[1] The precise contribution made by
King to this affair is difficult to determine: all available information on his role is contained in his *Political and Literary Anecdotes*,
and these are understandably devoid of details of the proposed
coup d'état. An insurrection had originally been planned in 1747,
which was to have had its beginning in September at Lichfield
races. It was later postponed, despite the fact that the English
Jacobites sent over £15,000 to the prince, who was now being
described as 'Charles III'. As late as September of 1749 King
attended Lichfield races in person and drew up a list of 275
loyal gentlemen who were present. Charles Edward's where-
abouts and immediate intentions were at this juncture a mystery to most English and continental Jacobites—even to their
principal protagonist in Oxford. The prince was rumoured to

---

[1] Sir Charles Petrie, Bt., 'The Elibank Plot, 1752–3', *Transactions of the Royal
Historical Society*, 4th Series, Vol. XIV (1931), pp. 175–96; *The Jacobite Movement*
(3rd edn. rev.; London: Eyre & Spottiswoode, 1958), pp. 413–31. On the continental background see Lesley Lewis, *Connoisseurs and Secret Agents in Eighteenth Century
Rome* (London: Chatto and Windus, 1961).

be in Poland: only the entourage of Pope Benedict XIV and a few other intimates knew that he was really in France, despite the fact that he had been officially expelled from that country in 1748 under the terms of the Treaty of Aix-la-Chapelle. King seems to have been completely unprepared for the appearance of Prince Charles in London during September of 1750.

In that month the Principal of St. Mary Hall received a note from Lady Primrose in which she indicated that she desired to see him immediately at her home in Essex Street, off the Strand. This communication eventually led to a complete *volte-face* in his political outlook. When he had reached Lady Primrose, she led him into her dressing room, and presented him to the Young Chevalier in person. On the circumstances of their meeting King wrote:

If I was surprised to find him there, I was still more astonished when he acquainted me with the motives which had induced him to hazard a journey to England at this juncture. The impatience of his friends who were in exile had formed a scheme which was impracticable; but although it had been as feasible as they had represented it to him, yet no preparation had been made, nor was anything ready to carry it into execution. He was soon convinced that he had been deceived, and therefore, after a stay in London of five days only, he returned to the place from whence he came.[1]

King relates later that, before leaving England, the Pretender came to his lodgings and drank tea with him. For some years afterwards they corresponded constantly, and during this period King informed himself of all particulars relating to Charles Edward both in public and private life.

The assessment of the Young Chevalier which appears in the *Anecdotes* is especially interesting in view of King's earlier pronouncements on the desirability of restoring the House of Stuart. After paying tribute to his 'tall and well-made' person, his 'handsome face', and his 'good eyes', King continues:

. . . but in a polite company he would not pass for a genteel man. He hath a quick apprehension, and speaks French, Italian, and English, the last with a little of a foreign accent. As to the rest, very little care seems to have been taken of his education. He had not

---

[1] *Political and Literary Anecdotes* (2nd edn., 1819), p. 197.

made the belles lettres or any of the finer arts his study, which surprised me much, considering his preceptors, and the noble opportunities he must have always had in that nursery of all the elegant and liberal arts and science [i.e. Rome]. But I was still more astonished, when I found him unacquainted with the history and constitution of *England*, in which he ought to have been very early instructed. I never heard him express any noble or benevolent sentiments, the certain indications of a great soul and good heart; or discover any sorrow or compassion for the misfortunes of so many worthy men who had suffered in his cause. But the most odious part of his character is his love of money, a vice which I do not remember to have been imputed by our historians to any of his ancestors, and is the certain index of a base and little mind.[1]

King further discusses the Chevalier's religious duplicity ('with the catholics he is a catholic; with the protestants he is a protestant . . .'), his insolent manner of treating his immediate dependants, and his drunken quarrels with his Scottish mistress, Clementina Walkinshaw. It is not surprising to find that King attributes to this man alone, rightly or wrongly, the ruin of the Jacobite cause.

King's role in the Elibank Plot seems to have been in the main negative. He was informed initially by the Prince himself of the details of the proposed rising. From the Stuart Papers in the Royal Library at Windsor Castle, the Rome and Tuscany State Papers in the Public Record Office, and other sources, it is possible to form a rather vague conception of the initial phase of the plot. During his five-day visit to London, Charles met the Duke of Beaufort, the Earl of Westmoreland, and about fifty other Jacobites at a house in Pall Mall, and offered to lead a rebellion if 4000 men could be mustered. He had already asked George Dormer, his agent in Antwerp, to procure 26,000 muskets for the same purpose. He hoped to seize the Tower of London during the course of the revolt, and contemplated blowing up one of the gates with a petard. The military details of the scheme he discussed with Colonel Brett, the Jacobite agent who had been secretary to the Duchess of Buckingham, the daughter of James II by Catherine Sedley. In order to gain greater public confidence, he renounced the Roman Church,

---

[1] Ibid., pp. 200ff.

and was admitted to the Church of England in St. Mary-le-Strand, as he himself subsequently announced in a draft proclamation of 1759:

In order to make my renountiation of the Church of Rome the most authentick, and the less liable afterwards to malitious interpretations, I went to London in the year 1750; and in that capital did then make a solemn abjuration of the Romish religion, and did embrace that of the Church of England as by Law established in the 39 Articles in which I hope to live and die.

I doubt that King discouraged the conversion of Prince Charles to the Anglican Communion, but he presumably poured cold water on all the prince's military projects, which he personally believed others had instigated, and desisted himself from being associated with them. He seems to have taken no active part in the melancholy attempts to organize the rising which were made subsequently, and which led to the execution on 7 June 1753 of Colonel Archibald Cameron, the last Jacobite to suffer the death penalty.[1]

The Young Chevalier made another clandestine journey to England in September 1752, when he again stayed at the home of Lady Primrose. His presence in the country was certainly known to the Secretary of State, Lord Holdernesse, who reported it to George II. On being asked what he wished to be done, the King is reported to have answered, 'I shall do nothing at all, and when he is tired of England he will go abroad again.' To commemorate this visit, which lasted for some weeks, a silver medal was struck on the Continent.[2] The exergue on the reverse contains the date

SEPT XXIII

MDCCLII

[1] Relevant background information is to be found in the Introduction to Sir Walter Scott's *Redgauntlet* and in Andrew Lang's *Pickle the Spy* and *The Companions of Pickle*.

[2] A formal description of this medal appears in Edward Hawkins, op. cit., Vol. II, p. 670. A reproduction of both sides is provided in R. W. Cochran-Patrick, op. cit., plate XIV, figure 5. This medal is unsigned. Its execution has been attributed to Thomas Pingo (e.g. in L. Forrer's *Biographical Dictionary of Medallists*, Vol. IV, p. 558), but Joseph Kirk, in one of his sales lists reprinted by William Till in 1838, claims it as being by himself. As the medal is dated, it was probably not issued until after the Prince's arrival in England. Specimens are preserved in the British Museum and the Heberden Coin Room of the Ashmolean Museum, Oxford.

The bust of Prince Charles is shown on the obverse, together with the legend REDEAT MAGNUS ILLE GENIUS BRITANNIAE. The influence of King's Radclivian oration is also apparent on some drinking glasses which date from about the same time and which have survived to the present day in the hands of private collectors. They have the word REDEAT engraved close to the rim.[1]

King *may* have continued for a little longer to play a purely advisory role in continental political intrigues, though the evidence is far from conclusive. In a letter written from Paris on 7 May 1753 to Frederick the Great, the Earl Marischal refers obscurely to a military scheme to aid the Jacobites in England, and comments:

Il me paraît que le mécontentement en Angleterre est si grand à l'heure qu'il est que peu de chose renverserait le gouvernement; mais ce peu de chose n'est pas facile à adjuster.

The Earl then refers to *un certain projet* and continues:

Les deux principales personnes en Angleterre dans le secret, outre Dawkins, sont le docteur King, homme d'esprit, vif, agissant, et milord Westmoreland, homme sage, prudent, d'une bonne tête, bon citoyen, respecté et respectable. Vous pourrez toujours vous fier à leurs sentiments, comme ils se fieront aux vôtres; mais ils ne se confieraient pas aisément à ceux d'aucun prince. S'ils avaient quelque chose à communiquer à Votre Majesté dans la suite, ils enverront un homme de confiance ou se serviront de mon canal.[2]

There is no reason for believing that either Frederick the Great or the Earl Marischal persevered in their plans once the Elibank Plot had definitely collapsed, and none that the Principal of St. Mary Hall, though he was acquainted with the Earl, had any intercourse with the King of Prussia.

While the Elibank Plot was spluttering indecisively in 1751, King produced *A Key to the Fragment* under the name of Amias Riddinge, B.D., with a Preface 'by Peregrine Smyth, Esq.' The

---

[1] Grant R. Francis, 'Jacobite Drinking Glasses and their Relation to the Jacobite Medals', *British Numismatic Journal*, Vol. XVI (2nd Series, Vol. VI, 1921–2), pp. 268ff. An indeterminate number of these glasses are earlier in date than King's oration, but the word REDEAT was engraved on them subsequently.

[2] *Politische Correspondenz Friedrich's des Grossen* (39 vols.; Berlin: Verlag von Alexander Duncker, 1879–1925), Vol. IX, pp. 437f.

entire publication has always been credited to him, and there is no cause for doubting this attribution. *A Key to the Fragment* is incomprehensible without a knowledge of the work it purports to explain, *A Fragment*, which appeared anonymously in 1750. Commentators on *A Fragment* have been very rare: the only one to provide an interpretation was Christopher Wordsworth in 1874.[1] No solution has been reached in the problem of the authorship of *A Fragment*. At different times it has been variously attributed to three writers in the University of Cambridge: Dr. Henry Stebbing, James Bickham, and Francis Coventry. It had two sequels: *Another Fragment* and *Fragmentum Est Pars Rei Fractae*, both of which were also issued anonymously in the same year. The Principal of St. Mary Hall probably acquired his knowledge of the controversy which is the subject of the fragments during the visits which he is known to have made to Cambridge about this time.[2]

A Fragment starts during the course of Chapter IX and concludes abruptly before the end of Chapter XI. Rows of asterisks indicate lacunae within the printed text. No information is provided on the missing portions: probably the author assumed that the readers for whom the book was primarily intended would readily see through the entire hoax. These portions of an imaginary larger work in fact constitute an allegory of the Duke of Newcastle's Chancellorship of Cambridge University, which had commenced with his election on 14 December 1748. He is represented in the guise of Tom Standish, who, the reader is told, is clerk to a Justice of the Peace in his neighbourhood. At the beginning of the fragment, Mr. Standish is anxious to wed an old gentlewoman who has a numerous family of sons and has had in the past a great many husbands. She owns several manors and many dependants, and Mr. Standish, who loves power, thinks that such a match will add greatly to his importance. So as soon as her ailing husband dies, Tom Standish and the old lady are married. Their story is then related from the time of the nuptials to the occasion when the old gentlewoman

---

[1] Christopher Wordsworth, *Social Life at the English Universities in the Eighteenth Century* (Cambridge: Deighton, Bell & Co., 1874), pp. 621–4.

[2] John Nichols, *Literary Anecdotes of the Eighteenth Century* (9 vols.; printed for the author, 1812–15), Vol. II, p. 608. Also relevant is Vol. I, p. 556.

swallows twenty pills prescribed by a group of learned doctors. From Wordsworth's commentary, King's *Key*, and the glosses written into several of the surviving copies, it is possible to interpret most of the allusions. The Justice of the Peace is George II, the marriage of Tom Standish represents the installation of the Duke of Newcastle as Chancellor of the University of Cambridge, the old lady is *Alma Mater Cantabrigiensis*, and the twenty pills represent the set of regulations which, having been rejected on 11 May 1750, were passed, against the inclination of a good proportion of the resident members of the university, on the following June 26. The learned doctors represent the Whig bishops and others who were in favour of the new regulations and recommended their acceptance.

A perusal of the text of these regulations may cause a modern commentator to wonder why King should be interested in them to the extent of writing a book to discredit them. They cover, for the most part, such conventional matters of university discipline as residence, attire, attendance at St. Mary's Church, and the keeping of servants, guns, and sporting dogs. Games of dice are forbidden within the precincts of the university, and playing at cards is permitted only under stipulated conditions.[1] The most obnoxious regulation was withdrawn: it had required that an annual account of the character and behaviour of every person in the university was to be transmitted to the Chancellor. King was not directly affected by these regulations, but he heartily objected to the Whig policies which the Duke of Newcastle was pursuing in the larger political sphere at Westminster, and probably saw the Chancellor's activities as a potential threat to Oxford.

There is no real doubt as to the historical personages who are represented by most of the other characters in *A Fragment*. The old lady's former husband is the Duke of Somerset, who was Chancellor of the University of Cambridge immediately prior

---

[1] For the text of and comments on these regulations see Charles H. Cooper, *Annals of Cambridge* (4 vols.; Cambridge: Warwick and Company, 1842–52), Vol. IV, pp. 278ff. Cooper also provides a list of 23 publications caused by the controversies over these regulations. On the administrative background see D. A. Winstanley, *The University of Cambridge in the Eighteenth Century* (Cambridge: at the University Press, 1922), pp. 145ff., and *Unreformed Cambridge* (Cambridge: at the University Press, 1935), pp. 1–37.

to the Duke of Newcastle. The Justice's eldest son represents the Prince of Wales. Mun is Dr. Edmund Keene of Peterhouse; Tom is Dr. Thomas Chapman, a former Vice-Chancellor. Tom Standish gained their good graces by talking to them of a jaunt to town and showing them Westminster Abbey and St. Paul's Cathedral: an obvious hint at Newcastle's encouragement of their preferment within the Church. Both Mun and Tom were pleased with the arrival of the box of pills which was brought by Tom Standish's own apothecary, Dr. Squirt, who represents Dr. Samuel Squire, chaplain to the Duke of Newcastle. A good deal of rather petty disagreement follows, during which time the reader is introduced to several of the leading figures in the controversy over the regulations, all under disguised names. Parts of the description of the old lady's illness and its treatment show a coarseness not unlike that in Swift's *Tale of a Tub*. In the end the old lady resigns herself to the pills, and Mun forces his 'quakeries' down her throat.

The importance of King's *A Key to the Fragment* is that its author clarifies the purport of the allegorical names in *A Fragment* by giving others which are still fictitious but considerably closer to the real ones. Thus he explains that the old lady and her numerous sons live in a manor named Bridgetown. Tom Standish, he writes, is really meant to be Sir Thomas Duke, Mun is Edmund Sharp, and Tom is Thomas Forward. Dr. Squirt is given the unmistakable name of Samuel Squib, and, in case any reader should still miss the allusion, is described as Sir Thomas Duke's chaplain. Several of the other characters are given new names over which there could be little margin for misinterpretation; thus Dr. George Rooke of Christ's College, who previously was given the appellation of Dr. Rock, is now rechristened George Crow.

King must have realized that his work was bordering on libel. Probably for this reason he claimed in his Preface, signed by 'Peregrine Smyth', that *A Fragment*, which had been published only the year before, was actually a reprint of a pamphlet which had first been issued in October 1658, and that shortly afterwards *A Key to the Fragment*, written by Amias Riddinge, B.D., had appeared. Peregrine Smyth was now taking the opportunity of reissuing the key of the long dead Amias Riddinge for

the benefit of those readers who had completely misinterpreted
A Fragment by applying the allegory to the business of the new
regulations in Cambridge. 'This Mistake,' observed Smyth,
'was very excusable, and the most sagacious Critic, or expert
Decypherer, would probably have fallen in with the common
Opinion, if they had never had an Opportunity of perusing the
KEY.'

The name Peregrine Smyth is purely fictitious, but Amias
Riddinge (or Ridding) was a real person. His dates were 1587
to 1661, and he is listed as a Bachelor of Divinity in *Alumni
Cantabrigienses*. It is not difficult to see why King chose the name
of this particular individual: he was a Fellow of St. John's
College who had been ejected in accordance with a writ of the
Puritan Earl of Manchester on 16 September 1644, and restored
to his Fellowship on 1 August 1660. Smyth's Preface explains
that Riddinge was

. . . a noted *Cavalier*, who had been ruined in his Fortune by the
Civil War; and 'tis no wonder therefore, that he explained the
FRAGMENT agreeably to his own Principles, and the Prejudices
of his Company and Education; that he painted the Characters of
his Adversaries in odious Colours, and perhaps, instead of his
Author's Meaning, imposed on us his own.

These prefatory observations continue to the effect that if a
roundhead had interpreted *A Fragment*, he would have done so
in a manner contrary to that of Riddinge, and would have
adapted it to the purposes of his own party. A disinterested
individual would not have suspected anything mysterious in the
narrative and would have interpreted it in its literal sense. The
suppositious Smyth comes to the conclusion that Riddinge's
Key cannot be presented as altogether clear and unexception-
able. He concludes, with an ingenuousness which is patently
intended to be hollow:

I deliver it out of my Hands, just as I found it in the *Harleyan* Collection; and, except a few immaterial Alterations in the Style, I have
reprinted it *Verbatim*. If any one should be so ill-natured as to doubt
my Sincerity, or so suspicious as to question the Age and Antiquity
of this *Tract*, I refer him to Mr OSBORNE, of whom I purchased it,
at an high Price, upon his assuring me, (and I had good Reason to

believe him) that there was not another Copy of the same Book in *England*.

Smyth's Preface includes parenthetically a story which is in all probability a true recollection of an incident in King's own life. This is the only place in his writings where it is recounted:

I remember, in the Year 1745, an old Acquaintance came into my Chamber, just as I had transcribed an Inscription out of *Gruter*, in which were these three Letters, *C.E.C.* a compendious way of writing among the Old *Romans*, to signify *Cives Ejus Coloniae*, and generally used in their monumental Inscriptions. My Friend having cast his Eye on the Paper, which lay wet on my Table, shook his Head, and said, That he wondered I would venture to write a treasonable Song at such a critical Juncture. For although, added he, you have disguised the rest in *Latin*, yet those three Capital Letters, which I suppose are the Burden of the Song, must be understood by the meanest Capacity, and can only signify, CHARLES, EDWARD, COME!

The Preface also contains what may reasonably be taken as confirmation that King himself was not the author of *A Fragment*. 'I cannot affirm,' he writes, 'in Truth I cannot, that the *Fragment* and the *Key* were written by the same Hand.'

In the text of *A Key to the Fragment*, the Principal of St. Mary Hall (under the guise of Amias Riddinge) provides many animadversions on the Whig Fellows of the University of Cambridge. The first is called Nehemiah Broomstick, 'tho' his true name is THOMAS BISHOP.' According to Wordsworth, Bishop Sir Thomas Gooch is intended. Successively the Ordinary of the dioceses of Bristol, Norwich, and Ely, Gooch had in 1751 succeeded to the baronetcy at the death of his brother William, Governor of Virginia. King's character of him in *A Key to the Fragment* is thoroughly biassed: he was indeed a Whig and attentive to the cause of his party in parliament, but he was also courteous, dignified, and punctilious in his pontifical duties, qualities for which the Principal of St. Mary Hall gave him no credit. According to the *Key*, Thomas Bishop named himself Nehemiah Broomstick, 'NEHEMIAH, because it is a Name of the Times, and BROOMSTICK, because he hath often declared, that if a *Broomstick* were Governor of this Realm, he would swear to the *Broomstick*, he would pray for the *Broomstick*, and preach for the *Broomstick*, and vote for the *Broomstick*, and scold for the *Broomstick*, and do anything but fight for the *Broomstick*.' Riddinge is then made to add an autobiographical reminiscence:

I remember this Man in very mean Circumstances; but he is now in possession of a vast Estate in Bishops Lands, which he acquired chiefly by the Favour and Interest of the present Lord of the Manour. He has therefore hung up Sir THOMAS DUKE's Picture at one end of his great Hall, with a Map of his own Estate at the other, with this inscription under it,

DEUS *nobis haec otia fecit.*

Other Cambridge subjects of King's ridicule include (according to Wordworth's key) Dr. John Newcome, Master of St. John's College, who is called John Comus or Belshazzar 'because he polluted the holy Vessels, and took the Plate, which had been consecrated for the Service of the Altar, to adorn his own Table'; Dr. Roger Long of Pembroke College, who appears as Roger Newton; and William Richardson and Henry Hubbard of Emmanuel College, who bear the easily identifiable names of William FitzRichards and Henry Hobbes. The latter had appeared in *A Fragment* as Boy Harry. He was, according to King, so well esteemed in the country that people thought him a cavalier at heart. Then he was seduced by a steward named Edmund Sharp, who invited him to dinner. The author provides the details on the hospitality of Sharp, who, 'at that very instant when he had loaded poor HAL'S Plate with fat Venison, or as others affirm, with excellent Plumb Pie, obtained a Promise of his Vote, in favour of the new Laws which were to be proposed at the next general Court.' *A Key to the Fragment* is full of this kind of trite academic scandal: it was perhaps entertaining at one time, at least to the sympathetic *cognoscenti*, but like so much gossip in writing is too lightweight to be of any permanent value.

King's one attempt to influence the trend of events at Cambridge was neither constructive nor positive. But at the same time he was engaged rather more fruitfully in activities at Oxford, one of which was his participation in the business of drawing up a body of statutes for the Radcliffe Library. In April 1750 Charles Pryor, clerk to the Trustees, had been told to ask King about the statutes.[1] One may assume that the Principal of St. Mary Hall started on their preparation, for on 18 August 1753 Dr. Richard Rawlinson wrote to George Ballard: 'I hope dr King, who I am told has the care of a body of Statutes for dr Radcliffes Library will take care to fix residence and attendance.'[2] The statutes could not have been produced with any immediacy: the Librarian, Francis Wise, was not an especially easy man to deal with and had his own ideas on what the statutes should contain. It is not surprising to read in an undated letter which he penned to Lord Guilford: '. . . I had the misfortune to be under the D. of Beau——t's displeasure, (which indeed would have been the case, with any body, who was put in against his will).'[3] There is no evidence to support Wise's rationalization of the Duke's displeasure, but a good deal which exhibits his own cantankerousness. As S. G. Gillam has shown, Wise did little to promote the interests of the almost bookless library, and 'tended to treat the position of Librarian as a sinecure, a position, moreover, made more difficult by his own failure to co-operate with the University authorities.'[4] In a letter to Rawlinson dated 23 August 1753, King is quite openly apologetic about an earlier communication written by Wise:

I defer'd answering your Letter, till I had an opportunity of communicating it to some of the Radcliffe Trustees. This morning I waited on the Duke of Beaufort and at the same time I saw Sr Walter Bagot. They were both greatly surprised, when they were informed of ye manner, in which Mr Wise had wrote to you. They accept books of any kind.[5]

The likelihood is that King and Wise were at variance over the content of the statutes for some considerable time; as late as December 1755 the Vice-Chancellor was still being requested to 'direct some person to form a Body of Statutes.'[6] Finally a

[1] Minutes of the Trustees, 9 April 1750.
[2] Bodleian Library, MS. Ballard 2, fol. 270.
[3] Bodleian Library, MS. North d. 7, fol. 176.
[4] S. G. Gillam, op. cit., p. xxxiii.
[5] Bodleian Library, MS. Rawl. Letters 114*.
[6] Minutes of the Trustees, 11 December 1755.

code of statutes was drawn up based on that of the Bodleian Library: a draft of it is in the University Archives, but it is undated.[1] Nothing is known for certain about the preparation of the text: it may be a composite work, but at least in the form which survives is more likely the product of a single compiler. He could have been King.

While the discussions over the statutes for the Radcliffe Library were in progress, the Principal of St. Mary Hall was putting together the *Opera Guilielmi King*: the volume of his serious Latin works which was completed only in 1760 and never actually published. This collected edition was a long time in preparation. The earliest surviving evidence relating to King's intention of compiling a collection of his Latin productions occurs in a letter from Lord Orrery of 30 November 1746. 'Your design of publishing your works together,' His Lordship declared, 'must give pleasure to your friends in general and to me in particular.'[2] King's original expectation was to issue his Latin works in one volume, but his plan was temporarily modified with a view to printing two, one of poetry and the other of 'orations, etc.', and subsequently altered to producing two volumes with his Latin pieces in chronological order. This sequence of prognostications is implicit in his letter to Orrery of 30 September 1747:

I have made great progress in preparing my Latin works for the press, having all the copper plates ready for the first volume. For, contrary to my expectation, I shall not be able to comprehend the whole in one volume. I had once resolved to print all the poetical pieces in one volume, and the orations, etc., in another. But, I have since considered it best, to observe the order of time, by which means, the whole will be better understood, as there are frequent references, not only in the satires, but likewise in the prose works, to something that was published before. I compute that what I have already published will be sufficient to complete the first volume: so that the second will consist of things entirely new. The Head-pieces and Tail-pieces, as well as the initial letters I have designed myself. For the Head-pieces of the presentation Speeches, I propose the several coats of arms, of those I presented. If you have any curiosity to see a

[1] Oxford University Archives, W. P. α S7(6).
[2] Countess of Cork and Orrery (ed.), op. cit., Vol. I, p. 302.

specimen of the engraving, I will enclose two or three in my next letter.[1]

More information on King's plans for selling the proposed two-volume edition of his collected Latin works is provided retrospectively in *Doctor King's Apology*, which appeared in 1755. He speaks of these matters as relating to seven or eight years beforehand, thus implying that they took shape in 1747 or 1748:

> Seven or eight years ago I advertised my friends, that I intended to publish my LATIN works in two volumes in Quarto, and desired, that those Gentlemen, who were inclined to purchase the books, would be pleased to leave, or send their names to the COCO TREE in PALL MALL. I fixed the price at two guineas, TO BE PAID WHEN THE BOOKS WERE DELIVERED. In a short time, with the names left at the COCO TREE, and others sent to me, I had about 450 subscribers, when I closed my subscription; having determined from the beginning to print no more than 500 books in that form. According to my proposals I neither required, nor received any part of the subscription money from any one of my subscribers, tho' many of them were so kind, as to offer me the whole . . . I would not oblige myself to fix a certain time for the publication, but be left to my own liberty and leisure.

The projected two-volume edition never in fact appeared. At an unascertainable time after 1748 King must have become convinced that two volumes were not called for and decided on one. The final compilation of the *Opera* will be discussed in Chapter VIII, but it is relevant to notice here that, at some time during the first half of the 1750s, five of King's Latin poems were entirely reset with a view to inclusion in the collected edition, while *Hydra* and *Monitor* were set in print for the first time.[2] The text of all these works was embellished with historiated initials and other copper plate engravings. By way of introduction to his *Opera* King wrote a new Latin prose Preface of some eight pages headed *Praesidibus Supremi Galliae Senatus*, which never appeared separately. It is dated MAII CALENDIS, MDCCLIV.

---

[1] The Houghton Library, Harvard University, MS. Eng. 218.2 (v. 5), pp. 64f.
[2] The works reset (and in varying degrees rewritten) during this period were *Miltonis Epistola ad Pollionem; Sermo Pedestris; Scamnum, Ecloga; Templum Libertatis;* and *Antonietti, Ducis Corsorum, Epistola ad Corsos.* This last poem acquired the revised title of *Antonietti, Corsorum Ducis, Epistola ad Corsos.*

There are various pieces of evidence which demonstrate the preparation of the collected edition during the early 1750s. Thus in *Doctor King's Apology* of 1755 we read that the author had been 'for some years out of pocket in a large sum for paper, print, copper plates, etc.' In the note to line 193 of *Hydra*, Lord Arran is said to have lived to the age of eighty years (*Ad octogesimum annum vixit*) in contradistinction to the information on the title-page to the effect that the work was written in 1746. Arran was born on 4 September 1671, and so King's note (at least in its present form) must have been composed on or at some time after 4 September 1751, that is to say some five years subsequent to the writing of the rest of the text. Several emendations to the existing editions of the Latin poems reveal King's gradual disenchantment with Jacobitism. For example, in the original text of *Templum Libertatis*, King refers flatteringly to the King over the Water, James III, during a note to verse 8 of Book Two: '*Britanniae vero Regnum legitimo & sacrato jure continetur: & Rex ipse ita est, ut Phoenix, avis magna, admiranda, unica.*' The revised version of this note in the *Opera* (quoted *supra*, p. 146) contains no reference of any kind to the Jacobite monarch. Other changes reveal the author's hardening attitude towards the Roman Catholic Church, a development which had its poetical acme in *Aviti Epistota ad Perillam, Virginem Scotam*, of 1760, and which was very probably connected with his growing antipathy towards the French hierarchy during the previous decade.

Perhaps most significant of all King's emendations are those in which he eradicates his references to Lord Orrery under the name of Laelius. In the *Opera* version of *Scamnum* the substitution is Carolus, and in the revision of *Templum Libertatis* it is Cadenus. The most plausible explanation of these changes is that King, like many other of Swift's admirers, was ill-pleased with the appearance in November 1751 of Orrery's *Remarks on the Life and Writings of Dr. Jonathan Swift*.[1] Indeed, it is difficult to imagine how King, who had referred to Swift as *amicissimus Cadenus*, could have reacted other than unfavourably to such observations as these which fell from Orrery's pen: '. . . it is certain, from SWIFT's settlement in *Dublin* as Dean of *St. Patrick's*, his choice of companions in general shewed him of a

---

[1] 1752 was the date of publication printed on the title page.

very depraved taste . . . Idleness and trifles engrossed too many of his hours: fools and sycophants too much of his conversation . . . his pride was so great as scarce to admit any body to the least share of his friendship, except such who could amuse him, or such who could do him honour.' No correspondence between King and Orrery survives after 1750, and there are no further references to His Lordship in any work which King subsequently wrote. The speech on Orrery in *Tres Oratiunculae* of 1743 was included in the *Opera*, but does not seem to have been reset. For this portion of the collected edition King simply incorporated remainders, a fact which is demonstrably clear from the nonsequential pagination.

Some discussion of the prose Preface *Praesidibus Supremi Galliae Senatus* is relevant here since it throws light on King's political thinking in the spring of 1754. This piece of writing is highly deferential to the contemporary *parlement* of Paris. In the controversies between the Catholic Church and the Jansenists, Louis XV had taken the side of the bishops while many of the leaders of France's principal *parlement* supported the Jansenists. King, who was in ideological conflict with the English Whig bishops, could scarcely help feeling a certain sympathy with the position of the Parisian *parlement*. The opening sentence of the Preface refers to 'these distinguished names', though in fact no names appear: '*Quandoquidem praeclara haec nomina, pro immortalibus vestris in patriam meritis, cum civitatis vestrae, tum gentium omnium consensu assecuti estis, jam diu est, cum ipse quidem, vir peregrinus, ut virtutibus vestris debitum cepisse testimonium, et quodammodo tribuisse videar, me et hoc opus meum vobis dicatum volo.*' There is another reference later to the now nonexistent names: '. . . *in fronte operis mei nomina tam venerabilia curavi inscribenda.* . . .' King presumably intended that a list of the French statesmen to whom he had dedicated his *Opera* should appear near the beginning of the volume. The most probable reason for its absence in the remaining copies is that it was removed before he finally prepared the sheets for binding. The declaration in 1756 of what subsequently became known as the Seven Years' War made France once more a formal enemy: King could hardly have wished towards the end of the war to perpetuate the names of the hostile leaders to whom he had earlier, and without any degree of foresight, dedicated a considerable portion of his life's work. His political outlook changed radically with the enthronement of George III, the appointment of a Tory Prime-Minister in the person of Lord Bute, and the end of the period of Whig oligarchy. In 1754 King had regarded the French as friends; by the early 1760s he no longer felt this sense of amity.

Nevertheless, when he was composing the Preface, King felt confident that his volume would be acceptable to the dedicatees, since it was devoted to the cause of liberty:

Porro autem totum hujus libri argumentum optimis civibus judici-busque integerrimis idcirco pergratum fore confido, quia libertatis causam complectitur, pro qua cum vobis semper fuit omnis conten-tio summa cum vestra laude, tum vero non commisistis, ut potentium minis, aut blanditiis malitiosis (in quibus ipsi se peccasse noverint) potius, quam sententiis et consiliis vestris religionis antiquitas, populi jus, et senatus auctoritas retineantur.

He refers to the French hierarchy in much the same tone as he habitually used when writing of the Whig bishops, and regards the Parisian *parlement* as being composed of custodians of justice and liberty and as constituting the only protection of the people:

Sed tamen id esse satis causae censent quidam, homines gratiosi, ex optimatibus et proceribus sacerdotum (at qui sacerdotes!) quare vos in suspicionem veniatis regni appetendi, aut, nescio cujus, conjura-tionis et maleficii; quum nihil est, quod mavultis, quam earum civitatum negotiis praeesse, quae legibus aequissimis contineantur, quaeque vos justitiae et libertatis custodes et unicum populi praesi-dium, contra gratiam aeque atque contra vim, esse sentiant.

He declares that it is not for him to undertake a defence of the innocence of the *parlement*, since the members have already demonstrated their eloquence in the cause of freedom, and then proceeds to warn them of the possibility of corruption of a kind which he sees all round him in Britain:

Atqui (fatendum est enim) quum video mores civium nostrorum omnium, praeter perpaucos majoribus suis et vetere Britannia dignos, adeo esse corruptos ac depravatos, uti prae lucro nullam, non dico reipublicae, aut posterorum, sed sui habeant rationem, mira hercle sunt, ni id quidem quosdam e civibus vestris, leves ac nummarios homines, (hodie enim late manat hujus sceleris contagio) ab integritate et fide sua deduxerit.

Immediately afterwards he offers his intended readers, whom he regards as the protectors of freedom in France, solace in their dealings with possible deserters to the cause of the purple-clad pontiffs:

Siqui sunt hujuscemodi, qui cum conjunctissimi cum vobis esse debeant communi patriae vinculo, ab ea tamen descivere, et pontificibus purpuratis ad vos opprimendos se adjutores praebuerunt, non possunt, ut non sibi statuant publici odii monimenta, vobis publici amoris, sempiterna.

He sees the motives of the French bishops as being fundamentally no different from those of their Whig counterparts in the Church of England, and expresses the wish that everyone will praise the piety, prudence, patience, and mildness of the members of the Parisian *parlement*, envisioned by the writer as being in some measure the Gallic equivalent of the English Tory Party:

Quinetiam si horum hominum perfidia, aut aulicorum vis, aut pontificalis authoritas, quae eo crevit, ut jam caeremoniis et religione laboret sua, acta et judicia vestra rescindere potuerit (pontifices enim et publicae religionis magistri, quantum de majestate et amplitudine vestra diminuerint, tantum gloriae et praesidii ad facultates et dominationes suas se adjecisse sperant) adversos eos casus, aut mala quaecunque fortuna curiae sanctissimae invexerit, si non vitare, aut sanare, at apte et sapienter ferre vos posse palam est. Enimvero facitis, ut cum pietatem et prudentiam vestram, tum patientiam et lenitatem laudent omnes, ament, admirentur.

A little later he implies that there may be difficulties ahead, but observes that strength of mind is especially perceptible *in rebus asperis et adversis, in aerumnis, in periculis, in naufragiis, in exiliis, in vinculis, in perpessione denique malorum omnium.*

When these sentiments have been briefly developed, the author expresses the hope that the authority of the French parliamentarians will eventually be restored, trusting, it may be assumed, that that of the Tories will likewise be resuscitated in the British Isles. He adds some advice in case matters should turn out otherwise on account of the iniquity of the times:

Sin autem aliter aliquando evenerit viris probatissimis propter temporum iniquitatem, atque adeo omnia jam vobis eveniant contra, ac quae boni omnes vehementer expetiverint, nos tamen persuasum habeamus, quo ea quidem aequiore animo sint ferenda, deum nihil facere, imperare, permittere, nisi summa ratione, et causam esse occultam, sed justissimam, quare providentiae suae cursum ipse aliquando impedire videatur.

His motives in addressing the members of the Parisian *parlement* are outlined in a manner both flattering and gracious: he is writing willingly and out of admiration towards them:

. . . Incorruptos libertatis custodes et vindices quaerebam: reperi, perspexi, cognovi, colui, atque ea observantia ac religione, qua vos ipsam illam libertatem et patriae jura usque coluistis. Nam cum ego is sum, qui haud sane in animum inducerem, etiam si vos essetis omnium mortalium beatissimi, ut ob eam causam, venalium scriptorum more, vos adularer; tum vero si miserrimi, si regni finibus in exilium infelicius pulsi essetis, neutiquam tamen ita me pigeret consilii et constantiae meae, ut virtutes vestras, suppliciis nullis deformandas, studiis et sermonibus meis celebrare unquam desinerem.

Thence he draws to a conclusion which puts the dedicatees into almost the same favoured category as he had placed Dean Swift:

Ubicunque terrarum eritis (pace theologorum sacerdotumque omnium ordinum dixerim) ibi erunt non modo GALLIAE vestrae, sed hujus seculi, sed humani generis decora et ornamenta.

The Latinity of King's Preface is on the same level as that of his published speeches: graceful and stylized, yet imbued with a considerable degree of animation. In King's handling of the Latin language lies the whole success of his Preface. The persons for whom it was intended probably never saw it. The political conditions which spurred him to write it evaporated not long after its composition. The author himself could not have subscribed to some of the sentiments contained in it for long after its completion. Above all, the cause of Jansenism, entirely different though it was from Jacobitism, was in the last analysis just as doomed: King's pejorative observations on the French hierarchy and his magnanimous expressions of encouragement intended for the men who opposed them, for all their non-academic worth, might just as well have been inscribed on the water of the Isis.

King wrote no more with regard to the French political scene. He was now involved in the more proximate problems stemming from the parliamentary election for the county of Oxfordshire, which had taken place between 17 and 23 April 1754. This was the last public election in which Jacobitism exercised any real influence: together with the undistinguished Rag Plot and Watch Plot, it had repercussions far outside the boundaries of the county.[1] Despite the accusations which filled the air during and after the event, the Tory supporters in the Oxfordshire countryside were in fact not Jacobite in any active sense, however strong Stuart sentiment may have been in the university. The failures of 1715 and 1745 had had their psychological effect. The charge of Jacobitism was used for the most part as a kind of election 'scare' by the two Whig or 'New Interest' candidates, Lord Parker and Sir Edward Turner, and usually ignored or circumvented by their Tory or 'Old Interest' opponents, Lord Wenman and Sir James Dashwood. After a warmly contested election the Whigs were defeated at the poll, but finally elected on a scrutiny by petition. The story of the election itself and its bellicose aftermath has been well told in R. J. Robson's *The Oxfordshire Election of 1754*, and valuable shorter surveys have been provided in W. R. Ward's *Georgian Oxford* and Sir Charles Petrie's *The Jacobite Movement*. The account that follows will therefore not be comprehensive, but merely sufficient to illustrate the role played by William King.

At the outset it should be emphasized that King had no official connection with the proceedings: his contribution consisted in his influence with the university authorities and his skill as a polemicist. But he did attend several meetings of Tory supporters to lend encouragement to the cause of Lord Wenman and Sir James Dashwood: the earliest of these took place

---

[1] By the 'Rag Plot' is understood the business involving the discovery on 17 July 1754 by Mrs. Carnall, wife of a Carfax grocer, of some 'treasonable verses' in a bundle of rags outside her husband's shop. The rags belonged to one Maria Duke, who had left them there to run an errand. The Tory claim that Horner, the butler of Exeter College, had, in the closing months of 1754, inserted a portrait of Prince Charles Edward in the back of the watch of a Tory elector in order to compromise him constitutes the sole evidence in support of the 'Watch Plot'. In a note in *Monitor*, which must have been composed in 1754 or later, King gives his opinion of the Rag Plot when he writes of a certain judge *qui Academiam Oxon. gravissime apud Cantabrigienses accusavit de ficta et ridicula ea conjuratione.*

in May 1753, when the Old Interest Society convened at the Crown and Anchor in the Strand. Here the election campaign was planned.[1] An irreverently burlesque account of this meeting was published in the second issue of *Jackson's Oxford Journal*: for this libel William Jackson was compelled to apologize to King.[2] Various authors have stated that King later contributed to *Jackson's Oxford Journal*, but I have been unable to find evidence in support of this assertion. Jackson occasionally included a brief quotation from King's works, but, as far as I am aware, nothing that could be regarded as specially written for his journal.[3]

On 15 January 1754 King published a collection of fanciful essays entitled *The Dreamer*. The date of publication is provided in an advertisement which appeared in Number 4081 of *The London Evening Post*, 5–8 January 1754. When charged by the Whig dons of Oxford as being the author, King was careful not to reply in the form of a denial. At the end of the book is a purported 'Advertisement by the Bookseller', which was undoubtedly written by King himself. This Advertisement explains that the manuscript was given to the bookseller 'by a dwarfish old man, whom I since recollected to have seen in Drury Lane, in the train of Oberon, the king of the Fairies.' Included in this Advertisement is an interpretation of the entire series of essays, written for the bookseller by 'an eminent mathematician who is well skilled in judicial astrology.' According to this interpretation, the essays in *The Dreamer* were intended as a satire on popery and some of the contemporary policies of the Vatican. They *could* indeed be thus interpreted, but in view of the political circumstances under which they were published, their author's immediate intention was no doubt to ridicule the Whigs and to expose further the venality

[1] See Cecil S. Emden, *Oriel Papers* (Oxford: at the Clarendon Press, 1948), p. 102.

[2] See *Jackson's Oxford Journal*, No. 2 (12 May 1753) and No. 3 (19 May 1753). In this latter issue, Jackson declared that the authorship of the account published in the previous week was unknown to him and confessed, '*I do hereby acknowledge my offence, and humbly beg Dr. King's Pardon. And as he has been so good as to forgive me, I promise never to offend in the same manner again, or suffer my Paper to be the Canal of private Scandal or personal Abuse.*'

[3] For example, see *Jackson's Oxford Journal*, No. 112 (21 June 1755), where a note is reproduced from the third edition of *Doctor King's Apology*.

which he saw all round him. No key to the book was ever published, but a partial key has been inserted in a copy in the
Bodleian Library, which is very probably in the hand of Horace
Walpole.[1] This, incidentally, is one of King's longer works: the
text proper runs to 240 pages, not including an unusually complete index of twenty-eight pages and the Advertisement, which
fills a further fourteen.

At the time of publication of *The Dreamer*, or perhaps soon
afterwards, there appeared *A Translation of the Latin Epistle in the
Dreamer*: it gives every impression of having proceeded from the
pen of King himself. In some surviving copies of *The Dreamer*
this translation of the Latin epistle is bound with the main work.
The translation contains a Preface which manifests its publication shortly before the general election of the same year:

An important conjuncture is now approaching, which will furnish
an ordinary capacity with the power of distinguishing truth from
falsehood, and a real man from a counterfeit. For, whoever shall
receive a bribe, or by any corrupt influence shall be induced to give
his vote in any county, city, or borough, at the next general election,
who has no checks within, and whose spirit is never disturbed by the
breach of his honour, or his oath; such a creature, we may conclude,
is descended from some species of the brute creation. And let me add
with an honest boldness, that every new member, from the son of a
peer down to an attorney, or stock-jobber, who shall be elected by
BRIBERY, or by any other base and dishonourable practices, with a
design to sell himself and his country, ought to be placed in the same
rank with his electors. We may with great justice deny his HU-
MANITY, and be assured, that altho' he may acquire the highest
honours in the state, he can never arrive to the dignity of a MAN.

To this paragraph is added a footnote indicating that the ——
of —— had told some foreigners of distinction who had recently
been in England that the —— shire election would cost him
twenty thousand pounds. It is not clear who was intended or
which shire was involved, but King quotes the occurrence as an
instance of 'the present corrupt state of this country.'

In the Introduction to *The Dreamer* the author announced

---

[1] Bodleian Library 270.f.62. A transcription of this key has been made in another
copy of *The Dreamer* in the Victoria and Albert Museum, Forster Collection,
4832.8.M.28.

what he considered the unprecedented nature of his intention:

... to trace out for myself a path, which has never been trod before
—*Nullius ante—Trita solo* ... What I contend for is, that no man
hath ever published a regular series of his dreams, or described the
variety of objects, which from time to time have presented themselves
to him in the realms of MORPHEUS. This is the singularity, which
I claim, and the scheme which I have pursued in these sheets, which
I now offer to my honest countrymen.

Actually he had been anticipated by several medieval authors
of regular series of dreams, of whom William Langland was the
greatest, but their works were neither in print nor easily
accessible when King was writing. Furthermore, the author
unwittingly represented his dreams as being in the nature of
those experienced by Piers Plowman: their significance is clearly
intended to be allegorical rather than literal or prophetic. The
allegorical papers in *The Spectator*, though not constituting a
regular series of dreams, are in other respects roughly comparable.

The events in *The Dreamer* are related in the first person, and
are supposed to take place in a country inhabited by the
Papyropolites. The author indicates that he has no idea of the
situation of the country, nor of the exact nature of the government,
since it was represented to him at various times as a
duumvirate, a triumvirate, an aristocracy, an oligarchy, and a
theocracy. He is certain, however, of what country it is not. It
is not Plato's Republic, nor Sir Thomas More's Utopia, nor
Gulliver's Brobdingnag, nor his land of the Houyhnhms. He
comments that it may be a part of New Holland, or it may be an
island in the Pacific Ocean. The author mentions that he has
since communicated his memoirs to a learned rabbi, 'who
corresponds in all parts of the world', and that the rabbi has
assured him that the Papyropolites are a nation of uncircumcised
Philistines.

During the course of his dreams about the Papyropolites, the
nameless dreamer visits a number of fantastic places. Perhaps
the most extraordinary is a paper mill, where the paper is made
from a mixture of linen rags, the most rare and valuable

vegetables, barley, hops, apples, Arabian berries, American nuts, dried leaves from a 'curious Chinese shrub', tobacco, raw silk and cotton, cochineal, indigo, soap, tallow, bees-wax, 'large shreds and pieces of all sorts of leather', and many other ingredients with barbarous names such as addaties, alliballies, baftaes, bendamnoes, chowtars, doozooties, goskees, gurrahs, humhums, mulmuls, peniascoes, sannoes, peerbands, seer-bettles, seerhaudconnaes, tanjeebs, terridaes, and tincal. The finest loaf sugar and salt must be added with all kinds of spices to season the paper and give it colour. Finally the whole mixture is moistened with the choicest wines, especially those of France. When the paper has been made, a quantity of it is put into a weird machine, and revolved in a hollow wheel, while the operator, Moses Monceca, beats time 'as exactly as HANDEL would do during the performance of an *oratorio*.' When the wheel starts to emit a rattling noise it is stopped and opened. There, in place of the paper, are pounds of gold dust which are immediately sent away to be melted into ingots. In the *Advertisement* at the end of the book the following interpretation is given: 'The PAPER MILL is the OFFICE or OFFICES in ROME, from whence the POPE'S BULLS, BRIEFS, INDULGENCES, DISPENSATIONS, and PARDONS are issued, which produce yearly such an immense sum, and in so easy a manner, that it may properly be called a quick TRANS-MUTATION of PAPER into GOLD.'

Other places visited by the dreamer include the College of the Rosicrucians, the Temple of Mercury, the Temple of Health, Pallantis or the City of Pallas, and the Temple of Hercules. Among the singular beings whom he meets are the Onocentaurs, who are obnoxious animals with some human characteristics, not unlike Swift's Yahoos. The Advertisement provides a deliberately misleading interpretation of most of these allegories: Hercules is the Pope, and the wealthy and elegant Temple of Hercules is the Court of Rome. The human sacrifices which are described as being offered on the altar of Hercules represent the cruelties of the Inquisition. The Rosi-crucians are the monks, who have departed from the rules of their primitive institution, and manifest a large number of vices which the author rehearses in detail. The City of Pallas represents the universities of Europe, and the Palladians, who are perpetually quarrelling with one another, represent the scholars in those universities. The Onocentaurs are the officers of the Inquisition. The Temple of Mercury represents the legal profession, and the Temple of Health the medical profession, both of which exhibit many abuses within their ranks.

The mere fact that King was attacked by Whig politicians as the writer of *The Dreamer* indicates that the religious interpretation of the allegory provided in the Advertisement was not credible to all his readers. However, in any attempt to interpret this work politically, one is faced with much the same difficulties as in the case of *Gulliver's Travels*: the general lines of the allegory are tolerably clear, but it is impossible for the reader of today to feel any degree of certainty with regard to many of the allusions. Some were intended to be obscure, while others could have had significance only to those readers who were intimately acquainted with academic politics in Oxford and the intricate historical relationship between the two parties. The brief and necessarily incomplete political interpretation that follows takes into account only those allusions that do not leave any significant latitude for doubt.

The country of the Papyropolites represents England under the government of the Whigs. The dreamer first visits the Temple of Mnemosyne in company with a band of four hundred, 'some being embroidered all over, others with the air of fribbles, some appearing to be very polite, others to be very clowns . . . all of the same trade': these represent the members of the House of Commons. The Intendants, who are in white satin with hats of the same colour, are the Duke of Newcastle and Henry Pelham. They constitute a duumvirate and employ the four hundred in the manufacture of paper 'of such an excellent sort, that it is the most valuable commodity in the land: which from hence is named the LAND of the PAPYROPOLITES.' The manufacture of this commodity had been improved when a knight adventurer, styled the Colossus, built a new and capacious paper mill. The Colossus represents Sir Robert Walpole; his mill is now administered by the two Intendants or 'White Hats':

The present INTENDANTS give their workmen great wages, and yet the latter have seldom thought themselves sufficiently rewarded. Even the Colossus was at last undone by refusing his BAND of workmen a largess over and above their salaries. When he thought himself most secure, they mutinied, and losing all respect for his person, they tumbled him headlong into his own MILL-POND; and, though he escaped with his life, yet he was compelled in his old age to quit his business, and abdicate his MILL. The WHITE-HATS, who have succeeded to him, were obliged to temporize, cajole the mutineers, raise their wages, and use many stratagems, before they could get into possession. And ever since that time they have managed their affairs with some difficulty. . . . They have been forced to take in many new hands, and yet not suffered to discharge any of those, who were grown old and useless.

The Intendants have lately presented a quantity of their paper to some distinguished foreigners: British subsidies to friendly foreign nations are here implied.

The mill itself seems to represent the contemporary chamber of the House of Commons. The dreamer is taken inside it, but

. . . the roaring of the water, the noise of the pounders, and the loud voices of the BAND of *Four Hundred*, who were all at work, talked all at once, and immediately forgot what they said, and repeated the same things again and again, almost stunned me; so that I imagined myself to be in the same *Bedlam*, where my old friend SWIFT had formerly placed his *Legion Club*. Wherefore I retreated as hastily as I could, without asking a single question.

The various commodities in the store room of the mill constitute articles on which taxes were levied and commercial profits made. One reads with some amusement that the teetotal author 'particularly observed vast heaps of barley, hops and apples'. Arabian berries and American nuts represent, I suppose, coffee and chocolate, and the 'small dried leaves plucked from a curious Chinese shrub' cannot be other than those of the tea plant.

Having left the mill, the dreamer is taken to the College of the Rosicrucians: the bishops are here intended, or rather less likely the clergy of the Establishment as a whole. Both the hierarchy and the lower clergy were juridically bound to obedience to the Hanoverian monarch in virtue of their oath of allegiance, but King seems most of the time to be alluding to the prelates. The dreamer comments that they had been greatly respected when they strictly observed the statutes of their founder: they were enjoined to be meek, humble, charitable, and hospitable, and indeed the primitive Rosicrucians had employed all their revenues in entertaining pilgrims and strangers and feeding the poor and hungry. As long as they practised these virtues they preserved their independence, but

. . . as they have now entirely departed from all the rules of their institution, and are become proud and luxurious, covetous and ambitious, they are likewise the most corrupt and servile crew in all the land of the PAPYROPOLITES. Some years have past, since they renounced the independency of their order, both for themselves and their successors, by a formal act, and agreed to obey implicitly all the commands, which from time to time they should receive from the INTENDANTS of the MILL. . . . while the ROSICRUCIANS are the most abject flatterers of men in power, they treat their inferiors, especially their younger brothers, of which there is a numerous tribe, with the greatest insolence and contempt, and suffer the latter, in violation of the most sacred injunctions of their common parent, to languish in poverty, and want even the common necessaries of life.

The dreamer adds that they are 'neither trained to arms, nor acquainted with those maxims of honour and gallantry, which form a modern hero. In case of a foreign, or domestick war, they rather chuse by their harangues to inspire their neighbours with courage, than give any proofs of it themselves.' This observation is followed by an indubitable allusion to Dr. Thomas Herring, the then Archbishop of Canterbury: 'However, there are some among them, who have been so bold as to gird their loins with the sword: and their present great master is as full of martial ardour, as he is of piety and devotion; and is ever prepared, in time of danger, both to pray and to fight for his friends and his country.' But the dreamer does not wish to appear prejudiced: he comments, 'I have known as excellent men of this order, as are to be found in the whole human species.'

The Temple of Mercury or Court of Judicature represents the legal profession and the Temple of Health the profession of medicine. The dreamer is taken to both of them. His accounts contain no criticism of a specifically religious or political nature, so there is no attempt to disguise their real purport. The Advertisement indicates that the satire in them is directed against those great cities in Europe where the legal and medical abuses which the dreamer ridicules are tolerated: in fact, the author was no doubt thinking mainly of the practice of these professions in the British Isles. The patron of laws was in classical tradition Apollo: the fact that King places the lawyers of the Papyropolites in a building dedicated to Mercury illustrates his general attitude towards them. The description of the Temple of Health gives King an opportunity to repeat what he considered to be the constituents of good health: cleanness, good hours, moderate exercise, temperance, and abstinence. The goddess of health calls these 'the only infallible rules, which can be given for the attainment and preservation of health and long life.' The dreamer adds his own observations on cleanness:

It is, according to my sentiments, the greatest beauty in a man or woman: and the *simplex munditiis* of HORACE, by which he has distinguished, and characterized PYRRHA, at the same time, that it gives us an example of the neatness and elegance of the poet's taste and style, hath made his mistress immortal . . . were I the governor of a kingdom, it should be my first law or ordinance, that every master of a family should be clean himself, and take especial care, that his house and his wife, his man servant, and his maid servant, and even his ox and his ass, and every creature, and every thing about him should be in the same condition; unless when by his trade or occupation he was necessarily employed in dirty work. But *dirty work*, or *dirty hands* should be no excuse for any persons above the degree of mechanics, especially for those, who make profession of the liberal arts, who serve at the altar of the gods, or form any part of the legislature.

Some of King's animadversions on the medical profession, put into the mouth of one of the priests of the Temple of Health, are highly unflattering. They might have been extended, but 'the good priests were called away to attend a person of distinction, who, having been perfectly cured of a most inveterate distemper by *abstinence* only, was come hither with an heart full of gratitude, to pay his devotions, and perform his vows to the

goddess of HEALTH.' The dreamer corroborates his report of
the priest's observations with a story of his own which he
inserts without comment:

When my old acquaintance, Dr. FRAMPTON of OXFORD, who
had acquired a large fortune by the practice of physic, was dying, all
the physicians in the city attended him. They consulted, they prescribed, and out of respect to a learned brother, they waited to see
their medicines administered. But when they were offered to
FRAMPTON, he rejected them with a half smile, and with this
expression: TAKE THEM AWAY: YOU KNOW, IT IS ALL A
FARCE!

Pallantis or the city of Pallas, the place next visited by the
dreamer, represents Oxford. It is a city 'of no great extent, but
beautifully situated near the conflux of two rivers, and has the
benefit of a wholesome and temperate air.' Formerly it had great
privileges, was free from all tributes and taxations, and was
governed by its own magistrates, 'as it is in some measure at
this day.' The ancestors of the Palladians were Greeks:

The citizens boast themselves to be descended from a colony of the
ATHENIANS, who left their native country, when the liberties of
GREECE were destroyed, and settled in ITALY. They urge, as an
argument to prove the antiquity of their descent, and the truth of this
tradition, that, as they have preserved the GREEK language in its
ATTIC purity to this day, so they both speak, and write the LATIN
of the AUGUSTAN age; and moreover, that they cultivate all the
liberal arts and sciences with unwearied application.

A few years previously Pallas had been attacked by the Onocentaurs, who represent the Whigs. The dreamer speaks of 'the
baseness and malignity of their nature' and describes them as
'noxious animals' who are 'little superior to any part of the
brute-creation'. Their great idol is the golden calf. They and the
Palladians have engaged for a number of years in a political
struggle, the historical origins of which are described in some
detail.

The ultimate cause of the controversy, we are told, resides
in the fact that the Papyropolitan government, which was once
free, has now become an oligarchy: the few nobles who govern
it cannot brook the existence in their dominions of a city

founded upon maxims so different from their own. They therefore supplied the Onocentaurs with money, arms, and all kinds
of warlike stores, and incited them to invade the city with a
view to settling in it. The Palladians withstood their attacks
with courage, but were at length obliged to give way to their
superior numbers and, by a formal treaty, to cede to them that
quarter of the city which they now possess. The Onocentaurs
could hardly have failed in their attack for they were well supported and the city was unfortified. How much longer Pallantis
can survive is questionable: the only recourse left to the inhabitants is prayer to their goddess.

While the dreamer is listening to a Palladian's explanation of
these matters, a messenger arrives to announce that a whole
legion of Onocentaurs is marching to the attack led by their
commander or *bray*, an obvious allusion to Thomas Bray of
Exeter College. They are supported by all the Palladian
deserters with Cornix (King's name for Sir Edward Turner) at
their head. The loyal Palladians march out to meet them under
the command of the count who had been the dreamer's guide.
As soon as the enemy forces catch sight of the count, they are
seized with panic and flee without striking a blow. They escape
'with the loss of a few prisoners, and one standard, which was
taken from the deserters, together with the standard bearer,
called PORCUS, who being covered over with brass from head
to foot, and having besides a protuberance of paunch, was an
overload for his horse.' Porcus, who represents Lord Parker,
and Vespa, who is described as 'a little fellow' but is not definitely identifiable, are referred to as 'the chief authors and pro-
motors of the present war.'

The last place visited by the dreamer is the Temple of
Hercules. This section of the work seems to be a general attack
on the power of money in contemporary society, but the allegory
is even vaguer than in the rest of the book. The Advertisement
provides no interpretation; the annotated copy in the Bodleian
Library indicates that Hercules is George II and the temple his
court. If these equations are correct, then the Anti-Herculeans,
according to Robson, may plausibly be identified with the
Jacobites.[1] The fact that King criticizes the Anti-Herculeans

[1] R. J. Robson, op. cit., pp. 71f.

for their factiousness provides corroboration for this interpretation: when he was writing *The Dreamer* there already existed a widening gulf between those Jacobites who desired political action and those whose attachment to the cause was almost entirely sentimental.

A qualified similarity between *The Dreamer* and *Gulliver's Travels* has already been implied: King perhaps acquired the general notion of his work from Swift's more famous story, though there are no unquestionable signs of direct indebtedness. King's style in *The Dreamer* is not reminiscent of the Dean's: it is, like that of his Latin orations, polished, elegant, and formal. *The Dreamer* is a product of a writer whose prose reaches its highest perfection in the form of Latin academic oratory, and whose English style was formed to a considerable degree by his reading of the classical authors. It is, in some respects, a typically Augustan piece of rhetoric, exhibiting an attrited quality, together with a certain magisterial stiffness which permeates the whole work and constitutes its principal strength. Like *Gulliver's Travels* its content is in places repulsive, especially in those passages relating to the Onocentaurs, but there is no attempt to reproduce the verisimilitude of Swift's work. The author makes it clear that he *dreamed* most of what he relates. Despite the fact that *The Dreamer* gives the impression of having been carefully written, it manifests neither Swift's depth, nor his sad ingenuousness, nor his ability to communicate a sense of intimacy to the reader. It shows a greater degree of internal consistency than *Gulliver's Travels*, but in most respects must be deemed a comparatively inferior piece of writing.

Critical pronouncements on *The Dreamer* in the author's own lifetime seem to have been coloured largely by the political bias of the writer. The most unsympathetic was made by Richard Blacow. In *A Letter to William King, LL.D.* he commented: '. . . a worse book than the *Dreamer*, both as to the shameless Abuses it is filled with, the principles it is calculated to recommend; and for poverty of composition, I think not easy to be found.' After the Whig attacks had subsided, the book was generally forgotten. It is not included in any of the standard bibliographies of Utopian literature, where one would most expect to find it, and, probably due to its anonymity, is not even included in some bibliographies of King himself. Its principal interest to literary scholars has consisted in the fact that it contains, in a long footnote, the text of *Paulus, by Mr. L——y* with *The Answer, by Dr. Swift*, neither of which was published by the Dean himself. In preserving these two poems of 1728, King performed a service to the cause of English literature which his contemporary critics seem to have ignored.

Whatever the reader may feel about the many vagaries which any interpretation of *The Dreamer* must necessarily leave undecided, there are good grounds for speculating on the author's reason for publishing when he did. The book appeared just a few months before the county election was held, and King probably hoped that during the intervening period *The Dreamer* would have some effect in influencing uncommitted voters against the Whigs. To judge from the later complaints in the press from outraged Whig correspondents it may have done so. But it would be as difficult to form a precise estimate of King's influence on this election as it would be to assess that of Sir Walter Scott on the American Civil War.

From the Tory point of view the most disturbing factor in the election itself was the conduct of the Fellows of Exeter College, and especially of their Rector, Francis Webber. Like all the other colleges, Exeter had been urged in a *Programma* from the Vice-Chancellor, Dr. George Huddesford of Trinity College, dated 15 April 1754, to observe political neutrality during the week of the poll. His position was unquestionably sound: this was a county, not a university election. The gates of all the colleges were to remain shut and all the occupants *in statu pupillari* not possessing a vote were forbidden to leave, except with permission. Dr. Huddesford forbade all of the students without exception 'to appear abroad without their respective Academical Habits; or bearing Clubs, Sticks, or any other Weapon whatsoever during the Days of the Poll; and This under the Penalty of having their Names put in the Black Register, and being farther proceeded against with the Utmost Severity.' Polling began on the afternoon of April 17 at the specially erected booths in Broad Street against the north side of Exeter College. A mob of Old Interest supporters had that morning established themselves in front of the booths, and so to protect the Whig voters (or to provide them with refreshment) the Rector of Exeter, in disobedience to the *Programma*, had admitted a party of them into his college. That afternoon he let them out of the *back* door of Exeter College so that they could approach the polling area from the rear. Protests by Sir James Dashwood were unavailing, and the door remained open. The Vice-Chancellor realized that the level of discipline implicit in the *Programma* could not be maintained, so on April 20 the demands were relaxed and the gates of all the colleges were reopened.

In this matter, as in several others occurring during this period, King's confidential advice to the authorities would appear to have been influential. The original owner of the Bodleian copy of Jackson's Poll-Book describes Huddesford in a note on the fly-leaf as 'an humble toadeater at the time of the Oxfordshire election to William King L.L.D.' Euseby Isham, commenting on Lord Arran's recent nomination of the Tory Earl of Westmoreland to the position of High Steward of the university, remarked, 'Dr. King is supposed to have been admitted into a great share of confidence with both the Earls, which may easily account for the nomination.'[1] A certain amount of his influence seems to have been exerted socially. Thus the following July he entertained the Earl of Westmoreland in company with Euseby Isham and some other guests in his lodgings at St. Mary Hall, and, wrote Isham, 'Dr. King gave us a proper dinner for him.'[2]

While the Principal of St. Mary Hall was helping behind the scenes to further the cause of the Old Interest, it was clear to everybody that the Rector and Fellows of Exeter College had actively assisted the Whig voters, a fact which led to a good deal of adverse comment from the Tories, and some disarming admissions from the Whig leaders. Thus on April 30 Lord Harcourt wrote to Bray:

All the Gentlemen that I have seen declare that we would not have polled a hundred votes, without the assistance of your College. But however we may be indebted to your Society, we are undoubtedly more so to you, than to allmost any other person of the Party. It is a

[1] Northamptonshire Record Office, Isham (Lamport) Collection No. 2185.
[2] Northamptonshire Record Office, Isham (Lamport) Collection No. 2705.

piece of justice I shall allways do you to acknowledge it, wherever I have an opportunity of mentioning Mr. Brays name.[1]

On the following July 5, when King presented some gentlemen for their degrees in the Convocation House, he alluded to the alleged revelry of the Whig voters in Exeter College and urged his listeners to observe the university statutes, *nisi nos facimus aedes nostras, ubi ingenuae artes florere debent, Ambulaiarum et Bacchantium collegia.*[2]

Meanwhile King had added more fuel to the flames in his speech delivered at the Commemoration of 1754. Speaking in the Sheldonian Theatre on July 2, he demonstrated 'his usual Spirit and Eloquence, and gained, as he always doth, the universal Applause of his audience.'[3] A few portions of this Latin presentation-speech are included in *Doctor King's Apology* of 1755, but the only account to have survived in any degree of detail is contained in a highly prejudiced letter written from Exeter College by Benjamin Kennicott to Samuel Richardson.[4] Kennicott explains that, after the long procession had entered the theatre, Dr. King stood at the Vice-Chancellor's right hand, 'and, as it soon appeared, not improperly: for the Vice-Chancellor was not very ready at the names of some of the now first-heard-of gentlemen intended to be Doctor'd—a difficulty which (you may be sure) was not owing to Mr. Vice-Chancellor's want of apprehension, but to the badness of the writing.' The account of King's speech commences a little later in Kennicott's letter:

Dr. King begun with telling us—he never intended to have turned orator again; but the insults of his enemies, the entreaties of his honest friends, and the commands of Mr. Vice-Chancellor, had prevailed. Then, his compliments to the High Steward, and the new Doctors—then the wickedness and corruption of the times—times

---

[1] Exeter College MSS., Harcourt to Bray, 30 April 1754.

[2] The text of the speech of 5 July 1754 is not preserved in its entirety: this extract is reproduced in *Doctor King's Apology*.

[3] *The London Evening Post*, No. 4159 (6–9 July 1754). A similar report appeared in *Jackson's Oxford Journal*, No. 62 (6 July 1754).

[4] Anna L. Barbauld (ed.), *The Correspondence of Samuel Richardson* (2 vols.; London: Richard Phillips, 1804), Vol. II, pp. 183–96. The date is given as 9 June 1754: this must be erroneous.

so irreligious (he said) that we were lately about to sell the birth-right of British Christians even to the *Jews*!—Times, so horribly corrupt, that we had agreed to sell our daughters by the late *Marriage* Act! Sweet creatures! (as the orator said) it was a thousand pities such fine girls as then filled the Theatre should be sold by their unnatural parents, and, perhaps, (dreadful thought!) even to *Whig* husbands!

There are variations between Kennicott's version of what followed and the very brief portions of the speech which King quoted in *Doctor King's Apology*. First, here are Kennicott's words:

But so beautiful, so elegant, were the ladies there assembled, he was sure they were of the right side; and he advised them, as the fair friends of liberty, to wear upon their rings, and embroider upon their garments, this sound maxim—*The man who sells his country, will sell his wife or his daughter*. (Upon which there was loud applause, the ladies *clapping their wings*, as well as the gentlemen; which the orator called *ominous*.)

King's account of the same part of the speech is somewhat different. According to *Doctor King's Apology* these tributes to the ladies came at the close of the speech rather than in the middle, and were followed by applause and some further remarks which had been completely misinterpreted by the 'Informers', by which the author meant principally the Whig dons of Exeter College, together with Richard Blacow of Brasenose. Thus wrote King:

In the close of this Speech I made a compliment to the Ladies, who were present, which I concluded with the following address, or exhortation: *Addam tria verba, quae vos, lectissimae matronae, vos, castissimae puellae, figite in mentibus, habete in annulis, acu pingite in vestibus:* QUICUNQUE SEIPSUM VENDIT, IS HERCLE CERTE HAUD DUBITABIT UXOREM, ET FILIAM VENDERE. This was received with a shout of applause; of which I took the advantage and proceeded in this manner: *Plausum hunc, Academici, accipio in omen bona praenuntians, saltem nos commonefaciens officii & virtutis nostrae, utque caveamus,* & c. How do you think the INFORMERS interpreted this expression? They said, that I was so indiscreet, *as to pronounce the applause which was bestowed on me, to be* OMINOUS, *or a* BAD OMEN.

The ending of the speech is reported by Kennicott in this wise:

Having done with the ladies, the old gentleman paid his compliments to our High Sheriff, that *unjust Judge*;—concluding, that if the good old cause should have no more justice *elsewhere*, farewell to British liberty.

It is a pity that King did not arrange for the printing of this oration: Kennicott's carping and partisan attitude does little to stimulate confidence in the fidelity of his summary. In reply to Kennicott, Richardson passed some comments on King which are quite unfair, but which constitute a little-known literary curiosity:

What strange people are some of your leading ones at Oxford! If your occasional orator were to choose his supreme governor, he would not find a Dr. King *permitted* to arraign the justice of his government, and to reflect on laws actually passed, and in force. There cannot be a greater instance of the lenity of the government he abuses, than his pestilent harangues, so publicly made with impunity, furnish all his readers with. I know not the gentleman. He is old, you say. Old, yet so abandoned of decency! So much a reviler of the powers that be! Such a rebel, as I may call him, to the doctrines of Christianity, and so great a stranger to that meekness and submission which are its characteristics! What encouragement to parents and guardians to send their youth to a seminary so governed![1]

The generally unsatisfactory conduct of the county election created a backwash of litigation at Westminster and domestic dissension at Oxford. The literary manifestation of the general ill-feeling took the form of a prolonged pamphlet war, the accumulated remains of which constitute a kind of farrago of very uneven quality. There is no necessity to elaborate on all of the publications emanating from the post-electoral controversy.[2] The chief cause was the Vice-Chancellor's speech to Convocation on 8 October 1754, when, according to *The London Evening Post*, he commented with a becoming zeal and severity on 'the infamous behaviour of *one college*, which despight of all

[1] Ibid., pp. 197f.
[2] Those specifically relating to Exeter College are listed in William K. Stride, *Exeter College* (London: F. E. Robinson, 1900), pp. 118–25. Also invaluable is the bibliography in R. J. Robson, op. cit., pp. 171–9.

Decency, opened its Gates, and its Cellars to the Refuse of Mankind, and prostituted itself, during the whole Poll, to be the Shop of *Corruption*, and the Factory of *Perjury*.'[1] There could be no doubt in anyone's mind as to which college was implied. About November 20 there appeared *A Defence of the Rector and Fellows of Exeter College*, issued anonymously but usually attributed to the Rector himself. The Vice-Chancellor during the following January responded in *A Proper Reply to a Pamphlet entitled A Defence of the Rector and Fellows of Exeter College*, and another Tory—it is impossible now to say who—joined in with *A Letter to the Author of the Defence of Exeter College*. At about the same time there were more charges and countercharges: it is in some cases difficult or impossible to determine the chronological order of the publications containing them. *An Address to Dr. Huddesford Occasioned by his Proper Reply* was perhaps the work of Benjamin Kennicott, while an unidentifiable Tory writer, using the pseudonym of *Cantabrigiensis*, was the author of the amusing piece entitled *The Conduct of [Exeter] College Considered*. This latter production contains a number of adverse reflections on Webber's *Defence*, but the writer's criticisms of the Exeter Whigs are mild compared to those of the Principal of St. Mary Hall in *Doctor King's Apology*.

This work appeared in February 1755, and had run through three editions before the end of the year. While it was being printed, the Vice-Chancellor excluded all Masters of Arts from the university printing-house on the top floor of the Sheldonian Theatre: even though he lamented the lack of political impartiality in Exeter College, he was at no pains to conceal the direction in which his own political preference lay. *Doctor King's Apology* was intended, so the initial Advertisement to the second and third editions explains, to answer the accusations of the 'Society of Informers', including his foremost antagonists in Exeter College: Francis Webber, Benjamin Kennicott, and

---

[1] *The London Evening Post*, No. 4199 (8–10 October 1754). No copy of the complete Latin text of the speech is now available, but an extract appeared in the Vice-Chancellor's (i.e. George Huddesford's) *A Proper Reply to a Pamphlet Entitled A Defence of the Rector and Fellows of Exeter College*. The Latin excerpt that the Vice-Chancellor published gives a slightly milder impression than the English quotation in *The London Evening Post*. King later published some brief remarks on the speech in *The Last Blow*.

Thomas Bray. The individual whom the author styles 'the Grand Informer' was Richard Blacow of Brasenose, who had become editor of *The Evening Advertiser* in October 1754, and was using this paper to attack the Tories in general and the Jacobites in particular.

Blacow's record for passing on information concerning anti-government activities to the Whig authorities had been impressive, a fact which becomes warrantably clear in the light of some of his confidential correspondence which has remained so far unpublished. It was he who had been responsible for bringing the principal miscreants in the Jacobite disturbance of 23 February 1747 to the Court of King's Bench. He knew about the Tory Journal *The Protester* before it had even been published, and passed his intelligence on to the Duke of Newcastle in his letter written on 31 May 1753 from Johnson's Court, Charing Cross:

The following I have just received as private intelligence, and I think it my duty as soon as possible to communicate it to Your Grace.——

'You will see on Saturday a new Anti-ministerial Paper under the title of *Protester*, which is supported by a powerful set of Noblemen and Gentlemen, who, I am told, are determined to hunt down the Minister and render him odious to the People.'

The person who wrote me this is a Printer, whom I have employed to print many of the papers on the *New Interest* side in the Oxfordshire Election. This I mention to satisfy Your Grace that I know him to be a trusty man and a fast friend to the Government, and that more material Intelligence concerning this base combination may therefore possibly be come at thro' his means.[1]

On 23 July 1754 Blacow had published a notice of the Rag Plot in *The Evening Advertiser*, and had thus brought the matter to the attention of official circles in London before it had gained any circulation in Oxford.[2] In the following October he wrote

---

[1] British Museum, Add. MSS. 32731, fol. 583. Later Blacow communicated to the Duke the names of the editor and some of the financial backers of *The Protester* (British Museum, Add. MSS. 32732, fol. 80). This periodical survived for 24 issues (2 June–10 Nov. 1753).

[2] *Informations and Other Papers Relating to the Treasonable Verses found at Oxford July 17th 1754* (Oxford, 1755), p. 6. Several letters on the subject appeared in *The*

to Thomas Bray asking for information 'in order that I may draw up a sort of History or connected account of this whole affair.' In the margin of this letter Blacow has written, 'Secrecy, Secrecy, Secrecy!'[1] He even descended to a mild form of blackmail after the Vice-Chancellor had written to him on the subject of the notice in *The London Evening Post*. Pleaded Huddesford, quoting in part from Blacow's own words, 'I desire you will, *as a common Piece of Humanity & Justice to the University of Oxford,* send me a true list of the names of *that Certain Number of Loyal Subjects—Members of the said University—* who authoriz'd you to insert in the Publick Papers an Advertisement so malevolent to the Generality of this Place—so regardless of Truth—and so Injurious to the real Character and deserved Credit of this University.'[2] Replied Blacow (with rather careless penmanship), '. . . unless you can think yourself at liberty . . . to oblige me with a copy of everything sworn against me . . . and transmitted to you, this whole affair between us must be brought before the Tribunal of the Publick, as that is the only Court you cannot hinder from being open to, Sir, Your Humble Servant, Richd. Blacow.'[3]

Not unnaturally Blacow expected to be rewarded for his pains, and ecclesiastical preferment from the Duke of Newcastle was the form he wanted. On 12 December 1748 he had sent the Duke a 'Humble Memorial'; on 18 October 1751 he had written, 'there cannot live a person to whom it would be more agreeable to me to owe my fortune to'; and on April 22 of the following year, 'there is now vacant a Prebend in the Church of Canterbury, which would make me extremely happy after above four years waiting.'[4] His loyalty to the Duke was even-

London Evening Post; see especially Nos. 4167 (25–7 July 1754) signed BRITANNI-CUS, 4169 (30 July–1 August 1754) 'from a Gentleman at Oxford to his friend in London', 4173 (8–10 August 1754) from 'OXONIAE AMICUS', 4177 (17–20 August 1754) signed 'A.B.', and 4184 (3–5 September 1754) from 'B.C.' A ballad entitled *The Rag Plot* was published in No. 4178 (20–22 August 1754), and 'an excellent new song' called *The Oxford Rag Plot* in No. 4195 (28 September–1 October 1754). *The Evening Advertiser*, according to *The British Union-Catalogue of Periodicals*, ran for 641 issues between March 1754 and April 1758. Very few numbers have survived.

[1] Exeter College MSS., Blacow to Bray, October 1754.
[2] Exeter College MSS., Huddesford to Blacow, 7 October 1754.
[3] Exeter College MSS., Blacow to Huddesford, 2 November 1754.
[4] British Museum, Add. MSS., 32717, fol. 427; 32725, fol. 309; 32726, fol. 491.

tually recognized when he was appointed to a canonry at Windsor. King was certain that this preferment was the result of his ability as an informer, and was equally sure that Blacow hoped to attain greater dignities by exposing the Tory villains involved in the Rag Plot. In *The London Evening Post* King expressed these sentiments by means of an epigram, and took the opportunity to broadcast an allusion to the fact that Blacow had at one time helped to promote his father's brewery:

> From selling bad ale which he found a poor trade
> Oates the second informed and a canon was made.
> But to show his new art, his reverence now brags
> He will pick out lawn sleeves from a heap of old rags.[1]

It is hardly any wonder that, when King wrote his *Anecdotes*, his sentiments towards Blacow and his like-minded colleagues had not mellowed. The Society of Informers became the *Blacones*, but King's attitude to them remained what it had been before:

> BLACONES apud Anglos sunt infames delatores, gigantum filii, quos natura malevolos spes praemii induxit in summum scelus: qui quum castos et integerrimos viros accusare soleant, omnia confingunt, et non modo perjuria sua vendunt, verum etiam alios impellunt ad pejerandum. Nomen sumunt a BLACOW quodam sacerdote, qui ob nefarias suas delationes donatus est canonicatu Vindsoriensi a regni praefecto D. de N. Quanta heu, heu, illo tempore fuerunt scelerum praemia![2]

The style of *Doctor King's Apology* is vituperative and setigerous, but the author does provide some well turned rebuttals to the invectives which his Whig adversaries had at various times hurled against him. The accusations of the Society of Informers, which King deals with one by one, are as follows:

1. That he was an Irishman.
2. That he had defrauded subscribers to an unpublished book or books to the extent of 3000 guineas.
3. That he wrote the Jacobite *London Evening Post*.
4. That he had written a book entitled *Political Considerations* in 1710, a work containing false English.

---

[1] *The London Evening Post*, No. 4187 (12–14 September 1754). Other verses on Canon Blacow appeared in Nos. 4189–94, 4196, 4199–201, and in several subsequent issues. There are also some criticisms in prose of 'the Dignified Informer'.

[2] *Political and Literary Anecdotes* (2nd edn., 1819), p. 216.

5. That he offered himself to sale both in England and Ireland, but was not found worth the purchase.

6. That he was the author of a book entitled *The Dreamer*.

First, King makes it clear that since he had been born in Middlesex he could not possibly be an Irishman. But even if he had been an Irishman, this fact would be no crime. In support of his contention he lauds the cultural standing of Ireland, alluding specifically to Dean Swift and quoting, *en passant*, from one of Swift's most distinguished readers on the continent, Cardinal Polignac, whom King had met in 1737:

... as to the liberal arts and sciences the IRISH [people] is in no respect inferior to ours, witness the immortal works of the late DEAN of ST. PATRICK's, of whom Cardinal POLIGNAC, who was himself one of the politest scholars in EUROPE, said to me, IL A L'ESPRIT CREATEUR; an elogy, in my judgment, preferable to all the monumental inscriptions in WESTMINSTER Abbey.

To answer the charge of fraud implied by his accusers, King explained the intentions which he had had in mind seven or eight years earlier for the two-volume collection of his Latin works. The author then proceeds to disclaim authorship of *The London Evening Post*, a trifle regretfully, since he acknowledges that many essays, letters, and political paragraphs in it are 'the productions of an excellent wit, and full of good sense; and prove the author to be well skilled in all the branches of our trade and commerce, and to have acquired a perfect knowledge of the English constitution.' He next points out that the book entitled *Political Considerations* was not his work at all: his enemies had confused him with Dr. William King of Christ Church. The accusation that King had offered himself to sale in England and Ireland was, he said, equally untrue, for at no time in his life, either in England or Ireland, had he sought, or endeavoured by any means to obtain employment of any kind from the present or any former government. Indeed, he had, so far, never even been once at court, either in England or Ireland.

With regard to the charge of being the author of *The Dreamer* King is unusually evasive. This part of King's *Apology* is the least satisfactory, since he does not really answer the accusation at all. He writes:

Now, as to an open acknowledgement, whether I am, or am not the author of this book, I do not conceive, it is of any concernment to the reader, or of any consequence to my own vindication; nor do I believe the equity and candor of the public will expect it from me. It will be sufficient, if I can free THE DREAMER from all unjust and malicious imputations. . . .

This argument clearly circumvents the charge. If he were not the author of *The Dreamer*, King would certainly have denied authorship, as he did in the case of *Political Considerations*.

Some of Blacow's accusations were, according to King, presented in *The Evening Advertiser* 'in wretched English metre.' He explains that the Grand Informer generally distinguished St. Mary Hall as *Aula Libertatis*, and adds: 'Under this title of AULAE LIBERTATIS PRINCIPALIS the same INFORMER hath bespattered me in some doggrel verses; in which, according to his manner, there is not a line of truth, or sense. So that I can now honestly boast, that I have been libelled by the *worst*, and celebrated by the *best* poet in *England*.' The verses of Blacow to which King alludes have not survived, so there is now no record to verify the charge that he was the worst poet in England. But since King immediately afterwards refers the reader to *The Triumph of Isis*, he evidently considered that in 1754 Thomas Warton was the best. Blacow himself King describes as being 'a fitter person to fill a sentry box, than a canon's stall,' and 'a snake or adder which was found in the highway perishing with cold and hunger.' He concludes the work with some general exhortations, among them a suggestion to the heads and Fellows of colleges to use great care and caution in admitting 'the sons of low mechanics'. In a footnote he answers one final charge.

. . . there is one CRIME, charged on me by the INFORMERS, which I must acknowledge to be true: tho' it will admit of some alleviation, as I could not prevent it, nor can I mend it. It is my AGE. I am an OLD SENSUALIST, an OLD TRUMPETER, or designed [i.e. designated] by some other elegant and severe Apellative, to which the Epithet, OLD, may be properly prefixed, to add a poignancy to the Satire. . . . I am willing on this occasion to return good for evil, and do most heartily wish, that this CRIME may never be imputed to any Member of the SOCIETY OF INFORMERS.

There appear to have been at least two replies to King's *Apology*, both of which appeared shortly after the work which they were intended to answer. The first, *A Letter to Doctor King, Occasioned by his Late Apology*, is described on the title-page as being by 'a friend to Mr. Kennicott.' It is sometimes regarded as being the work of Kennicott himself. If it is, it does little justice to one of the great Hebrew scholars of the eighteenth century. As a piece of pamphleteering this work is combative but circumlocutory, much of it never rising above the level of anti-Jacobite propaganda. It contains a number of petulant observations on *The Toast* and *The Dreamer*, together with much irrelevant personal abuse of King and several mistakes both logical and factual. For example, it is taken for granted that King must be an Irishman because O'Donald, the supposititious translator of *The Toast*, calls Ireland 'his own country'; the Principal of St. Mary Hall is confused more than once with the other William King of Christ Church; and it is implied that the Principal knew no Greek, whereas he shows himself a competent writer of Greek in several places, especially in the third book of *The Toast*. However, it is significant that even this work contains one flattering reference to King's ability as an orator, an indication that even his enemies were impressed by his *expertise*:

One thing, which the world is generally agreed in, is *your just fame*, as an *Orator* . . . How masterly your ELOCUTION! What a graceful propriety of ACTION! *Action;* that essential part of true Oratory, however unfortunately discontinued by the *Readers* (for one cannot call them *Speakers*) of the languid and unanimated Discourses in modern times!

The other reply was Blacow's *A Letter to William King*, in which the author attempted to prove that the Principal of St. Mary Hall was responsible for the disturbance of 23 February 1747/8. Even though three editions of this pamphlet appeared in 1755, it exerted no special influence: Blacow's case against King rested on a minor undergraduate disturbance which had taken place some seven years previously.

Meanwhile the flood of pamphlets and booklets continued unabated, many of their writers repeating arguments which had already been used again and again. Of these publications, the only one which is definitely attributable to King is *The Last Blow*, described on its title-page as 'An Unanswerable Vindication of the Society of Exeter College. In Reply to the Vice-Chancellor, Dr. King, and the Writers of the *London Evening Post*.' At least two editions were published dated MDCCLV. This 'vindication' is actually an attack on the dons of Exeter College ingeniously presented in the guise of a defence, and yet another example of its author's facility for arguing one case while seeming to argue its opposite. In common with many of King's other writings, this brief work requires a key for the reader's full comprehension. A partial key is provided by Stride, but some allusions remain unclear.[1]

There is nothing especially new about the content of *The Last Blow*, and a good deal of it is no more than chaff. A few pieces of information are given on the Rag Plot and the Watch Plot which are not provided anywhere else, and there are some additional comments on the Vice-Chancellor's speech of 8 October 1754. Thomas Bray is ridiculed under the name of Boots, and Benjamin Kennicott under almost no disguise at all:

> But *hic vir! hic est!* here comes the man, here comes the glory of the tribe, *Little* BENJAMIN *their Ruler*, or in simple terms the Rev. Mr. K–NN–C–T! This gentleman has entirely exploded the old axiom in philosophy, *ex nihilo nihil fit*: for though he came from *nothing*, his very enemies are now obliged to acknowledge him to be *something* of consequence. Indeed these very enemies were the people that made him so. They lifted him from the dirt in which he lay groveling in obscurity, and added splendor to his character by an University Degree.

Other Whigs coming under King's lash include Francis Webber, James Cosserat, and Richard Blacow. The observations made on these gentlemen are sometimes marred by unnecessary condescension and coarseness: again, the reader is conscious of the influence of Swift. Perhaps the most noteworthy feature of this pamphlet, if it is judged as a historical document, is the remarkable accuracy of its prophecies. Thus King wrote of Francis Webber, 'we make no doubt but he will be shortly advanced to some high dignity in the Church.' Sure enough, in

---

[1] William K. Stride, op. cit., pp. 123f.

the next year, Webber was made Dean of Hereford. Of Thomas
Bray, King prognosticated:

> *A Canon! that's a place too mean;*
> *No, Thomas, thou shalt be a Dean.*

A little over two decades later Bray became Dean of Raphoe in
Ireland. And of Benjamin Kennicott, the reader is assured:
'Although . . . this *fellow* came originally from the cobler's stall,
it is by no means fit that he should be sent thither again. Nor,
we trust, will he; he will rather rise on account of his extraordinary merits by gradual promotions, till he fills a nobler
STALL. . . .' This nobler stall turned out to be at Westminster
Abbey, where Kennicott was appointed to a canonry in July
1770. Some five months later he resigned this position for the
fourth stall at Christ Church, Oxford.

The Last Blow was King's final contribution to the literature
of the county election of 1754. Perhaps it is not too much to say
that this small work was also the last blow of any significance
to be struck for the non-juring members of the Tory Party,
whose confidence in the eventual restoration of the House of
Stuart was shrivelling. It is difficult to gauge the extent to which
King himself could be called a Jacobite at this time, but to
judge from *The Last Blow*, the charge of Jacobitism was still
being bandied with frequency:

How disaffected a place is *Oxford*! The *Vice-Chancellor* is a Jacobite.
Why? because he reprimanded Our College. In the dutiful expressions of his attachment to the King and Royal Family he certainly
meant the Pretender; at least *we represented his words so to ourselves in
English*. Every minute circumstance in this place is an evidence of
jacobitism. The picture-shops are stuck full of prints of Mr. *Rowney*,
with a *Latin* motto under them, *Pro Patria*; which means the Pretender. One of the principal coffee-houses in the *Highstreet* is called
James's coffee-house. Can any thing be more flagrantly jacobitical?
There is also an inn in the *Highstreet* called *The King's Head*; and
whose Head is it? Not King GEORGE's, no, King CHARLES's.
Besides all this, one of the chief *Old Interest* inns is the *Flower de Luce*,
which, by a very slight knowledge of *Inuendo*, may denote the con-
nexions and attachment of that party.

It may be assumed that King's criticisms of the dons of Exeter

College were virtuously motivated, even though they were expressed in a bellicose and far from disinterested fashion. What the Principal of St. Mary Hall could not have foreseen in 1755 was the speed with which the entire issue would become, for all practical purposes, completely moribund.

VIII

The Final Years

EVEN though in the mid-1750s he was engaged in more or less constant personal dispute, King was not neglecting his academic duties. Of special interest is the fact that in February 1755 he gave Dr. Samuel Johnson his diploma of M.A., which had been awarded by decree in the same month. Boswell in his *Life of Johnson* commented of this event: 'We may conceive what a high gratification it must have been to Johnson to receive his diploma from the hands of the great Dr. KING, whose principles were so congenial with his own.'[1] The author of the text of the diploma is not known, but he was quite possibly King himself.

On 10 March 1755 a collection of some 130 statues and other antiquities was presented to the University by Henrietta Louisa, Countess Dowager of Pomfret. As one of the several gestures of thanks made to her on the part of the authorities, King composed an inscription to be exhibited with them. This collection has been moved on more than one occasion: today it is in the Ashmolean Museum, together with the inscription. King commemorates in two sentences both the donation by the Countess and the fact that William Fermor, Baron Lempster, had originally purchased the collection:

MARMORA HAEC SPIRANTIA, ET EXIMIAS GRAECIAE ET ROMAE ANTIQUAE RELIQUIAS, AB EXTERIS REGIONIBUS UNDIQUE SUMMA CURA ATQUE DILIGENTIA CONQUISITAS MAGNO SUMPTU COMPARAVIT SOLERTISSIMUS RERUM ANTIQUARUM AESTIMATOR GULIELMUS BARO DE LEMSTER. HUIC ACADEMIAE DONAVIT, EX VOLUNTATE ET CONSILIO CHARISSIMI ET SPECTATISSIMI CONJUGIS MUNIFICENTISSIMA

---

[1] James Boswell, *Life of Johnson*, ed. G. B. Hill and L. F. Powell (6 vols.; Oxford: at the Clarendon Press, 1934–1950), Vol. I, p. 282. The Latin text of Johnson's M.A. diploma appears on pp. 281f.

LITERARUM PATRONA HENRIETTA LOUISA COMI-
TISSA DE POMFRET ANNO DOMINO MILLESIMO SEP-
TINGENTESIMO QUINQUAGESIMO QUINTO.[1]

King's estate at Ealing was also receiving his attention. On
25 August 1755 he leased nine acres of the glebe land of the
rectory of Ealing known as Parson's Hault.[2] Three deeds now
among the records of the Church Commissioners, dated in 1755
and 1756, show King making a number of changes in the
arrangements under which he and the other persons mentioned
in these documents held the leasehold of the rectorial property.
The ultimate ownership of the rectory and its estate remained,
as it had been for a considerable length of time before, in the
hands of the Chancellor of St. Paul's Cathedral. The signature
of the then Chancellor, Dr. Peniston Booth, is on all three
documents.[3]

In the following year King engaged in his last significant
controversy. His opponent this time was the recently appointed
Regius Professor of Civil Law, Robert Jenner of Trinity College.
During the Commemoration of July 1756, Jenner had delivered
a Latin speech, in the course of which he had slighted the
Principal of St. Mary Hall. According to Jenner, the remarks
against King took the form only of an 'oblique lash or two',
but his adversary's sensitivity was evidently stung. On the
following October 27 King spoke in Convocation and made a
contumelious Latin reply to Jenner's previous assault. Jenner
shortly afterwards published his English version of King's short
oration, accompanied with introductory material and sixteen
pages of notes under the title *A New Speech from the Old Trumpeter
of Liberty Hall*.[4] This pamphlet was signed OXONIENSIS and

---

[1] A printed version of the text appears in John Gutch's edition of Antony Wood,
The History and Antiquities of the University of Oxford (2 vols.; Oxford: Printed for the
Editor, 1792–6), Vol. II, part 2, p. 811. 10 March 1755 was the date of the indenture which effected the legal transfer of the collection. The name of Lempster
sometimes appears as Leominster; the alternate form of Pomfret is Pontefract.

[2] Greater London Record Office (Middlesex Records), Acc. 112/5.

[3] Church Commissioners' Records, Deeds No. 1537–9, dated respectively 19
March 1755; 12 March 1756; and 28 May 1756. In the case of the first two of these
documents, William King's signature appears on the counterpart.

[4] According to *The Oxford English Dictionary*, the earliest known instance of the
phrase 'Liberty Hall' occurs in Goldsmith's *She Stoops to Conquer*, written in 1773.
In point of fact, it is quoted on page 16 of *Doctor King's Apology*.

dated 18 November 1756. Early in 1757 King published his Latin version of the speech, ostensibly edited by Jenner, though really intended as a parody on his Latinity. Such are the basic facts of this rather petty dispute: the two short publications which it engendered alone constitute whatever interest in it still remains.

The content of both published versions of King's speech in Convocation is roughly similar, though the order of the material is rearranged in Jenner's edition, perhaps because he was writing from memory, and presented to the reader in such a way to show the speaker in as unfavourable a light as possible. There is little point in rehearsing all of King's accusations: their full significance is now impossible to assess since most of them were intended primarily as rebuttals to Jenner's Commemoration speech, no text of which is today extant. In *A New Speech from the Old Trumpeter of Liberty Hall* King's banter on the subject of Jenner is Englished in this tone:

How ridiculously did he exhibit himself, like a public Fool, or rather as frantic in his fury, vomiting forth whatever abuse came uppermost, foaming at the mouth, brandishing his cane, menacing the young men, and applauding himself! I heard, with fix'd attention, the raging of his voice; and I saw him leave the [Sheldonian] Theatre, as a vile actor quits the Stage, amidst the hisses of the whole assembly . . . Fie upon it!—the King's Professor to act the Part of a *Terrae Filius*! . . . And then, how ridiculously absurd the man was, with his little scraps of Latin; fond of shewing some of the commonplace Sentences he had noted down in his younger days, and now us'd without either Rhyme or Reason. (*Populus me sibilat, at mihi plaudo.*)

King's edition of his speech—what Jenner calls 'this last of all his last speeches'—is only a little more dignified. From the Latin text of the piece just quoted, it will be clear that Jenner took considerable liberties in his version.

. . . Sed, quanquam huic calumniatori sive insipientiam, sive amentiam, sive malignitatem suam, ego adducor, ut ignoscam; dehinc tamen his omnibus ita occurrendum esse arbitror, ita consulendum Academiae dignitati, ut homo iste ne quidem eodem modo iterum bacchari, ac furere permittatur, usq; adeo, donec odio et strepitu juvenum nostrorum e loco coactus sit excedere.

Atqui hoc ipsum illi vitio dari posset: Qui excessit, immo vero
erupit e venerabili coetu, tanquam ex histrionum scena; tanquam
si morionis, aut quod ipse de se nunc affirmat, TERRAE FILII
ageret partes (pro pudor! PROFESSOR REGIUS TERRAE
FILII ageret partes!) ore spumans, baculum quassans, pueris
minitans, sibi plaudens:

> Populus me sibilat, at mihi plaudo
> Ipse domi.

Jenner's pamphlet incidentally contains an anecdote relating
to a satirical work on the plan of Alain Le Sage's *Le Diable
Boiteux* entitled *The Devil Upon Crutches*, which was published
in London in 1755 and whose author remains undetermined.
Soon after its appearance, there was printed in a newspaper *A
letter to the old Trumpeter at Liberty Hall, occasion'd by his Devil upon
crutches &c.* According to Jenner, King was highly indignant:

And now, what truly does the peevish old man, but advertise
immediately, in one of the daily papers, with *his own name* (I mean
the name he has gone by since his arrival from *Ireland*) and with *the
name of his Hall*, as follows; *Whereas a scandalous advertisement has
appear'd, declaring that I* (that I!) *am the author of a book, entitled The
Devil &c.* so that he takes to himself (you see) the Fool's Cap, the
title of *the old Trumpeter* without the least ceremony and with the
greatest promptitude; as if, in all the fitness of things, it could possibly fit no pate but his own. Wherefore, for fear of offending against
the old Trumpeter's own proclamation, this must be henceforth *the
name*, the name of his own public adoption.

However justified Jenner considered his case to be, he demonstrated that he was one of those who was ready to taunt the
Principal of St. Mary Hall with the aspersion of being an
Irishman. 'Cork was the real place of his birth,' he proclaims in
the notes, 'and his first name *Peregrine O Donald* (near relation to
Peregrine Pickle). . . .' Somehow or other Jenner had secured a
copy of *The Toast*—he quotes from it and calls it 'that most
infamous of all books'—and based his opinions on the information that he found therein. It is quite possible that Blacow's
copy fell into his hands. He had either not read or not been
convinced by the refutation which had been set out in *Doctor
King's Apology* of the statements made by the Principal's enemies
relating to his supposed Hibernian origin.

Even though his view is constantly coloured by personal antipathy, Jenner can occasionally provide a glimpse of his adversary which shows a certain descriptive talent, as in his picture of King entering Convocation

. . . most elegantly bepowder'd, and strutting beneath the pomp of scarlet, yet with infinite obsequiousness *bowing* to the first, *nodding* to the second, *smiling* on the third, and *whispering* to the fourth; whilst his eyes darted every way at once, to discover *who* and *who* and *who* was arriv'd, and whether *he was likely to have a full house*—now fear damping his hope, now hope getting the better of his fear—in short, with every symptom of that anxiety, with which a third-rate player is seen peeping thro' the curtain, about the second music, upon his own *Benefit-night.*

Jenner is not known to have published anything else besides *A New Speech from the Old Trumpeter of Liberty Hall,* despite the fact that he held the Regius Professorship of Civil Law until 1767. Whatever the merits of their dispute, King seems to have been instrumental in inspiring his legal colleague's one appearance in print.

The Latin text of King's speech, professedly edited by the Regius Professor of Civil Law, was published under the title *Oratiuncula Habita in Domo Convocationis, Oxon. Die Oct. 27, 1756.* It is preceded by an introductory *Epistola Dedicatoria ad Honoratissimum Dominum,* the *Dominus* in this case being the Chancellor, Lord Arran. This letter, dated 1 February 1757, *ex mea domo in Sancto Puteo* (Holywell), is comparable in style and satirical intention to the *Epistola Canonici* of 1744. Jenner's Latin is represented as being no better than that of Bishop Gilbert, very shortly to become Archbishop of York, as may easily be seen in the opening sentence of the *Epistola Dedicatoria*: '*Post commendationem mei ipsius vestrae DOMINATIONI, dedico vobis hoc meum primum opus, ut ego debeo, quia honorabilem locum, quem ego nunc teneo in hac Universitate, teneo a vestro favore, praeter multas alias benignitates, quae mihi significantur a VESTRA DOMINATIONE de tempore in tempus.*' The entire *Epistola,* covering some thirteen pages, is deliberately intended to make Jenner look a fool. For example, he is made to claim that corroboration for his arguments may be found *in uno magno et divino Poeta, Tertulliano.* At the bottom of the page there is a footnote: *Ego nondum legi hunc*

Poetam. He is also represented as behaving in a ridiculous manner when he was listening to the speech which he is now editing:

... Tum unus *Bedellorum,* qui stabat proxime mihi, et qui solet ambulare ante me, quando ego eo in solenni pompa ad juridicas disputationes, dicebat mihi in aurem, *Fuge, fuge; nunc est vestrum tempus fugere.* Quare ego fugi, metuens aliquid malum ulterius. Sed postquam eram ex Theatro, et recuperavi meum halitum, unus amicus veniebat mihi dicens, quod non erat bonum consilium fugere, et quod iste *Bedellus* est male versutus homo, et deridebat me. Tum ego commovebar ira ita magna, ut meum caput videbatur vetere circum et circum, et jeci meum corpus super pavimentum in Schola Divinitatis, et spumabam, et clamabam vehementer. Tum servus meus portabat me domi, ubi non potui dormire tribus totis noctibus.

The text of King's speech follows the *Epistola Dedicatoria*; at the end of it, there are almost sixteen pages of *Notae et Observationes,* an *Avisamentum Lectori,* and a list of *Errata,* all of which are written to show Jenner as a laughing stock. In the *Errata,* for example, this note appears:

Pag. 9 Not. 3.

Pro coepit bene *aliquis contendit, quod debemus legere* bene coepit. *Sed haec alteratio, sive transpositio verborum non videtur necessaria; quia non facit ullam alterationem, aut ullam minimam differentiam in sensu.*

As in the *Epistola Canonici,* there is a skit on the antiquated logical methodology of the schoolmen. This one occurs as a note to King's opening sentence '*Peto jus dicendi, pauca dicturus, quae ad Academiae dignitatem spectant.*' In the note, Jenner is made to resort to a sorites of a kind:

Valde ominosum est Principali ita cespitare in limine sui operis, ut is plane appareat omnibus esse malus homo, et iniquus sua ipsius confessione; quod ego vero sic probo logicaliter et syllogistice:

Qui *petit jus,* petit bonum et aequum:
Principalis *petit jus;*
Ergo Principalis petit bonum et aequum.
Qui petit bonum et aequum, petit quia id
non habet in seipso:

Principalis petit bonum et aequum;
Ergo petit, quia id non habet in seipso.
Probatur Major; Quia nemo petit id, quod habet.

The mock *apparatus criticus* contained in King's edition of his *Oratiuncula* is wittily written but extremely spiteful. Reading it, one is tempted to wonder whether King would not have achieved his purpose just as well by ignoring Jenner's animadversions altogether. By this time, the Principal of St. Mary Hall was capable of exerting an influence in Oxford almost as formidable as that of the Chancellor or the Vice-Chancellor, and certainly greater than that of the Public Orator, the comparatively colourless Roger Mather of Brasenose College. Jenner had held his appointment for a little over two years; King had held his for more than thirty-seven. It is difficult to imagine that the reputation of so senior a member of the university was enhanced, even in his own day, by an extended piece of highly unsympathetic mimicry, avowedly intended to make the comparatively young holder of one of the most important chairs in the university appear completely asinine.

On 28 October 1756, the day after King's oratiuncle against Jenner, the senior Trustee of the Radcliffe Library, the fourth Duke of Beaufort, passed away and was buried in Badminton Church, Gloucestershire. King composed the Latin epitaph for the Duke's tomb: it is the earliest of his known surviving compositions in this *genre*. The virtues attributed to the Duke in this respectfully phrased tribute were among those which King most admired:

Patriae fuit amantissimus,
Verae religionis cultor assiduus,
Libertatis publicae vindex indefessus,
Et, nisi procerum invidia, aut temporum iniquitas
Tantum virum a reipublicae muneribus exclusisset,
Britanniae nostrae caput et lumen futurum.
Dum vero boni omnes
Principem hunc excellentissimum
Regni negotiis praeesse frustra optant,
Eum maxime sunt admirati,
Et observantia summa coluerunt

Privatum:
Quippe cujus otium
Omni imperio aut regum favore fuit honoratius.

He discharged well the duties of his state in life:

Maritus fidelissimus,
Pater optimus,
Amicus certus et constans,
Hospes munificus et jucundus
Academiae suae Oxoniensis praesidium,
Et eruditorum omnium patronus
Ipse eruditissimus.

His only enemies were those of his country:

Inimicum habuit neminem
Nisi qui patriae et reipublicae fuit inimicus.
Etenim is illi erat vultus decor, is animi candor,
Et in laudabili severitate tam come ingenium,
Ut hominibus demerendis natus videretur.

The epitaph closes with some noble aspirations on the subject of his son and heir, Henry, who became the fifth Duke at the age of twelve:

. . . unicum filium,
Summae spei puerum optimaeque indolis;
Quem incolumem servet Deus,
Ut nobilissimam domum,
Principis hujus illustrissimi,
Immatura morte labefactatam
Avitis virtutibus restituat, sustineat, et exornet
Filius patri quam simillimus.

A little over two years later, there occurred the death of the aged Earl of Arran, Chancellor of Oxford University. He was buried at St. Margaret's, Westminster, on 23 December 1758, and with his passing the dukedom and marquessate of Ormonde became extinct. His possible successors in the Cancellariate were three in number: the Earl of Westmoreland, the Earl of Lichfield, and the Bishop of Durham. Westmoreland had the blessing of the Principal of St. Mary Hall, who had described him as 'learned himself . . . a lover of learned men, and a steady asserter of the liberties of his country.'[1] In due course King's candidate was elected. His installation ceremonies took place in July 1759, the earlier part of which is thus described in *The Gentleman's Magazine*:

... the ceremony began with a grand procession of noblemen, doctors, &c., in their proper habits, which pass'd through St. Mary's, and was there joined by the masters of arts in their proper habits; and from thence proceeded to the great gate of the Sheldonian theatre, in which the most numerous and brilliant assembly of persons of quality and distinction were seated, that had ever been seen there on any occasion.[2]

The arrangements for seating in the Sheldonian theatre during this festivity are described in a set of Orders issued by the Vice-Chancellor, Dr. Thomas Randolph, on the previous June 27:

The rising Semicircle of the *Theatre* is reserved for the Noblemen and Doctors. The Enclosure within the Rail is the Place for Masters of Arts. The Gallery behind the Doctors in the circular Part of the *Theatre* and the East and Westward Side-Galleries are reserved for Ladies and Strangers, among whom all Gownsmen are forbid to intermix. The upper Gallery above the Noblemen and Doctors is appointed for Gentlemen-Commoners and Bachelors; and the upper Galleries East and Westward are for Undergraduate Scholars of Houses and Commoners. The rest of the Area for Battlers and Servitors.

Dr. Johnson was in Oxford for the solemnity and wrote some relevant (but not impeccably grammatical) comments which were later quoted by Boswell:

I have been in my gown ever since I came here. It was at my first coming quite new and handsome. I have swum thrice, which I had disused for many years. I have proposed to Vansittart climbing over the wall, but he has refused me. And I have clapped my hands till they are sore, at Dr. King's speech.[3]

The speech to which Johnson refers was delivered on Friday,

---

[1] *Doctor King's Apology*, pp. 36–7. King wrote a letter to William Huddesford, Keeper of the Ashmolean Museum, dated 9 February 1758, to which he added this postscript: 'If you give yourself the trouble to write to me again, direct under cover to my Lord Westmoreland. I am now with him in Hanover Square.' (Bodleian Library, MS. Ashmole 1822.)

[2] *The Gentleman's Magazine*, Vol. XXIX, 1759, p. 342.

[3] James Boswell, *Life of Johnson*, ed. G. B. Hill (Oxford: at the Clarendon Press, 1934), Vol. I, pp. 347f. See also R. W. Chapman (ed.), *The Letters of Samuel Johnson* (3 vols.; Oxford: at the Clarendon Press, 1952), Vol. I, p. 123.

July 6; it came at the close of four days of Latin oratory inter-
spersed with musical events and other festivities.[1]

It is a pity that we possess no copy of the speech at which
Johnson demonstrated such plauditory enthusiasm. The entry
in the Register of Convocation for July 9 contains only the
statement that King *comitia clausit oratione Latina copiosa et per-
polita.* According to the diary of Sir Roger Newdigate, the
Principal of St. Mary Hall spoke for fifty minutes.[2] A brief
report which was printed in *Jackson's Oxford Journal* the day
after the event declares:

> Then the Solemnity of the Installation and Commemoration was
> closed by Dr. King, Principal of St. Mary Hall, who in a spirited
> and eloquent Oration, delivered with his usual Grace and Dignity,
> enlarged on the Propriety of the Choice the University had made;
> displayed his Lordship's eminent Abilities; introduced Lady Pom-
> fret's and Mr. Dawkin's late Benefactions; and concluded with an
> exhortation to the Youth of this Place, and his ardent Wishes for the
> perpetual Peace and Prosperity of the University.[3]

One sentence, claimed by Charles Churchill to be taken from
this speech, is used as the motto on the title-page of *The
Prophecy of Famine,* published in 1763. It reads '*Carmina tum
melius, cum venerit IPSE, canemus.*'[4] These shreds of evidence
constitute all that remains of what was in all likelihood one of
the Old Trumpeter's great solos.[5]

King had one new work printed in 1760, *Aviti Epistola ad
Perillam, Virginem Scotam.* This was never published, but is sometimes included in the collected *Opera.* No author's name appears,
but the work is described as EDITORIS ECPHRASI ET

---

[1] A complete list of the speakers on all four days appears in *The London Evening
Post,* No. 4938 (28–30 June 1759). The actual installation of the Chancellor took
place on the first day, Tuesday July 3.

[2] County Record Office, Shire Hall, Warwick, Diary of Sir Roger Newdigate,
July 1759.

[3] *Jackson's Oxford Journal,* No. 323 (7 July 1759). The same report appeared
verbatim in *The London Evening Post,* No. 4942 (7–10 July 1759).

[4] Douglas Grant (ed.), *The Poetical Works of Charles Churchill* (Oxford: at the
Clarendon Press, 1956), p. 510.

[5] Worlidge painted a picture of the installation of Lord Westmoreland as
Chancellor; according to John Nichols, King, 'a tall, lean, well-looking man', is
in the orator's rostrum. See John Nichols, *Biographical Anecdotes of William Hogarth*
(3rd edn., 1785), p. 594, and *Illustrations of the Literary History of the Eighteenth
Century* (8 vols.; London: Printed for the Author, 1817–58), Vol. I, p. 609.

ANNOTATIONIBUS ILLUSTRATA, a reference to the ecphrasis (a short preface) and the twelve pages of notes by the supposititious editor. In the ecphrasis, addressed to a nameless *Vir Illustrissimus*, the 'editor' (King himself) explains that these small verses (*versiculos*) were written by a certain young Italian pretending to be an elderly Englishman (*scriptos fuisse ab Italo quodam juvene, quanquam se hominem Anglum simulat esse, et senem*). The reason for the anonymity of the writer is then explained: '*Etenim ita libere locutus est, et jocatus de re severissima, de religione et cultu Romano, ut siqui ex Pontificiis expiscarentur, qui, et cujas sit, omnia mehercule ei essent pertimescenda.*' The editor then injects some views of his own on life in Rome. It seems highly likely, on the basis of King's known views about Catholicism in general, as distinct from his attitude towards individual Catholics, that the opinions expressed are his own. What he says is unflattering, especially on the monks who preach poverty while acquiring riches for themselves, but it is consistent with his general attitude of hostility towards clerical acquisitiveness and secular ambition.

Several of the mysteries concerning this work, which the reader might have hoped to find solved in the ecphrasis, remained unexplained. Who was Perilla? Is *Avitus* to be taken as a proper name or as meaning a grandfather? What significance is to be attached to the notation at the end of the ecphrasis ROMAE *Calendis Januariis* MDCCLX? Was King really writing this work in Rome or merely pretending to be? The author explains at the beginning: '*MINUS decennium est, quod Londini sex fere menses ego commoratus, dulci tuo colloquio saepissime fruebar, (neque spero te cepisse oblivionem consuetudinis nostrae) quo ingenium tuum, et liber spiritus, et animi candor satis mihi esset perspectus.*' When was this period during which King sojourned for almost six months in London? Why was he away from St. Mary Hall for so long? Who was the *vir illustrissimus* to whom the work is dedicated? Of Perilla, the editor intimates merely: '*DE PERILLA (et hoc fortasse fictum est nomen) nihil compertum habeo. Scoti nobiles, hospites tui, de virgine ea, siqua est, formosa et erudita te certiorem faciant. Certe equidem tam rarae animi dotes prohibeant eam latere.*' And on his method of obtaining the text of the poem, he adds in a rather cavalier manner, '*QUO casu carmen hoc in manus meas pervenerit, haud operae pretium est referre.*' In short, the ecphrasis is yet another example of King's exercises in purposeful equivocation.

The actual poem is written in elegiac couplets, and extends to 190 verses. It commences with a brief description of the conditions under which it is being written:

> DUM tristi frangor morbo, longaque senecta,
> Et mea vix calamum sustinet aegra manus . . .

The poet is delighted that Perilla is skilful in the Latin language, and enquires about the effects on her of the classical authors. For him they have always been the masters of life and manners:

> Hi mihi semper erant vitae morumque magistri,
> Quos juvenis colui, quos sequor usque senex.

Furthermore they teach the hoarse pulpits what they are unable to preach:

> Qui, quo te melius noscas, et vivere quid sit,
> Pulpita quod nequeunt rauca docere, docent.

Passing from the classics to contemporary Europe in the midst of the Seven Years' War, the poet finds a lamentable situation:

> Vastantur terrae, urbes incenduntur, et ignes
> Qui modo vitabant, heu! periere fame.
> En quoque, ne rabidi desint ursique lupique,
> Omnia qui lacerent, Russicus hostis adest.

In a footnote he describes the Muscovites as 'that enormous and barbaric people', and indicates that those who seek their help, and invite the army of the *Sarmatae* into Germany, will feel remorse for their plan (*eos consilii sui olim poenitebit*).[1] The present ruin, he continues in the text, could scarcely be worse if Etna were to extend its flaming forces to the whole world:

> Vix equidem, Aetna suas si toto extenderet orbe
> Flammiferas vires, tanta ruina foret.

But who would believe such things to be the work of Christians?

> At quis Christicolum talia credat opus?
> Mitis erat CHRISTUS, praeceptaque mitia CHRISTI:
> Ille hominum, ille almae pacis amator erat.

---

[1] The *Sarmatae* were described by Herodotus as being beyond the Don.

However, when war ceases, the condition of religion continues
to exhibit shortcomings:

> Ast ubi non bellum est, neque gloria quaeritur armis,
>   Relligio voluit cuncta licere sibi.
> Ecce igne, aut ferro tolli, quicunque negarint,
>   Quod non credibile est, credere, saeva jubet;
> Et scelere immanes superans Busiridis aras,
>   Innocuos cives immolat illa suis.
> Aut crede, aut simula vestros renuisse penates,
>   Judaee, ut tandem sit tibi salva domus.
> Semideus vanos stimulat dum Loiola reges,
>   Plena ferae caedis Gallica regna vides.
> Regibus Austriacis, mihi dic, insignior ecquis
>   Cum clade infanda, tum pietate fuit?
> Quas vastas subigit, gentes exterminat omnes,
>   Et raptas populi tollit Iberus opes:
> Haec quia non coluit CHRISTUM pars altera mundi,
>   Cui CHRISTUS nullo nomine notus erat.

In case any reader should miss the point, the footnotes provide
generous amplifications of the principal ideas which are versified in the text. For example,

Religio Christiana pacem amat, cupit, conciliat, servat. Principes
Christiani, etiam Christianissimi pacem aversantur, aspernantur,
indignantur, finitimis et vicinis caedes et excidia utique meditantur.

Or again,

Ea scilicet superstitio qua imbuitur maxima pars Europae, gens
potissimum Hispanica, et Lusitanica, Dei omnipotentis pio cultui
quam dissimillima. Quot enim homines, crudeliter excruciatos, et
vero etiam quot millia hominum necari, et cremari jussit? . . . Si
CHRISTUS terram reviseret, ubi inveniret doctrinam et religionem
suam, simplicem, puram, humilem, benevolam, pacificam? Frustra
equidem eam quaereret in tristi et inexorabili INQUISITIONIS
domo, frustra fortasse in ulla regali aula.

A good deal of the invective that follows in the text is directed
against the Roman Church, in particular the monks (*in tunicis
foedisque cucullis*) and continental mariolatry. Speaking of the
city of Rome he writes:

Reginam coeli, mutato nomine, adorat,
  Junonisque locum Virgo Maria tenet...

Not content with criticizing Rome, he turns, in an acid footnote,
to Loreto:

B.M. Virginis imago, quae in *Laureti* domo posita est, induitur
corona aurea, magnis, pretiosissimis, et fulgentibus gemmis illumin-
ata: totusque ejus ornatus tot tantisque gemmis distinctus est, ut
maximorum regum coronas, diademata, vestimenta, uniones et
gazas omnes vix tanti aestimares. Ipsa autem statua, quae ex ligno
facta est, adeo est informis, ut non e coelo cecidisse, sed ex veneficae
cujusdam cella ablatam fuisse diceres.

A brief comparison is made between Rome and Scotland.
Although King is a little less protracted on the subject of Scottish religion, he is scarcely more charitable:

Roma colit quaecunque, ea numina Scotia damnat;
  Romaque quae damnat, Scotia cuncta colit:
Templis inque suis, si fas ea templa vocare,
  Si decoris quidquam est, id putat esse nefas.
Rusticitas nam sola placet; reverentiaque hic est,
  Debita siqua homini, debita nulla deo.

Turning to the Calvinistic doctrine of predestination, he proceeds to put into verse one of the standard theological objections against it:

Nam magnum faciunt coeli implacabile numen,
  Humano generi quod nocuisse juvat:
Totum perque diem dum supplice voce precantur,
  Posse preces ullas vincere fata negant.
Fata trahunt omnes: cedamus et omnia fatis:
  Libera nec cuiquam mens animusque datur.
Cantantes eadem quo tu discrimine noris,
  Seu CHRISTI, flamen sive Dialis erit?
De grege Calvini rigido nisi jure timerem,
  Ne tibi quis noceat, plura monenda forent.

The conclusion of the poem consists of an exhortation to Perilla
not to marry:

At neque conjugium tibi suadeo. Virgo maneres,
  Tu poteris Musis aptior ire comes.

But whether she marries or not, the author, in the final couplet, wishes her all prosperity:

> Sive autem mater, seu mavis virgo vocari,
> Eventura tibi prospera cuncta precor.

This unusual performance, considered as a whole, is not great poetry. It contains some fine single lines, and exhibits the careful use of *figurae etymologicae* and other devices of the classical poets. But it lacks the sophistication of King's earlier works, especially of *The Toast* and *Templum Libertatis*, and in its place one is conscious of a shrillness which does not always seem to blend appropriately with the benign and endearing terms which are used in profusion to describe the Scottish maiden. The attack on the Roman Church immediately reminds one of the *Franciscanus* and its companion work, *Fratres Fraterrimi*, of George Buchanan, though the *Aviti Epistola* does not exhibit their author's particular kind of virile pungency. Indeed, it is difficult to avoid the feeling that King's increased aversion to certain forms of religion was due, to a considerable degree, to his lack of political sympathy for large numbers of persons calling themselves Christians.

The choice of the elegiac distich, a metre not usually employed by King, was made in all probability to add an extra overtone of plaintive mournfulness. Sidney, in the *Defence of Poesie*, had written of the lamenting elegiac 'who bewayleth ... the weaknesse of mankinde,' and King presumably saw himself as fulfilling some such role in *Aviti Epistola*. But I question the extent to which this poem could be called an elegy in the classical sense of the word. In places it is not so much a lamentation on certain aspects of the times as an indictment of them. Perhaps for this reason King was content to use the term *Epistola*.

Despite its denunciatory power and breadth of coverage, *Aviti Epistola* exhibits several examples of one of King's most irritating mannerisms, namely his habit of making sweeping generalizations without bothering to qualify or to substantiate them. Thus in the notes we read: '*Scoti minus reverenter Deum colunt, quam regni satrapas, vel etiam aequales suos. Gentis hujus religio in una hac re posita videtur, ut quam longissime absit ab institutis,*

ritibus, et caeremoniis Ecclesiae Romanae, nec non et Anglicanae.'
Admittedly, the meaning of the term *regni satrapas* is not entirely plain, but whoever they and their equals were, it was
uncondign to generalize on their collective piety to the detri-
ment of the Scots as a whole. Furthermore, the subsequent
comments on the contemporary Scottish religious position
vis-à-vis that of the Roman and Anglican churches were not
equally true of the Episcopal Church in Scotland, which
officially recognized the Stuart monarchs until 1788, the
Moderate Presbyterians, and the Popular Prebyterians. King's
descriptions of Catholicism and Calvinism exhibit the
same lack of precision, as well as a considerable degree of
bias.

Nevertheless, *Aviti Epistola* contains portions of incidental
interest which have no precise counterparts in King's other
poems. One of these, placed among the *editoris annotationes*,
is a long *Elogium*, which, the supposititious editor claims, had
been fastened to the door of a noble Swedish senator. Which
dignitary is its subject remains undetermined, but it seems most
likely that King intended this *Elogium* to commemorate Count
Karl Gyllenborg, who had been the Swedish ambassador to
Great Britain from 1715 to 1717, and had been imprisoned for
several months as a result of his becoming too intimately involved in Jacobite activities. He became President of the
Chancery (i.e. Premier) and Chancellor of the University of
Uppsala in 1739, prior to launching the Swedish campaign
against Russia in 1741. This was a complete fiasco: military
preparations were inadequate and the Swedish army suffered
from bureaucratic corruption among the Hats. Two years later
Gyllenborg was forced to make peace with Russia under the
terms of the Treaty of Abo. I assume that this is the treaty to
which King refers in the preamble to the *Elogium*: '*At vero per
mihi visum est mirum, Sueciae optimates foedus cum Muscovitis fecisse,
qui amplissimas et fructuosissimas Suedorum provincias occuparunt, et
sub imperium ditionemque suam subjunxerunt, caeteras omnes mox
devoraturi. Aut senatores Suecici largitione turpissima corrumpuntur, aut
in maximarum rerum ignoratione versantur.*' Though most of the
Elogium is critical of the senator, it commences with a passage
of praise with reservations:

HIC SITUS EST
SENATUS PRINCEPS, ET REGNI PRAEFECTUS;
Vir nobilis, splendidus, affabilis, blandus,
At animo non magno, nec magna corporis dignitate,
Cujus nomen et laudes tota jamdiu celebrat Academia;[1]
Quem sacerdotes aulici omnes imprimis observant;
Quem reverendissimi Praesules, ut Deum colunt.

The alloyed flattery over, King elaborates at some length on
what he regards as the senator's many shortcomings: the subject
appears in some respects remarkably like a Swedish version of a
Whig prime-minister as seen by one of his political enemies.
Indeed, these lines could be applied just as appropriately to
the image in their author's mind of the Duke of Newcastle:

Semper vehementissime occupatus,
Ac res permagnas visus agere,
Omnino nihil agit.
Semper festinans, properansque,
Atque ad metam tendere prorsum simulans,
Nunquam pervenit.

The *Elogium* concludes with eight lines which may possibly have
been influenced by the celebrated epitaph of Swift which today
hangs on the south wall, above the door of the vestries, in St.
Patrick's Cathedral, Dublin:

Haec fortassis, Viator, rides:
Sta vero, et tristem lege Epilogum:
HUJUS unius hominis inscitia
Tantum impressit dedecus,
Tantum attulit detrimentum reipublicae,
Ut omnibus appareat,
Nisi SUECIAE Genius, siquis est, sese interponat,
SUECIAM futuram non esse.

The incidental comments provided in this *Elogium* and its
preamble on the contemporary Swedish political situation under
the rule of the Hats are disagreeably querulous. Indeed, one
wonders how reliable King's comments are on the senator him-

[1] In a footnote King indicates that *Academia* is to be taken as the University of
Uppsala.

self: even though the Old Trumpeter was in all probability involved in the earlier Jacobite intrigues with the Swedes and Russians, there is no proof that he was as intimately connected with the secrets of the *Riddarhus* as this *Elogium* would seem to imply. It is also arguable that he may have been unconsciously jealous of the wide following which his subject had enjoyed among the clergy, an advantage which the English Tories had not experienced since 1714. At best, King's observations on Sweden and her nameless senator are those of a foreign observer, given to strong but not always consistent political partialities, whose sources of information may or may not have been dependable.

A further item hidden away in the *annotationes* is a short, untitled poem in hendecasyllabics, another metre which King seldom used. It is introduced by this preamble:

Quos dies festos nos agimus, et celebramus, Scoti nefastos ducunt, et lugubria, puto, canunt. Quum in hac boreali Britanniae parte olim peregrinabar, hospitis mei vicinus (ex iis unus, quos *ministros* appellant) in judicium fuit vocatus, et damnatus sceleris, quia anserem ausus est prandere natali Christi, aut festo die Michaelis Archangeli. Nam eo die Anglis mos est patrius mensas suas assis anseribus extruere, haud quidem religione obstrictis; sed quia, circiter id anni tempus anseres sunt pinguissimi, et jucundi saporis. Nonne autem hic reus judicium subiit iniquissimum? Quid si improbum hunc Anglorum morem ignorabat? Quid si ignorabat, cujus praecipue dies esset, siquidem in Scotorum calendario Archangelus, nullum, ni fallor, locum obtinuit? Quid denique si vir bonus nihil praeter unum anserem habebat, quod ederet?

The poem follows immediately afterwards. The influences of Petronius, Catullus, and Presbyterianism are all, in their different ways, in evidence. The result is a pleasantly facetious *jeu d'esprit*:

> Tres Encolpius anseres necavit,
> Ut nos Arbiter ille fabulator
> Jucundus docuit, sacros Priapo.
> Id propter vetulae crucem minantur.[1]
> Quid vero meus ille Scotus hospes,

[1] The *vetulae* are the priestesses of Priapus.

Unum cum necat anserem profanum,
  Quo natos aleret puellulasque,
Nunc in judicium reus vocatur?
Utrum sit sacer anser, an profanus,
  Nil refert: sed inexpiabile hoc est,
Siquis Scotus homo die nefasto
  Convivis jubet anserem parari.
Si, sic nota tibi Dei voluntas,
  Qui sint, dic bone vir, dies nefasti,
Ut prandentibus error absit omnis.
Omnem credideris diem nefastum,
  Inque ipso ansere daemonem latere,
Angli quem celebrant ineptiores,
  Festum coelicolis suis dicatum.
At ut, praecipue, valere si vis,
  Festum, Scote, caveto Michaelis.

Though they are comparatively brief, perhaps the most revealing parts of *Aviti Epistola* are those praising the status of Britain in 1760 under the House of Hanover. Having spent most of his life preaching the doctrine that true British liberty would return only with the restoration of the Stuart monarchy, King now saw fit to adopt a more optimistic tone:

Quod tantum potuit, quod nunc majora facessit,
  Et solis nixa est viribus ipsa suis;
Insula, et extremi sit quamvis angulus orbis;
  Sedem hic Libertas maluit esse suam.

And in the footnote to these lines, the reader is assured: '*Populi Britanni propria est ea perfectae libertatis, et reipublicae species, qua nihil dulcius, et homine dignius: et quae quidem nunquam amitti potest, nisi eam vendat ipse senatus.*' In a fuller development of his political position, the author not only justifies the King's war, but for perhaps the first time in his life pens some sentiments complimentary to the existing British government:

Bellum justissimum (siquod est justissimum) a populo Britanno cum Gallis hodie geritur. Cum hujus belli initia prospera essent Gallis, et rempublicam nostram administrarent quidam purpurati, in quibus neque quid scientiae militaris, aut consilii, aut dignitatis, fuit, omnia sibi promittebat gens inimica, etiam opes et possessiones nostras omnes, et totius oceani imperium. Simul autem ac novi homines singulari prudentia, alta mente, et authoritate praediti ad capessendam rempublicam accesserunt, O quam subito commutata est hujus insulae fortuna! O quae temporum inclinatio! quae repentina rerum Gallicarum conversio, quas in extremum casum deductas esse magno cum nostro gaudio ac beneficio hodie videmus!

These passages reveal that King's political outlook had been undergoing a profound change, the course of which deserves discussion. Gradually his trust in the Stuart claimants had been waning, while at the same time he was becoming much better disposed than ever before towards at least some of the Whig members of the administration. Horace Walpole, in a letter to George Montagu of 4 May 1758, provides evidence that King's antipathy towards the long deceased Sir Robert Walpole had already somewhat mellowed. In his book entitled *A Catalogue of the Royal and Noble Authors of England*, Horace Walpole had written of his father, 'Sir Robert Walpole, Earl of Orford, is only mentioned in this place in his quality of author: it is not proper nor necessary for me to touch his character here— sixteen unfortunate and inglorious years since his removal have already written his elogium!' Of this passage, King commented (according to Horace Walpole) 'It is very modest, very genteel, and very *true*.' Walpole described this remark as the most extraordinary thing he had heard about his book.[1] Although King was later, in his *Anecdotes*, to make some fractious criticisms of Sir Robert's administration, he seems to have felt some sympathy for the retired Prime-Minister, admitting that 'my Lord ORFORD was consulted by the ministers to the last day of his life.'[2]

The fact that King was increasing his contacts with a few of the aristocratic Whigs, and notably the Earl of Shelburne, is balanced by the fact that at the same time his confidence in his fellow-Tories was being put to a severe test. On 15 September 1759 General Robert Clark wrote to Lord FitzMaurice with reference to a recent visit to Oxford: 'I had a *tête à tête* for six hours with old Doctor King where we talked a great deal of you. He says the Tories have not one man amongst them at

---

[1] W. S. Lewis (ed.), op. cit., Vol. 9, p. 219.
[2] *Political and Literary Anecdotes* (2nd edn., 1819), p. 43.

present capable to be put at their head.'[1] With the death of George II, and the commencement of the new reign on 25 October 1760, the exclusive royal patronage of the Whig party came to an end. A hearty pledge of loyalty was offered to the new monarch by the University of Oxford, and the old barriers between the two principal parties gradually weakened in a new spirit of *rapprochement*. The motivation behind the Jacobite movement was gradually dissipated, as the now seriously ailing James III relinquished hope of ever recovering the crown for himself. Though Pope Benedict XIV had ordered in 1756 that all James's subjects should style him King of England, the number of persons who regarded themselves as his subjects had become in fact so small that even the Italians would jestingly refer to him as 'the local king.'

After the accession of George III, King seems to have lost all interest in the cause of the Catholic claimant. Shortly after Sir Francis Dashwood was appointed Treasurer of the Chamber in March 1761, the Old Trumpeter sounded his felicitations to a new tune: 'Amongst the congratulations of your great friends accept the sincere compliments of an old Recluse, who loves and honours you; and who without the gift of prophecy can foretell, that a few gentlemen of your character, placed about a young King, will make him as well as his people easy and happy.'[2] King's formal abandonment of Jacobitism may be said to date from 16 September 1761, when he accompanied a delegation representing the University of Oxford to present George III with a congratulatory address on his recent marriage to Princess Charlotte Sophia of Mecklenburg-Strelitz. At the Court of St. James, he was personally introduced to the King by the young Lord Shelburne.[3] When he was an undergraduate at Oxford, Shelburne, in his own words, 'fell into habits with Dr. King,' whom he describes as 'a Tory and Jacobite, but a

[1] Shelburne MSS. at Bowood, General Robert Clark to Lord FitzMaurice, 15 September 1759.

[2] British Museum, MS. Eg. 2136, f. 66.

[3] Reports of the occasion, with the text of the addresses to the King and Queen and Their Majesties' gracious answers, appeared in *The London Evening Post*, No. 5288 (19–22 September 1761); *The London Gazette*, No. 10140 (15–19 September 1761); *The St. James's Chronicle*, No. 83 (19–22 September 1761); and *The Public Advertiser*, No. 8386 (21 September 1761).

gentleman and an orator.'[1] On 4 August 1761 Sir William Blackstone had assured him of King's complete renunciation of the Jacobite cause:

I yesterday saw our Friend Dr King, & discoursed with him on the Subject which Your Lordship gave me in Charge. The Doctor desired me to assure You, upon his Word and Honour, that he had no Attachments whatever, either public or secret, to that Cause in which the Sentiment of the World has usually ranked him as a Principal:– That he honours and sincerely loves the Character of that most respectable Person, to whom Your Lordship is with Justice so warmly and affectionately attached; and has no Scruples about waiting on him, together with the rest of the University. But he thinks that, at his time of Life, a special and particular Introduction, to a Place where he has never before been, might occasion more Talk & Banter than his Spirits & Infirmities might now perhaps support; and it therefore requires some little Consideration on his part, before he takes & executes a Resolution so entirely new. He added, that in a short time he intends to wait on Your Lordship, at either Hanover Square, Whitton, or Wycombe; & will there discourse with You upon this Subject more at large.[2]

On the following August 18, Shelburne wrote to the *de facto* Prime-Minister, Lord Bute, explaining that the Principal of St. Mary Hall intended going to court to kiss the King's hand:

In consequence of . . . the respect he thinks due to the present King and Government, he takes the opportunity of going with the Address. I take the liberty to mention it to Your Lordship, that if the King does not think a man who has indulged himself in Republican Sentiments worse than a Jacobite, he may oblige an old, and I have reason to think, a good man, consequently a vain one, who has nothing left to ask but an exception from absolute insignificance at the end of his days.[3]

After the presentation, King's relations with Shelburne remained excellent. His Lordship wrote a highly complimentary letter to the Principal of St. Mary Hall, and received the following reply, dated 22 October 1761:

You have done me great honour by y^r letter, which you have been pleased to write to me, and I have had some thoughts of depositing

[1] Lord FitzMaurice, op. cit., Vol. I, p. 15.
[2] Shelburne MSS. at Bowood, Blackstone to Shelburne, 4 August 1761.
[3] Shelburne MSS. at Bowood, Shelburne to Bute, 18 August 1761.

it in yᵉ Archives of the University as yᵉ best testimonial I need ever desire to receive. To be praised *a laudato viro* is the best and truest kind of praise, and will always give a man of sense a real pleasure. I persuade my self, that I know you perfectly well, & therefore I am not insensible, how great a portion of esteem a man must necessarily derive from your good opinion, especially if you are pleased to honour him with your friendship.[1]

King's presentation at court met with a certain amount of censure. In November 1761 a newspaper advertisement appeared, written by the last non-juring bishop of the regular succession, Robert Gordon, who used to reside next to his oratory on Theobald's Road, near Gray's Inn. His congregation was dwindling: he understandably expressed resentment when King defected to the Hanoverian monarchy. The Old Trumpeter waxed angry at his words:

QUUM A POTENTISSIMIS illis viris, qui hujus Imperii res et rationes procurant, et gubernant, nulla praemia aut munera mihi petii, aut fortasse unquam exoptavi, sane quidem miror, quo malo fato natus tot inimicitias ego contraxerim, aut quae sit causa, quamobrem viri nequissimi me praecipue ex omnibus elegerint, in quem inveherentur; etiam quem accusarent graviorum criminum, et eorundem flagitiorum, quae insani, quae perjuri, atque ut uno verbo omnia dicam, quae ipsi fecerunt et prope quotidie faciunt; ut haud sciam profecto, an malus iste Deus horum hominum et calumniatorum omnium princeps et magister usque adeo maledicere et mentiri auderet.[2]

He called the advertisement infamous and inserted on purpose to defame him for no other reason 'but because as a member of the University I attended my brethren, when with the whole body (our chancellor at their head) they waited on the King with an address of congratulation on his Majesty's marriage

---

[1] Shelburne MSS. at Bowood, King to Shelburne, 22 October 1761. Whether or not King deposited His Lordship's previous letter in the university archives, no such document survives today.

[2] *Political and Literary Anecdotes* (2nd edn., 1819), p. 189. Information on Bishop Robert Gordon is provided in J. H. Overton, *The Non-Jurors* (London: Smith, Elder & Co., 1902), esp. pp. 232–8, and Henry Broxap, *The Later Non-Jurors* (Cambridge: At the University Press, 1924). Like King, he had maintained a regular correspondence with Charles Edward; unlike King, he never deserted the Jacobite cause. Among the 'suffering remnant' who were still faithful when he died in 1779 was the young Thomas Bowdler, who later acquired immortality of a kind in the field of Shakesperian editorship.

with the Princess of Mecklenburgh. I have been reviled hitherto as a jacobite, and now I am censured for going to court.' His attendance on the monarch he describes as 'an act of duty, which was required from me by the body corporate of which I am a member.' The appearance of the newspaper notice came as a complete surprise to him, for 'it never entered into my thoughts that a nonjuring clergyman, who values himself much upon the sanctity of his manners, and with whom I had once lived in some degree of friendship, should conspire with two or three villainous attorneys, who for a small bribe would swear away any man's life, to traduce me by a public advertisement.' In disparaging Bishop Gordon, King manifests the complete reversal which his political outlook had undergone. He complains that this Non-juror would be 'content to see the nation involved in a general ruin, and the extirpation of three or four millions of our people, if by that means the House of *Stuart* might be restored.' To these remarks he adds that 'the non-jurors are now become a very insignificant and contemptible party' and apropos of the gradual weakening of the barriers between Whig and Tory observes that the combination of a series of military victories and the successful conduct of public affairs 'may justly be alleged as one of the principal causes of uniting many of those (however they have been distinguished by party) who are real lovers of their country.'[1]

The Principal of St. Mary Hall has sometimes been criticized by historians of the Jacobite movement for defecting from the cause, but it is only condign to admit that he remained loyal to the King over the Water for as long as, if not longer than, there was any reasonable prospect of his being restored to the throne in London. After two generations of Stuart loyalists had attempted to assert the principle of legitimate monarchy, the chances of success in 1761 were dimmer than ever before. At home, the outstanding competence of William Pitt the Elder was allowed by men of all political persuasions; abroad, the brilliant victories of 1759 at Lagos, Quiberon Bay, Masulipatam, and Quebec had raised even King's confidence in the abilities of Britain's rulers. The attitude of George III towards the Tories was far more conciliatory than that of either of his Hanoverian

[1] Ibid., pp. 190ff.

predecessors, and as a result Tory statesmen began to exercise a much larger influence both at court and in the affairs of parliament. The Tory leaders could hardly have felt displeased as some of the greatest Whig magnates, including the Duke of Newcastle, were obliged to resign from their offices in the household or their lord-lieutenancies in the counties. The twenty-two year old monarch was also thoroughly Anglicized: having been born and educated, for the most part, in London, he was far more British than either of the two Pretenders. While the steadily ailing King over the Water continued to hold 'court' at the Palazzo Muti in Rome's Piazza Santi Apostoli, he was not only losing the interest of many of his former supporters in the British Isles, but failing to provide adequately for the circle of expatriated aristocrats who still remained part of his entourage. His heir had by this time declined, through chronic and prolonged demoralization, into a drunken reprobate: his public altercations with Clementina Walkinshaw, before she left him in 1760, had stimulated court gossip throughout Europe. The only political attachment that many Tories felt towards the end of the 1750's was for Pitt, and even King had admitted that the party had no acknowledged leader. Under these circumstances his tergiversation is at least understandable.

King was by no means the only personage in Oxford whose political outlook underwent a change about this time, but he was the most conspicuous example among the wave of political converts. The situation in the autumn of 1762 was described succinctly in a letter by Samuel Horne of University College in these terms:

Such a tumble of parties was surely never known before! Only imagine to yourself Bilstone and Jenkinson, Allen and Bray united together in support of the same interest!! As for old King, He wonder'd what people meant by opposing the Court when such fair advances had been made to us, and said with a grave face that He could account for it no otherwise than by supposing that they were *Jacobites*.[1]

---

[1] British Museum, Add. MSS. 39311, fol. 121 b. W. R. Ward, op. cit., pp. 222, 291, attributes this letter to George Horne, the Hutchinsonian. The signature seems to me to read 'S. Horne', and the heading is 'Univ. Coll. Oct. 6, 1762'. On this date George Horne, Samuel's brother, was residing at Magdalen College.

One may add that Oxford has never seen a comparable tumble of parties since Horne wrote. The two years between 1760 and 1762 constitute the last time in the history of the university when unanimous—or practically unanimous—loyalty to the monarch could be regarded as uncustomary. The reconciliation between Oxford and the court, which took place, broadly speaking, between 1768 and 1780, was a logical consequence of the new fidelity to the crown implicit in *Aviti Epistola*.

King's other noteworthy literary endeavour of 1760 was the final compilation of his *Opera*. In Chapter VII the long history of the preparation of the author's collected works was traced to 1754: it now remains to complete the story. The sheets of the entire *Opera*, except those of *Aviti Epistola ad Perillam, Virginem Scotam*, were in print by that year, and yet King appears to have made no attempt to publish or to distribute the collection. The various elements of the *Opera* seem not to have been bound into one volume for at least another six years. The most likely reason why he continued to hesitate is to be found in the anti-Jacobite sympathies of the government. In 1754, the Elibank Plot was not far behind, and the decline of the Whig ascendancy was still some seven years in the future. King was a marked man, whose identity was well known to the authorities. The Prime-Minister was the Duke of Newcastle, whom King had ridiculed in *A Key to the Fragment*. Many of the other Whigs whom King had satirized in his works, in either Latin or English, held high positions in Church and State. He was demonstrating a very reasonable prudence in not publicly attaching his name to a group of works, parts of which could have been established at law to be subversive, treasonous, or libellous.

The *Opera* was never published. A few copies may have been bound in 1760 or during the period before King's death, but it seems indisputable that the majority, if not all of the surviving copies were bound after he had passed away. There are two reasons for making this statement. First, there is to be found in most of the surviving copies a title-page which reads in part:

OPERA
GUL. KING, LL.D.
AULAE B.M.V. APUD OXONIENSES
OLIM PRINCIP.

Since King was Principal of St. Mary Hall until his death, the most palpable explanation of the phrase OLIM PRINCIP. is that this page was not printed during his lifetime.[1] Secondly, there is an account of the arrangements made for binding the volume provided in a letter of King's executor, Richard Bullock, dated 18 December 1799, and preserved in a copy of the *Opera* in the Beinecke Rare Book and Manuscript Library of Yale University. Bullock writes on the subject of the *Opera*:

Dr. King left 500 of this collection ready for binding; but understanding, from good authority, that he was sensible before his death of the severity (not to say more) with which he had treated most of his subjects, when they fell into my hands I resisted the temptations of Dr. King's bookseller (to whom he had devised the copy-right when this impression should have been sold) and, preserving only fifty, committed the rest to the flames. These 50 were almost immediately dispersed amongst Dr. King's old friends, with the reservation of a very few for myself and friends; so that the book, such as it is, may be deemed scarce.[2]

Bullock's observation on the scarcity of this handsome quarto volume is truer today than in 1799. As far as it is possible to form an estimate, there are at the present time in various libraries and private collections approximately twenty surviving copies, at least five of which are in the United States.[3] The sequence of the contents is not always consistent. In all the copies which I have seen, the five poems which King specially revised for his proposed collected edition (*Miltonis Epistola ad Pollionem; Sermo Pedestris; Scamnum, Ecloga; Templum Libertatis;* and *Antonietti, Corsorum Ducis, Epistola ad Corsos*) come first, followed by *Hydra* and *Monitor* which were never printed separately. At the conclusion of *Monitor* the sequential pagination ceases. The rest of the collection consists of remainders. There is some variation of items from volume to volume, but *The Toast*, with or without the author's handwritten alterations, is always placed last. Some volumes also include the errata slip for the 1736 edition of *The Toast* and a manuscript key to the characters.

---

[1] Where this title page occurs it is always in the form of an unsigned leaf.
[2] The Beinecke Rare Book and Manuscript Library, Yale University, Ik K589 + B760 Cop. 1.
[3] One of these is defective (Yale University, Ik K589 + B760 Cop. 2).

Many of the head- and tail-piece illustrations were devised by William Green the Younger and engraved on copper plates by Fourdrinier. There is usually a frontispiece by Hubert Gravelot.[1] Owing to the variations among the separate volumes of the *Opera*, there would be little value in formulating a collation of the whole.[2]

The surviving evidence does not by any means solve all the unanswered questions relating to the *Opera*. Why did King not have his speeches reset as he did in the case of his Latin poems? Why were some of his major speeches never printed at all? What right had Bullock to burn 450 unbound copies, when the author had already stipulated that the copyright should be reserved for his bookseller? To these and several similar problems there are no certain solutions.

The fact that King had determined on the final form which his collected Latin works should take did not terminate his literary career. The *Opera* makes no claim to be complete. In 1761 he printed two more short Latin works: the *Elogium* on Dr. John Taylor, the oculist, and the *Epitaphium Richardi Nash*. These pieces are both remarkable in their separate ways.

King had met Taylor at Tunbridge Wells in 1758. It is indeed interesting to peruse King's character of this eccentric individual who liked to be addressed as 'Chevalier', and whom Johnson regarded as 'an instance of how far impudence will carry ignorance.' Perhaps he is most often remembered nowadays (if he is remembered at all) for his habit of making inflated speeches before his treatments, starting each sentence with the genitive case, and concluding with the main verb. This singular kind of therapeutic oratory he described as 'the true Ciceronian, prodigiously difficult and never attempted in our language before.' Despite many of the characteristics of a pompous mountebank he possessed a not inconsiderable degree of medical expertise, as is evidenced from time to time in his publications. Among those who consulted him were many of

[1] Information on these continental designers and engravers may be found in Thieme and Becker's *Allgemeines Lexikon Der Bildenden Künstler* (Leipzig, 1912). The details are not always reliable.

[2] A very incomplete bibliographical description is included in Harold Williams, 'The Old Trumpeter of Liberty Hall', *The Book-Collector's Quarterly*, Vol. I, No. 4 (1931), pp. 54f.

the more prominent members of the continental aristocracy, and at home he counted Edward Gibbon and King's second cousin, Sir William Smyth of Warden, Bedfordshire, among his patients. In his *Anecdotes*, King remarked:

He seems to understand the anatomy of the eye perfectly well; he has a fine hand and good instruments, and performs all his operations with great dexterity; for the rest, *Ellum homo confidens!* who undertakes any thing (even impossible cases) and promises every thing. No charlatan ever appeared with fitter and more excellent talents, or to a greater advantage. . . .[1]

The *Elogium* was probably penned in 1761, and is a mixture of genuine praise and compliments of a distinctly dubious nature. The earliest form of it appears in the *Anecdotes*, but King improved this version with some new features, and printed a few copies to oblige his friends. It appears on a folio sheet folded. In it, Taylor is described as

> Caecigenorum, caecorum & caecutientium
> Quotquot sunt ubique,
> Spes unica, solamen, salus.

His travels in Europe are alluded to sympathetically together with his skill in languages. While some commentators regarded his 'true Ciceronian' orations as sheer fustian bombast, King described him as

> Orator summus non factus, sed natus.

But immediately afterwards, there follows an odd and perhaps purposely obscure reference to his activities in the field of amatory endeavour:

> Vultu compto, corpore procero, fronte urbana gloriosus,
> Ingenioque praeditus prope singulari,
> Artem amandi, et amoris remedium
> Plenius et melius Nasone ipso
> Edidicit, docuit, exercuit.

Sometimes it is difficult to tell whether King is sincere or not.

---

[1] *Political and Literary Anecdotes* (2nd edn., 1819), p. 131.

Statements of the following kind seem to me to have a definite tongue-in-cheek quality:

Mirificus fabulator, magnificus promissor,
Rerum copia, artiumque varietate abundans,
Sese exhibet, effert, praedicat
In gymnasiis, in gynaeceis, in conviviis, in triviis;
Philosophando gloriam magnam adeptus,
Maximam saltando.

Or again, on the subject of Taylor's wealth, King seems purposely to leave ample opportunity for differences of interpretation:

Praemia, dona, permulta, amplissima accepit.
Permulta corrasit, pecuniae appetentior:
Et nondum, eheu! locupletatur.

The statement made by King in the *Anecdotes* that Taylor entreated him to publish this effort, conceiving that it would do him honour, could at least cause some eyebrow raising. Did Taylor realize that some of King's flattery was written with a *double entendre*? Or did he feel that a certain notoriety would promote his fame? It is possible that, having been the subject of several satires, including the ballad opera *The Operator* of 1740, he may have decided to turn a blind eye to a few more mild jibes in Latin. But at least King's opinion of Taylor was higher than Johnson's.

Though the Principal of St. Mary Hall had mixed feelings on the subject of the oculist chevalier, the same is certainly not true in the case of his attitude to Beau Nash. I do not know of any derogatory comment that King ever made concerning the Monarch of Bath and Tunbridge Wells, bar one or two brief allusions to what he regarded as pardonable faults. The earliest reference to Nash in King's writings occurs in *The Dreamer*, where he is called 'the greatest monarch in Europe.' The author thus expatiates on this appellation:

For, although he is possessed of absolute power, he governs with universal esteem, and by the unanimous consent of a warlike and opulent nation. During the course of a long reign (of more than forty years) he has convinced the whole world, that he would have been worthy of empire, *si non imperasset*. He has never committed any acts of violence or oppression. His taxations have been very moderate, and he has required no other subsidies, than what have been just necessary for the service of his government. He has promulgated no laws or ordinances, but such, as are evidently calculated to promote the welfare and happiness of his people, maintain decency and order, and encrease all innocent diversions. I must further add, that this excellent monarch hath greatly embellished his feat of empire with many magnificent monuments, erected at his own expense. His citizens have followed his example. Several new streets have been lately built; and this place [i.e. Bath] is at present one of the most beautiful cities in EUROPE. So that Mr. NASH may say of BATH, what AUGUSTUS said of ROME, a little before his death, *Lateritiam inveni; marmoream reliqui*. When he shall have finished his last act, he may likewise demand a PLAUDITE; but with much more reason and justice, than the ROMAN Emperor.

These were King's opinions in 1754, and they did not alter.

Richard Nash died on 3 February 1761, at the age of eighty-seven.[1] King must have composed his *Epitaphium* shortly afterwards, for it seems to have been in print by the following April 2. On that day he wrote to Sir Francis Dashwood, in language that implies that a copy is enclosed with his letter: 'Some years ago I promised *Nash*, that if I survived him, I would write his Epitaph. If he had died sooner, before my own faculties were so much impaired, the picture would probably have been better drawn.'[2] Two settings of the *Epitaphium* were printed under King's purview: both are now rare. One is on a folio sheet folded: the text covers three unnumbered pages and the last page is blank. There is no imprint. The other setting is in the form of a booklet: it contains eight pages, of which the last is blank, and bears the imprint of C. Pope and J. Leake in Bath.[3] There are no material differences in the text of the two

[1] The *Dictionary of National Biography* gives the date of his death as 3 February 1762: this is a mistake. It is repeated in the *Cambridge Bibliography of English Literature*, where Sir Harold Williams postulated that Nash's epitaph was printed in the year before his death. On the details of Nash's burial see Willard Connely, *Beau Nash* (London: Werner Laurie, 1955), pp. 170ff.

[2] British Museum, MS. Eg. 2136. f. 66.

[3] An example of the text in three pages is in the Bodleian Library, MS. D. D. Dashwood (Bucks.), J. 6/2. Two of the best preserved copies of the seven-page text are in the Bath Municipal Library, Bath Pamphlets B 920, NAS No. 2343, and the Library of the State University of Iowa, f. CT788. N33K5.

settings. The *Epitaphium* was reprinted by Oliver Goldsmith in his biography, *The Life of Richard Nash*, which appeared in 1762, again twelve years later in Edward Popham's *Selecta Poemata Anglorum Latina*, and once more by Richard Warner in his *Modern History of Bath* of 1801. In addition to the Latin text, Goldsmith also provided his readers with a more or less literal translation: he did not indicate whether or not this vernacular rendering was his own.

In an age when florid Latin epithalamia were almost *de rigeur* for the mighty and the prominent, King's elaborate tribute to Nash, a hundred lines in length, excelled in grandeur many which had been composed in memory of sovereign rulers. Judged as a piece of literature, it exhibits a degree of elegance which, within its compass, would be difficult to surpass. Even though Nash had been born *obscuro loco* (actually Swansea) and of mean ancestors (*nullis ortus majoribus*), he was exalted by his epitaphist as an example to kings and, as a lawmaker, superior to Solon and Lycurgus. Besides endowing Bath with incomparable benefits, he also ordered well his 'celebrated province' of Tunbridge Wells:

> Quam admirabili consilio et ratione
> Per se, non unquam per legatos, administravit;
> Eam quotannis invisere dignatus,
> Et apud provinciales, quoad necesse fuit,
> Solitus manere.

He was not personally a seeker of regal splendour; instead of wearing a crown, he was content to be distinguished by a large, white hat:

> In tanta fortuna
> Neque fastu turgidus Rex incessu patuit,
> Neque, tyrannorum more, se jussit coli,
> Aut amplos honores, titulosque sibi arrogavit;
> Sed cuncta insignia, etiam regium diadema rejiciens,
> Caput contentus fuit ornare
> GALERO ALBO,
> Manifesto animi sui candoris signo.[1]

[1] The Intendants in *The Dreamer* wear white hats. Though King's feelings towards them were far from sympathetic, he may have been influenced by the head-

Nash's other generally accepted virtues are alluded to with deference: though he was a provider of pleasures, he conducted them with gravity and decorum, repressing licentiousness severely, and preventing obscenity from offending the modesty of the fair sex. With no enemies of any significance, he was a friend to rich and poor alike. He possessed the happy secret of uniting the vulgar and the great, the rich and the poor, the learned and the ignorant. Despite the fact that his power was limitless, liberty never flourished more than under his rule. He had faults, but they were venial:

> QUICQUID peccaverit,
> (Nam peccamus omnes)
> In seipsum magis, quam in alios,
> Et errore, et imprudentia magis quam scelere, aut improbitate,
> Peccavit;
> Nusquam vero ignoratione decori, aut honesti,
> Neque ita quidem usquam,
> Ut non veniam ab humanis omnibus
> Facile impetrarit.

The final section constitutes a graceful threnody in melopoeic periods, thus providing a fitting climax to a work generously studded with rhetorical ornaments. It may be noticed that anaphora occurs in the second, third, and fourth lines, and that the second and third lines also constitute isocolon. The seventh line is an example of brachylogia.

> TALEM virum, tantumque ademptum
> Lugeant Musae, Charitesque!
> Lugeant Veneres, Cupidinesque!
> Lugeant omnes juvenum et nympharum chori!
> Tu vero, O BATHONIA,
> Ne cesses tuum lugere
> Principem, praeceptorem, amicum, patronum;
> Heu, heu, nunquam posthac
> Habitura parem!

gear of Nash. William Hoare's portrait of Nash *galero albo* hangs at present in the Pump Room at Bath. It is reproduced as the frontispiece of A. Barbeau, *Life and Letters at Bath in the Eighteenth Century* (London: William Heinemann, 1904) and in the *Book of Bath* (1925), p. 68.

Whether or not this extended eulogy was justifiable depends largely on the degree of greatness which can reasonably be attributed to Beau Nash. In this matter one should not be misled by the hosts of obituary writers who produced 'characters' of Nash during the year or so after his death, many of whom were hoping principally to distinguish themselves in the reflected glory of this particular *elegantiae arbiter*. On the whole, the sentiments contained in King's epitaph seem to be those of the majority of persons who knew Nash in life, though even some of his most ardent admirers might well have felt reservations about this lofty proposal:

> Hujus vitae morumque exemplar
> Si caeteri reges, regulique,
> Et quotquot sunt regnorum praefecti,
> Imitarentur;
> (Utimam! iterumque utinam!)
> Et ipsi essent beati,
> Et cunctae orbis regiones beatissimae.

Goldsmith, in *The Life of Richard Nash*, provided the most influential answer to King's suggestion: 'To set him up, as some do, for a pattern of imitation, is wrong, since all his virtues received a tincture from the neighbouring folly; to denounce peculiar judgments against him is equally unjust, as his faults raise rather our mirth than our detestation. He was fitted for the station in which fortune placed him.' Goldsmith considered that no great abilities were needed to fill this station; King felt the opposite.

In attempting to determine whether King or Goldsmith was nearer to the truth, the literary historian should take into account the qualifications which both of these writers possessed in relation to their common subject. King had visited Bath intermittently over a long period of time, and could draw on a considerable fund of personal knowledge concerning his subject. Goldsmith, on the other hand, probably never set eyes on Nash, and wrote his biography primarily to pay for his expenses in the city, which he visited for the first time in 1762. *The Life of Richard Nash* was a piece of hackwork produced for

John Newbery, the bookseller, in return for which the thirty-three-year-old author received fourteen guineas. King's epitaph was clearly a labour of love. If the Old Trumpeter's estimate appears unduly sympathetic, Goldsmith's is, in places, disagreeably condescending, as in his description of Nash as 'a weak man governing weaker subjects.' Neither writer was impartial, but it would be difficult to deny convincingly that King wrote with greater authority.

Some time after Nash had been buried beneath the south nave of Bath Abbey, King's epitaph to him, engraved on a large slab of marble, was laid on the floor over the coffin. It is not normally visible today, for when the whole of the nave was fitted with permanent pews and wooden flooring, most of the memorials on the nave floor were covered over. There is on the south aisle wall not far from the tomb an epitaph to Nash composed in the early 1790s by Dr. Henry Harington: compared to King's composition, it is of pygmy proportions. When King came to compose the introduction to his own epitaph, he commented of the one to Nash:

> I promised NASH, a few years before he died, that if I survived him, I would write his epitaph. I performed my promise, and in my description of this extraordinary phenomenon, I think I have written nothing but the truth; one thing I omitted, which I did not reflect on until after the epitaph was printed, that a statue had been erected to him whilst he was living; and this great honour had been conferred on him with more justice than to any other of his contemporaries or brother kings.[1]

After 1761 the Principal of St. Mary Hall published nothing. But during the infirmities of his seventy-sixth year, to beguile the languor of the sickroom, he wrote his last book, which did not appear in print until 1818, sixty-five years after his death. It was then issued by the house of John Murray under the title *Political and Literary Anecdotes of His Own Times*, edited by Philip Bury Duncan. A second edition, the most recent, appeared in 1819, and during the same year the book was reprinted and published in the United States by the Boston house of Wells and Lilly. This short work, covering a little over 250 pages,

---

[1] *Political and Literary Anecdotes* (2nd edn., 1819), p. 248.

consists of detached pieces of table-talk, on the whole pleasantly written. Its special significance consists in the fact that it
contains stories and opinions about prominent figures of King's
own time which are not found in the works of any other
author, and also some original criticisms of the Latin poets.
Most of the anecdotes are written in English, but there is also an
engaging trifle in Latin entitled *Somnium Academici Alterum*.

The character of the Young Chevalier provided by King in
this book has already been discussed. Another anecdote, with
Pope as the subject, has a peculiar value, since it is not referred
to or mentioned in any of the standard biographies of that
poet. King writes:

POPE and I, with my Lord ORREY and Sir HARRY BEDING-
FIELD, dined with the late Earl of BURLINGTON. After the first
course POPE grew sick, and went out of the room. When dinner
was ended, and the cloth removed, my Lord BURLINGTON said
he would go out, and see what was become of POPE. And soon
after they returned together. But POPE, who had been casting up
his dinner, looked very pale, and complained much. My Lord asked
him if he would have some mulled wine or a glass of old sack, which
Pope refused. I told my Lord BURLINGTON that he wanted a
dram. Upon which the little man expressed some resentment
against me, and said he would not taste any spirits, and that he
abhorred drams as much as I did. However I persisted, and assured
my Lord BURLINGTON that he could not oblige our friend more
at that instant than by ordering a large glass of cherry-brandy to be
set up before him. This was done, and in less than half an hour,
while my Lord was acquainting us with an affair which engaged our
attention, POPE had sipped up all the brandy. POPE's frame of
body did not promise long life; but he certainly hastened his death
by feeding much on high-seasoned dishes, and drinking spirits.[1]

Having put forward the suggestion, which is neither provable
nor disprovable, that Pope's early death was caused partly by
alcohol, the teetotal author proceeds a few pages further on to
suggest that Swift's troubles in his later years were not improved
by the same addiction. The events which King describes presumably took place in the Deanery of St. Patrick's Cathedral,
Dublin, and its garden:

The last time I dined with Dean SWIFT, which was about three

[1] Ibid., pp. 12f.

years before he fell into that distemper which totally deprived him of his understanding, I observed, that he was affected by the wine which he drank, about a pint of claret. The next morning, as we were walking together in his garden, he complained much of his head, when I took the liberty to tell him (for I most sincerely loved him) that I was afraid he drank too much wine. He was a little startled, and answered, "that as to his drinking he had always looked on himself as a very temperate man; for he never exceeded the quantity which his physician allowed and prescribed him." Now his physician never drank less than two bottles of claret after his dinner.[1]

Scattered throughout the book are anecdotes relating to the Earl of Chesterfield, the Duke of Wharton, Lord Bath, Lord Gower, the Duke of Buckingham, Bishop Butler of Durham, Bishop Burnet of Salisbury, and many other prominent contemporaries. Some of the most mordant sentiments in the book are reserved for Sir Robert Walpole: 'He unhinged all the principles and morals of our people, and changed the government into a system of corruption. He openly ridiculed virtue and merit, and promoted no man to any employment of profit or honour, who had scruples of conscience, or refused implicitly to obey his commands. . . .'[2] One anecdote provides an interesting, though perhaps exaggerated, sidelight on the problem of tipping servants:

The CUSTOM of giving money to servants is now become such a grievance, that it seems to demand the interposition of the legislature to abolish it. How much are foreigners astonished, when they observe that a man cannot dine at any house in *England*, not even with his father or his brother, or with any other of his nearest relations, or most intimate friends and companions, unless he pay for his dinner! But how can they behold without indignation or contempt a man of quality standing by his guests, while they are distributing money to a double row of his servants? If, when I am invited to dine with any of my acquaintance, I were to send the master of the house a sirloin of beef for a present, it would be considered as a gross affront; and yet as soon as I shall have dined or before I leave the house, I must be obliged to pay for the sirloin, which was brought to his table, or placed on the sideboard . . . Suppose there were written in large gold letters over the door of every man of rank: THE FEES FOR DINING HERE ARE THREE HALF CROWNS

---

[1] Ibid., p. 16.   [2] Ibid., pp. 39f.

OR TEN SHILLINGS TO BE PAID TO THE PORTER ON ENTERING THE HOUSE: PEERS OR PEERESSES TO PAY WHAT MORE THEY THINK PROPER. By this regulation two inconveniences would be avoided: first, the difficulty of distinguishing amongst a great number, the quality of the servants. I, who am near-sighted, have sometimes given the footman what I designed for the butler, and the butler has had only the footman's fee: for which the butler treated me with no small contempt, until an opportunity offered of correcting my error. But secondly, this method would prevent the shame which every master of a family cannot help feeling whilst he sees his guests giving about their shillings and half-crowns to the servants. . . .[1]

Occasionally, the author makes observations of a rather intimate nature, which are without precedent in his earlier books. For example, he had appeared in *The Toast* to be concerned with lesbianism and at the same time repulsed by it, but in the *Anecdotes* he not inconsistently expressed his admiration for clerical celibacy. 'I have often wished that the canons which forbid priests to marry were still in force', he wrote. 'Chastity certainly adds a grace and dignity to their function. . . . To the celibacy of the bishops we owe almost all those noble foundations which are established in both our Universities.'[2] And his sensitivity to the Latin authors is revealed especially clearly in his disarming admissions of his own responses to them. Thus in regard to Horace he confessed, 'I could never read the first stanza in the *Carmen Seculare* without falling into a fit of devotion,' and the story of Ceyx and Halcyone in Ovid's *Metamorphoses*, he disclosed, 'I never read without weeping.' In view of such acknowledgements, one can fully accept the ingenuousness of his declaration: 'I have a veneration for VIRGIL: I admire HORACE: but I love OVID.'[3]

While King was recording these confessions of his personal partialities, the consciousness of his own approaching death was impinging upon him. His son, Charles, had already been buried. His daughter, Dorothy, died on 21 June 1761, and was interred five days later in Ealing churchyard.[4] Ill health

---

[1] Ibid., pp. 50–55.   [2] Ibid., pp. 186f.   [3] Ibid., p. 30.
[4] The date of her interment is given as 26 June 1761, in the contemporary Burial Register of the parish church of St. Mary, Ealing. She is described simply as 'wife of William Melmoth, Esqr.'

continued to plague him. He took no official part in the installation of the Earl of Lichfield as the new Chancellor of the University of Oxford on 5 October 1762. On the following April 1, he wrote to Sir Francis Dashwood in a quavering hand: 'I have been confined for three months past to my chambers & chiefly to my bed by a fever, tormented during the same time by fits of yᵉ stone & gravel. I am now slowly recovering, and 'tis only within a few days past, that I have endeavoured to use my pen.'[1]

The Principal of St. Mary Hall delivered his last oration on 8 July 1763, at the conclusion of that year's Encaenia. As usual, the four festal days in the Sheldonian Theatre had been replete with music and Latin declamations. On the morning that King spoke, Handel's anthem *Zadok the Priest* had been performed, and the Old Trumpeter could at last associate himself fully with its iterations of 'God Save the King'. Two brief accounts of the speech survive. One is in *Jackson's Oxford Journal*, couched in a manner similar to that of the 1759 oration:

. . . the whole Solemnity of this Grand Encaenia was closed by Dr. King, Principal of St. Mary Hall, who in a most spirited and elegant Oration, delivered with a Grace and Dignity, which notwithstanding his acknowledged Powers, could scarce be expected from a Gentleman in his 79th Year [*sic*], enlarged on the salutary Effects arising from a general Peace; complimented his Majesty for his particular Regard to Arts, to Literature, and to the University of Oxford; and, after taking a most affectionate Farewell of the Youth of this Place, concluded with a polite Address to the Chancellor.[2]

The other account is contained in a letter written from Balliol College on the following August 1 by Charles Godwyn to John Hutchins:

. . . Dr. King spoke in a strain very different from anything which we had heard from him before: but his strength and memory, and the applause which he received, were just the same as usual. The purport of his Speech was this: 'that we had gained great honour by acting with steadiness and integrity in a time of general corruption: and that now, without any alteration in our conduct, we had the

---

[1] Bodleian Library, MS. D. D. Dashwood (Bucks.), B. 11/10/7.

[2] *Jackson's Oxford Journal*, No. 532 (9 July 1763). The mention of 'a general Peace' refers to the conclusion of the Seven Years' War with the Treaty of Paris.

happiness of being in some degree of favour with a Prince, who is one of the best that ever lived.' He said, 'it was his happiness that he was born an Englishman; and he reckoned it an additional circumstance of happiness that he was *Oxoniensis.*' That we may not grow vain upon these compliments, Churchill [i.e., Charles Churchill] is to apply, by way of remedy, a little cooling satire. A large dose of it is prepared for the Chancellor, and Lord Despenser, and Sir John Phillips, and Jack Burton. How Dr. King is to escape, I don't know. Churchill expressed great approbation for his manner of speaking; but from the notes which were taken down in writing, we apprehend, that there is a great deal laid up in store, and to be applied by way of correction.[1]

The 'little cooling satire' appeared in Churchill's poem *The Candidate*, published later in the same year. It was little enough: two lines only, addressed to the actor Garrick:

> King shall arise, and, bursting from the dead,
> Shall hurl his *piebald* Latin at thy head.[2]

King's last surviving letter, dated 7 September 1763, is largely an endorsement of the policy of George III. It constitutes an answer to an earlier letter from Sir Francis Dashwood, in which King had been told of the severe demands which a group of politicians close to the monarch were making in opposition to the terms of the Treaty of Paris. The reply from St. Mary Hall could hardly have been more indulgent to the reigning Hanoverian: 'If his M. should not have firmitude enough to reject these demands, he would hereafter have no more power than a Doge of Venice, and the people would be governed by an oligarchy, which history & our own experience have taught us, is yᵉ worst species of tyranny.'[3]

In the same letter King offered his hopes to Sir Francis that they would meet again, 'before I go to Bath.' His health continued to deteriorate, though he decided to undertake the journey. Despite the fact that he had earlier in his life expressed doubts on the medical efficacy of the spa waters, he presumably still felt that he could obtain some therapeutic benefit from

[1] John Nichols, *Literary Anecdotes of the Eighteenth Century* (9 vols.; printed for the author, 1812–15), Vol. VIII, p. 236.

[2] Douglas Grant (ed.), op. cit., p. 548.

[3] British Museum, MS. Eg. 2136, f. 67.

another visit. In this respect his attitude towards taking the waters was no different from that of Pope and a hundred other distinguished visitors: grumbling could have had cathartic benefits. Whether he should have made the journey across England in the depth of winter is more problematical. He left St. Mary Hall after the Christmas Gaudy (or so the Buttery Book entries would seem to indicate) and died at Bath, at the age of seventy-eight, on 30 December 1763. During the following days his body was carried back by coach to Ealing, where his funeral took place, in St. Mary's Church, six days after his death.[1] The obituary which appeared in *Jackson's Oxford Journal* was brief but dignified. King was 'the oldest Head of a House in Oxford', and, the writer continued, 'a Gentleman whose Character in the polite and literary World is too well known to need any Encomium; and who was universally allowed to be the most celebrated Orator in all Europe.'[2]

Shortly after King's demise, the lease of Ealing rectory was purchased from his estate manager by Thomas Bramley of East Acton and Thomas Harrington of Old Brentford.[3] It is perhaps appropriate to add that this edifice, of which King for a good part of his life had been the lessee, was subsequently to have a noteworthy history as the principal building of Great Ealing School. Under the former rectory roof, at various times, such diverse figures as John Henry Newman and his brother Francis, Thackeray, Sir William Gilbert (who rose to be head boy), Captain Marryat, Thomas Huxley (whose father was a member of the staff), Bishop Selwyn, Sir Henry Rawlinson, Lord Lawrence, Sir Henry Lawrence, Lord Truro, Richard Westmacott, Sir Robert Sale, William Hicks Pasha, and dozens of lesser lights all received part of their education. Today, thanks to the

---

[1] According to the Burial Register for 1761–76, the date was 5 January 1764. Most of the eighteenth century tombstones in the churchyard are now defaced or have been moved. Only a small number of memorials from the interior of the church which was opened on Trinity Sunday, 1740, were incorporated into the present building, the greater part of which dates from 1866. Today there is no tombstone or memorial to King at Ealing.

[2] *Jackson's Oxford Journal*, No. 558 (7 January 1764). A similar notice appeared in *The London Evening Post*, No. 5642 (31 December 1763–3 January 1764). The writer in *Jackson's Oxford Journal* mistakenly gives King's age at death as eighty.

[3] Thomas Faulkner, op. cit., p. 177. Edith Jackson, op. cit., gives the name of the second purchaser as Thomas Harrison.

activities of the death watch beetle, there remains of Ealing rectory not a stone upon a stone.

In addition to the enemies whom King acquired during his lifetime, one other person was made indignant by the announcement of his decease. He was Charles Jennens of Gopsall in Leicestershire. Thereby hangs a tale. Exactly seventeen years to the day before King's expiration, on 30 December 1746, Edward Holdsworth, Jacobite, neo-Latin poet, classical scholar, and designer of the New Buildings in the Palladian style at Magdalen College, Oxford, had passed away, and a few days later was buried in the parish church of Coleshill in Warwickshire. Charles Jennens, another Oxford Jacobite, friend of Handel and patron of the arts, one whose grand style of living caused him to be known as 'Solyman the Magnificent', was so much an admirer of Holdsworth that he erected an Ionic temple to his memory in the grounds of Gopsall Hall, and had his exhumed body brought there from Coleshill. In this small building he decided to place a cenotaph with a Latin inscription extolling the not inconsiderable virtues of his departed hero. Who better to write the inscription than William King? Jennens, since his undergraduate days at Balliol, had been acquainted with the Doctor, and not long after Holdsworth's death approached him with a view to obtaining a suitable epitaph. For some reason which cannot now be ascertained, King did not comply with this request, but promised, or so Jennens afterwards maintained, that he would compose an appropriate inscription in the future. For over a decade and a half Jennens waited, with growing impatience, but King's Latin sentiments on Holdsworth were never forthcoming. After the Doctor had died, the now thoroughly disgruntled Jennens was forced to write the inscription himself, but to prove to his temple pilgrims that the long delay was none of his fault, he added, lower on the cenotaph beneath a bust of Holdsworth, a second inscription of an explanatory nature. King is not named, but Jennen's despair at his long procrastination is made amply evident:

E. HOLDSWORTH, natus 1684, mortuus 1746.
Inscriptionem praestolatus usque ad 1764.

Miraris forsan, Lector, nec immerito,
hunc omni laude dignissimum virum
sine saxo et sine nomine corpus
jamdiu jacuisse!
Verum iste Regulus, qui Eloquium pollicebatur,
dum per plures annos
Orationibus vel Oratiunculis,
et Versibus Satyrico-Politicis,
scribendis, dicendis, et agendis,
suo denique suipsius Elogio
inanem sibi gloriam aucupatur,
Famae interim melioris oblitus,
amicis quam dederat fidem fefellit.
Quod Genius diu solicitatus negavit,
promisit enim, nec tamen praestitit,
id demum impar quidem conatui,
sed indignata
praestat Amicitia.[1]

The temple collapsed in 1835 and Gopsall Hall was demolished in 1951, but the cenotaph, with its twin inscriptions to honour Holdsworth and to dishonour King, still stands.

Before the interment at Ealing, King's heart, at his own request, was taken from his body, enclosed in a marble vase, and returned to St. Mary Hall. Later, the vase was set in the north wall of the chapel, over the epitaph which he had composed for himself.[2] The engraving of this epitaph could not have been carried out with any great urgency, for on 2 April 1764 Charles Godwyn wrote again to John Hutchins:

Dr. King's picture is just put up in the Picture-gallery, and placed, by his desire, next to Butler's. His heart is to be lodged in the Chapel at St. Mary Hall, with an inscription which he drew up himself. The most remarkable part of it is this: *Permultos habui*

---

[1] The text is printed in John Nichols, op. cit. ult., Vol. III, pp. 69f. Additional relevant information appears on p. 126. Jennens's present reputation in the musical world is due largely to his being the author of the words of Handel's oratorios *Saul* and *Belshazzar*, and the compiler of the scriptural passages in *The Messiah*.

[2] Some authors (e.g. John Nichols) have written of a 'silver case', though there is no evidence that King's heart ever rested in any receptacle other than the closed marble urn which may still be seen at the present time. The date of composition, *pridie Nonas Junii, die natali Georgii III, MDCCLXII*, is included in the inscription.

amicos, at veros, stabiles, gratos (quae fortasse est gentis culpa) perpaucissi-mos. Plures habui inimicos, sed invidos, sed improbos, sed inhumanos. This, and the whole of it, might, I think, very well have been omitted.[1]

The exact date of the erection of this monument is now unas-certainable.

The text of King's epitaph was published first by Edward Popham, and has since been reprinted several times.[2] The monument itself remained in the chapel until the merger with Oriel College took place on the death, in the summer vacation of 1902, of the last Principal of the Hall, Dr. Drummond Chase. It was then taken down and reset in the west wall of the chapel of Oriel College. There are slight variations in the printed ver-sions of the epitaph; the text in the *Anecdotes* reads thus:

FUI
GUILIELMUS KING, LL.D.
Ab Anno MDCCXIX ad annum MDCCLX
Aulae B.M.V. in Academia Oxon. Praefectus.
Literis humanioribus a puero deditus,
Eas usque ad supremum vitae diem colui.
Neque vitiis carui, neque virtutibus,
Imprudens et improvidus, comis et benevolus;
Saepe aequo iracundior,
Haud unquam, ut essem implacabilis.
A luxuria pariter ac avaritia
(Quam non tam vitium,
Quam mentis insanitatem esse duxi)
Prorsus abhorrens,
Cives, hospites, peregrinos
Omnino liberaliter accepi;
Ipse et cibi abstinentior, et vini abstinentissimus.

---

[1] John Nichols, op. cit. ult., Vol. VIII, p. 241.

[2] Edward Popham, *Selecta Poemata Anglorum Latina* (Bath, 1774), pp. 171f.; Antony Wood, *The History and Antiquities of the Colleges and Halls in the University of Oxford* (Oxford, 1786), p. 675; John Nichols, op. cit. ult., Vol. II, p. 609; James Ingram, *Memorials of Oxford* (3 vols.; Oxford, 1837), Vol. II, pp. 7f.; William King, *Political and Literary Anecdotes* (2nd edn., 1819), pp. 251f.; John Sparrow, *Poems in Latin* (Oxford: at the Clarendon Press, 1941), pp. 51f., with notes on p. 67. A trans-cription taken from King's monument appears in the same author's *Lapidaria* (Oxford: privately printed, 1943). Some copies of the *Opera* also contain the epitaph.

Cum magnis vixi, cum plebeiis, cum omnibus,
Ut homines noscerem, ut meipsum imprimis:
Neque, eheu, novi!
Permultos habui amicos,
At veros, stabiles, gratos
(Quae fortasse est gentis culpa)
Perpaucissimos.
Plures habui inimicos,
Sed invidos, sed improbos, sed inhumanos:
Quorum nullis tamen injuriis
Perinde commotus fui,
Quam deliquiis meis.
Summam, quam adeptus sum, senectutem
Neque optavi, neque accusavi,
Vitae incommoda neque immoderate ferens,
Neque commodis nimium contentus:
Mortem neque contempsi,
Neque metui.

DEUS OPTIME,
Qui hunc orbem et humanas res curas,
Miserere animae meae!

On the monument itself, the third line of the epitaph appears as

Ab anno MDCCXIX ad annum MDCCLXIV.

No indisputable explanation can be offered for the discrepancies in the date of King's terminating the Principalship of St. Mary Hall. He was still Principal when he died: the correct date of termination should therefore be 1763. The dates 1760 and 1764 are both impossible.

In comparison to the amorphous and flattering generalities in which most epitaphs of the time were couched, King's is unusually frank and self-critical. It gives the impression of being phrased in terms as candid as its maker could formulate. From 1722, when he had rashly contested the university seat in Parliament with his senior colleague George Clarke, he had on various occasions shown signs of the side of his nature which was *imprudens et improvidus*, witness especially the long lawsuit in Ireland which led him to write *The Toast*. The fact that he was also *saepe aequo iracundior* almost inevitably led him into a long series of controversies which continued despite the fact that he was *haud unquam . . . implacabilis*. To these personal shortcomings should be added his tendency to blame others on questionable premisses, illustrated by his lamenting that his very small number of *amicos veros, stabiles, gratos* was *fortasse gentis culpa*. That he could claim not to have despised or feared death may well be a reflection of what he wrote in *Monitor* and repeated in 1755 among the concluding lines of his *Apology*:

> Attamen aequo animo, non ullis rebus egenus,
> Non inhonoratus vixi. . . .

With his heart in its marble urn and his epitaph engraved and erected, the career of William King was, properly speaking, ended. But it had a strange and prolonged epilogue. For well nigh a century and a half afterwards, in fact until St. Mary Hall ceased to exist as an institution, gentlemen whose rooms were close to the chapel would sometimes be woken up during the night by the eerie sound of beating which came from the direction of the marble urn in the chapel. Writers on the subject offered sundry explanations of this bizarre phenomenon, but none with more authority than Dr. Lancelot Phelps, who was Provost of Oriel College from 1914 to 1929. In a letter to John McGrath, Provost of Queen's College, of 15 February 1916, Phelps discusses the marble vase, and then continues:

As to the heart, let me add a reminiscence. It was always held that so restless and so turbulent was King's life that after his death the heart went on beating in its vase. Now it so happened that when I lived in St. Mary Hall the head of my bed abutted on the wall in a recess in which the vase stood. Rarely, if ever, did I go to bed without hearing a sound as of tapping on the wall, the origin of which I could find nothing to explain, except the action of the heart. More than that, shortly after I had left the rooms, I met my successor in them and expressed the hope that he was comfortable. 'Yes,' he said, 'in every way—but did you ever hear a curious kind of tapping on the wall near your bedhead?'

'But,' I said, 'you know what that is?'

'Indeed, I do not, and cannot imagine.'

22—W.K.

'That is the heart of Dr. King.'
Can further proof be needed of the truth of the tradition?[1]

The Reverend Dr. Phelps, in his day an acknowledged expert on the history of poor law administration, was not regarded as a superstitious man, or as one given to credulity. When he died in 1936, his opinion on the subject of the heart in the urn was still unchanged. The question of whether he was right or wrong is best left to historians of psychic phenomena, for now that St. Mary Hall is no more, the Old Trumpeter's heart has finally ceased to beat.

[1] *Notes and Queries*, 12th Series, Vol. I, pp. 194f.

IX

An Assessment of King's Achievement

OXFORD, wrote Matthew Arnold, is the home of lost causes,
forsaken beliefs, unpopular names, and impossible loyalties.
William King was one of those persons who have contributed
to whatever truth this description possesses. Through no fault
of his own, he devoted most of his energies for the greater part
of his life to a political cause which proved to be a failure and
which he himself finally came to abandon. It does not by any
means follow that his life's work may therefore be dismissed as
of no consequence. His writings exerted at least some influence
in learned circles in his own time, and would probably be more
widely read today, were it not for the decline in the educational
importance of the classics.[1] His significance would seem to be
fourfold. First, he was by general consent the leader of the
Jacobite party in Oxford and England's most forceful literary
polemicist for the Jacobite viewpoint. Secondly, he was one of
the most artistically competent writers of Latin in the eighteenth
century, a language which he could wield with an exceptional
degree of grace, clarity, and fluency. Thirdly, he is noteworthy
as a humorist, satirist, and allegorist, in both the Latin and
English Languages, and fourthly, through his connections with
such figures as Swift and Pope, he is memorable for the minor,
though not wholly unimportant part which he played in the
history of English literature.

Vigorous and dedicated though they were, his purely political activities have now only a historical interest. If the cause of
Jacobitism were ever to be revived in the future, his efforts on

---

[1] Some explanations are provided in R. M. Ogilvie, *Latin and Greek: A History
of the Influence of the Classics on English Life from 1600 to 1918* (London: Routledge
and Kegan Paul, 1964) and M. L. Clarke, *Classical Education in Britain, 1500–1900*
(Cambridge: at the University Press, 1959). For informal observations on the subject see Gilbert Highet, *The Classical Tradition* (Oxford: at the Clarendon Press,
1949), pp. 490–500.

its behalf would perhaps be reassessed in a more favourable light, but since none of the Stuart claimants since the theoretical accession of Charles Emmanuel IV of Sardinia in 1807 has made any attempt to regain the power to which, it could be argued, he is *de jure* entitled, the possibility that King's thinking will ever again be politically important seems remote. The present Stuart claimant, His Royal Highness Duke Albert of Bavaria, who was staunchly anti-Nazi and spent most of the Second World War in Ravensbrück concentration camp, has indicated that he is not interested in reviving the Jacobite cause. His predecessor, Crown Prince Rupert of Bavaria, was visited shortly after the First World War by Lieutenant-Colonel Stewart Roddie, and showed himself to be of a similar mind. Said Roddie:

"You—you are the direct heir through the Stuarts to the throne of England. You are the 'King across the Water'."

"How did you know?" he asked with some interest.

"Because I heard no less a person than His Majesty King George of England himself say so," I said.

"Oh! He knows? . . . Well," he added laughingly, "if you have the opportunity, please assure His Majesty from me that I have no intention of pressing my claim."[1]

King's principal achievement was literary, and his best work was written in Latin. The English works are either too slight or too ephemeral to lend themselves to serious literary criticism, and the small macaronic productions are more in the nature of oddities, entertaining in themselves, but not especially rewarding to the critic. *The Toast*, though also an oddity, is in a class by itself: it cannot appropriately be considered with any of the author's other works, but invites separate treatment.

Very little modern criticism applied to neo-Latin poetry and prose has appeared in print. Even today, there is no treatment of Latin and neo-Latin literature comparable to David Daiches's *Critical History of English Literature*. A. E. Housman remarked in 1892 that no rightminded man would go to a classical scholar for judgements on literature: the kind of aca-

---

[1] Lt.-Col. Stewart Roddie, C.V.O., *Peace Patrol* (London: Christophers, 1932), p. 290.

demic mentality which led him to make that comment has by no means disappeared. But an evaluative approach to the works of William King or any comparable Anglo-Latin writer is surely possible, and it seems to me that the critic may proceed in two different ways. One method is to judge the author's output by classical standards of criticism, using the principles of such authorities as Cicero, the anonymous author of the *Rhetorica ad C. Herennium*, Dionysius of Halicarnassus, Quintillian, and Longinus, and he may augment these with the kind of theory to be found in the works of Renaissance scholars such as Erasmus, Petrus Mosellanus, Melanchthon, Juan Luis Vives, and Daniel and Nicolaas Heinsius. That is to say, he may regard his subject's product as an extension of the Latin language into the modern period, bearing constantly in mind the fact that criticism of Latin literature is relevant only if measured against what the best writers of that language were intent to put into their literature, and not against what modern vernacular authors strive to put into theirs. His procedure will be that of the classical critics, who regarded good style, in its broadest sense, as the touchstone of the literary artist. The second method available to the modern critic consists in the evaluation of neo-Latin poetry and prose as a part of the literature of England, reflecting strongly the conditions of the age in which it was produced, and showing the influence of other authors who wrote entirely or mainly in the vernacular. Since these two procedures are to some extent complementary, it is appropriate first to comment on the purely stylistic aspects of King's Latin works before the second and broader approach is discussed.

William King was a consummate Latinist. Probably the most conspicuous characteristic of his Latinity, despite the objections of John Burton and his ilk, is the purity of his classical diction. True, he exhibits the kinds of shortcomings that were the result of imperfect scholarship in his own day: there are occasional examples of unclassical orthography, and, like most other neo-Latinists, he invents questionable neologisms now and again. But these cases are exceptional. On the whole, King's grammatical, syntactical, and metrical correctness are remarkable, and they still remain so when his prosody is considered in the light of the work of modern theorists.[1] A few of the prosodical devices which he employed have been indicated with examples: anaphora, asyndeton, and isocolon amongst them. These and similar embellishments are used by the poet with some frequency: they add considerably to the elaborately wrought character of his high style. In keeping with practically all writers of Latin in his time, King regarded such ornaments as far more integral than most modern authors conceive them to be. In this respect he was in the tradition of the humanists who conceived of Latin style largely in terms of the traditional figures of speech. Of these approximately two hundred were recognized at the time when the Renaissance critics were writing, though individual authorities differed among themselves as to the scope and number of the figures, their relative importance, and the manner of their division into tropes and schemes.

Perhaps the most pervasive of the figures used by King is the species of hyperbaton known as anastrophe: there are instances of it throughout his Latin poetry and prose. Examples could be given *ad nauseam*, most of which would merely corroborate the fact that his word order is as a rule more artistically effective than the normal order would be. Very rightly, King's usual tendency is to put his strongest words at the end of the sentence, but he does not invariably employ this procedure. Metrical convenience sometimes appears to have been a determinant, and, in a few other instances, the reader is deliberately surprised. Thus in *Monitor*, after Aulicus has been lecturing Aulus for some time with considerable severity, the reader is pleasantly jolted by this example of aposiopesis:

Si modo desieris, monitusque HEROA, DUCEMQUE —
AUL. Aulice, quo properas, horrenda, extrema minatus
Indigno?

[1] See, for example, S. E. Winbolt, *Latin Hexameter Verse* (London: Methuen & Co., 1903); William Hardie, *Res Metrica* (Oxford: at the Clarendon Press, 1920); J. P. Postgate, *Prosodia Latina* (Oxford: at the Clarendon Press, 1923); Maurice Platnauer, *Latin Elegiac Verse* (Cambridge: at the University Press, 1951); Freidrick Crusius, *Römische Metrik* (7th ed. revised by H. Rubenbauer; Munich, 1963); D. S. Raven, *Latin Metre* (London: Faber and Faber, 1965). Some relevant matters of orthography and metre are discussed in W. Sidney Allen, *Vox Latina* (Cambridge: at the University Press, 1965). See especially his treatment of vowel length and quantity, pp. 64–77, 89–94.

Parallelism of expression is in King's verse, as in that of Vergil, one of the principal means of obtaining a heightened and sonorous quality. This effect is achieved with an especial degree of leisurely lucidity in the poet's descriptive passages. Thus in *Scamnum, Ecloga,* he writes:

> Huc veniunt pueri, & tenerae per prata puellae:
> Huc satyri veniunt, Faunique. Hic Naiadas inter
> Nunc Galatea suos, nunc Aegle narrat amores.

In *Templum Libertatis* there are likewise many excellently balanced lines; for instance, these three individual cases:

> Hi pomis gaudent variis, hi floribus halant.
> Perque informe Chaos, perque aspera viscera terrae.
> Certa deum mens est: certo regit omnia fine.

Sometimes symmetry is accomplished between lines as well as within them. Again, these examples come from *Templum Libertatis:*

> Tuque ingeniosa
> Dum lustras, hospes, lautae miracula villae,
> Alcinoique solo lucos & culta vireta
> Dum Vari praefers; tamen hic potes hospita sacra,
> Hic potes Alcinoi faciles cognoscere mores.

> Nec licet, aut fas est coelum incusare querelis:
> Nec potis, aut fas est scrutari arcana deorum.

> Queis modo tot comites, queis primos emerat aulae,
> Queis sibi tot servos, queis primos emerat urbis . . .

The fourfold repetition of *queis* in the last example is especially felicitous.

Dozens of examples could be quoted from King's poetry of the threefold repetition in a couplet which is so marked a characteristic of Vergilian style, but it is worthwhile quoting a septuple repetition from *Miltonis Epistola ad Pollionem* as an example of how he can use the hexameter in a manner which is as oratorical as it is poetic:

> At quid tu possis? quid pars sincera senatus?
> Quid socii proceres? quid virtus dura Catonis?

Quid Bruti? Si vel totum Cicerona sonares,
Quid tibi, quid patriae divina Philippica prosit?

King occasionally achieves symmetry by the simultaneous use of isocolon and homoeoteleuton, as in this couplet in *Templum Libertatis*:

Haec etenim rapuit, qui possidet omnia, Cyclops.
Haec etiam vendit, qui vendidit omnia, Cyclops.

The use of *vendit* with *vendidit* is an added embellishment. Though homoeoteleuton is sometimes regarded as a device to be generally avoided, the repetition of *Cyclops* is clearly intentional. Vergil had occasionally employed repetitions of a comparable nature, putatively for rhetorical effect:

Transfossi ligno veniunt. Vix unus Helenor
Et Lycus elapsi: quorum primaevus Helenor,

for example.[1]

There are several instances in *Templum Libertatis* and elsewhere of parallel effects worked out within a larger parallelism. This kind of counterpoint manifests a considerable degree of artistic and technical expertise:

Hic est, hic ille est, cujus nunc dicitur orbis
Librari ingenio; cui nunc sua prospera Plutus,
Cui rerum summam, cui se quoque tradit: &, omnis
Hic opifex infandi operis, celer itque reditque
Nuntius huc, illuc; & praemia magna reportat.

Templum Libertatis also contains many excellent examples of the symmetry that can be achieved by the judicious placing of light and heavy sense-pauses.[2] In the following period, the sense-pauses have, with one exception, been placed within the separate verses, so as to allow for the elasticity and easy flow

[1] *Aeneid*, Book IX, ll.544f. The most comprehensive treatment of the repetitions in the *Aeneid* is in John Sparrow, *Half-Lines and Repetitions in Virgil* (Oxford: at the Clarendon Press, 1931), pp. 55–154.

[2] I am of the opinion that a comma in King's Latin poetry is generally to be taken as indicating a light sense-pause. Referring to classical elegiac verse, Maurice Platnauer does not regard the comma as a sense-pause; see his *Latin Elegiac Verse* (Cambridge: at the University Press, 1951), p. 24. For a different division of pauses as applied to hexameter verse see S. E. Winbolt, op. cit., pp. 1–69.

from stich to stich which is one of the charms of developed hexameter composition.

> Illa artem docuit Batavos, qua stagna colantur,
> Qua vada, qua rupes; sterilis qua reddat arena
> Frugiferas messes; qua dulcia praebeat arbos
> Poma, vel invita terra; qua cuique colono
> Fiant magna satis sua, quamvis parvula, rura.

There are occasions, however, when the author, for the sake of metrical variety, may achieve equally artistic symmetrical effects with the use of verses ending in heavy sense-pauses. In the period from *Templum Libertatis* which follows, King exhibits this kind of paratactical symmetry, with the additional embellishments of isocolon and two instances of anaphora:

> Qualia vix quisquam sine divum numine speret;
> Qualia vix reges, vix poscat regia pellex;
> Vix aut Socraticae chartae, vel pagina Tulli,
> Vix aut carminibus vates meruere priores.

King's subtle manipulation of different rhythmical patterns is an essential ingredient of his art and of the musical quality perceptible in a good deal of his Latin verse. His metre rarely, if ever, becomes monotonous, thanks largely to the constantly changing variety of verse patterns which he exhibits, and to his judicious interplay of dactyls and spondees. Two short examples must suffice to illustrate the manner in which the poet manipulates the possible combinations of *metra*. The first example comes from *Templum Libertatis*:

> Ausus opus cum sim tantum, tu, diva, canenti
> Ingenium uberius, magnas & suffice vires,
> Atque animos, quibus ipsa cales, viridemque senectam.
> Et potes haec; & cuncta potes. Nec te sine quicquam
> Sublime exoritur; *neque sit vel amabile quicquam,*
> *Vel sine te laetum.* Quin tu, si numine dextro
> Nunc adsis, faveasque; aderit mihi magnus Apollo,
> (Quo venias, veniet) faciles aderuntque Camoenae.
> Et nitor, & numeris accedant pondera nostris;
> Atque aliquem hoc vati praestet quoque carmen honorem.

The combinations of dactyls and spondees in the first four feet of the individual verses are as follows:

D S S S
D D S S
D D D D
D S D S
D D D D
D S S S
S D D D
D D D D
D D S S
D S S D

It will be noticed that here, as in Vergil's poetry, there is a predominance of dactylic first feet. The structure of feet in the first and sixth verses

D S S S

is that which is most commonly found in Vergil: it is used by King with frequency. The structure of feet in the second and ninth verses

D D S S

is the second most commonly used by Vergil. The combination

D D D D

occurs twice, but neither the two cases of this structure nor any other two similar arrangements are consecutive. There is a notable predominance in this passage, as in King's poetry as a whole, of the strong caesura. It is also noteworthy that the poet makes use of elisions, of which there are five in these ten lines, in a proportion similar to that of the *Aeneid*.

The second example is taken from the commencement of *Aviti Epistola ad Perillam, Virginem Scotam*, and is in elegiac distichs.[1] The variety of rhythmical patterns employed eliminates the dullness that this metre, in the hands of less skilled

---

[1] In this metre, each dactylic hexameter verse is followed by a pentameter, which is historically a defective hexameter. The pentameter is divided into two hemistichs which are alike in that each is a catalectic dactylic trimeter, but different in that only the first admits the substitution of a spondee for a dactyl. Thus the dactylic pentameter verse calls for an unvarying sum of four short syllables in

writers, sometimes acquires from repetitive smoothness. This variety is best illustrated by scansion:

Dūm trĭs-|tī frăn-|gŏr ‖ mŏr-|bŏ, lŏn-|gāquĕ sĕ-|nēctă,
    Ēt mĕă|vīx călă-|mūm ‖sŭstĭnĕt|āegrā mă-|nŭs:
Quā nŏn|ĭpsĕ frŭ-|ŏr, ‖ tĭbĭ |mītŏ, Pĕ-|RĪLLĀ, să-|lūtĕm,
    Pīgnŭs ă-|mĭcĭtĭ-|āe, ‖ chără pŭ-|ēllă, mĕ-|āe.
Scōtŭs ăd-|ēst hōs-|pēs, ‖ quī|dē tĕ|mūltă rŏ-|gātŭs,
    Nīl, ăĭt, |īngĕnĭ- |ō ‖ pūlchrĭŭs| ēssĕ tŭ-|ō,
Tēquĕ, quŏd| ōptā-| băm, ‖ lĭn-|guăm căl-|lērĕ Lă-|tīnăm,
    Ōrĕquĕ|Rōmā- |nō ‖ jăm dĭdĭ-|cīssĕ lŏ-|quī.

Several observations on the rhythmic subtleties in these verses are apposite. The first line contains as many spondees as it is possible for the dactylic hexameter to incorporate: the resulting impression of ponderous sadness is highly appropriate to the admission of sickness and old age conveyed by the words. In the third line, *mitto* exhibits, *metri gratia*, an example of shortening. Following the custom of the Augustan poets, the author has used mostly end-stopped couplets throughout this work, but the comma at the end of the sixth verse creates one of several enjambments. By way of counterbalance, the pauses in the seventh verse break the flow in a pleasing manner. Perhaps it is also germane to add that, in the fourth and sixth lines, the poet has successfully followed the Ovidian tendency to end the two hemistichs of the pentameter with a rhyming noun and adjective.

The artistic use of repetition, especially in the form of epanalepsis, constitutes another method by which King achieves his musical effects. Many of the best instances are to be found in *Templum Libertatis*; as, for example, in these individual lines:

Ut nequis vir sit castus, nec foemina casta.
Sacra mari seu sit, seu sacra sit insula coelo.
Tu modo da veniam; da, rex, mihi visere terras.

---

the second hemistich, while allowing a variation of four, two, or no short syllables in the first. The last syllable of the line is technically *anceps*. For some doubts on the generally accepted theory of the pentameter see L. P. Wilkinson, *Golden Latin Artistry* (Cambridge: at the University Press, 1963), pp. 227f.

And there are more mechanical (but quite justifiable) instances of repetition, as in this verse also taken from *Templum Libertatis*:

> Patriciosque senes: iterumque iterumque repulsus . . .

Occasionally, King's inclination for this device takes the form of epanastrophe or anadiplosis. Thus he wrote in *Templum Libertatis*:

> Tot mala, dii, merui? Merui: neque enim grave quicquam
> Conquerar . . .

And the last line of this elaborately ornamented period in *Miltonis Epistola ad Pollionem* could be regarded as quasi-epanastrophic:

> Novit Fuscus (qui omnia novit)
> Quo casu, quo animo infelicis carminis auctor,
> Qua prece, quo pretio cuncta haec memorare volebat:
> Et voluisse sat est: satis est voluisse videri.

The poet's use of epistrophe, though not frequent, is generally effective: he is notably competent at achieving an echoic effect in such couplets as occur in this period, taken from *Antonietti, Corsorum Ducis, Epistola ad Corsos*:

> At vos, o cives, dum daedala prodit imago,
> Dicite gratantes, Rex nobis ligneus esto!
> Sylvicolae acclament, Rex nobis ligneus esto!

Very rarely King lapses into a more pedestrian style of repetition, as in *Monitor*:

> Te tamen excepto semper, clarissime Prisce,
> Te tamen excepto semper, charissime Caeli. . .

But in the composition of jingling couplets, the verses of which are metrically interchangeable, King is not nearly so frequent an offender as Lucan.

A few of King's other musical devices deserve at least passing reference. He makes considerable use of the five-worded line to achieve a resonant and majestic effect: it could be argued that, like Ovid, he overdoes this technique from time to time. Occasionally he employs a four-worded line for the same purpose: one of these in *Sermo Pedestris* acquires added sonority with the inclusion of Greek proper names. The verse following completes the sense:

> Pasiphae tauri, Pygmaei Penthesilea
> Concubitu indulget, nec vult servire marito.

His tripartite lines often have an impressive ring; in *Monitor* he provides a few in a period which also includes asyndeton and carefully placed principal, secondary, and tertiary caesuras. Despite its large number of pauses, the fact that the separate parts of this sentence are well dovetailed prevents it from sounding disjointed and gives it organic unity:

> Expers militiae, clarus tamen induperator
> De portu solvit; mare transit; terret Iberas,
> Gallorumque acies: quid deinde? hostilibus oris
> Appellit naves; expugnat, diruit, urit
> Tres piscatorum casulas, urbique minatus
> Excelsae horrendas strages, incendia, praesensque
> Excidium, redit incolumis, poscitque triumphum.

The effect of a tripartite stich with an ablative absolute is especially concinnous, as in this example taken from *Templum Libertatis*:

> Additur infernus, mutato nomine, Plutus:
> Nam sibi dat Marci nomen.

Another kind of embellishment sometimes used by King is hypermetre; one finds it, for example, in *Miltonis Epistola ad Pollionem*:

> Servique & satrapae, gemmae, longa atria, pluresque
> Uxores . . .

The reader is also intermittently conscious of the deliberate collocation of vowels and consonants appropriate to the mood which the author wishes to convey. Thus in *Scamnum, Ecloga*, when the poet, who is seated in Vergilian manner in the shade of a beech-tree, sees Lacon and Tityrus approaching, he captures the warm, languid atmosphere of the occasion well, with the use of the repeated sounds *u*, *m*, and *n*, in this melodious line:

> Cantatum veniunt: apta est cantatibus umbra.

All the ancient critics who wrote on the subject were agreed that an excess of sibilants produced a cacophonous effect: King employs this device at the commencement of *Hydra*, where he seems to be attempting to reproduce Vergil's use of *s* to create a serpentine feeling. He augments the sibilation with the repeated employment of the appropriate vowel *i*:

> Semper ego satirae scriptor? Sic omina nostros
> Significant nondum pacatos laeva Penates?[1]

On the other hand, especially mellifluous are those liquid lines in which every word ending in a consonant is followed by one beginning with a vowel, and every word ending in a vowel is followed by one beginning with a consonant. Fortuitously, the first line of *Miltonis Epistola ad Pollionem* and the last line of *Aviti Epistola ad Perillam, Virginem Scotam* both conform to this pattern. Thus their author commenced his first poem in the *Opera* with these words:

> Si vis ingenii, mihi si concessa potestas
> Carminis . . .

and concluded his career as a maker with a pentameter composed in equally perfect contrapuntal fashion:

> Eventura tibi prospera cuncta precor.

Whether writing verse in hexameters or elegiac couplets, King was a scrupulously careful observer of the niceties of the best Roman metrical usage. He avoided undue coincidence of metrical ictus and word stress, and thus saved himself from the pitfalls into which some classical and neo-Latin composers had fallen, preceded by Ennius in his banal line

> Sparsis hastis longis campus splendet et horret.

Though all his serious Latin poetry is characterized by a formal grandeur and a richly patterned texture, it is seldom merely pretentious and never elephantine as are the arid stretches in the products of dozens of his contemporaries on the continent. Nor are his works centonisations: though he used

---

[1] Compare the *Aeneid*, Book II, lines 209–12. Dionysius of Halicarnassus considered that *i* was the least sonorous of the vowels.

phrases drawn from the Augustan poets, he developed an individual style which is not quite like that of any other Latin poet. It is, in fact, difficult to find fault with his poetry on purely technical grounds. Perhaps one may feel irritated by such prosaic, enumerative sequences as this one in *Sermo Pedestris*:

> Nimirum emendat, regit, auget, donat & aufert
> Res, urbes, gentes, commercia, foedera mundi,
> Magnanimumque heroum fata . . .

But these are not common, and, when they do occur, are certainly no worse than some of the less inspired repetitive periods in Lucretius.

Only five of King's Latin orations have survived in their entirety, and four of them are described by him as *oratiunculae*. That so little of his oratory remains can only be a matter of regret. It is indeed saddening to think of the hundreds of Oxford orations which were irretrievably lost prior to the modern practice of printing them in the *Oxford University Gazette*. But the few remnants of King's Latin speeches, together with the short examples of his prose, are sufficient to provide evidence of the artistic ability of their author in non-poetical literature. Some of the ornaments which he used in his prose pieces are the same as those which appear in his poetry. Anaphora, for example, is the principal decoration in the third *Redeat* petition towards the close of the oration of 13 April 1749:

> REDEAT, efficiatque, cum nihil hoc conventu cernere est illustrius, ut caeteri cives, et ii maxime scilicet, quibus aula et curia patet, pares sint honestissimis hisce senatoribus, pares sint vobis, ACADEMICI, si non ingenii et doctrinae gloria, et probitate et industria, at magnitudine animi, at libertatis studio! Ut foeminae omnes sint quam simillimae praestanti huic Nympharum cohorti, si non specie et pulchritudine oris, at pudicitia et sanctimonia, at corporis cultu, at morum elegantia! Ut deinde populus noster universus sit laboriosissimus ac temperantissimus, et aliquando tandem cum bonorum consiliis consentiat ad conservandam imperii majestatem: utque Britannia nostra non tam suo mari, et classibus pulcherrimis instructissimisque, (etsi his ipsis utinam usque valeamus!) quam incolarum robore ac virtute, et summa rerum gerendarum prudentia muniatur!

Brachylogia of a definitely Ciceronian kind occurs on a number of occasions; for example, in the ecphrasis of *Aviti Epistola ad Perillam, Virginem Scotam,* where one period contains two separate sequences:

> Scis cuipiam licere more suo Romae vivere, si modo taceat de religione, de summi Pontificis authoritate, de praesulum superbia, de monachorum praestigiis; qui, dum paupertatem, uti summum bonum, clamant, praedicant, prae se ferunt, vigilantes et dormientes aureos montes cogitant, et reperiunt.

It is also significant that the rhythm of King's Latin prose is clearly influenced by that of Cicero: this fact is especially evident in those cadenced *clausulae* consisting of a brief trochaic sequence which are purposely placed at the conclusion of a period. Even though the Ciceronian model is manifest in rhythm and diction, it is not followed slavishly: King was successful, as so many other neo-Latin orators have been, in giving his rhetoric a personal stamp, while at the same time remaining within the limits of this particular convention. The Ciceronian archetype permits more freedom than is sometimes realized: in modern times Sir John Sandys, Sir Robert Tate, Cardinal Bacci, and Thomas Higham have composed many extended piece of Latin prose, all of which could be called, in a broad sense, Ciceronian; however, their author's individuality is never completely submerged. In reading such compositions—King's included—one feels that thus Cicero might have expressed what, in many instances, he could never have felt.

The possible influence of Quintilian on King has already been indicated. Since comparatively little of King's Latin prose has been preserved, it would be unwise to draw any general conclusions, but he does conform to the recommendations of the *Institutio Oratoria* in such respects as these:

> Nobis prima sit virtus perspicuitas. . . . Felicissimus tamen sermo est, cui et rectus ordo et apta iunctura et cum his numerus opportune cadens contingit. . . . Quamvis enim vincta sit, tamen soluta videri debet oratio. . . . Compositio debet esse honesta, iucunda, varia . . . sit dissimulatio curae praecipua, ut numeri sponte fluxisse, non arcessiti et coacti esse videantur.[1]

[1] Quintilian, *Institutio Oratoria*, Book VIII, ii, 22; Book IX, iv, 27, 77, 147.

Quintilian also expatiates on the ancient distinction between the two kinds of prose style: 'one closely welded and woven together, while the other is of a looser texture, such as is found in dialogues and letters.'[1] King's non-burlesque Latin prose is of the first kind: in its architectonics it exhibits the best qualities of order, connection, and rhythm which are elaborated upon at some length in the *Institutio Oratoria*.

There is no reason to doubt that King was also intimately acquainted with such works of Cicero as *De Oratore*, *Partitiones Oratoriae*, *Brutus*, and *Orator*, and that their precepts affected his own practice. However, the advice given in these treatises is of such a nature as to make it difficult to point to specific examples of King's indebtness in his speeches. Nevertheless, the reader is always more or less conscious of a richness of vocabulary, an amplitude of expression, and a lambent beauty of phrasing which constantly recall the Ciceronian prototype. King did not have the passion of a Demosthenes: his orotundity, though ingenuous and heartfelt, was consistently lapidary and formal. But his prose style is never turgid, and because his speeches were delivered on academic occasions, he could avoid the forced swagger which mars some of Cicero's orations, such as those delivered in 57 B.C. relating to his exile. While King's personality unfailingly radiates outwards from his prose pieces, he avoids showing the least sign of flagging or exhaustion. The tension in his finely molded periods is always carefully controlled and disciplined. His rhetoric is Gorgianic and for the most part epideictic in quality, but it is not meretricious. Like Cicero, he neither shouts nor bores.

Although King's technical excellence as a Latin author was admitted in his day by all but his most biased critics, this fact did not prevent William Melmoth the Younger from publishing a number of charges against neo-Latin poetry in general and, by implication, that of his father-in-law in particular. Melmoth's basic assertions were first, that 'a poet who glows with the genuine fire of a warm and lively imagination will find the copiousness of his own native English scarce sufficient to convey his ideas in all their strength and energy'; and secondly, that 'a pregnant imagination disdains to stint the natural

[1] *Ibid.*, Book IX, iv, 19.

growth of her thoughts to the confined standard of classical expression.' On modern poems written in Latin he comments:

The style of these performances always puts me in mind of Harlequin's snuff, which he collected by borrowing a pinch out of every man's box he could meet, and then retailed it to his customers under the pompous title of *tabac de mille fleurs*. Half a line from Virgil or Lucretius, pieced out with a bit from Horace or Juvenal, is generally the motley mixture which enters into compositions of this sort.[1]

Any writer of poems of this kind, Melmoth continues, is guilty of a kind of theft:

For to express himself with propriety, he must not only be sure that every *single* word which he uses, is authorized by the best writers; but he must not even venture to throw them out of that particular combination in which he finds them connected: otherwise he may run into the most barbarous solecisms. To explain my meaning by an instance from modern language: the French words *arene* and *rive*, are both to be met with in their approved authors; and yet if a foreigner, unacquainted with the niceties of that language, should take the liberty of bringing those two words together in the following verse,

> Sur la rive du fleuve amassant de l'arene;

he would be exposed to the ridicule, not only of the criticks, but of the most ordinary mechanick in Paris. For the idiom of the French tongue will not admit of the expression *sur la rive du fleuve*, but requires the phrase *sur le bord de la riviere*; as they never say *amasser de l'arene*, but *du sable*. The same observation may be extended to all languages whether living or dead. But as no reasoning from analogy, can be of the least force in determining the idiomatick properties of any language whatsoever; a modern Latin poet has no other method of being sure of avoiding absurdities of this kind, than to take whole phrases as he finds them formed to his hands. Thus instead of accommodating his expression to his sentiment, (if any he should have) he must necessarily bend his sentiment to his expression, as he is not at liberty to strike out into that boldness of style, and those unexpected combinations of words, which give such grace and energy to the thoughts of every true genius. True genius indeed, is

[1] Sir Thomas Fitzosborne (i.e. William Melmoth), *Letters on Several Subjects*, Vol. II, Letter XLIX. The first edition of the second volume appeared in 1749. Copies of this edition are rare.

as much discovered by style, as by any other distinction; and every eminent writer, without indulging any unwarranted licences, has a language which he derives from himself, and which is peculiarly and literally his own.[1]

Melmoth's criticisms contain some truth, though his clearly unsympathetic attitude towards neo-Latin poetry does nothing to strengthen his case. To do his contention justice, one may concede that there is an imitative element in most of the best neo-Latin poetry, and that in the eighteenth century, imitation on the part of the poet was considered a literary virtue to a greater extent than either before or since. It may also be allowed that, in any artistic endeavour, academic correctness in itself is not of overriding importance: if it were, Ebenezer Prout would be accounted one of the great composers of the nineteenth century. But Melmoth's main charges are answerable on the principle that certain kinds of artistic anachronism not only are justifiable but indeed may be commendable. A good deal of his argument could be applied, *mutatis mutandis*, to the modern architect who designs a Gothic building: he also must necessarily bend his aesthetic sentiment to this particular form of architectural expression rather than *vice versa*. Yet no one would seriously suggest that Augustus Welby Pugin, Sir Charles Barry, Sir Giles Gilbert Scott, and Sir Ninian Comper were all at various times guilty of artistic theft and that none of them was at liberty to achieve boldness of style within the aesthetic limits which are imposed by the neo-Gothic convention. There is a place in literature, as in architecture, for pure traditionalism. In the hands of an author with the necessary degree of training, the Latin language can be as relevant to his own day as a style of architecture which became crystallized in an age which has long passed.

Melmoth was probably influenced in his objections by the products of the large number of inferior neo-Latin poets of his own time, but their failures—which are legion—do not entitle a critic to infer that every eminent writer should express himself only in the vernacular. King's Latin works are best regarded as living literary anachronisms in the same sense that

[1] Ibid.

Pugin's neo-Gothic edifices were living architectural anachronisms when they were erected. King and Pugin were both imitators, but they possessed enough force of personality to prove that, through their art, anachronism is not incompatible with a significant degree of aesthetic achievement. There is surely no need to labour this point: in the field of modern music, the *Classical Symphony* of Prokofiev and the polyphonic compositions of Edmund Rubbra alike provide evidence that an anachronistic medium can actually enhance rather than detract from the expression of genuine artistry. To the age-old objection that the proportion of readers who can comprehend a non-vernacular language is always limited, one can only reply that no work of art derives its aesthetic merit from the number of persons who are in a position to understand it. In King's favour it may also be added that the subject matter of all his Latin works was created out of the stuff of contemporary events: in this respect he was at once thoroughly modern and, at the same time, a faithful imitator of the great Roman literary artists.

On quite different grounds, it is fair to criticize King's Latin works as reflecting several of the limitations common to the literature of eighteenth-century England in general. One of these is, paradoxically, that of simplicity. Though King's literary medium is a non-vernacular often highly elaborate and embellished, the thought which it conveys is, as a rule, simple and confined to the notions which the average cultured gentleman of his day could appreciate without taxing his powers too heavily. King in this matter is at one with most of the other poets of his own period. The mind of the age was set firmly in the direction of the simplicity without which, as Swift expresses it, 'no human performance can arrive to any great perfection.' [1] The most significant poets of the time aimed at achieving the kind of unified simplicity which they found in architecture inspired by classical models. It was in this respect that they differed most profoundly from the Metaphysicals. Pope expressed the comparison between poetry and classical architecture well in the *Essay on Criticism*:

[1] *A Letter to a Young Gentleman, Lately enter'd into Holy Orders* (London, 1721). Reprinted in Jonathan Swift, *Irish Tracts and Sermons*, ed. Herbert Davis (Oxford: Basil Blackwell, 1948), p. 68.

Thus when we view some well-proportion'd dome,
(The *world's* just wonder, and ev'n *thine*, O Rome!)
No single parts unequally surprize;
All comes *united* to th'admiring eyes;
No monstrous height, or breadth, or length appear;
The *whole* at once is *bold*, and *regular*.[1]

The cult of simplicity in poetry was, then, simply one aspect of the contemporary neo-classical preference for order and unity of design.

King's thought is simple in another sense which he shared with many of his contemporaries: the philosophy underlying it has neither complexity nor profundity. It is a rather shallow combination of legitimism, *laissez-faire*, and the kind of Leibnitzian metaphysic that was popularized by Pope in the *Essay on Man*. This mixture, combined with a tendency to regard the Whig government as the source of most of the evils in Britain, was by no means unusual among the more highly cultured Jacobites. King's metaphysic is expressed tersely in his letter to Lord Orrery of 17 September 1741:

I believe, *that every thing, that happens, is best.* This short sentence makes the whole of my Philosophy and my religion too.[2]

It is not difficult to appreciate the similarity between this outlook and the superficial theodicy implicit in Pope's epigram, 'Whatever is, is right.'

When writing to Lord Orrery on 1 January 1741/2, King included a few semi-facetious comments on his own philosophical outlook:

... I am now able to resolve whatever may be called human happiness, into two Words, which is more than was ever done by all the old Sages of Greece and Rome and all the modern Philosophers. I may add the Divines likewise, of France and England. I have therefore some thoughts of setting my self up as the founder of a new sect of Philosophers, which shall be called the *Laconic*. My System will certainly be well received by the World, since it will

[1] *Essay on Criticism*, ll. 248ff.
[2] Bodleian Library, MS. Eng. hist. d. 103, p. 35.

be sufficiently explained in less than ten words, and yet be of ye most general use to mankind.[1]

Unfortunately, he never divulged what the two words to explain the mystery of human happiness actually were, nor did he ever provide the explanation in less than ten words of his philosophical system. In his *Anecdotes* he gave insight of a somewhat more luminous nature into what might be loosely termed his philosophy of life:

I DO NOT KNOW any better rules or maxims than the three following, which were framed by the old monk, to enable a man to pass through life with ease and security:

Nunquam male loqui de superioribus.
Fungi officio taliter qualiter.
Sinere insanum mundum vadere, quo vult; nam vult vadere, quo vult.

The first of these may be greatly improved by adding St. Paul's precept, *To speak evil of no man.*[2]

These few informal comments contain everything of consequence that King wrote concerning his own personal philosophy.

Under the circumstances, it is not incongruous to observe that King's poetry is lacking in breadth, another characteristic which it shares with that of several English Augustans. A good deal of the poet's polemical method consists of casting aspersions on his opponents: he is constantly guilty of the *argumentum ad hominem*. Despite his acumen in corroborating his contentions by appropriate historical parallels, his ability to formulate purely abstract premises is limited. And in spite of his considerable powers of argumentation, the ratiocinative content in such poems as *Sermo Pedestris*, *Hydra*, and *Monitor* has a dialectically constricted quality: one often feels that the poet is not so much attacking evil as the people whom he considers to be committing evil. This unwillingness (or inability) on the part of many contemporary poets to envisage social evils in terms of the kind of moral abstractions to be found in the work of Shakespeare, Milton, or Wordsworth was not peculiar to King: it was an almost inevitable concomitant of the homo-

---

[1] Bodleian Library, MS. Eng. hist. d. 103, p. 50.
[2] *Political and Literary Anecdotes* (2nd edn., 1819), pp. 143f.

centricity of the age.[1] Furthermore, as a satirist, he was pre-
cluded from adopting an impartial attitude; by nature of his
genre he was limited to pleading one point of view by castigating
its opponents.

The ill will and the sometimes petty vindictiveness which
disfigure parts of King's work likewise have their counterparts
in the poetry of his contemporaries. Pope's *Dunciad* immediately comes to mind: the peevish invective and tetchy abuse in
this work, the first edition of which appeared in 1728, two years
before *An Ode to Mira*, may have encouraged King to write
likewise. But the comparison between Pope and King should
not be pressed too far. Pope's spleen has a heatless quality
and is often indistinguishable from cantankerousness; King, on
the other hand, can on occasions, especially in *Templum
Libertatis*, project considerable warmth through his fulmina-
tions. King's Latin verses exhibit a sonorous dignity which Pope
could rarely attain with the English heroic couplet: King had
fewer stops at his disposal, but his diapason can resound with
un-Popean thunder. In common with Swift, King was capable
of expressing his antipathies with a brutal cynicism: underneath
his formalism, elegance, and polish lay a penetrating intellec-
tual force and a ferocious ability to mangle his enemies with
his words. These corrosive powers he used, like Swift, beyond
the limits of polite gentility. Indeed, in his ability to combine
derogation and sardonic humour he often exceeded the Dean.
But King rarely uses flippancy for its own sake: he is always
motivated by a serious underlying purpose. However amoral—
or, at times, immoral—his work may appear on the surface,
the moralist in him is seldom out of sight.

In this connection it is significant that the antipathy towards
the contemporary love of material wealth and luxury, which
figures predominantly throughout King's writings, was also a
bête noir of the Dean of St. Patrick's. Indeed luxury, interpreted variously to mean riches, vanity, sensuality, self-indul-
gence, or a combination of these, became one of the favourite
whipping boys of the eighteenth century. Thomas Gray provided merely one example of the common attitude of severe

---

[1] This observation may justifiably be applied to Swift as a poet: he achieved
better results in his sermons.

moralists and those poets who shared their feelings, when he
wrote his celebrated lines:

> The struggling pangs of conscious truth to hide,
> To quench the blushes of ingenuous shame,
> Or heap the shrine of Luxury and Pride
> With incense kindled at the Muse's flame.[1]

Authors such as Swift and Gray could quote numerous classical precedents in support of their opinions: Herodotus had connected material wealth with moral decline, Xenophon had
warned that civilizations fall through the type of luxury that
results from an attitude of self-indulgent superiority, Strabo
had compared the luxury of the Athenians to the ascetic poverty
of the barbarians with no compliment intended to the former,
and dozens of later writers, including Cato, Varro, Diodorus,
Livy, Tacitus, Justin, Appian, and Florus, had expressed
roughly comparable opinions. Their views were applied to
English history by such men as Polydore Vergil, Samuel Daniel,
Raphael Holinshed, Lord Clarendon, Gilbert Burnet, and
Swift's patron, Sir William Temple. The latter, like King, was
convinced that the Norman Conquest had been in certain
respects a disadvantage to England: one of these, he argued,
was that through the Normans luxury was first introduced into
the country:

... *England* by the Conquest lost, in a great measure, the old
Plainness and Simplicity of the *Saxon* Times, and Customs of Life,
who were generally a People of good Meaning, plain Dealing, con-
tented with their own, little coveting or imitating their Neighbours,
and living frugally upon the Product of their own fruitful Soil: For
the Profusion of Meats at our *English* Tables, came in with the *Danes*,
and the Luxury of them was introduc'd first by the *Normans*, and
after increased by the frequent Use of Wines, upon the Accession of
Guienne to this Crown.[2]

Swift's thinking on luxury, in its broadest sense, must have
been well known to King. The sentiments of the Dean in this
matter are often reflected in the poetry of the Old Trumpeter.
In a letter addressed to Pope on 10 January 1721, which King

---

[1] *Elegy Written in a Country Church-Yard*, ll. 69–72.
[2] *The Works of Sir William Temple, Bart.* (2 vols.; London, 1720), Vol. II, p. 584.

would likely have read in its published form, the Dean commented:

It is true, the Romans had a custom of chusing a Dictator, during whose administration, the Power of other Magistrates was suspended; but this was done upon the greatest emergencies; a War near their doors, or some civil Dissention, for Armies must be governed by arbitrary power. But when the Virtue of that Commonwealth gave place to luxury and ambition, this very office of Dictator became perpetual in the persons of the Caesars and their Successors, the most infamous tyrants that have any where appeared in story.[1]

This outlook is reflected in the arrogant speech of Plutus to the hosts of Tartarus in the second book of *Templum Libertatis*:

Ars siqua est, vigili siqua experientia vestro,
Dictis siqua fides; en, vestra potentia, viresque,
Armaque! (& ostendit massas, quas fecerat, auri)
Siquando terras Libertas dura petivit,
Regum saeva ultrix, & amicis parcere regum
Nescia, quos Ditis numen praefecerat orbi;
Mene ausa est contra causam contendere plebis?
Mene pati auratum potuit? Nonne ipse fugavi
Et divam, et vates divae sociosque ministrosque,
His solis usus, solisque his utilis, armis?
Graiae, divitiis & libertate potentes,
Nunc ubi sunt urbes? Ubi nunc est libera Roma,
Conscriptique patres? Neque nostram illuserit artem
Gens, hodie quaecunque cupit respublica dici.
Quid? Veneti, Batavi, Ligures parere recusant
Unius imperio? vexantur mille tyrannis,
Sanguine quos animisque aequant, servire coacti
Civibus, ecce, suis.

A letter of Swift written to William Pulteney on 8 March 1735 shows that the Dean and King were alike in their gloomy forebodings for the future: 'But it is altogether impossible for any nation to preserve its liberty long under a tenth part of the present luxury, infidelity, and a million corruptions.'[2]

---

[1] Harold Williams (ed.), *The Correspondence of Jonathan Swift* (5 vols.; Oxford: at the Clarendon Press, 1963-5), Vol. II, p. 373. Pope later indicated that he had never received the letter. It was printed by Faulkner in 1741.

[2] Ibid., Vol. IV, p. 303.

The laments of the condition of the contemporary Church, and especially the higher clergy, in several of King's writings have their parallel (and may have had their source of inspiration) in Swift's essay 'Concerning That Universal Hatred Which Prevails Against the Clergy.' The Dean's argument is fundamentally no different from that used by King and by numerous puritan moralists: the vices of ecclesiastical institutionalism had brought about the present degeneracy of the established Church:

> In a very few centuries after Christianity became national in most parts of Europe, although the Church of Rome had already introduced many corruptions in religion; yet the piety of early Christians, as well as new converts, was so great, and particularly of princes, as well as noblemen and other wealthy persons, that they built many religious houses, for those who were inclined to live in a recluse or solitary manner, endowing these monasteries with land. It is true, we read of monks some ages before, who dwelt in caves and cells, in desert places. But, when public edifices were erected and endowed, they began gradually to degenerate into idleness, ignorance, avarice, ambition, and luxury, after the usual fate of all human institutions.[1]

This kind of thinking underlies the whole of the preface to the *Opera*, that part of *The Dreamer* dealing with the College of Rosicrucians, and most of the *Aviti Epistola ad Perillam, Virginem Scotam*. It led King to declaim in the latter work:

> Ecquis rite colit te, coeli magne CREATOR?
> Legatus CHRISTI quaerit avarus opes.
> Sacrilegum vidi, quem mitra et purpura vestit;
> Vidi, eheu, doctos credulitate trahi.[2]

The note to these verses is a *cri de coeur* which is close in spirit to Swift's contention:

> Perpaucos usquam gentium cognovi ex purpuratis iis, qui Archipraesules, Praesules, Antistites, Episcopi honorificentissime appellantur, ad priscae veraeque sanctitatis imaginem factos, aut quorum libri, praecepta, orationes cum eorum vita non pugnarent. Multos

---

[1] Jonathan Swift, *Directions to Servants and Miscellaneous Pieces, 1733–1742*, ed. Herbert Davis (Oxford: Basil Blackwell, 1959), p. 124.
[2] The first word of this line is printed *Vide*: it is corrected in the Errata.

equidem novi ambitiosis hisce nominibus potitos, qui nihil cogita-
bant, nisi quo divitias congererent, familiam ornarent, censum
augerent, sacerdotia alia aliis ampliora ditioraque consequendo.
Unde fit, ut quos majores nostri tanquam sanctos Christi Apostolos
colebant, nos quidem nulla prorsus veneratione dignos putemus.
Quae enim infamia! quae eorum impietas! quos pecuniam, quam
ecclesiae, quam pauperibus, quam Deo debent, in uxorculas, liberos,
consanguineos, et affines suos conferre minime puduit.

To these evidences may be added King's comments in the
Anecdotes on the same subject:

To speak freely, I know nothing that has brought so great a re-
proach on the Church of England as the avarice and ambition of our
bishops. CHANDLER, Bishop of Durham, WILLIS, Bishop of
Winchester, POTTER, Archbishop of Canterbury, GIBSON and
SHERLOCK, Bishops of London, all died shamefully rich, some of
them worth more than £100,000. I must add to these my old
antagonist GILBERT, predecessor to DRUMMOND, the present
Archbishop of York. Some of these prelates were esteemed great
divines (and I know they were learned men), but they could not be
called good Christians. The great wealth which they heaped up, the
fruits of their bishoprics, and which they left to enrich their families,
was not their own; it was due to God, to the church, and to their
poor brethren. The history of the good *Samaritan*, which was so
particularly explained by Christ himself to his disciples, ought to be
monitory to all their successors.[1]

Most of the other particulars in which King's Latin works
reflect the English Augustan age have been alluded to in earlier
chapters. On almost all his pages, the decorum, smoothness,
perspicuity, and air of refinement common to the English
Augustans in general are in evidence: like them, and in contradistinction to several of the Romantics, he regarded poetry
primarily as the art of writing poems.[2] There is a rather greater
proportion of censorious and comminatory material in his work
than in that of most of his contemporaries: his lack of tolerance
for human weakness is one of the least attractive features of his
outlook. On the whole, his derogations tend to be stronger than

---

[1] *Political and Literary Anecdotes* (2nd edn., 1819), pp. 183ff.

[2] 'Coleridge and Shelley, you might almost say, wrote poetry: Dryden and
Pope wrote poems.' See James Sutherland, *A Preface to Eighteenth Century Poetry*
(Oxford: Oxford University Press, 1963), p. 120.

his compliments, which, like his other pleasantries, sometimes exhibit a tincture of blandness. However, whether praising or blaming, he maintains an undeniable candour.

There are two respects in which, as a serious Latin poet, he is peculiar. One is that he never completely ceases to be an orator, even when he is writing verse. Of all the English neo-Latin poets, he is the most declamatory in tone. To a greater degree than Vergil, he regularly applies to his poetry the ornamentation of oratorical prose: if his poetry is read aloud, the *ear* is seldom dissatisfied. He is one of the most perfect practitioners of the dictum enunciated by Joseph Trapp in his *Praelectiones Poeticae* of 1711 that eloquence should be common to both poetry and oratory. The modern reader will inevitably notice the rhetorical deliberateness with which King set out to gain his poetical effects. Like the best formal declamation, the poetry in the *Opera* is not so much a free expression of personal emotion as a calculated attempt to win the approval and arouse the sympathy of its readers by the artistic use of a non-colloquial medium. In this sense, his poems are carefully wrought rhetorical artifacts: though they are invariably fluent, they seldom, if ever, sound spontaneous.

The other peculiarity was dimly perceived by Lord Orrery in his letter written to King on 9 May 1744, when Pope was slowly dying: 'Poor M^r. Pope, who is so kind as to write often to me, is I fear in a declining State of Health. He can only dictate & sign his letters. When he is gone, farewell to English Poetry, & when you are gone, farewell to Latin Poetry.'[1] To suggest that the death of Pope would mark the end of English poetry was an unpardonably pessimistic prognostication, but the prophecy regarding its Latin counterpart was nearer the truth. King was the last example of a Latin poet in the grand manner. Perhaps his nearest contemporary counterpart was Giovanni Volpi—he latinized his name as Joannes Vulpius—but the resemblances are not particularly close. Volpi was, *inter alia*, the editor of the poetry of Andrea Navagero and Giacopo Sannazaro, the author of a number of Latin orations, and a poet who is best known for his *Carmina*. These were first pub-

---

[1] The Houghton Library, Harvard University, MS. Eng. 218.2 (v. 2), no page number.

lished in 1725 at Padua in the form of three books, which in later editions were augmented to five. By classical standards King wrote the purer Latin, but Volpi displayed in his poems a lively charm which, of its kind, has not since been surpassed.[1]

That King has had no rivals since his death may be unequivocally conceded. Latin poetry has continued to be written to the present day, as is made manifest by the prize poems issued from university presses and the quarterly appearances of *Latinitas*,[2] but much of the former sublimity and spaciousness have disappeared. The most prolific of the Anglo-Latin poets since King's demise has been Walter Savage Landor, but even though not all of his Latin compositions were printed, there is ample evidence that the Muse did not often inspire him with more than a rather pedestrian competence. His elegiac epigrams constitute his best work, but his reputation as a Latinist inevitably suffers from his comparatively small amount of really excellent writing in that language, and from the fact that so much of his English verse is apodictically superior. Of the other modern English writers of Latin verse, Bishop Charles Wordsworth, Charles Calverley, William Cory, Lionel Johnson, Herbert Kynaston, Sir Richard Jebb, and Allan Ramsay deserve special mention, but they confined themselves largely to occasional poems and *jeux d'esprit*.[3] On the continent there have been neo-Latin poets in greater profusion: of these Pope Leo XIII was one of the most magisterial, but the majority of his poems are brief and do not display any sustained flight.[4] Antonio Braus, Guiseppe Petrucci, Innocenzo Polcari, Diego Vitrioli, and Guiseppe Morabito, to mention only a few other poets by name, have all written Latin verse with ability, but none has an artistic stature comparable to that of the leading figures of the eighteenth century.

[1] I deliberately exclude from consideration the slightly younger Dalmatian contemporary of King, Raimondo Cunich, who lived from 1718 to 1794. He was primarily a translator: his principal importance is that he was the last to attempt a Latin version of the *Iliad*.

[2] Published in Rome *Typis Pontificiae Universitatis Gregorianae*.

[3] It is perhaps worthwhile recalling that Swinburne published two Latin poems: *In Obitum Theophili Poetae* and *Ad Catullum*.

[4] Two of the best are *Tenui Victu Contentus Ingluviem Fuge* and *Ineuntis Saeculi Auspicia*. See W. T. Henry (ed.), *Poems, Charades, Inscriptions of Pope Leo XIII* (New York: The Dolphin Press, 1902).

Of King's major works in the *Opera*, only *The Toast* remains to be appraised. As far as it can be fitted into any literary tradition, *The Toast* belongs to that of Menippean satire, the mélange of prose and verse invented by Menippus of Gadara three centuries before the Christian era, and developed in Rome by Varro, Petronius and others.[1] The characteristic content of Menippean satire was its commentary on life and morals, together with a strong element of humour and fantasy. These ingredients are present throughout King's poem. But any attempt to argue more than a very general similarity to the other works in this tradition is doomed to failure. There are abundant evidences of the influence on King of earlier authors, both within the Menippean tradition and outside it, but none of these ever attempted to synthesize a large body of notes with his text in order to evolve a single integrated art form. One is conscious throughout *The Toast* of the indirect influence of Petronius, though the unique combination of the scholastic and the burlesque, which gives King's work its special oddness, has no place in the pages of Nero's *elegantiae arbiter*. On the other hand, the sense of indefinable sorrow that haunts all human achievement, the *triste post coitum*, and the nostalgia of the gutter, all of which contribute towards the peculiar melancholy of the *Satyricon*, are absent from King's product. The Old Trumpeter has left no doubt as to his feelings towards Petronius:

A STORY TELLER is the most agreeable or disagreeable character we can meet with . . . of all the ancient authors of this character, I have a partiality for PETRONIUS. There is a certain grace and pleasantry peculiar to himself in whatever he relates: his history of the EPHESIAN MATRON is allowed by all the critics to be a master-piece: it is concise and elegant; it is simple and sublime: but what distinguishes the excellent judgment of the author, there is not a circumstance which can be added to it or taken from it without lessening its value; and MONSIEUR ST. EVREMOND, thought I acknowledge him to be an admirable writer, and one of the greatest geniuses which this or the last age hath produced, hath yet, in my opinion, done no honour to PETRONIUS by para-

[1] The only comprehensive treatment of Menippean satire is F. Giroux, *La Composition de la Satire Ménippée* (Laon, 1904).

phrasing the EPHESIAN MATRON, and lengthening the narrative.[1]

Whatever one may think of King's classing Saint-Évremond among the greatest geniuses of the age, his preference for the text of the *Satyricon* is admitted and is evident in *The Toast*. Both works share a kind of elegant indecency, and both presuppose in the reader a fair knowledge of the Homeric epics from which their respective themes and some of their subsidary motifs are drawn. The theme of *The Toast* is the wrath of Apollo; that of the *Satyricon* is the wrath of Priapus; the wrath of Apollo and Poseidon in Homer's epics, however much subject to mockery, is their common archetype. But once these facts are allowed, it remains true that King was as far from his classical prototypes as Pope was when composing *The Rape of the Lock*.

Within the limits which I have suggested, *The Toast* is best taken to be *sui generis*. Despite a general indebtedness to classical precedents, King produced a work which has no real counterpart in either classical or modern literature. For this reason it is difficult, if not impossible, to trace any works in English which had any special influence on him while *The Toast* was being written. Something of the atmosphere of Swift's satires and of Pope's *Dunciad* is present, but there are no particular verbal echoes.[2] The idea of the burlesque 'monkish verses' in the notes, which contain some of King's most characteristic humour, seems to have been his own.

The author's description of *The Toast* on the title-page is 'an heroic poem', a term which was, for all intents and purposes, synonymous with epic, as George Puttenham makes clear: 'Such therefore as gave themselves to write long histories of the noble gests of kings and great Princes entermedling the dealings of the gods, halfe gods or Heroes . . . they called Poets Heroick, whereof Homer was chief and most auncient among the Greeks,

---

[1] *Political and Literary Anecdotes* (2nd edn., 1819), pp. 72, 76f.

[2] Dryden's *MacFlecknoe* is in a different category: it is more in the nature of a lampoon than a satire—despite the author's describing it as a 'Varronian satire'—and was written primarily to vex Thomas Shadwell rather than to preserve a record of specific historical incidents. In any case, Dryden is the least personal of the English poets; King, on the contrary, is both personal and individualistic.

Virgill among the Latines.'[1] The fact that the reader very soon learns that this work is technically a parody (in the Augustan sense) does not mean that its author intended to ridicule the epic as an art form: King's intention in writing the English text of the poem was the same as that of any writer of what may be broadly termed mock-epic, namely to turn a dignified genre to witty use, principally by the device of incongruity. The main structural features of the poem are modelled on the epic: the invocation to the Muse, the introduction of Olympian divinities in a human setting, the speeches, the descriptions, the moralizing asides, the assembly of the gods presided over by Jupiter, and the combat at the conclusion all have their parallels in the pages of Homer and Vergil. But the peculiarity of *The Toast* is that the poem itself is not intended to be read continuously: the parodistic apparatus was compiled to be followed *pari passu* with the supposititious translation. Furthermore, the story is not consistently mock-heroic. The underlying satire sometimes predominates over the parody, a feature which is especially noticeable in the observations on the general behaviour of Mars and in the physical descriptions of Myra. In short, *The Toast* does not fit perfectly into any of the accepted literary categories.

The sheer *bizarrerie* of this production renders it as unamenable to conventional literary criteria as the Alice books of Lewis Carroll. One may concede that it exhibits a type of learned whimsy and a level of academic caprice which are never likely to be reproduced. Judged as a satire, it is indubitably a powerful piece of writing, with a structural compactness and a degree of systematization which are remarkable in view of its length. It also exhibits an epigenous geniality which somewhat softens the underlying spleen. But the poet's phenomenally uncharitable attitude towards his characters and the generally repulsive nature of its contents do nothing to raise one's opinion of *The Toast*. Whether a work can be considered aesthetically successful which derives so much of its power from its own emetic feculence is debatable. It was a pity that King decided to incorporate so high a percentage of matter which, even to the strong-stomached, can be highly objectionable.

Though the entire work is tendentious, it is not at all clear

[1] George Puttenham, *The Arte of English Poesie*, Book I, xi.

whom King hoped it would please. At the end of the Appendix he wrote: '. . . I am sure my Friends are obliged to me who have put myself into a very perilous Situation to afford them two or three hours Entertainment.' One may seriously question the extent of the author's wisdom in voluntarily placing himself in so perilous a situation. Of the few contemporary readers of *The Toast*, only Swift is known to have praised it. During the frustrations resulting from his prolonged period of Irish litigation, with all its attendant delays, the composition of this work may have given its author the psychological benefits of catharsis, but, even so, the poem's sordidness is not *ipso facto* justifiable. It is difficult to avoid the conclusion that *The Toast* was an original and ingenious conception, which was spoilt by its author's prurience and lack of reticence.

Gilbert Highet has in recent years revived the ancient differentiation of satirists into two kinds which may be typified by their principal representatives, Horace and Juvenal.[1] Satirists of Horace's type like the subjects of their satire, but think they are blind and foolish. Satirists of Juvenal's type hate or despise them, their aim being not to cure, but to wound, punish, or destroy. According to this distinction *The Toast* would appear to have been in the tradition of Juvenal rather than of Horace. In the notes and observations to 'The Author's Preface' O'Donald writes:

. . . there are Crimes which the Hand of Justice cannot reach, and are not otherwise to be punished, than by being exposed; and which ought to be exposed in Order to prevent honest Men from being deceived by Appearance, and circumvented under the Colour and Masque of Friendship. This in my Opinion is the best Apology for Personal Satire.

Presumably these words express King's own sentiments in the matter.

But in attempting to investigate further the motivation which drove the Principal of St. Mary Hall to produce this macaronic freak, one is reminded of the comment that Dr. Johnson made with reference to Swift: 'The greatest difficulty that

[1] Gilbert Highet: *The Anatomy of Satire* (Princeton: Princeton University Press, 1962), p. 235.

occurs in analysing his character is to discover by what depravity of intellect he took delight in revolving ideas from which almost every other mind shrinks with disgust.'[1] These words may be applied with equal veracity to King, at least as the progenitor of this particular work. Astute critic though he was, Johnson never solved the difficulty which he propounded. I am inclined to doubt if any lesser critic could solve what would appear to be a comparable difficulty in the case of the Old Trumpeter.

Finally, it is perhaps apposite to comment briefly on King as a person. On this subject there is little evidence of an unbiassed nature: though his friends and enemies were not slow to pen their views on King's writings, there were few who touched on the more general subject of the man himself, and even then their observations were, as a rule, incidental. The only writer to discourse at any length in this regard was William Melmoth the Younger: what he asserted on the subject of his father-in-law was far from disinterested in tone. Thus he wrote of King under the name of Mezentius:

Mezentius, with the designs and artifice of a Catiline, affects the integrity and patriotism of a Cato. Liberty, justice, and honour, are words which he knows perfectly well how to apply with address; and having them always ready upon proper occasions, he conceals the blackest purposes under the fairest appearances. For void, as in truth he is, of every worthy principle, he has too much policy not to pretend to the noblest; well knowing that counterfeit virtues are the most successful vices. It is by arts of this kind, that notwithstanding he has shewn himself unrestrained by the most sacred engagements of society, and uninfluenced by the most tender affections of nature, he has still been able to retain some degree of credit in the world: for he never sacrifices his honour to his interest, that he does not in some less considerable, but more open instance, make a concession of his interest to his honour; and thus, while he sinks his character on one side, very artfully raises it on the other. Accordingly, under pretence of the most scrupulous delicacy of conscience, he lately resigned a post which he held under my lord Godolphin; when at the same time he was endeavouring by the most shameful artifices and evasions, to keep a friend of mine out of the possession of an

---

[1] Samuel Johnson: *Lives of the Poets*, 'Jonathan Swift (1667–1745)'.

estate, to which, by all the laws of honour and honesty, he had a most indisputable right.[1]

The exact circumstances that Melmoth refers to are not now ascertainable. Who was Melmoth's supposedly wronged friend? On what grounds could Melmoth claim that King had sequestered an estate?[2] What was the post which King had held under Lord Godolphin?[3] These questions cannot be answered. But one can say with certainty that it was grossly untrue and discourteous on Melmoth's part to assert that his father-in-law was void of *every* worthy principle and uninfluenced by the most tender affections of nature. I am not sure what Melmoth means when he says that King was 'unrestrained by the most sacred engagements of society': he provides no verifiable corroboration, so his argument remains unproven. But Melmoth does provide a few more insulting generalizations:

But will you not suspect that I am describing a phantom of my own imagination, when I tell you after this that he has erected himself into a reformer of manners, and is so injudiciously officious as to draw the enquiry of the world upon his own morals by attempting to expose the defects of others. A man who ventures publickly to point out the blemishes of his contemporaries should at least be free from any uncommon stain himself, and have nothing remarkably dark in the complexion of his own private character. But Mezentius, not satisfied with being vitious, has at length determined to be

---

[1] Sir Thomas Fitzosborne (i.e. William Melmoth), *Letters on Several Subjects*, Vol. I, Letter XXIII. This letter is addressed to 'Palamedes', and is dated 'March 10, 1703'. This date seems to be a deliberate attempt on Melmoth's part to shroud the real personality of Mezentius.

[2] I assume that King's estate at Ealing is the one to which Melmoth alludes. King states as much in the Notes and Observations to *Elogium Famae*, during his observations on Sir Fitz: '. . . I have always been of Opinion, that a Writer, who is capable of publishing a Forgery, to rob a Man of his good Name, will use the same Means to rob him of his Estate. . . .'

[3] Presumably the first Earl of Godolphin (1645–1712) is here intended: though he went over to the Whigs towards the end of his life, he continued to maintain a correspondence with the exiled Stuarts. The second Earl of Godolphin (1678–1766) was described by Hearne as 'a pitiful, mean-spirited, half-witted, whiggish, snivelling person'; even if one makes allowances for Hearne's bias, the second Earl was not the kind of individual under whom King would willingly have served. Lord Macaulay, whose political leanings were in his favour, called him 'an insignificant man, of whom Lord Chesterfield said that he came to the House of Peers only to sleep, and that he might as well sleep on the right as on the left of the Woolsack'.

ridiculous; and after having wretchedly squandered his youth and his patrimony in riot and dissoluteness, is contemptibly misspending his old age in measuring impotent syllables, and dealing out pointless abuse.[1]

What value can be placed in this testimony? There is no evidence that the Principal of St. Mary Hall squandered his youth wretchedly or his patrimony in rioting and dissoluteness. There is a good deal of information which suggests that King probably spent his youth studiously, and that he was given neither to rioting or dissoluteness. He was certainly a teetotaler, a fact that hardly supports his son-in-law's contentions. His Latin poetry could not justly be called impotent, even though the point of some of his abuse is not always clear to a modern reader. Whatever caused Melmoth to write this character, it is clearly warped and in several respects patently wrong. As evidence on which to form a disinterested picture of King, it is best ignored.

Probably the most impartial conceptions of King as a person are to be found in the paintings of contemporary artists. The two principal portraits of King are by John Michael Williams and Thomas Worlidge. The former was presented by the executors of King's estate to the Bodleian Library in 1764 where it hangs today; the latter is in the Upper Senior Common Room of Oriel College.[2] Both show him as an ascetic, dignified personage, his gravity of demeanour lightened slightly by a trace of humour about the eyes and lips. This is the kind of impression that his writings also create: a curious mixture of imperiousness and facetiousness, of severity and whimsicality. But despite his considerable literary and oratorical powers, he was not a great man: he had neither the breadth of vision, nor the foresight, nor the forbearance that go with greatness. He could never have been universally popular: the promptings of his own nature and the fact that he enjoyed disputation for its own sake to-

---

[1] Ibid.

[2] For descriptions see the *Catalogue of Oxford Portraits*, Vol. I, pp. 101, 104, and Vol. II, p. 88. A portrait similar to that of John Michael Williams was engraved by J. Faber in 1751: a copy of this engraving is in the Ealing Public Library. There is also a minute copperplate portrait of King in the historiated initial Q on the first page of the preface to the *Opera*. For references to other depictions see *Notes and Queries*, 12th Series, Vol. II, p. 467.

gether formed him to be a controversialist, and at times a ruthless one. Like the exiled James III, he was destined to see the principal objects of his life's work elude him when they seemed almost within his grasp: as the twilight of Jacobitism gradually faded, and he himself ultimately abandoned the cause to which he had devoted practically his entire career, he could have felt grateful that protracted frustration had been the worst fate decreed for him by destiny.

APPENDIX I

List of King's Works

1730   *An Ode to Mira*
        [?] *Myra's Answer*

1732   *The Toast*
        Subsequently expanded for the versions of 1736 and 1747.

1734   *A Letter from Mr. Lewis O Neil to Peregrine O Donald, Esq., with Mr. O Donald's Answer*

1737   Article [no title] in *Common Sense*, 28 May 1737

1738   *Miltonis Epistola ad Pollionem*
        The translation of 1740, published under the title *Milton's Epistle to Pollio*, may have been made by King.

1739   *Sermo Pedestris*

1740   *Scamnum, Ecloga*

1742   *Templum Libertatis, Liber Primus*

1743   *Templum Libertatis, Liber Secundus*
        Tres Oratiunculae Habitae in Domo Convocationis Oxon.

1744   *Epistola Objurgatoria ad Guilielmum King*
        To this is annexed the *Epistola Canonici Reverendi Admodum ad Archidiaconum Reverendum Admodum*
        [?] *A Letter to a Friend Occasioned by Epistola Objurgatoria*
        [?] *A Chiding Letter to S.P.Y.B. in Defence of Epistola Objurgatoria*
        Antonietti, Ducis Corsorum, Epistola ad Corsos
        The title in the *Opera* text is *Antonietti, Corsorum Ducis, Epistola ad Corsos*

1746   *Hydra*

1748   *A Proposal for Publishing a Poetical Translation, Both in Latin and English, of the Reverend Mr. Tutor Bentham's Letter to a Young Gentleman of Oxford*

1749 *A Poetical Abridgement, Both in Latin and English, of the Reverend Mr. Tutor Bentham's Letter to a Young Gentleman of Oxford*

[?] *A Certain Proposal of a Certain Little Tutor for Making Certain Reformations in a Certain Method of Education Most Certainly Practis'd in a Certain University*

Oratio In Theatro Sheldoniano Habita Idibus Aprilibus, MDCCXLIX. Die Dedicationis Bibliothecae Radclivianae Monitor

1750 *The Wonder of Wonders or Fresh Intelligence from Eton* Subsequently expanded under the title *An Answer to Dr. King's Speech: By the Rev. Mr. John Burton, Batchelor in Divinity, and Fellow of Eton College.* A folio half-sheet broadside issued twice as a folio whole-sheet broadside.

The Old Lady in Her Tantarums

Elogium Famae Inserviens Jacci Etonensis, sive Gigantis

1751 *A Key to the Fragment*

1754 *The Dreamer*

[?] *A Translation of the Latin Epistle in The Dreamer*

Praesidibus Supremi Galliae Senatus Intended to serve as the Preface to the *Opera* and found only in that volume.

1755 *Doctor King's Apology*

The Last Blow

1756 Inscription for a collection of statues presented to the University of Oxford by the Countess Dowager of Pomfret.

Epitaph for the fourth Duke of Beaufort, ob. 28 October 1756, buried at Badminton, Gloucestershire.

1757 *Oratiuncula Habita in Domo Convocationis, Oxon. Die Oct. 27, 1756*

1760 *Aviti Epistola ad Perillam, Virginem Scotam*

Opera Guilielmi King

1761 *Elogium* to John Taylor the Oculist. The date of printing is approximate only.

Epitaphium Richardi Nash

Political and Literary Anecdotes of His Own Times
Published posthumously in 1818; second edition in 1819.
Reprinted in the United States in 1819. The Preface
was written 'in my seventy-sixth year'.

In addition to these works, a few others have been attributed to King on very slender evidence, and without
reference to stylistic criteria. I have not treated these as
part of the canon. The principal cases are:

1740 *Reasons and Proposals for Laying a Tax upon Dogs*
Written in fact by a William King of Reading.

1749 *Carmen Rhythmicum Monachicum Momo Dicatum*
Attributed to King by Leicester Bradner in *Musae
Anglicanae*, presumably on the authority of the *Catalogus
Bibliothecae Bodlianae*. W. R. Ward in *Georgian Oxford*,
p. 184, indicates an anonymous author other than King.
Sir Harold Williams did not regard this as one of King's
authentic works.

1754 *Serious Reflections on the Dangerous Tendency of the Common
Practice of Card Playing*
Sir Edward Turner considered that this work was written
by King, but no grounds for this unlikely attribution
have ever been suggested. The author's pseudonym (or
perhaps his real name) is Gyles Smith.

1756 *A New Speech from the Old Trumpeter of Liberty Hall*
Though this short work is sometimes attributed to King,
all the intrinsic evidence points to Robert Jenner as the
author.

1768 *Animadversions upon the Conduct of the Rev. Dr. Rutherforth
in the Controversy which has Followed the Publication of the
Confessional*
The author of this short booklet is undetermined, but
he was not the Principal of St. Mary Hall.

1771 *An Answer to a Second Scandalous Book, that Mr. B—t is
Now Writing*
Attributed to 'Dr. William King' in Halkett and Laing's
Dictionary of Anonymous and Pseudonymous English Literature.
Since the dates given for King's birth and death are

erroneous, it is impossible to ascertain which King was here intended. This pamphlet is occasionally credited to the Principal of St. Mary Hall, though he could not possibly have been the author.

It has also been suggested that King may have contributed to *Mist's Journal*. This error presumably arose from the fact that Nathaniel Mist seems to have had an apprentice by the name of William King. On this matter see *A Dictionary of the Printers and Booksellers . . . in England, Scotland and Ireland from 1726 to 1775* (Oxford: Printed for the Bibliographical Society at the Oxford University Press, 1932 for 1930), p. 147. There are no other grounds for suggesting any association of Mist with the Old Trumpeter.

APPENDIX II

List of *King's Extant Letters*

Correspondent	Date[1]	Place	Source[2]
Lord Arran	11 June 1721	St. Mary Hall	National Library of Ireland, Ormonde MSS., Vol. 177, p. 221
Captain Charles Halsted	2 Sept. 1721	Bagshot	PRO, State Papers Domestic, 35/28, Item 66
Captain Charles Halsted	24 Oct. 1721	St. Mary Hall	PRO, State Papers Domestic, 35/28, Item 89
Captain Charles Halsted	4 Feb. 1722	St. Mary Hall	PRO, State Papers Domestic, 35/30, Item 27
Jonathan Swift	20 Sept. 1735	London	Williams, Vol. IV, p. 394
Mrs. Whiteway	14 Sept. 1736	Edinburgh	Williams, Vol. IV, p. 529
Mrs. Whiteway	9 Nov. 1736	Paris	Williams, Vol. IV, p. 541
James Edgar	24 Nov. 1736	Paris	The Royal Library, Windsor Castle, SP 191/168
Jonathan Swift	7 Dec. 1736	London	Williams, Vol. IV, p. 550
Mrs. Whiteway	24 June 1737	St. Mary Hall	Williams, Vol. V, p. 51
Jonathan Swift	24 June 1737	St. Mary Hall	Williams, Vol. V, p. 53.
Mrs. Whiteway	2 March 1738	London	Williams, Vol. V, p. 93
Deane Swift	15 March 1738	St. Mary Hall	Williams, Vol. V, p. 99[3]
Deane Swift	25 April 1738	St. Mary Hall	Williams, Vol. V, p. 107
Lord Orrery	8 July 1738	London	Bodleian Library, MS. Eng. hist. d. 103, p. 3
Jonathan Swift	23 Jan. 1739	London	Williams, Vol. V, p. 135
Mrs. Whiteway	30 Jan. 1739	? St. Mary Hall	Williams, Vol. V, p. 136
Mrs. Whiteway	6 March 1739	London	Williams, Vol. V, p. 139
Lord Orrery	2 July 1739	St. Mary Hall	Bodleian Library, MS. Eng. hist. d. 103, p. 5

Lord Orrery	23 Sept. 1739	St. Mary Hall	Bodleian Library, MS. Eng. hist. d. 103, p. 7
Lord Orrery	15 Jan. 1740	St. Mary Hall	Bodleian Library, MS. Eng. hist. d. 103, p. 9
Lord Orrery	25 March 1740	London	Bodleian Library, MS. Eng. hist. d. 103, p. 11
Lord Orrery	1 June 1740	St. Mary Hall	Bodleian Library, MS. Eng. hist. d. 103, p. 13
Lord Orrery	5 Aug. 1740	Ealing	Bodleian Library, MS. Eng. hist. d. 103, p. 15
Lord Orrery	28 Oct. 1740	London	Bodleian Library, MS. Eng. hist. d. 103, p. 17
Lord Orrery	15 Jan. 1741	St. Mary Hall	Bodleian Library, MS. Eng. hist. d. 103, p. 19
Lord Orrery	20 May 1741	St. Mary Hall	Bodleian Library, MS. Eng. hist. d. 103, p. 21
Lord Orrery	4 June 1741	St. Mary Hall	Bodleian Library, MS. Eng. hist. d. 103, p. 23
Lord Orrery	5 July 1741	St. Mary Hall	Bodleian Library, MS. Eng. hist. d. 103, p. 25
Lord Orrery	14 July 1741	St. Mary Hall	Bodleian Library, MS. Eng. hist. d. 103, p. 27
Lord Orrery	24 Aug. 1741	St. Mary Hall	Bodleian Library, MS. Eng. hist. d. 103, p. 29
Lord Orrery	4 Sept. 1741	St. Mary Hall	Bodleian Library, MS. Eng. hist. d. 103, p. 31
Lord Orrery	9 Sept. 1741	St. Mary Hall	Bodleian Library, MS. Eng. hist. d. 103, p. 33
Lord Orrery	17 Sept. 1741	St. Mary Hall	Bodleian Library, MS. Eng. hist. d. 103, p. 35
Lord Orrery	24 Sept. 1741	Bath	Bodleian Library, MS. Eng. hist. d. 103, p. 37
Lord Orrery	29 Sept. 1741	Bath	Bodleian Library, MS. Eng. hist. d. 103, p. 38b
Lord Orrery	3 Oct. 1741	Bath	Bodleian Library, MS. Eng. hist. d. 103, p. 40
George Faulkner	5 Oct. 1741	Bath	Faulkner's An Appeal to the Public (1758)
Lord Orrery	6 Oct. 1741	Bath	Bodleian Library, MS. Eng. hist. d. 103, p. 42
George Faulkner	12 Oct. 1741	Bath	Faulkner's An Appeal to the Public (1758)

[1] For sake of convenience, the year appears consistently in New Style.

[2] In the case of published letters, only the most recent source is listed. 'Williams' indicates Sir Harold Williams, *Correspondence of Jonathan Swift*, 5 vols. (Oxford: at the Clarendon Press, 1963–5); 'Dickens and Stanton' indicates Lilian Dickens and Mary Stanton, *An Eighteenth-Century Correspondence* (London: John Murray, 1910); 'Cork and Orrery' indicates the Countess of Cork and Orrery, *The Orrery Papers*, 2 vols. (London: Duckworth, 1903).

[3] Here misdated 'March 13th, 1737–8.'

Correspondent	Date[1]	Place	Source[2]
Lord Orrery	14 Oct. 1741	Bath	Bodleian Library, MS. Eng. hist. d. 103, p. 44
Lord Orrery	10 Nov. 1741	London	Bodleian Library, MS. Eng. hist. d. 103, p. 46
Lord Orrery	1 Jan. 1742	St. Mary Hall	Bodleian Library, MS. Eng. hist. d. 103, p. 48
Lord Orrery	16 May 1742	St. Mary Hall	Bodleian Library, MS. Eng. hist. d. 103, p. 50
Lord Orrery	18 Aug. 1742	St. Mary Hall	Bodleian Library, MS. Eng. hist. d. 103, p. 52
Lord Orrery	3 Sept. 1742	St. Mary Hall	Bodleian Library, MS. Eng. hist. d. 103, p. 54
Lord Orrery	4 Oct. 1742	St. Mary Hall	Bodleian Library, MS. Eng. hist. d. 103, p. 56
Lord Orrery	6 Oct. 1742	St. Mary Hall	Bodleian Library, MS. Eng. hist. d. 103, p. 58
Lord Orrery	31 Oct. 1742	St. Mary Hall	Bodleian Library, MS. Eng. hist. d. 103, p. 60
Lord Orrery	29 Dec. 1742	St. Mary Hall	Bodleian Library, MS. Eng. hist. d. 103, p. 62
Lord Orrery	5 Jan. 1743	St. Mary Hall	Bodleian Library, MS. Eng. hist. d. 103, p. 64
Lord Orrery	19 Jan. 1743	St. Mary Hall	Bodleian Library, MS. Eng. hist. d. 103, p. 66
Lord Orrery	31 Jan. 1743	St. Mary Hall	Bodleian Library, MS. Eng. hist. d. 103, p. 68
Lord Orrery	27 Feb. 1743	St. Mary Hall	Bodleian Library, MS. Eng. hist. d. 103, p. 70
Sanderson Miller	April 1743	Bath	Dickins and Stanton, p. 94
Lord Orrery	9 April 1743	St. Mary Hall	Bodleian Library, MS. Eng. hist. d. 103, p. 72
Lord Orrery	19 April 1743	St. Mary Hall	Bodleian Library, MS. Eng. hist. d. 103, p. 74
Lord Orrery	6 June 1743	St. Mary Hall	Bodleian Library, MS. Eng. hist. d. 103, p. 76
Lord Orrery	9 Sept. 1743	St. Mary Hall	Bodleian Library, MS. Eng. hist. d. 103, p. 78
Lord Orrery	6 Oct. 1743	Bagshot	Bodleian Library, MS. Eng. hist. d. 103, p. 80
Lord Orrery	20 Oct. 1743	St. Mary Hall	Bodleian Library, MS. Eng. hist. d. 103, p. 82
Lord Orrery	23 Nov. 1743	St. Mary Hall	Bodleian Library, MS. Eng. hist. d. 103, p. 84
Lord Orrery	24 April 1744	London	Bodleian Library, MS. Eng. hist. d. 103, p. 86
Lord Orrery	25 May 1745	St. Mary Hall	Bodleian Library, MS. Eng. hist. d. 103, p. 88

Lord Orrery	St. Mary Hall	24 June 1745	Bodleian Library, MS. Eng. hist. d. 103, p. 90
Sanderson Miller	St. Mary Hall	July 1745	County Record Office, Shire Hall, Warwick, Miller Collection, CR 125B/159
Lord Orrery	St. Mary Hall	8 July 1745	Bodleian Library, MS. Eng. hist. d. 103, p. 92
Lord Orrery	St. Mary Hall	10 April 1746	Cork and Orrery, Vol. I, p. 312
Sanderson Miller	? St. Mary Hall	May 1747	Dickins and Stanton, p. 129
Lord Orrery	London	20 Nov. 1747	The Houghton Library, Harvard University, MS. Eng. 218.2 (v. 5), p. 77
Lord Orrery	London	6 Feb. 1750	Cork and Orrery, Vol. II, p. 68
Lord Orrery	London	24 April 1750	The Houghton Library, Harvard University, MS. Eng. 218.2 (v. 5), p. 71
Dr. Richard Rawlinson	St. Mary Hall	23 Aug. 1753	Bodleian Library, MS. Rawl. Letters 114*
?	London	30 July 1757	Bodleian Library, MS. Add. A. 64
William Huddesford	London	9 Feb. 1758	Bodleian Library, MS. Ashmole 1822
Sir Francis Dashwood	St. Mary Hall	2 April 1761	BM, MS. Eg. 2136.f.66
Lord Shelburne	St. Mary Hall	22 Oct. 1761	Shelburne MSS. at Bowood
Sir Francis Dashwood	St. Mary Hall	1 April 1763	Bodleian Library, MS. D. D. Dashwood (Bucks.), B. 11/10/7
Sir Francis Dashwood	St. Mary Hall	7 Sept. 1763	BM, MS. Eg. 2136. f.67
Dr. Thomas Nowell	Carey Street	'Tuesday Morning'	County Record Office, Shire Hall, Warwick, Newdigate Letters, MS. B 2028
Sanderson Miller	St. Mary Hall	'Friday noon'	County Record Office, Shire Hall, Warwick, Miller Collection, CR 125B/158

King also wrote a postscript to a letter from Robert Duncan to Thomas Hearne, dated 6 May 1721.
Source: Bodleian Library, Rawl. Lett. 7, fol. 200.

1, 2 For footnotes see page 367.

APPENDIX III

Extracts from the Ealing Poor Rate Book for 1719–29

It is Ordered and Agreed in Publick Vestry at the Cross House on Wednesday, 31st day of Oct. 1722 and We do in our own Names and in the Names of all the Inhabitants of the sd Parish Of Ealing also Zealing promise and engage to indemnify the present Churchwardens and Overseers of the poor of and from all manner of Action or Actions, Suit or Suits of Law which Dr. Wm. King shall bring against them or any of them for making a Distress or Seizure of or upon his Goods & Chattells for not paying the sum or sums of money now in Arrear and charged upon him for his Tythes and parsonage of the parish afores^d towards the relief of the poor of the s^d parish, provided such Churchwardens and Overseers of the poor do maintain a Lawfull warrant in the first place. Witness the Hands and Seals of His Majesties Justices of the Peace for the County & Witness o^r Hands the day & year above s^d.

> Maurice Boheme ⎫
> Wm Lonsdale ⎬ Churchwardens
> ⎭

B, the Mark of ⎫
Thomas Bishop ⎬ Overseers of ye poor.
Daniel Dean ⎭

Whereas by an Order of Vestry dated the 31st day of Oct^b last past the present Churchwardens and Overseers of ye poor of ye sd parish of Ealing were thereby indemnified of and from all manner of Action or Actions, Suit or Suits in Law which Wm King Esq L.L.D. should bring against them or any of them for making a Distress or Seizure of or upon his Goods and Chattells for not paying the sum or sums of money now in arrear & charged upon him for his Tythes and parsonage of the said parish of Ealing towards the relief of the poor of the said Parish

provided such Churchwardens & Overseers of the poor did
obtain warrant in the first place under the Hands and seales of
his Majesties Justices of the peace for this County and was
signed by the Inhabitants of the sd parish who were there in
vestry p'sent. But whereas some Disputes have arisen since the
said order was made whither it was a sufficient Security to indemnify them and sd. Churchwardens & Overseers of the poor
against the sd Wm King Esq. touching the sd Distress by reason
publick Notice was not given in the Parish Church of Ealing the
Sunday before the sd vestry was held as above mentioned for
the making of the said order, therefore the sd Church wardens
& Overseers of the poor did on Sunday last past imediately
after morning service give Publick Notice in the sd parish
Church desiring the inhabitants of the sd parish to meet at the
Cross House on this day at ten of the Clock in the forenoon to
make an order to indemnify them & every one of them from all
charges, trouble & expense whatsoever which the above sd
William King should putt them or any of them to for or by
reason and means of making a Distress or Seizure upon his sd
Goods & Chattels for his refusing to pay the sum of twenty six
pounds seventeen shillings and six pence which the sd. William
King now stands charged with and is in Arrear being for & towards the relief of the poor of ye sd parish of Ealing. It is therefore Ordered and Agreed in Publick Vestry duly called and
held at the Cross House on Wednesday ye 12th day December
1722, by the sd Churchwardens & Overseers of the poor and the
inhabitants of ye sd parish for the sole and only purpose above
mentioned. And we the said Inhabitants do hereby Ratify &
Confirm the said Order of Vestry made the 31st of Oct. last past
and do further Order & Agree that the sd Churchwardens &
Overseers of the poor & every person concerned in making a
Distress upon the sd. William Kings Goods & Chattells shall be
Reimbursted and paid All and Every Sum or Sums of Money
which they or any of them shall expend & layout in defending
the Suit or Suits in Law against the sd William King touching
the payment out of the Monies raised for the relief of the poor
whether a Verdict or Verdicts shall pass for ye Defendants in
such Suit or Suits or not and in Case no sufficient Distress can
or may be found and the sd Churchwardens & Overseers should

obtain a Warrant to seize and secure the person of him the sd Wm King Esq. for such deficiency. We also promise, order and agree to indemnify all & every person concerned in seizing his person in the same manner and out of the sd Rates as if an Action or Actions, Suit or Suits in Law had been brought against them or any of them for making ye Distress on his Goods & Chattells as aforesaid.

In Witness whereof we have been here set our Hands ye sd 12th day of December, 1722.

[Here follow the signatures of the Churchwardens and the Overseers of the Poor. Some are only partially legible.]

APPENDIX IV

King's Places of Residence

From the time that he was appointed Principal, King regarded St. Mary Hall, Oxford, as his normal place of residence. Very little evidence is available relating to his other domiciles. Thomas Faulkner indicates that, when King was living in Ealing, he resided for many years on an estate called Newby, near the church. This seems to have been part of or adjoining the rectorial estate, the lease of which he acquired from the Chancellor of St. Paul's Cathedral. Three legal documents now in the possession of the Church Commissioners (Deeds 1534, 1535, and 1536) provide some information on this holding. The first is a Surrender, dated 26 November 1730, of a previous lease of the rectorial estate granted to William Pope and Ambrose Adams. This Surrender significantly states that during the term of the lease to be surrendered, William King, his brother-in-law Charles Wither, and James Munro had acquired a beneficial interest in it. No definite indication is provided of the time when King first invested in the property. It is clear that the estate was extensive: pastures, woods, closes, and underwoods are included. Two days later, on 28 November 1730, a bond for the performance of covenants was signed by William King; also named are his brother John, Charles Wither, and James Munro. On the same day the new lease was signed: it was intended to run for the lives of William King, his brother John, and his son Charles. The yearly rent was fixed at £24. This lease made William King responsible for the maintenance of the chancel of St. Mary's Church: for this reason his name is sometimes listed among those of the Rectors of Ealing. It is questionable, however, to what extent successive Chancellors of St. Paul's Cathedral, in leasing the rectorial property at Ealing, divested themselves of the title of Rector. Today in the vestry of St. Mary's Church there is a list of Rectors, many of

25—W.K.

whom were also Chancellors of St. Paul's Cathedral: Dr. Edward Jones appears as Rector from 1719 to 1733, and Dr. Peniston Booth from 1733 to 1761. Edith Jackson in *Annals of Ealing* indicates that King was Rector of Ealing from 1739 to 1761, but at most he would have been a lay impropriator. I also question the reliability of this author's dates. King seems to have relinquished most of his interest in the property by the lease dated 28 May 1756, cited in Chapter VIII.

Even though King was a Barrister-at-Law of Gray's Inn, there is no proof of his having resided there. But he did maintain chambers in the Temple. A letter from Swift to Lord Orrery of 2 July 1737 establishes this fact:

> I have corrected the inclosed as well as my shattered head was able; I intreat Your Lordship will please to alter whatever you have a Mind; and please to deliver it with Your own Hand to Doctor King at his Chambers in the Temple.[1]

And on 24 April 1744, King wrote to Orrery from 'London' on the subject of the rooks in the Temple:

> An old friend, who frequently makes me a morning visit, and who I must tell you, is a bigotted Pythagorean, insists that these same Rooks were formerly all Preachers or other eminent Lawyers of the two Temples. Tis a matter I never dispute with him, because yᵉ Metempsychosis is a doctrine I have never studied, and therefore I neither know nor remember any thing of what I was, before I was born. Whereas my learned friend remembers distinctly the several transmigrations of his Soul, and can tell you (as well as Pythagoras) who he was at yᵉ time of the Trojan War. If my Soul should enter hereafter into yᵉ body of a Rook (as my friend tells me may probably be my fate, because I have been so long an inhabitant of the Temple), I shall most certainly . . . fly immediately to Marston and dwell in one of the old Elms in your Garden.[2]

No record of King's residence survives today in the archives of either the Inner Temple or the Middle Temple, but it was a not uncommon practice, then as now, for Members of Gray's Inn to have chambers in the Temple. The Temple receipt books

---

[1] Harold Williams (ed.), *The Correspondence of Jonathan Swift* (5 vols.; Oxford: at the Clarendon Press, 1963–5), Vol. V, p. 59.

[2] Bodleian Library, MS. Eng. hist. d. 103, pp. 86f.

survive, but King's name does not occur in them, probably because his fees were paid to the Head of Chambers rather than directly to the Treasury.

It is likely that he relinquished his chambers in the Temple soon after Christmas 1747. Writing from 'London' on 20 November 1747 to Lord Orrery, he confessed:

I came to this place about a month since, in order finally to settle my private affairs so that I might be in a condition to retire for the rest of my life without any disturbance or interruption to my monastery. I thank God, I have in a measure finished every thing to my satisfaction, and at my next trip to London, which will be soon after Christmas, I shall have nothing to do, but to execute some writings and to take my leave. I don't however, mean by this, that I will never see London again; my friends and my country, notwithstanding my age, shall, upon any urgent occasion call me out of my cell. But I have done with ambition, and the busy world: and for the pleasure of it (I mean those which are so esteemed) I have no relish left.[1]

King seems to have been as good as his word. He paid visits later to London, Bath, Ealing, and other places, perhaps including Rome, but until his death regarded St. Mary Hall as his monastery and his home.

[1] The Houghton Library, Harvard University, MS. Eng. 218.2 (v. 5), pp. 77f.

APPENDIX V

The Arms Ascribed to King by Warburton

At various times historians have been misled by the ascription of arms to William King by John Warburton in his *London and Middlesex* (1749). The blazon is as follows:

Arms: *Or on a Pale Azure three Coronets of the Field.*
Crest: *Issuant from a Mural Crown Or an Eagle displayed Azure charged on the Breast with a Ducal Crown Or.*
Mantling: *Gules doubled Argent.*
Motto: *Virtus Gemma Coronis.*

The armorial bearings so described are actually not those of William King at all, but those granted by Edward Bysshe, the intruding Garter King of Arms, on 20 February 1649, to Joseph King, son of John King of Weston Patrick in Hampshire, and captain of the Trained Band of Odiham. As these arms were granted during the Commonwealth period, they are null and of none effect.

INDEX